BELOVED
FROM GOD'S HEART TO YOURS

A DAILY DEVOTIONAL

KAY ARTHUR

HARVEST HOUSE PUBLISHERS
Eugene, Oregon 97402

BELOVED

Copyright © 1994 by Kay Arthur
Published by Harvest House Publishers
Eugene, Oregon 97402

Library of Congress Cataloging-in-Publication Data

Arthur, Kay, 1933–
    Beloved : from God's heart to yours / Kay Arthur.
        p.   cm.
    ISBN 1-56507-198-0
    1. Devotional calendars.   2. God.   I. Title.
BV4811.A76   1994
242'.2—dc20   94-10728
                                                                          CIP

Printed in the United States of America.

94   95   96   97   98   99   00   —   10   9   8   7   6   5   4   3   2   1

"I am my beloved's and
my beloved is mine"
(Song of Solomon 6:3).

—*Kay Arthur*

JANUARY

What Is God Truly Like?

"The people that do know their God shall be strong, and do exploits," says the prophet Daniel. As we begin our year together in this daily devotional book, we will spend these first months of January and February looking at God's sovereignty and His character. We will explore what it means to say that God rules over all. You will come to understand, my friend, that all that comes into your life is literally filtered through His fingers of love!

As we walk through these days, I'll share, too, how God has used some difficult experiences in my life to mold me more and more into His image. You will see how He is doing the same in you, and how He will use you as a result!

God's Sovereignty...
Your Strength

I WILL NEVER FORGET the first time I really saw the passage in Daniel. I had begun to read J. I. Packer's outstanding book, *Knowing God,* when I came across his quote of Daniel 11:32b: "but the people that do know their God shall be strong, and do exploits" (KJV). Suddenly it was as if my Divine Guide, the Holy Spirit, had taken me into a magnificent museum of truth. On the walls hung exquisite pieces of art, each one a portrait of my God.

Awestruck, I fell to my knees as I knew the presence of the Sovereign God. Then, like a lightning bolt, the realization of Daniel 4:34,35 hit me: God does according to His will in the army of heaven and among the inhabitants of the earth, and no one can say to Him, "What doest Thou?"

He rules! The reality of the words throbbed in my head. Nothing happens by happenstance. I am not in the hands of fate, nor am I the victim of man's whims or the devil's ploys. There is One who sits above man, above Satan, and above all heavenly hosts as the ultimate authority of all the universe. That One is my God and my Father!

As suddenly as I had entered that museum of truth, my mind raced back to my first days as His child. Once again I could see Dave Pantzer standing in my living room. He had taken off his ring, placed it in his palm, and then tightly wrapped his fingers around it. "Kay," he said, "you are just like this ring now that you belong to God. God has you in His hand, and no one can touch you, peek at you, or say anything to you without God's permission." I will never forget how Dave's other hand tried to pry open those whitened knuckles, how he bent down to peep at the ring—all to no avail. The hand held fast to the ring so that nothing or no one could touch it or even look at it until the hand permitted it! Now I truly understood what Dave had been teaching me in those early days of my faith. My God is sovereign!

This year, Beloved, God wants me to take you into this museum of truth so that you, too, might behold your God and, knowing Him, stand firm and do exploits. As we stand before each portrait of His character, I will share with you some of what He has taught me. Together we will grow to know Him more intimately.

God's Sovereignty . . . Your Security

I NEVER READ ANY MORE of *Knowing God*. Yet Dr. Packer's book served its purpose, for it drove me immediately into God's Word to search out all I could learn about the sovereignty and the character of this One who sits on His throne, supreme over all. In that magnificent museum of truth my eyes widened in wonder as they fell on engraved plates of gold beneath each portrait:

Omniscience . . . Omnipotence . . . Omnipresence . . . Mercy . . . Justice . . . Righteousness.

As I read each inscription, the swell of a great orchestration of violins, harps, trumpets, and cymbals provided the background for heavenly choruses singing, "Holy, holy, holy, is the Lord God, the Almighty, who was and who is and who is to come" (Revelation 4:8). Yet, although caught in this glorious swell of praise, I could hear the Spirit's whisper, "Behold your God . . . and live." Suddenly concerns about myself—my well-being, my security, my loved ones, my needs, my hopes, my dreams, my ambitions—fell into insignificance. Standing in the knowledge and the presence of One far greater than man or angels or Satan, I was enveloped in a security I had never experienced before. I had found my dwelling place.

> He who dwells in the shelter of the Most High will abide in the shadow of the Almighty. I will say to the LORD, "My refuge and my fortress, my God, in whom I trust!" For it is He who delivers you from the snare of the trapper, and from the deadly pestilence. He will cover you with His pinions, and under His wings you may seek refuge; His faithfulness is a shield and bulwark (Psalm 91:1-4).

Then I knew, as never before, "LORD, Thou hast been our dwelling place in all generations. Before the mountains were born, or Thou didst give birth to the earth and the world, even from everlasting to everlasting, Thou art God" (Psalm 90:1,2).

God's Sovereignty...
Your Peace

IF WE ARE TO KNOW our God, we must have correct definitions of those terms which describe His being. When I say that God is sovereign, I mean that He rules over all, that nothing can happen in His universe without His permission. People who cannot accept or believe this will oppose the idea of God's sovereignty with rebuttals about the free will of man. "But if God rules over all, then that makes man a puppet!" they argue. "If God is sovereign and nothing can happen without His permission, then man cannot be accountable to God. He is only doing whatever God wants!" Yet the truth—the heavenly paradox, if you will—is that although God is sovereign, we still retain our free will and, consequently, are totally responsible and accountable to God.

We have been given a free will. Yet in His grand, eternal universe God so rules and overrules that no man or angel, no demon or devil, no circumstance of life can thwart His desire or His plan. Neither necessity nor chance nor Satan's malice controls the sequence of events or their causes. Rather, God rules supremely over all.

Stop and meditate on this. Think it through and talk to God about it. Ask the Holy Spirit to guide you into all truth. When it comes to having total peace of mind, I honestly do not believe there is a more reassuring message in all of Scripture than the sovereignty of God. I know of so many people who truly have been able to pass through trials as more than conquerors because they have realized that God is sovereign and have rested in that truth.

The doctrine of the sovereignty of God does not originate with me. It has been the mainstay of saints throughout all the ages. So meditate on this. Write down your questions, your "ifs," your "buts." Seek His face and trust Him by His Spirit and through His Word to guide you into all truth as we continue to look at His sovereignty together.

Daniel's Diary

HAVE YOU EVER READ the book of Daniel? It's quite a book! Many historians and liberals say that it could never have been written by Daniel; it is far too accurate historically, they say. Therefore, it must have been written after the fact. Nor can they contend with its miracles; there is too much of the supernatural! However, those who accept the Bible as the verbal, plenary (complete in every respect), inspired Word of God point out that the prophet Ezekiel referred to Daniel three times and that Jesus warned His own followers to take heed when they saw the "ABOMINATION OF DESOLATION . . . which was spoken of through Daniel the prophet" (Matthew 24:15).

As he does with all God's truth, the enemy of our souls seeks to destroy the veracity of the book of Daniel. The father of lies once again hisses his age-old "Hath God said?" But we will not fall captive to his empty deceptions. Rather, we will believe our Lord Jesus Christ, who constantly attested to the truth of the Old Testament.

Remember, Daniel declares that "the people who know their God will display strength and take action. And those who have insight among the people will give understanding to the many" (Daniel 11:32b,33a). God will use your knowledge of His character not only to strengthen your own life, but to enable you to give understanding to others, to those who will listen.

Listen, Beloved, listen.

If you will take the time to read through Daniel, you will notice that at chapter 4 Daniel stops writing and another person takes up Daniel's pen and adds a personal word of testimony! I can see it all. Apparently Daniel, led by God, began writing a chronological account of the events in his life after he was taken captive by the Babylonians, when Nebuchadnezzar was king. In his diary, Daniel recorded the various dreams and decrees of Nebuchadnezzar. However, when Daniel came to the story of the king's humiliation by God, Nebuchadnezzar had to tell his own story! For Nebuchadnezzar had finally recognized that, as for the King of heaven, "all His works are true and His ways just, and He is able to humble those who walk in pride" (Daniel 4:37).

We will read his story tomorrow.

From Generation to Generation

AS NEBUCHADNEZZAR TAKES UP his pen to give his testimony, he gives his reason for writing: "It has seemed good to me to declare the signs and wonders which the Most High God has done for me. . . . His kingdom is an everlasting kingdom, and His dominion is from generation to generation" (Daniel 4:2,3b).

Obviously, Nebuchadnezzar is concerned that all who live upon the earth should recognize God's sovereignty (Daniel 4:1). But did King Nebuchadnezzar always feel this way? No! Not until after God visited him through a prophetic dream, which was interpreted by Daniel and then came to pass in Nebuchadnezzar's life. As humbling as it was, the king needed to see "that it is Heaven that rules" (Daniel 4:26). Thus the interpretation of his dream and the decree of the Most High came upon the king, as Scripture says, so "that you be driven away from mankind, and your dwelling place be with the beasts of the field . . . until you recognize that the Most High is ruler over the realm of mankind, and bestows it on whomever He wishes" (Daniel 4:25).

Twelve months later, the dream was fulfilled. As you read Nebuchadnezzar's account, note why he had to be humbled. Then tomorrow we will look at the end result of it all.

> He [Nebuchadnezzar] was walking on the roof of the royal palace of Babylon. The king reflected and said, "Is this not Babylon the great, which I myself have built as a royal residence by the might of my power and for the glory of my majesty?" While the word was in the king's mouth, a voice came from heaven, saying, "King Nebuchadnezzar, to you it is declared: sovereignty has been removed from you, and you will be driven away from mankind, and your dwelling place will be with the beasts of the field. You will be given grass to eat like cattle, and seven periods of time will pass over you, until you recognize that the Most High is ruler over the realm of mankind, and bestows it on whomever He wishes" (Daniel 4:29-32).

Who Rules Your Affairs?

HUMANISM. IT HAS COME to the forefront in our vocabulary, and yet it is as old as Satan's enticement: "You will be like God" (Genesis 3:5). However, the first public declaration of humanism recorded in God's Word came at the Tower of Babel.

> And they said, "Come, let us build for ourselves a city, and a tower whose top will reach into heaven, and let us make for ourselves a name; lest we be scattered abroad over the face of the whole earth" (Genesis 11:4).

God's command to man after the flood had been to "be fruitful and multiply, and fill the earth" (Genesis 9:1). At Babel, however, Nimrod instigated a rebellion against that command. No, they would not obey. Instead, they would maintain their unity and make a name for themselves. Man, not God, would be supreme.

Men and women do not want to acknowledge that there is a God in heaven who has a direct role in their affairs. We see this in King Nebuchadnezzar, who became caught up in his own importance. He had built Babylon by his own power, for his own glory (Daniel 4:30)! Yet, when brought face-to-face with his own impotence before God, he honored God as God.

> "For His dominion is an everlasting dominion. . . . And all the inhabitants of the earth are accounted as nothing, but He does according to His will in the host of heaven and among the inhabitants of earth; and no one can ward off His hand or say to Him, 'What hast Thou done?'" (Daniel 4:34,35).

Who is at the center of your universe? Do you envision yourself the captain of your own destiny? Do you imagine yourself in the hands of some fickle power called fate? Or have you bowed your knee to the Sovereign Ruler of the universe and said, "My Lord and my God, I recognize that I exist because of Your will and that I was created for Your pleasure. I humble myself before You, my King."

A Future and a Hope

DO YOU READ THE NEWSPAPERS and tremble? No wonder. It seems as if today's news serves only as a prophet of doom. If you do not become the victim of some atrocious crime, then surely unemployment or inflation will price you right out of a decent life. If you manage to escape becoming one of those statistics, perhaps you will find yourself devastated by flood, earthquake, or tornado. If not, it is still possible that a routine examination will proclaim the frightening news, "Cancer." And what about AIDS and its rapid spread? And should you remain untouched by all of the above, is there not the possibility of suddenly finding yourself a statistic of divorce or a broken home? Or, escaping this, is there not always talk about total economic collapse?

Is it any wonder that multitudes are committing suicide while others escape into the oblivion of drugs or alcohol, and still others live in the darkness of depression? Psychiatrists, psychologists, and counselors abound; yet they seemingly cannot treat the sickness that plagues the souls of mankind.

Is this what God designed for us—a future without hope? No, Beloved, no! This is what happens when man chooses to believe Satan, the father of lies. For those who are His, God "plans for welfare and not for calamity to give you a future and a hope" (Jeremiah 29:11).

Christians must never look to the future or even at today except from the perspective of God's sovereignty. For if God is not sovereign, then you cannot give thanks in all things (1 Thessalonians 5:18); and if God is not sovereign, He cannot cause all things to work together for good to those who love Him and are called according to His purpose, and the events of your life can never be used to make you into His image (Romans 8:28,29). Rather you are the victim of man, Satan, nature, or fate.

No, Beloved, God is sovereign. And He assures you: "Surely, just as I have intended so it has happened, and just as I have planned so it will stand. . . . For the LORD of hosts has planned, and who can frustrate it? And as for His stretched-out hand, who can turn it back?" (Isaiah 14:24,27).

God . . . Over All Adversity

"DOES GOD PERMIT CANCER, murder, starvation, poverty, danger, and every other conceivable kind of tragedy in a Christian's life?"

"Do you mean to tell me that a God of love permits such things?"

"No, thanks! If that's your God, then I want no part of Him!"

Have you ever heard statements like these? If you have ever discussed the sovereignty of God, you have. Possibly you have even had these thoughts yourself. I understand. They are natural and normal reasonings of the human mind. Yet the human mind cannot understand truth apart from God's Word.

> "For My thoughts are not your thoughts, neither are your ways My ways," declares the LORD. "For as the heavens are higher than the earth, so are My ways higher than your ways, and My thoughts than your thoughts" (Isaiah 55:8,9).

Let us answer these questions about adversity and sickness from God's Word and humbly submit to what He speaks, whether we can rationalize it or not. We must take one precept at a time, day by day. So be patient, listen, and wait for His revelation. Just beware that you don't lean on your own understanding.

First we want to look at adversity and how it fits into God's sovereignty. This will take several days. For now, listen to what God says of Himself through the prophet Isaiah; then meditate upon it, and we'll talk about it tomorrow.

> "I am the LORD, and there is no other; besides Me there is no God. I will gird you, though you have not known Me; that men may know from the rising to the setting of the sun that there is no one besides Me. I am the LORD, and there is no other, the One forming light and creating darkness, causing well-being and creating calamity; I am the LORD who does all these" (Isaiah 45:5-7).

Filtered Through God's Love

IN ISAIAH 45:7, God tells us that He is the One who causes well-being or peace and that He is the One who creates calamity.

The word "calamity" comes from the word *ra* in the Hebrew, and in the King James Version it is translated "evil." It refers to distress, affliction, sorrow, or trouble.

The word "create" comes from *bara*, which means "to create, to cut down, to select, feed, choose, dispatch." It is used in this passage to show the unfolding of God's purposes in history.

This does not, however, make God the author or instigator of evil, for "let no one say when he is tempted, 'I am being tempted by God'; for God cannot be tempted by evil, and He Himself does not tempt anyone" (James 1:13). Rather, what God is saying is that if evil occurs, He permits it, and He will use it to achieve His ultimate goal and glory. For He makes even the wrath of man praise His name (Psalm 76:10; Exodus 9:16).

Thus, when adversity comes into your life, precious one, you can rest in the fact that first it had to be filtered through His sovereign fingers. And those are fingers of love, for God is love! If you are familiar with the Old Testament and the history of God's chosen people, Israel, you know that many times God used the adversity brought by other nations to chasten Israel. Yet that chastening (discipline) came because He loved them (Hebrews 12:5,6; Proverbs 3:11,12). However, God then held those nations accountable to Him for their evil behavior toward Israel.

"I can't understand it. It doesn't seem fair!" Is that what you are thinking? Remember, God's ways are not your ways, His thoughts are not your thoughts. Faith submits, taking God at His word and resting in His character.

In the days to come you will see that this Sovereign One who sits upon the throne of the universe is just, merciful, holy, righteous—a God of love. Rest and listen. Remember Job? In fact, why not read the first chapter of Job? When you do, think about who permitted Job's adversity or calamity. Then we will discuss it tomorrow.

Triumphant Through God

LET'S GO BACK to the questions we asked several days ago: "What about adversity in a Christian's life? Does God permit that? Cancer, murder, starvation, poverty, danger? Do you mean to tell me that a God of love could permit such things?"

Did God permit adversity in Job's life? Yes, He did. When Satan challenged the reason for Job's fear (or reverence) of God, God said to Satan, "Behold, all that he has is in your power, only do not put forth your hand on him" (Job 1:12). And what did Satan do? Why, he brought calamity upon calamity, wave upon wave, as he literally wiped out all that Job had. And what did Job do after learning of the destruction of his livestock and the death of his servants and his sons and daughters?

> Then Job arose and tore his robe and shaved his head, and he fell to the ground and worshiped. And he said, "Naked I came from my mother's womb, and naked I shall return there. The LORD gave and the LORD has taken away. Blessed be the name of the LORD" (Job 1:20,21).

Where did this calamity come from? Job said, "The LORD gave and the LORD has taken away."

Job looked beyond secondary causes to the sovereignty of God, and he bowed his knee without bitterness. "Through all this Job did not sin nor did he blame God" (Job 1:22). Yet the adversity was not over. For once again Satan was permitted to touch Job, this time with boils. Yet he could not take Job's life; God would not give him permission. "So the LORD said to Satan, 'Behold, he is in your power, only spare his life'" (Job 2:6).

O precious child of God, are you in great travail of soul because of some adversity? Fear not! Your Father is filtering it all through His fingers of love. As it was with Job, so it will be with you. Trust in Him, and it will result in good.

God's Perspective

"BUT HOW?" YOU SAY. "How could what I'm going through ever result in good? There's no way!"

No, there doesn't seem to be any way, does there? It all seems so senseless, so painful, so unjust. I understand. Yet we have to remember how limited our perspective is. Bound by our humanity, our vision is so shortsighted, our perspective so temporal (1 Corinthians 2:9).

No, Beloved, the whys and wherefores of pain and suffering cannot be understood by our human senses; they must be revealed by His Spirit (1 Corinthians 2:10). May God grant you that revelation according to your deepest need. And may you give Him time to speak to you.

Job's suffering affected every area of his life, from his material possessions to his loved ones to his own physical condition. He even endured an excruciating outbreak of boils. Yet in the midst of all this, when his wife suggested that he "curse God and die," Job responded, "'You speak as one of the foolish women speaks. Shall we indeed accept good from God and not accept adversity [evil]?' In all this Job did not sin with his lips" (Job 2:9,10).

No, Job did not sin with his lips. Even so, his adversity only increased as pious friends came to point out his seeming transgressions as reasons for his pain.

What riches we glean from Job's situation and his response to it! If he were here, I'd share these thoughts with him:

> O Job, I know it must have seemed unbearable at times, but I thank you for going before me. I know, my dear brother, it must have caused you anguish of the soul that I have never known; yet your tragedy has left me a legacy of untold wealth. And not me alone, but millions besides me. Because of your testimony, Job, I now understand that, "Whether for correction, or for His world, or for lovingkindness, He causes it to happen" (Job 37:13).

> O Job, I bow with you before our God, and I say as you did during the days of your great affliction, "I know that Thou canst do all things, and that no purpose of Thine can be thwarted" (Job 42:2).

Refined by God

ADVERSITY. WHY DOES GOD PERMIT IT? Can you not see its purpose by now?

Adversity is to refine us, to consume the dross so that we can come forth as pure gold, tried in a furnace of fire seven times. Remember, His plans for us are good, not evil, to give us a future and a hope (Jeremiah 29:11). And what is that future but to share in His glory?

> For I consider that the sufferings of this present time are not worthy to be compared with the glory that is to be revealed to us (Romans 8:18).

> In this you greatly rejoice, even though now for a little while, if necessary, you have been distressed by various trials, that the proof of your faith, being more precious than gold which is perishable, even though tested by fire, may be found to result in praise and glory and honor at the revelation of Jesus Christ (1 Peter 1:6,7).

When Job's trial was over and Satan had seen that he truly feared God and did not have a fair-weather faith of bless-me-God-and-answer-my-prayers-but-don't-make-it-rough-and-I-will-worship-You, then God restored Job's fortunes and increased all that he had twofold. But was that all? Was it simply a matter of material gain for Job once the trial was over and his faith was proved? No! It was far more than that. Job himself said, "I have heard of Thee by the hearing of the ear; but now my eye sees Thee; therefore I retract, and I repent in dust and ashes" (Job 42:5,6). Now Job knew his God as he had never known Him.

This, Beloved, is the purpose of adversity in our lives. It is filtered through God's fingers of love so that we might say with the psalmist, "It is good for me that I was afflicted, that I may learn Thy statutes" (Psalm 119:71). "But the people that do know their God shall be strong, and do exploits" (Daniel 11:32b KJV).

Through adversity Job came to know God even better, and it will be the same for you and for me.

The Refiner's Fire

TODAY I FEEL that God would simply have me share with you this precious poem, "The Refiner's Fire." These meaningful verses were given to me by a dear saint of God, although I do not know who wrote them for they bear no author's signature.

He sat by a furnace of sevenfold heat,
    As He watched by the precious ore,
And closer He bent with a searching gaze
    As He heated it more and more.
He knew He had ore that could stand the test
    And He wanted the finest gold,
To mold as a crown, for the King to wear,
    Set with gems of price untold.
So He laid our gold in the burning fire,
    Tho' we fain would say Him, "Nay";
And watched the dross that we had not seen,
    As it melted and passed away.
And the gold grew brighter and yet more bright,
    But our eyes were dim with tears,
We saw but the fire—not the Master's hand,
    And questioned with anxious fears.
Yet our gold shone out with a richer glow
    As it mirrored a Form above,
That bent o'er the fire, tho' unseen by us,
    With a look of ineffable love.
Can we think it pleases His loving heart
    To cause us a moment's pain?
Ah, no! but He sees through the present cross
    The bliss of eternal gain.
So He waited there with a watchful eye,
    With a love that is strong and sure,
And His gold did not suffer a bit more heat
    Than was needed to make it pure.

Accepting God's Sovereignty

HAVE YOU EVER WONDERED what purpose prayer serves if God is sovereign? After all, if something is going to happen in God's sovereignty, then it's going to happen. So why should I pray?

These thoughts have occurred to me, although I must admit they have come as a result of preparing myself as a teacher of God's Word rather than as personal questions of my own heart.

To me, accepting God's sovereignty doesn't mean that I must make every other truth in God's Word submit to the logic of His sovereignty. Maybe it is my naïveté or my lack of formal education, but I just don't have trouble trying to make all my doctrines fit into a logical sequence with one doctrine totally supporting, explaining, or amplifying the other according to my human reasoning.

To illustrate my point, let me ask you how you explain the doctrines of election, predestination, and the free will of man. If you are like many people, you will buy one and discard the other because you cannot make them "fit"! Yet others of us accept all three doctrines because we believe that if Scripture says it, we are to accept it and believe it even if we cannot totally understand it! When I cannot make everything fit together, I simply say:

> Oh, the depths of the riches both of the wisdom and knowledge of God! How unsearchable are His judgments and unfathomable His ways! FOR WHO HAS KNOWN THE MIND OF THE LORD, OR WHO BECAME HIS COUNSELOR? OR WHO HAS FIRST GIVEN TO HIM THAT IT MIGHT BE PAID BACK TO HIM AGAIN? For from Him and through Him and to Him are all things. To Him be the glory forever (Romans 11:33-36).

To me this is far better than taking doctrines to extremes.

Why don't you stop and ask God how balanced you are? Are you a real student of His Word, or are you an opinionated follower of men? If you are the latter, you are still precious, but you are carnal. I say that in love. Such division over doctrine was the problem in Corinth. Read 1 Corinthians 1:10-17; 3:1-5 and see what God says about this.

The God Who Answers Prayer

IF GOD IS SOVEREIGN, if He wounds and heals, kills and makes alive (Deuteronomy 32:39), then why pray when we or one of our loved ones becomes sick? Because, Beloved, God bids us pray.

> Is anyone among you sick? Let him call for the elders of the church, and let them pray over him, anointing him with oil in the name of the Lord; and the prayer offered in faith will restore the one who is sick. . . . Therefore, confess your sins to one another, and pray for one another, so that you may be healed. The effective prayer of a righteous man can accomplish much (James 5:14-16).

How God's sovereignty and our prayer fit together I do not completely understand. Yet laced throughout the tapestry of God's Word is the golden thread of His sovereignty. And looping over and under it, in a beautiful and intricate pattern, is the silver thread of the redemptive power of prayer. Neither distracts from the other nor mars God's perfect pattern.

In the Old Testament God takes pains to let us see Asa's failure to turn to Him when "in the thirty-ninth year of his reign Asa became diseased in his feet. His disease was severe, yet even in his disease he did not seek the LORD, but the physicians" (2 Chronicles 16:12).

In contrast, God also gives us an account of King Hezekiah, who in his illness cried out to God and was healed. God sent the prophet Isaiah to tell the king to set his house in order because of his impending death. "Then he turned his face to the wall, and prayed to the LORD, saying, 'Remember now, O LORD, I beseech Thee, how I have walked before Thee in truth and with a whole heart, and have done what is good in Thy sight.' And Hezekiah wept bitterly" (2 Kings 20:2,3). And God stayed Hezekiah's death, saying, "I have heard your prayer, I have seen your tears; behold, I will heal you" (2 Kings 20:5).

Oh, yes, our times are in His hands. He holds the keys to hell and death; yet He bids us pray (Psalm 31:15; Revelation 1:18). Don't try to figure it all out! Just believe Him, do what He says, and rest in Him.

"God, I Am Hurting"

I RECEIVE MANY LETTERS from people who are hurting and confused, and they are usually hurting in the area of interpersonal relationships, often involving divorce, or in the area of physical illness. Their confusion comes because they have believed God will alter their situation and He hasn't.

For example, I read a letter last night from a woman who had been married and divorced five times. Then she was saved. And what is her heart's cry now? "I'm very alone. However, I don't just want someone, anyone, and I definitely don't want an affair! My greatest desire is (only if it's possible without going to hell) to meet and marry a good Christian man! To fulfill what God intended for my life!" Her confusion is over whether or not she can have a good marriage, and if not, why not? After all, a good marriage, to her, is fulfillment.

This woman's letter is not unique. Most people who write have not been divorced five times, but many have been divorced at least once. And if they are not divorced, then it is a matter of infidelity, and they want the infidelity stopped or they want to be set free from the marriage so they can find someone else and live happily ever after.

It is the same with those who are physically ill. Someone wrote: "I was left with an injured nerve in my leg (I'm 65). I'm not able to do much. I believe God has saved me, and I have prayed so much for my healing. Sometimes I feel like He doesn't hear my prayers because the nerve hasn't healed back. God made that leg, and I believe He can make it back as He did the first time. Am I deceived, or is it not God's will to heal me?" For people like this, physical healing is foremost in their minds.

Whether it involves a relationship or a physical problem, their confusion is, "Doesn't God want me to be happy? Surely if I am a child of God I'm not to suffer such disappointments—am I?"

Are we? If God is God, if He is sovereign, if He honors faith and answers prayer, why doesn't He always intervene and alter our situation? Good question, isn't it? What's the answer? Ask God and then we'll talk about it tomorrow.

A Portrait of Love

WHEN WE WALK THROUGH God's magnificent museum of truth, surveying the various portraits of the Sovereign Ruler of the universe, do we catch grotesque or fearful images of different aspects of God's character that show Him to be a malicious despot? No, of course not! The One who sits upon the throne of the universe is a God of love. The Scriptures state it plainly: "God is love" (1 John 4:8); and God's actions demonstrate it clearly: "For God so loved the world, that He gave His only begotten Son" (John 3:16). The very essence of God's being is love.

Love is not merely an attitude with which God clothes Himself at certain times; rather, it is an attribute that so permeates His being that He could never divest Himself of it. To do so would make Him less than God. Therefore, whatever actions or commandments issue forth from His throne must come from love. Even His judgments! Why? Because God Himself is love.

Yet how well do you understand love?

Can we, as redeemed sinners not yet made perfect, begin to comprehend "the breadth and length and height and depth, and to know the love of Christ which surpasses knowledge" (Ephesians 3:18,19)?

Can we, with our finite reasoning power, even begin to judge whether or not God is acting in love? After all, He is the very source and author of love. Could we even begin to know love or to act in love if it were not for Him? Would we have a clear, untainted demonstration of the purity of love if we had not seen and heard of it from Him? How then can we sit in judgment of God and accuse Him of not being loving if He does not conform to our evaluation of love's behavior? What folly!

Yet, isn't this what we do when God's actions do not live up to our expectations? Surely a loving God will not leave us with our prayers unanswered when we have prayed in faith believing, will He?

O precious one, if you are hurting, if you are confused, if you are disappointed in God, don't be. Believe Him when He says, "I have loved you with an everlasting love; therefore I have drawn you with lovingkindness" (Jeremiah 31:3).

God . . . Over All Disappointment

"DISAPPOINTMENT—His *appointment*,"
Change one letter, then I see
That the thwarting of my purpose
Is God's better choice for me.
His appointment must be blessing,
Tho' it may come in disguise,
For the end from the beginning
Open to His wisdom lies.
"Disappointment—His *appointment*,"
Whose? The Lord, who loves me best,
Understands and knows me fully,
Who my faith and love would test;
For, like a loving earthly parent,
He rejoices when He knows
That His child accepts UNQUESTIONED
All that from His wisdom flows.
"Disappointment—His *appointment*,"
"No good thing will He withhold,"
From denials oft we gather
Treasures of His love untold.
Well He knows each broken purpose
Leads to fuller, deeper trust,
And the end of all His dealings
Proves our God is wise and just.
"Disappointment—His *appointment*,"
Lord, I take it, then, as such.
Like the clay in hands of potter,
Yielding wholly to Thy touch.
All my life's plan is Thy moulding,
Not one single choice be mine;
Let me answer, unrepining—
Father, "Not my will, but Thine."

—Edith Lillian Young

God ... Over All Shattered Hopes

HAVE YOU EVER WANTED something so badly that you wondered how you could survive without it? Yet it never came to pass! You begged, you pleaded, but it didn't happen. God did not answer your prayers. And when all your hopes, dreams, and expectations were dashed against the hard, cold wall of reality, you finally saw that it would never be. How did you handle it then?

Did you thank God, accept it, and walk away from the rubble, trusting in His sovereign love?

Or did you stoop down to examine the broken bits of what might have been, shedding tears of pity? Maybe you gathered all the pieces in a box carefully marked "Shattered Hopes, Dreams, and Expectations" and stored them in the attic of your memories.

Many times, in my early years as God's child, that is what I did. Then on rainy days of disappointment I would dig them out of the attic and work on restoring them. Carefully I would examine each piece, dreaming of what-could-have-been-if-only-I-had-done-things-differently. When I did this, I would plunge into a season of depression. In turn, the depression would make me angry with the reality of my present relationships or situations, for they seemed usurpers of what could have been, if only I had had my way or if only God had answered my prayers.

The gloom of depression would last as long as I let it. For I learned that all I had to do to end it was to put the broken pieces back in the box and remove them from my thoughts. I would again store them in the attic, safely tucked away for another rainy day of disappointment, when once more I would go through the same process.

Then one day, when I fully accepted His word that "His way is perfect," I quit struggling and snuggled into the arms of His sovereign, infinite wisdom and love. Resting there, I threw the box away. "Forgetting what lies behind," I determined I would always reach "forward to what lies ahead" and "press on toward the goal for the prize of the upward call of God in Christ Jesus" (Philippians 3:13,14).

What about you? Have you decided to fully trust? Or are you going to indulge yourself on rainy days of disappointment?

The One Who Cares

DO YOU SOMETIMES WONDER if there even is a God who cares, who loves, who sees, who knows what is going on in your life? At times does it all seem so frustrating, so futile that you just want to run away? Or maybe just escape into the oblivion of alcohol, or the temporary, quiet, anesthetic bliss of drugs, or the warmth and seeming security of illegitimate arms?

I understand. I was there once. Caught in a marriage that was a nightmare compared to my idealistic dreams, I felt enslaved—a prisoner in a dungeon of misery and wretchedness from which I might never escape. I had been taught that marriage is permanent. Only death could sever my chains. And yet, I reasoned, if Tom died before me it probably wouldn't happen until I was an old woman. And who wanted old women? Oh, would I never know the one thing I had ever really wanted, a marriage where two people were head over heels in love with each other—totally content, totally fulfilled because they belonged to one another forever?

I tore the platinum wedding band from my hand and threw it across the room. My finger was naked for the first time in six years. Round and round it rolled, making a mockery of the words engraved inside, "Our Love Is Eternal."

Disillusioned, hurt, longing for unconditional love, I gathered my sons in my arms and ran. I ran to a wilderness filled with illegitimate arms offering warm but temporal security, not knowing there was a God who sees, who cares—who, if I had turned to Him, would have sent me back and saved me so much grief.

What about you? Where are you? He knows. He sees. He cares. Your God is omniscient, all-knowing, and he understands your infirmities (Hebrews 4:15). You don't have to run away. Stay. In faith, pour out your heart to Him. He will meet you where you are and sustain you.

JANUARY 21

The One Who Sees

THE HARSH TREATMENT was too much. She ran. Leaving the security of home, she fled to the wilderness. It wasn't fair. It wasn't her idea that she sleep with her mistress's husband. She could not stand the jealousy. Then He found her. Face-to-face with the angel of the Lord, Hagar realized that there was a God. He saw. He understood. And because she knew that He knew, she could go back to Sarai and Abram. She could endure.

God had revealed Himself to a mere slave! How awesome it was to have seen God and remained alive! "Then she called the name of the LORD who spoke to her, 'Thou art a God who sees'" (Genesis 16:13). Hagar could stop running because she knew that God lived, that He cared, and that she had His promise.

Does your situation sometimes seem too hard to bear? Does it seem unfair, unjust? A situation not of your choosing, not really of your making? You look at others and they don't seem to be experiencing your pain, your hardship, your suffering.

Has God cheated you? Did He cause it all to happen? Or are your circumstances simply the awful wages of sin—the sin of mankind or your own personal sin?

Obviously all suffering ultimately exists because man chose to believe the serpent's lie in the Garden. With that, sin entered the world, bringing with it death—its awful wages (Romans 5:12; 6:23).

Yet, there is a God who sees. A God who loves. A God who reigns. A God who redeems.

O precious one, quit looking at your circumstances. Quit feeling cheated. Quit running away. Instead, run to the One who can take it all and make it result in good. Turn to the Redeemer.

> If He causes grief, then He will have compassion according to His abundant lovingkindness. For He does not afflict willingly, or grieve the sons of men.... Why should any living mortal, or any man, offer complaint in view of his sins? (Lamentations 3:32,33,39).

God . . . Always There

MUCH OF MY PAST has faded into the insignificance of years gone by, but I can still recall one scene as vividly as if it happened yesterday.

I was not even a year old in Christ. The boys and I had just come home from church when the phone rang. It was the admissions desk at Johns Hopkins Hospital where I was to go for surgery that afternoon. They gave me a message to call a number in Cleveland, Ohio, and I recognized it immediately as my in-laws' phone number. Little did I realize what they would say to me.

My husband, Tom, and I had been divorced for several years. Yet my heavenly Father had finally brought me to the place where I was willing to go back to Tom.

Tom had been on my heart recently; I had even thought of writing him. He had been concerned about my surgery, and since this was the day I was to enter the hospital, I assumed that Tom was trying to reach me and wish me well. I did not know that an entirely different message awaited me and that I would never hear Tom's voice again.

When I reached my father-in-law, his first words were, "Tom is dead. He hung himself." I was sitting on the edge of the bed, but that wasn't solid enough. Hearing that news, I slid to the floor and sought refuge on my knees where I could get my bearings. Our conversation was brief; talking was too difficult. I assured Dad Goetz I would be home as soon as I could get there.

The receiver never left my hand as I hit the buttons, waited for the dial tone, and frantically called my pastor. The phone rang and rang. I just *knew* the pastor was home. Finally, in numbness, I accepted the fact that, need him or not, he was not there. If it were not for God, I would almost have felt betrayed. *Where were you when I needed you?*

"Where were you?" It may be a question you can ask of others, but you can never ask it of God. For He can say, "I'm omnipresent, My child. I am there all the time."

O Beloved, He is there. You can find Him, on your knees. Call on Him.

God's Word...
Your Refuge

"BEHOLD, I AM THE LORD, the God of all flesh; is anything too difficult for Me?... Call to Me, and I will answer you, and I will tell you great and mighty things, which you do not know" (Jeremiah 32:27; 33:3).

I will be eternally grateful to my God that my pastor was not home. For if he had been, I might have missed what God said to me that day. And over the years, when the past has come back like a flash flood to drown me in morose memories, my Heavenly Father's words, which He quickened to my heart that day, have kept my head above the waters.

When I hung up the phone, I cried out, "O God...." And, as I said, He had been there all the time, waiting for me to call. "O God" was all I had to say. He knew it all. He had known it before the foundation of the world, and He would provide the way of escape. I could bear it, or He would not have allowed it to happen.

When I said, "O God," He quickened three things to my heart in that intimate yet inaudible still, small voice. Now, mind you, I was only months old in the Lord. No one had taught me to memorize Scripture, yet I had read and read God's Word, literally devouring the pages of the New Testament in wonder and awe. Thus, the first thing God said to me was, "All things... work together for good." It was Romans 8:28, a verse I had read and thought upon, though I didn't know just then where to find it.

Here was a sure promise from my God and Father in which, believing, I could find solace. God is in control and, because He is sovereign, He can take each and every situation in a believer's life and cause "all things to work together for good."

The good, the end result of it all, will be to conform His children to the image of His Son. If that is God's goal and everything in a believer's life has that end, then I could believe the next thing God said to me. What was it? We will look at it tomorrow.

For today, let me ask you a question: Precious one, where do you run to in the day of trouble? To the arms of flesh or to the God of all flesh who said, "Call upon Me in the day of trouble" (Psalm 50:15)?

Believe God . . . Live in Peace

THE SECOND THING God said to me that memorable day was, "In everything give thanks." At the time, that was enough for His new babe in Christ. And so I said, in childlike trust, "Thank You, Father." I couldn't have told you where that verse was then, but I can tell you now—1 Thessalonians 5:18. And I can tell you, looking back on it in its fullness and its context and from the perspective of God's sovereignty, that all untoward circumstances of life, all ploys of men or of Satan, and even all mistakes are so watched and so supremely governed and overridden by God that ultimately they will be used to achieve God's will for each one who belongs to Christ Jesus. This, Beloved, is our heritage as children of the Sovereign God.

And does this promise cover only the days of my life after I came to know Jesus Christ as my Lord and Savior? No, I do not believe so. When God says, "All things . . . work together for good," I believe He means all the things that have happened in your life since you were first conceived in your mother's womb. Even the way you were formed, even the parents that conceived you are part of God's plan to conform you into His image, "just as He chose us in Him before the foundation of the world" (Ephesians 1:4). Because of this, you can give thanks in everything, "for this is the will of God in Christ Jesus concerning you" (2 Thessalonians 5:18b KJV).

Do you realize what peace would be yours if you would only believe what God has said and bow your knee in humble, trusting thanksgiving? Then you would cease replaying bitter memories of horrible days gone by—days that have been overruled by His promises and His sovereign rule. With a touch from His scepter they have been turned into good—your eternal good.

Now, as you go back and reread today's devotional, may God grant you the blessed ability to see all of life through the prism of His infallible Word.

God's Faithfulness . . .
Your Sufficiency

THE THIRD THING God said to me when I learned of Tom's suicide was, "I will not give you anything that you cannot bear." Oh, what a promise that was to me! A year or two later I would memorize four assurance verses, including 1 Corinthians 10:13. In studying the meaning of temptation in that verse, I would understand that it could also be translated "trial" or "testing."

> God is faithful, who will not suffer you to be tempted [tried or tested] above that ye are able; but will with the temptation also make a way of escape, that ye may be able to bear it (KJV).

It was true, and it was mine for the obedience of faith.

Meanwhile, however, those three things God had spoken to my heart, plus the hours I had spent reading God's Word, enabled me to sit in the pew and look at Tom's casket, which rested on the very spot where we had once stood and pledged our vows to each other. "In sickness and in health . . . ." Tom had been sick, mentally sick, manic-depressive. "For richer or for poorer . . . until death do us part." But death had not parted us. I had. When the marriage got so bad I thought I couldn't take it any longer, I had walked out. But not before lacerating him irreparably with a tongue "set on fire by hell" (James 3:6).

I might as well have put the rope around his neck myself. I knew it. I was guilty, and I could have kept on chasing "what ifs" or "if onlys" down the corridors of my imagination forever. But to do so would have been to deny what I knew about God and what He had said to me.

No, I had acknowledged my sin; I had sought His forgiveness; I had heard His cry from Calvary's tree as He hung there cursed for me: "Father, forgive Kay, for she knows not what she does." And I really had not known, at least not from the true perspective of life, for I was blind. If I had seen then as I do now, I never would have left Tom. However, it was done. Tom was dead. I had to live.

And how would I live? I would live by every word that proceeded out of the mouth of my God (Matthew 4:4).

God's Faithfulness . . . Your Provision

ONE OF THE NAMES for God is Jehovah-jireh. It means "the Lord will provide." Abraham was the first to use this name for God when God tested him at Mount Moriah. Until this time, Abraham had received all of the benefits of God's covenant. Now it was time to test Abraham's covenant commitment to God. Would Abraham love God enough to give up his only son?

You probably know the story; it's recorded in Genesis 22. As Abraham took the knife to slay his son at God's command, "the angel of the LORD called to him from heaven, and said, 'Abraham, Abraham! . . . Do not stretch out your hand against the lad, and do nothing to him; for now I know that you fear God, since you have not withheld your son, your only son, from Me'" (Genesis 22:11,12).

It was then that Abraham learned that when God tested, He also provided. There is always His provision for every situation of life, every trial, every testing, every temptation. Genesis 22:14 says, "And Abraham called the name of that place The LORD Will Provide, as it is said to this day, 'In the mount of the LORD it will be provided.'"

Mount Moriah, the "mount of the LORD," is where the temple would one day be built. There men would meet with God and in time learn of the Savior through whom God would provide all of man's needs. "And my God shall supply all your needs according to His riches in glory in Christ Jesus" (Philippians 4:19).

The Father knows how to give good gifts to His children, for "every good thing bestowed and every perfect gift is from above, coming down from the Father of lights, with whom there is no variation, or shifting shadow" (James 1:17). And He is the same yesterday, today, and forever (Hebrews 13:8). The Jehovah-jireh of Abraham is your Jehovah-jireh, the God who provides.

To whom do you run in time of trouble? O precious one, whatever your need, learn to run first to the outstretched arms of Calvary where you will find His all-sufficient grace . . . grace to help in time of need (Hebrews 4:16). Then wait on the Lord, that He might provide in His perfect time all your need. Not to do so is to end up in the horrible distress that comes when we will not walk in obedience of faith.

Living in His Sovereignty

I HAVE KNOWN GOD as my Father for over thirty years, and I could tell you one story after another of how He has faithfully provided all I have needed.

After Tom's death, I began to feel that God wanted me to attend Bible school. Having had surgery on my neck and being locked into an immobilizing neck brace, I was on leave of absence from Johns Hopkins where I worked on a research team as a registered nurse. After much prayer and a period of recovery, I met a couple who were leaving soon to go to school in Chattanooga, Tennessee. Having sought out positions as a school nurse, only to have those doors close, I felt God wanted me to go to this Bible school too.

I had read the biographies of George Mueller, Dwight L. Moody, Charles Haddon Spurgeon, and Madame Guyon. And I knew their God—the God who provided all their needs—was also my God.

I made application, but there was no time to wait for a response. So by faith I rented the other half of a U-Haul truck from my new friends. With a small amount of cash in my pocket, $350 in the bank, and a station wagon loaded down with two sons, a dog, and a potted tree, I set off with His promise: "Faithful is He who calls you, and He also will bring it to pass" (1 Thessalonians 5:24).

I was a little like Abraham, who went out not knowing exactly where he was going. I knew I was headed for Chattanooga, Tennessee, but that was all. The only people I knew there were the two new friends I was traveling with. I had no job, no home, and, as of yet, no school!

We arrived in Chattanooga with the morning sun. But now what was I going to do? As I walked into my friends' empty house, I was thinking of our needs, the boys' and mine. We had to live somewhere, but where? As I walked into their house, I did, I guess, what every woman does when she walks into a new house. I went to the window over the kitchen sink to survey the rest of the neighborhood. And there, across the backyard, was a little brick house. I couldn't believe my eyes! It looked empty! Was it? I had to find out.

Jehovah-jireh—THE LORD WILL PROVIDE. Do you know His name?

Your Extremities . . . God's Opportunities

I DASHED ACROSS THE BACKYARD crying out, "Maybe this is what God has for us." Nose pressed against the glass, hands cupped over my eyes to shut out the glare, I twisted and turned to see all that I could through those glass patio doors. It looked empty. Then I ran to the front of the little three-bedroom brick house. There it was—*For Sale.*

I flew back to my friends' home saying the telephone number over and over again so that I wouldn't forget it. The real estate salesman didn't waste any time getting out there. He could spot a prospective buyer when he heard one! Why, he couldn't have missed! Or at least he thought so until he met me and found out that all I had to my name was $350, no husband, and no job—just two boys and a dog! And not only did I want to buy his house, I also wanted him to let me store my furniture in its garage until the loan was approved. I would apply for the loan on Monday. He was probably thinking, *Who would approve her loan?!* Yet God overruled his better judgment.

O Beloved, if only we could see that man's extremities are God's opportunities! When do we need God? At all times. But when do we usually turn to Him? Right! When there is no other way of escape. When we can't swing it ourselves. It's sad, but it's true, isn't it?

Yet, when we find that we cannot handle it ourselves and we run to Him, what do we find? We find a God of mercy, a God of compassion, a God who does not give us what we deserve, but a God who rules from a throne of grace—unmerited favor.

> The LORD's lovingkindnesses indeed never cease, for His compassions never fail. They are new every morning; great is Thy faithfulness. "The LORD is my portion," says my soul, "Therefore I have hope in Him." The LORD is good to those who wait for Him, to the person who seeks Him (Lamentations 3:22-25).

Think upon these things, and tomorrow I will continue our story. His and mine.

"Call Unto Me"

THE DOWN PAYMENT on the house was supposed to be $600, but since they had not installed an air-conditioning unit, they would let me have it for $350 down. I was so excited! Yes, I could store my furniture in the garage, the real estate agent said. But I did have to get a job before I went to apply for that loan.

Monday morning, I arrived bright and early at the hospital closest to our new home-to-be and walked out with a job. Then I went back to look at the house again. I remember walking across its backyard to a place where I stopped and prayed. I could probably take you to that spot today. "Father, I want this house only if it's Your will. If it's Your will, make them approve the loan. But if it's not, don't let them approve it, for You will have to make the payments on this house."

That afternoon as I sat in the FHA office, answering all the questions, I timidly said, "If the Lord wants me to have this house, He'll have this loan approved."

A muffled "What?" came from the head bent over my forms. Although she never looked up, I repeated what I had said, this time a little louder. Having gotten it out once, I now had more boldness: "If the Lord wants me to have this house, He will have this loan approved."

With that she dropped her pencil and asked incredulously, "Who?"

"The Lord God. He will have this loan approved. I've prayed about it." Her head went back down, still shaking.

The loan was approved. And was the real estate agent surprised! "Do you know how many couples have tried to buy this house and could not get their loans approved?" No, I didn't know, but it didn't matter; God had set aside that house for me, and I would live there for only $90 a month (including utilities) until His next provision came along.

Now there was only one other thing that I felt we needed, and that I asked God to provide—a husband!

"Behold, I am the LORD, the God of all flesh; is there anything too hard for Me? . . . Call to Me, and I will answer you, and I will tell you great and mighty things, which you do not know" (Jeremiah 32:27; 33:3).

Be Strong

IT'S TRUE, BELOVED. The people who know their God not only can stand firm, but they can do exploits for Him, even in the midst of adversity. Within the year I was to learn another aspect of His sovereignty as God allowed someone to reach between His omnipotent fingers and touch me in a hurtful way.

"For promotion cometh neither from the east, nor from the west, nor from the south. But God is the judge: he putteth down one, and setteth up another" (Psalm 75:6,7 KJV). God, in His sovereignty, would put me down. When He knew my faith was mature enough to bear it, I would lose my job and run out of money. Yet even that would be filtered through fingers of love; and it would only be for a season, so I might learn more about the character and ways of my Sovereign Father.

I will share all this with you next month, Beloved, and I will tell you how God brought Jack and me together. For as we continue through the Museum of the Character and Sovereignty of Our God, I want you to see the practicality of it all and to apply it to your life so that, no matter what, you may stand firm. It is hard for me to convey the sense of urgency I feel, and the burden. I am so concerned because I feel the time is coming even closer when our faith will be tested to the core. And we are so ill-prepared because we do not know our God. We know *of* Him, but we really do not know *Him* because we are too busy, too involved, too entangled with the affairs of this life.

The setting of Daniel 11:32b—"But the people that do know their God shall be strong, and do exploits" (KJV)—is the end times. As you read from Daniel 11:32 through the end of Daniel, you will see several references to "those who have insight." Many of these people will endure great difficulties, yet they are the ones who "will give understanding" to others (Daniel 11:33) and who "will shine brightly like the brightness of the expanse of heaven" (Daniel 12:3).

Beloved, I am preparing for that time. I have determined that I will stand for my God no matter the cost. But to stand, I must know Him. And to know Him, I must have time with Him—time alone and time in His Word. What about you? Will you get to know your God?

Rest in Him

HER LETTER WAS VERY BRIEF. I ached as I read it. She was desperate, confused. "Our two sons, ages 19 and 31, were found murdered in their older brother's car. Where was God? How could He allow such a thing?"

Have you ever heard of some horrible tragedy and wondered the same thing? Where was God?

Some time ago I was given a message while speaking at Mount Hermon conference center. When I told the girl at the desk my name, she said, "I'm afraid I have bad news for you. Your husband just called. Dan DeHaan was killed in a plane crash."

My response to her was a simple, "Thank you," but to God I said, "Father, this is so hard to understand."

Dan was only 33. He loved his God and served Him fully. When Dan was still single, we taught teens side by side. Then God brought Penny, a widow with two sons and a daughter, into his life. Her first husband had been killed in a plane crash also.

I couldn't understand why God would let this happen, just as that dear mother couldn't understand why God would allow her two sons to be murdered. I still do not understand.

"Maybe it was an accident." That is what some would say. But if that were the case, then God had nothing to do with it! And if God had nothing to do with it, then where was God? Dan was God's son. Did God not know that Dan was in trouble as he piloted that little single-engine plane through the fog at night?

And what about the two sons who were murdered? Did God not know they were in danger? How could God allow Dan to die? How could God allow this woman's two sons to be murdered?

I do not know how God could allow either; I only know that He did. And although I cannot understand it or explain it, it is all right, for I know my God. "See now that I, I am He, and there is no god besides Me; it is I who put to death and give life" (Deuteronomy 32:39).

"But," you say, "what kind of a God is that?" We will see as we continue to look at God's character and His sovereignty.

————

Resting in His Sovereignty

If I were permitted to share only one truth with you, I would choose to teach you the character and sovereignty of our God, for this truth anchors my soul when I do not understand the circumstances of life. In this truth I find the peace, security, and rest that make me a conqueror over doubt and distress. It is my prayer as we move together in these days that you, too, will find great stability and endless hope in the knowledge of who your God is, and in the certainty that He is on His throne!

————

God . . . All That You Need

IF THERE IS ONE TRUTH that I want to know and fully understand, it is the sovereignty of God. This truth holds everything else together. It's the truth I run to, crying, "Abba, Father." There, in childlike trust, I can bury myself in the folds of His garment. There I can shut out all the whys, wherefores, and hows as God lifts me up in outstretched arms and looks straight into my eyes. There my questions disappear, for I see His face—a face that reveals His character. And that is all I need to see! Just Him . . . "for He cannot deny Himself" (2 Timothy 2:13). Whether I can understand what has happened or not, it is all right; for I know that, as my God rules from His sovereign throne, He cannot deny who He is!

God is first and primarily a loving, holy God. He is a wise and just God, righteous in all His ways, merciful and long-suffering. He is immutable—never-changing—and never, never failing. True, His righteousness requires that His wrath punish all unrighteousness. Yet this is only right; for to let unrighteousness go unjudged would be wrong. God cannot do what is wrong.

And from where did such a God come? He has always been. He is the eternal, self-existent, self-sufficient God who is infinite in His realm and truthful in all His words. Omniscient, omnipotent, omni-present, He is incomprehensible. He is a jealous God who will share His glory with none.

This is my God. This is the One to whom I run when everything seems wrong. In His presence I find answers that enable me to cope with life. There I can live in the absolute certainty "that all things work together for good to them that love God, to them who are the called according to his purpose" (Romans 8:28 KJV).

And you, precious one, what is your God like? How far can you trust Him?

You will be able to trust Him only to the extent that you know Him! And that is what I pray will happen as never before for you—that you will know your God.

Kept in His Perfect Peace

BELOVED, KNOWING YOUR GOD and understanding His sovereignty will hold you when nothing else will. When we say to Him, "God, I cannot understand why," we still need to know that we can trust Him—understand or not!

If a child of God can understand early in his or her Christian walk that God is in control of everything, it will save much heartache. It is a truth that will give you inexplicable peace—peace that will shelter you in the worst of storms, peace that will calm the overwhelming waves of depression that seek to slap you down and catch you in an undertow of despair, peace that will enable you to see far beyond today and tomorrow to the shores of eternity, peace that will cause you to endure as seeing Him who is invisible (Hebrews 11:27).

"Thou wilt keep him in perfect peace, whose mind is stayed on thee: because he trusteth in thee," says Isaiah 26:3 KJV. A mind stayed upon God is a mind at peace.

But what does it mean to stay your mind upon God? Is it simply saying over and over again, "I believe in God"? No, I do not believe so. Rather, it is concentrating on the aspects of the character of God that appropriately apply to the situation in which you find yourself.

For instance, where was God when Dan DeHaan got into trouble as he flew into the fog? Or where was God when those two sons were being shot to death? God was there. He is present everywhere. And even in that time of human tragedy, God was there operating in His mercy. He could have stopped it all, changed the circumstances, and come to their rescue. Yet He did not. Why? I do not know. I do not understand. I only know that, understand it or not, it is all right. I can say this because of His character.

God cannot lie; He is righteous. His promises, which are yea and amen (true and so be it), were theirs in their moment of distress. "For He Himself has said, 'I WILL NEVER DESERT YOU, NOR WILL I EVER FORSAKE YOU'" (Hebrews 13:5).

This month may God grant us deeper insight into His character and the marvelous peace that results from such knowledge.

Standing on His Word

IT WAS AUGUST 1978. Karen and Sarah (not their real names) had taken several days off to bask in the Florida sun and study God's Word. They were settled in their room one evening, listening to tapes on prophecy from Moody Bible Institute. The porter had just delivered the cheeseburgers they had ordered from the motel restaurant, and he was returning to get their Cokes. He left the door to their room ajar . . . he would return in just a minute or two.

Suddenly the door flew open. In burst two men with black stockings covering their faces. Each had a gun.

"One held a gun on us while the other went through our luggage," says Sarah. "One said, 'If anyone comes through that door, they're dead.'

"Because of having been at Precept Ministries and having studied the Word, we were able, I think, to stand in the midst of all of this," Sarah continued. "We had learned that God is sovereign and that everything that happens is filtered through His fingers of love. We knew we were in His hands."

When this happened, Sarah was only two years old in Jesus Christ. She and Karen drove about forty-five minutes from a nearby city to Precept Ministries each week to attend our course on Romans. Sarah was saved while we were studying Romans 3. Now, two years later, both were teaching Sunday school.

"I had just taught Romans 8:28 before we left for Florida," Sarah says. "As I sat in that motel room, it kept going through my head, 'And we know that all things work together for good to them that love God, to them who are the called according to his purpose.'"

She and Karen had learned about God's sovereignty in the Word, but they experienced it in that motel room.

I will continue their story tomorrow. But before you read on, let me ask you: What if that had been you? Would you have been ready to die? Would you have realized you were in God's hands rather than the gunmen's?

Your Help and Shield

"THEY CONTINUED TO HOLD US for about twenty minutes," Sarah said of their ordeal. "I kept wondering where the porter was. They searched all over our room. They made me take my watch off. Then one took his shirt and began wiping off fingerprints.

"When the porter knocked, the men opened the door and got behind it so that he couldn't see them. As the porter walked through the door, he must have seen the fear on our faces, and he turned toward them. One of them shot him right below the eye. He was killed instantly. The man who shot him ran out the door. The other one stepped across the porter's body, reached out with his gun and shot Karen under her right eye. The bullet came out just beneath her left ear. Karen fell backward onto the bed and lay there drowning in her own blood. Then he turned and shot me. The bullet went in my left cheek and exited under my left ear. I knew that was my last breath. I just knew that anyone who was shot in the head would die!

"Before he shot us, I thought my heart would beat out of my body from sheer fright. But as soon as I thought I would die any minute, all I could think about was seeing Jesus. I didn't think about my children; I didn't think about my husband. There was just a kind of anticipation. I thought, 'I'm going to see Jesus at any time.' I wasn't sad. When the man ran out of our room, I remember saying, 'Father, forgive him.'

"I called the desk and told them that we had been robbed and shot. At the very moment that the motel called the police and the ambulance, there was a paramedic passing by on his way home from work. When he heard the call going out to the police over his radio, he came straight to our room and saved Karen's life."

> The king is not saved by a mighty army; a warrior is not delivered by great strength. . . . Behold, the eye of the LORD is on those who fear Him, on those who hope for His lovingkindness, to deliver their soul from death (Psalm 33:16-19).

We will finish the story tomorrow. For now, meditate for a few minutes on this Scripture. It is God's Word.

The Keeper of Life

NOT ONLY HAD KAREN been wounded worse than Sarah, she had also lost a lot of blood. As she lay in the hospital the first three days, all she said over and over was, "No man can take my life. God is sovereign, and He holds the keys to life and death" (Revelation 1:18).

"When I was shot, I had an anticipation," recalls Karen. "I don't know how else to explain it except I had an anticipation, and I saw a light. My next thought was that I would see Jesus. When I came to myself, I thought, 'That's no light; that's the ceiling!' Then I remembered telling Sarah to telephone for help. And I remembered her saying to me, 'Turn over! Turn over!' but I couldn't. I felt just like my head was pinned to the bed. Then the paramedic came in the door. Immediately Sarah told him to turn me over. . . .

"At the hospital all that night when I kept saying over and over, 'No man can take my life. God is sovereign, and He holds the keys to life and death,' a lot of those doctors couldn't get over what I was saying. One of them said, 'I would sure like to know your God!'

"You know, when those men were in our room we never begged or pleaded. Even when we were shot, we never moved or flinched. I have thought of it so many times. The doctor said if I had moved even a fraction either way, the bullet would have hit my jugular vein. It was so close that it clipped a nerve. Being shot at such close range blew my eyeball out, but it also saved my eye. Isn't that something! If my eye had not been blown out, it would have been destroyed. Also, because I was sitting on the edge of the bed with my feet on the floor, and because the gunman was above me, the bullet went in at such an angle it just missed everything. God had it all under control."

That is it, Beloved. No matter what happens, whether good or bad, God is in control. If that were not true, we would be in the hands of mere men or victims of the whims of fate! But listen:

> "For I am God, and there is no other; I am God, and there
> is no one like Me, declaring the end from the beginning
> and from ancient times things which have not been done,
> saying, 'My purpose will be established, and I will
> accomplish all My good pleasure' " (Isaiah 46:9,10).

His Peace . . . His Promise

OUR MINDS ARE MEMORY BANKS, able not only to call up the details of events that have happened to us, but also to flash on the screen such vivid pictures that we feel the emotions all over again. Even the slightest touch and the scanner is at work searching out the past. A word, a look, a sight, a sound, a fragrance, a certain time of year, a certain type of day—and the whole event is recalled.

How do you handle this when the event has been a tragedy? Never talk about it? Become bitter? Blame God? Take pills? Drink? Never get over it? Or live with "what ifs" or "if onlys"?

Karen said, "I relived that porter's death so many times. Every time I saw a black person, it was like triggering a tape recorder. I kept wishing I had cried, 'Don't come in here!' so that maybe I could have saved his life. Finally, I realized that I had to set my mind on things that were pure and lovely and worthy of praise . . . I had to 'Philippians 4:8' it! When I obeyed God, I had peace. I quit reliving it, and the peace of God mounted guard around my heart and mind."

And you, Beloved, how do you handle your tragedies? Have they maimed, crippled, or destroyed you? Or do you "Philippians 4:8" them?

> Finally, brethren, whatever is true, whatever is honorable, whatever is right, whatever is pure, whatever is lovely, whatever is of good repute, if there is any excellence and if anything worthy of praise, let your mind dwell on these things (Philippians 4:8).

If you will bring every thought under the inspection of Philippians 4:8 and reject each thought, each memory that does not meet its qualifications, then, Beloved, "the peace of God, which surpasses all comprehension, shall guard your hearts and your minds in Christ Jesus. . . . and the God of peace shall be with you" (Philippians 4:7,9b).

This is God's promise to you. It is yours for obedience!

Eternity . . . With Him?

BUT HOW CAN SUCH TRAGEDY, such pain, ever work together for good? What's the good in Dan's plane crash or in being shot through the head or in anything that brings distress of any kind? How can a God of love and mercy, if He is sovereign, allow such things?

First of all, we must remember that we are eternal beings. All of life, whatever it brings, is God's means of preparing us for eternity. Every human being will live forever—either in heaven (Matthew 7:21) or in the lake of fire (Matthew 25:40-46). Our passing from physical life into physical death is not the end.

Therefore, the death of a Christian brings distress only to the ones who are left behind. For the true child of God, to be absent from the body is to be present with the Lord (2 Corinthians 5:8); to die is gain (Philippians 1:21). I promise you that anyone who has ever entered into heaven would never choose to come back to earth.

But what if the one who dies is not a Christian? How can a tragedy like that work together for good?

For the one who dies without Christ, it does not work together for good; God did not promise that it would. His promise is only to those "who love God, to those who are called according to His purpose" (Romans 8:28). Yet, Beloved, that person never would have been saved, even if he or she had lived hundreds of years. God knew that (John 6:37,39; 10:26-29). He knew that person would refuse to come to Him so that he might have life; therefore, another aspect of God's character, His wrath, is shown.

> For the wrath of God is revealed from heaven against all ungodliness and unrighteousness of men, who suppress the truth in unrighteousness, because that which is known about God is evident within them; for God made it evident to them (Romans 1:18,19).

That person knew God was God, but because he refused His righteousness, he experienced His wrath.

If you were to die, how would it be for you?

You Are Eternal

DEATH SERVES AS A CONSTANT REMINDER that this life, as we know it, is temporal. The wail of sirens, the ink on newspapers, the coverage of television, the tears of the bereaved ever herald the truth, "It is appointed for men to die once" (Hebrews 9:27). All men and women know this, even if they do not believe the remainder of the verse: "and after this *comes* judgment."

And so God, in His sovereignty, uses death to bring life. At Dan DeHaan's funeral the pastor gave an invitation from God. When Karen and Sarah share their testimony, they give an invitation from God. And what is God's invitation?

"Will you believe on the Lord Jesus Christ so that you might have life? Will you bow before Me and say, 'My Lord and my God'? Will you give up and surrender your all to Me, deny yourself, take up your cross, and begin following Me for the rest of your life?"

Thus death and tragedy work together for good, for they become a platform for the gospel of Jesus Christ. From that platform the dead can yet speak (Hebrews 11:4), testifying by their lives as to where they will spend eternity, for true faith has works which others can see (James 2:14-26). Or if there has been a near-death conversion, there is the testimony of a life that came so close to eternity without God that it cried out, "For what does it profit a man to gain the whole world, and forfeit his soul?" (Mark 8:36).

The verse God gave us that explained the whole purpose of our seeming tragedy was Genesis 50:20: 'And as for you, you meant evil against me, but God meant it for good in order to bring about this present result, to preserve many people alive.' Through our testimony many people have been saved, and that makes it all worthwhile."

And you, precious one for whom Christ died, if you have not accepted God's invitation, may I ask why not? Why don't you think about your answer and consider whether or not it is worth it? Remember: You are eternal.

Prepared for Eternity

ALL OF LIFE, WHATEVER IT BRINGS, is God's means of preparing us for eternity. Understanding this can keep you from bitterness.

The dear woman who wrote me about the murder of her two sons said, "Sometimes I think there is no God. Why did my two sons have to die? Why?"

I understand her pain. My sons were not murdered, but their father murdered himself. I hurt with her.

Does a God who is in control sit on His heavenly throne and idly watch such things and not have a purpose for them? Does He waste pain, tragedy, suffering, tears, broken hearts? Or does He redeem them from the waste bins of life's marketplace and recycle them, using them for His glory and our ultimate good? He recycles them, of course. And although that process may be very painful, someday we will see "that the sufferings of this present time are not worthy to be compared with the glory that is to be revealed to us" (Romans 8:18).

His grace is there, available to all, sufficient for any and every circumstance of life (2 Corinthians 12:9). It is ours through the appropriation of faith. We must simply take God at His word: "See to it that no one comes short of the grace of God; that no root of bitterness springing up causes trouble, and by it many be defiled" (Hebrews 12:15).

Not to receive His grace will result in a greater tragedy than the one that caused your bitterness. And your bitterness will defile others.

Our tragedies are permitted for two reasons: that we might become more like Jesus and that others might see the reality of our God and long to know Him as we know Him.

"For we who live are constantly being delivered over to death [death to my will, my way, my life] for Jesus' sake, that the life of Jesus also may be manifested in our mortal flesh" (2 Corinthians 4:11).

The more trials we experience, the more we become like Jesus, if we appropriate His grace. Therefore, all of life, whatever it brings, prepares us for eternity.

FEBRUARY 10

His Higher Ways

"Can you discover the depths of God? Can you discover the limits of the Almighty? They are high as the heavens, what can you do? Deeper than Sheol, what can you know? Its measure is longer than the earth, and broader than the sea. If He passes by or shuts up, or calls an assembly, who can restrain Him?" (Job 11:7-10).

BECAUSE GOD IS GOD, He is beyond our understanding. Incomprehensible! That is what God is. Try as we may to make Him logical, to confine Him to our box of human reasoning and comprehension, we cannot. He will not, He cannot, be put into a box. He is God. His ways, His acts, His character are higher than ours.

Oh, the depths of the riches both of the wisdom and knowledge of God! How unsearchable are His judgments and unfathomable His ways! For WHO HAS KNOWN THE MIND OF THE LORD, OR WHO BECAME HIS COUNSELOR? OR WHO HAS FIRST GIVEN TO HIM THAT IT MIGHT BE PAID BACK TO HIM AGAIN? For from Him and through Him and to Him are all things. To Him be the glory forever. Amen (Romans 11:33-36).

Have you realized that you can only understand that which God chooses to reveal to you? Have you accepted the fact that He is God and that you are mere man, and that because He is incomprehensible, there will have to be times when you will need, by faith, to cease trying to figure Him out and simply rest in His character and His sovereignty?

Oh, how good it is to become a child, to *snuggle* rather than *struggle,* to see that it is enough just to accept the fact that He is the Father and you are the child. Young children do not try to understand their father; they simply take him at his word.

Have you been struggling? Are you confused because you cannot figure Him out? Do you wrestle with "whys" and "hows"? Snuggle— just snuggle like a child. You are in His arms. When you do, what rest you will find for your tormented soul!

You Can Know Him

"THAT I MAY KNOW HIM" (Philippians 3:10). This was the passion of the apostle Paul's life. It is also the passion of my life. Is it the passion of your life?

And how do we come to know Him? I believe it happens primarily in three ways. First, we come to know Him through His Word as the Holy Spirit guides us into all truth and reveals the things of God to us (1 Corinthians 2:9-16). Second, our various life experiences teach us more about Him. For instance, how will you realize that God is faithful if He never permits you to be in a situation where you can see His faithfulness? Third, we come to know Him through the experiences and testimonies of others.

If you were to know God through His Word and yet never experienced its reality in the test tube of life, how well do you think you would know Him? Not very well! It takes experience. This is the meaning of the word *know* in Philippians 3:10. It means "to know experientially."

Tomorrow, I will begin sharing with you some of the experiences that have given me a deeper, personal knowledge of God. To be honest, at times they were challenging and painful; yet I would not have missed one of them. For along with His Word and the testimonies of others, they are what have made me what I am in Him. And they have given me a confidence in my God that I would not exchange for anything on this earth.

"But if it brings pain, then I'd rather not know Him," you may say.

To that, Beloved, I would say, "But can you bear to live without knowing Him? That truly is unbearable pain."

Take a few minutes and talk to God about Paul's words in Philippians 3:8:

> More than that, I count all things to be loss in view of the surpassing value of knowing Christ Jesus my Lord, for whom I have suffered the loss of all things, and count them but rubbish in order that I may gain Christ.

What does the Spirit bring to your mind as you meditate on this verse?

My Test of Faith

YOU HAVE, IN ALL PROBABILITY, sung the chorus, "God is so good, God is so good, God is so good, He's so good to me." It's sweet and simple and the words are easy to remember. But is it true?

Yes, it is true. The psalmist wrote, "Praise the LORD! Oh give thanks to the LORD, for He is good; for His lovingkindness is everlasting" (Psalm 106:1). If God is good, then He can never act apart from His goodness, and I can sing this chorus at any and all times, even when things do not seem to be going my way!

I was on duty one evening at the hospital, and as I made my rounds, I came upon one dear old man who was absolutely terrified. From what I had heard at report he was a patient to be avoided, yet my heart went out to him. He needed peace. So after asking him if he would let me read God's Word to him, I took the Gideon Bible from his bedside drawer and read him passage after passage. Peace came for him, and it was precious.

The next day, however, I was asked to report to the Director of Nursing where I learned that another nurse had reported my conversation with the elderly patient.

"Kay," she said, "your nursing is beautiful, but you will have to stop telling your patients about Jesus."

"Have my patients complained?" I asked.

"No, but you can't talk about Jesus. God Almighty doesn't need people like you to go around telling them of His existence."

"I'm sorry. I cannot stop. I will just have to quit my job."

"No, we don't want you to do that. Your nursing is beautiful. You just need to be quiet about God and the Bible."

But I couldn't quit telling people about Jesus. They needed Him. Without Him there was no peace.

So, I quit. I had no savings, and my boys and I already lived from hand to mouth. My two boys and I—and our God . . . who is so good.

A trial came for me, and it was precious. Through that trial I would come to know God as my Jehovah-jireh (the Lord will provide) in an even deeper way. And through that trial the reality of my faith would once again be confirmed to me.

Jehovah-jireh . . . My Provider

THE NEXT DAY I WAS out looking for a job. I had a school bill to pay, children to feed, and house payments to make. By that afternoon I had a job offer. The only problem was that nothing was right about it, and I knew it wasn't where God wanted me.

It would be two weeks before I would work again, and two weeks more before my first paycheck. Before that, my money ran out.

I began every day singing to my Jehovah-jireh, my God who promised that He would supply all my needs (Philippians 4:19)! The gas gauge on Bluie, my faithful station wagon, was broken, so every morning when the boys and I piled into the car to go to school, we sang, "Give me gas in my car, keep me going, going, going. Give me gas in my car, I pray." I wish I could sing it for you! Then you would understand why the Lord kept us waiting only weeks instead of months. *You should hear my singing!*

The day I ran out of gas I was on the school campus, so there were plenty of friends to come to my rescue. Also, that day someone gave me $2. Then a bag of groceries appeared in our kitchen.

God is good, so good, but would I have ever realized just how good if I had never found myself between a rock and a hard place? When those times come, He is still good. He never changes. His lovingkindnesses are new every morning.

The job He eventually provided was at the Diagnostic Hospital. There, in the year to come, I would freely share Jesus Christ with my precious patients. But even more exciting, I would witness to one of the doctors who hired me, Dr. Maurice Rawlings. Years later Maurice would be saved and would author three bestselling Christian books. And who would help him with the scriptural part of *Beyond Death's Door* and *Before Death Comes*? I would!

I will never forget the first night we went over the manuscript of *Beyond Death's Door*. We were sitting on the couch praying. I looked up and Maurice was shaking his head. "Kay," he said, "who would ever have thought we'd be holding hands praying?!"

"He indeed is good for His lovingkindness is everlasting" (2 Chronicles 5:13b).

Nothing Too Difficult

"FATHER, DO YOU WANT ME to have a husband?" I needed to know. I had looked all over our Bible school and college campus and our church and hadn't seen any likely candidate. The prospect of finding a husband seemed pretty dismal! Yet if God wanted me to have a husband, He certainly wasn't limited by our campus or the membership of our church. There was a whole big world out there and my omniscient Father knew everyone, so I decided to discuss the matter with Him in prayer and commit the entire situation to Him.

"Father, You are omnipresent and there is nothing too hard for You; You are omnipotent. Therefore, will You please search the world over and bring me the husband of Your choice. You know I have trouble picking out men, so You pick one for me and bring him to me." I had prayed according to the attributes of my God. Now I would wait and see what He would do.

I prayed that in November or early December 1964. What inspired it was a paper I was writing on Genesis. Before we left on Christmas break, we had to hand in a paper that dealt with some aspect of the first 25 chapters of Genesis. I chose Genesis 24, for the theme of that chapter had become dear to me as a young widow with two sons. (In Genesis 24, Abraham sends out his servant to find a bride for his son, Isaac.)

I titled my paper, "On Hunting Husbands and Winning Wives," and in it I showed, first of all, how God sends His Holy Spirit out to obtain a bride for His Son, the Lord Jesus Christ. Then I explained how God, because He is omnipresent, can search the whole world over and find the perfect mate for each of us. If He is sovereign and omnipotent, then, in His own way and in His own time, He can bring a man and a woman together to become one with Him. "Is anything too difficult for the LORD?" (Genesis 18:14).

I think I got an A on my paper. I know I got an A + on my prayer. I will tell you about it tomorrow.

For today, why don't you think about Genesis 18:14: "Is anything too difficult for the LORD?"

Comforted in God's Hands

DURING CHRISTMAS BREAK the boys and I drove to Michigan to be with my family. As a one-and-a-half-year-old child of God, I had written to every member of my family, explaining how to be born again. Well, that went over like a porcupine in a balloon factory. No one wanted to discuss the subject; my porcupine needles had already done their damage. The whole family became upset, and we went to our separate rooms to cry.

As I talked with God there on my knees beside the bed, I felt like Elijah—so alone. I was just kneeling, saying nothing, just hurting and needing comfort. I loved my family. We're lovers, not scrappers! I loved my God. I didn't want to hurt either. Then He spoke, in a still, small voice in my mind. What He said really caught me off guard!

"You are going to marry Jack Arthur." That was all. That was enough! It certainly took my mind off my hurt. I wouldn't be alone any more; I'd have a husband, a husband who understood me.

Someone had told me about Jack. "He's a bachelor who really loves the Lord." Jack was a missionary with the Pocket Testament League serving in South America. Our church had prayed for him because he had been stoned for preaching the gospel.

I had heard about Jack, but I didn't know what he looked like. So the first thing I did was get his missionary prayer card with his picture so I would recognize him when he came along! God had searched the world: There Jack was in Argentina and there I was in Chattanooga, Tennessee. Now, He would have to bring Jack to me.

I would wait almost six months before I would see Jack face-to-face when we met for the first time in the Happy Corner, the ice cream shop at the school I was attending. At one time, as an older student, Jack had managed the Happy Corner, never realizing that it would be the "field" where he would meet his Rebekah—and her two sons!

"The righteous, and the wise, and their works, are in the hand of God" (Ecclesiastes 9:1 KJV).

"I Commit My Cause"

IT WAS JUNE, beautiful June, when the evenings are long and warm and you just want to be out enjoying it all—going somewhere, doing something, anything, just to be outside.

Late that Friday I received a call from the hospital. "Kay, we won't need you tonight. We have no patients."

They may not have needed me, but I needed them. I needed that twelve hours of pay. Even though we had no patients, someone might come to the clinic during the night.

Immediately I was praying, "Father, why did You let them close the hospital? You know I have a school bill to pay. I need that money."

His answer came quickly. "In everything, give thanks."

"All right, Father, I don't know why, but thank You anyway."

An unexpected night off . . . a warm June evening. The boys and I would go to a recital at school. Little did I know that someone else had the same idea.

That same day, Jack Arthur was passing through Chattanooga on his way home to visit his grandparents. Mom and Pop, his grandparents, had raised him, and Pop's life seemed to be ebbing away. However, on the way to Indiana there was another father to be visited, Jack's spiritual father, Dr. Charles Weigel.

So on that lovely, warm June evening, Jack and Dr. Weigel decided to walk over to Philips Memorial Chapel to hear the recital. Oh, how Dr. Weigel loved to sing! As students, our hearts thrilled when he stood in chapel, threw up his hands, pulled out all the stops, and sang his favorite, "No One Ever Cared For Me Like Jesus." Little did I realize that Jack was his beloved son in the gospel. If I had, I probably would have become friends with Dr. Weigel!

I had thought seriously, at first, about helping God bring Jack and me together. I thought about writing Jack in South America and telling him that this young widow with two sons was praying for him as she attended his alma mater! But then I came to my senses. "No, Father, if this is of You, then You can bring it to pass without my help."

"Unto God would I commit my cause; which doeth great things and unsearchable; marvellous things without number" (Job 5:8,9 KJV).

"Truly I Have Spoken"

AFTER THE RECITAL the boys wanted an ice cream cone from the Happy Corner, and I wasn't in any hurry to get home.

The young man at the soda fountain had just placed two chocolate ice cream cones in my hands when I heard the words, "Mr. Arthur, would you please sign my Bible?"

I had the boys praying for Jack, so they had recognized him from his picture. Of course, I hadn't told them what God had told me!

I gladly delivered the ice cream cones to my sons and immediately introduced myself. How I did it I don't know, but I made sure Jack knew he was talking to a widow. I really don't remember too much of our conversation that night. I was too nervous and excited.

However, I do remember one thing Jack said. He said, "In December I'm going back to South America." And in my mind I said, *Well, you don't know it, but I'm going with you!*

Jack left Chattanooga the next day, and I went to see the school registrar. If I was going to South America, I had better go to summer school and graduate so I'd be ready.

Well, I graduated. But still no Jack! So I enrolled in more classes. And just when I had gotten into my Greek alphabet, he once again appeared on the scene.

We bumped into one another on the corner of Orchard Knob and Union right there on campus. That night we went out to dinner. And in November Jack asked me to marry him. To which I replied, calmly, "Jack, I have something to tell you. God told me I was going to marry you eleven months ago!"

When we told the boys, Mark said, "Well, God says, 'Ask and you shall receive.' "

Jack said laughingly, "I never had a chance!"

He didn't. Our Father knew we needed to be together!

"Truly I have spoken," God says. "Truly I will bring it to pass. I have planned it, surely I will do it" (Isaiah 46:11b).

What, precious one, has God spoken to you? If He has spoken, then rest assured; if He has planned, none shall frustrate Him.

God Is Holy

WHEN YOU READ or hear about how God blesses and deals with others, do you feel a twinge of jealousy? Sometimes it's hard to take, isn't it? Others seem to have so much, more than they really need, while you can hardly make ends meet! And where is the just God you have heard and read about? Where is the God who is no respecter of persons?

He is there, Beloved—holy, righteous, just in all His ways. Do not walk by the sight of your eyes, nor by the passions of your heart. Do not listen to that subtle voice of accusation. You cannot see or know all that God is doing. Do not try to figure Him out. Instead, learn of Him. You cannot trust someone that you do not really know.

For the next several days I want to talk with you about God's holiness, righteousness, and justice—the three aspects of His character that will help you when the liar seeks to defame your God and Father. You need to be prepared to stand when he whispers, "If God really loved you then . . ." or, "See, you're not special to God like that one. If you were, God would . . ."

Let me arm you with several Scriptures that describe your God. As you read them, underline any significant words or phrases that describe His character. Then meditate on the implications of calling such a God "Father."

> Then the LORD spoke to Moses, saying, "Speak to all the congregation of the sons of Israel and say to them, 'You shall be holy, for I the LORD your God am holy'" (Leviticus 19:1,2).

To be holy means to be morally excellent. Holiness is purity of being in every aspect; holiness is that which is set apart and, therefore, untainted with ungodliness.

> "The Rock! His work is perfect, for all His ways are just; a God of faithfulness and without injustice, righteous and upright is He" (Deuteronomy 32:4).

God Is Always Just

HE WAS 120 YEARS OLD, and he blew it! For the last 80 years of his life he had been waiting for this event. The whole thrust of his existence had been to bring the children of Israel out of the land of Egypt, the house of bondage, so that he might take them into Canaan, the land of promise. Now Moses himself would never set foot in the land, for he had disobeyed God by failing to treat God as holy.

Oh, how my heart ached for Moses the first time I read that passage in Numbers 20:1-13. Here was something else that was hard for me to understand.

The children of Israel had come, by God's leading, to the wilderness of Zin, where they found themselves without water. It was the second time in their 40 years of wilderness living that this had happened. The first time occurred at Rephidim on their way to Mount Sinai. That time God brought water from the rock after Moses struck it, as God had commanded (Exodus 17:6).

Now, as was their custom when things became difficult, the Israelites complained bitterly, "Why then have you brought the LORD's assembly into this wilderness . . . to die here?" (Numbers 20:4).

For 40 years Moses had put up with this! Whenever anything went wrong, the people always murmured—not against God, their Divine Leader, but against him. Now it was happening again. And once again Moses fell on his face before the Lord, and God met him there.

"Take the rod," God said. "Assemble the congregation and speak to the rock . . . that it may yield its water" (Numbers 20:8).

This second time God did not ask Moses to strike the rock, but simply to speak to it. And this is where Moses failed. He blew it because he did not treat God as holy. He did not do God's work God's way. He struck the rock rather than just speaking to it.

And because God is immutable, because He cannot change, He had to punish Moses. And what a hard punishment it was! Hard, but just. God is always just. You can rely on it.

So do as Moses did. Bow before your God and say, "All His ways are just . . . righteous and upright is He" (Deuteronomy 32:4).

Jesus Christ... Your Rock

WHAT WAS SO BAD about Moses striking the rock? you may ask. It worked the first time, didn't it? Water came out both times, didn't it? Both times the people and their cattle drank and were satisfied, weren't they?

Of course it worked. *But it was still wrong!* Because Moses disobeyed. Because Moses got provoked.

> Moses and Aaron gathered the assembly before the rock. And he said to them, "Listen now, you rebels; shall we bring forth water for you out of this rock?" Then Moses lifted up his hand and struck the rock twice with his rod; and water came forth abundantly, and the congregation and their beasts drank (Numbers 20:10,11).

The rock, according to 1 Corinthians 10:4, was a symbol or picture of the Lord Jesus Christ: "And all drank the same spiritual drink, for they were drinking from a spiritual rock which followed them; and the rock was Christ." Thus, the water from the rock became symbolic of the Holy Spirit given to each one who believes in the Lord Jesus Christ (John 7:37-39).

The Holy Spirit could be given only through Jesus Christ's death, burial, resurrection, and glorification. And once the Holy Spirit comes to indwell us, we are complete in Jesus (Colossians 2:9,10). Anything we need will be ours by virtue of Christ's sacrificial death which sanctified and perfected us once for all time (Hebrews 10:10,14).

Thus, when Moses struck the rock a second time, it was a picture of crucifying Jesus a *second* time. You cannot crucify Him over and over; His one death was sufficient for all time.

Think about this. To understand it is to have your thirst satisfied.

> "If any man is thirsty, let him come to Me and drink. He who believes in Me, as the Scripture said, 'From his innermost being shall flow rivers of living water'" (John 7:37,38).

God . . . Perfect, Just, Faithful

REMEMBER NOW, we are looking at the character of our God. We want to know—we need to know—the attributes of this One who is the Sovereign Ruler of the universe.

God wants you to be strong in Him. But to do this, you must know Him. For He has said: "The people that do know their God shall be strong, and do exploits" (Daniel 11:32b KJV). So hangeth thou in there, precious one. Learn, apply, and grow.

"The Rock! His work is perfect, for all His ways are just; a God of faithfulness and without injustice, righteous and upright is He" (Deuteronomy 32:4). This verse is part of a song Moses wrote, and do you know when he wrote it? After God told him that he could not go into the land of Canaan with the children of Israel.

God's judgment was not easy for Moses to accept. As a matter of fact, Moses pleaded with God to rescind his punishment:

> " 'O Lord God, Thou hast begun to show Thy servant Thy greatness and Thy strong hand. . . . Let me, I pray, cross over and see the fair land that is beyond the Jordan, that good hill country and Lebanon.' But the LORD was angry with me on your account, and would not listen to me; and the LORD said to me, 'Enough! Speak to Me no more of this matter' " (Deuteronomy 3:24-26).

And why didn't God give in to Moses? "Because," God said, "you did not treat Me as holy in the midst of the sons of Israel" (Deuteronomy 32:51).

But how could a God of love be so hard on Moses?

He had to be, Beloved, because He is also a just God, righteous in all His ways. Whether He deals with men, angels, or demons, He acts in total equity by rewarding righteousness and punishing sin. Since He is omniscient, knowing all, every one of His decrees is absolutely just.

Moses knew this, for just before he went up to Mount Nebo to die at 120 years of age, he sang his song: "The Rock! His work is perfect. . . ."

O Beloved, will you not sing Moses' song?

Fair and Righteous

PLEASE DO NOT THINK I am saying that if others have something and you do not, it is because you must have done something wrong. Oh, no! I am *not* saying that. I simply used Moses' situation to show you that Moses knew God's character.

Remember, the murmuring, complaining children of Israel were permitted to go into Canaan, but Moses wasn't. Yet Moses never said, "God, that is not fair! I never complained in all the forty years we spent in the wilderness. I never refused to go into the land that You had the twelve men spy out from Kadesh-barnea. Why aren't You treating me the same as everyone else?"

No, Moses never said any of this, because Moses knew God's character. He knew that God deals with each of us in a fair and righteous way. His actions are always consistent with His character, which is love. Love always seeks another's highest good (1 Corinthians 13:4-8). And nothing can ever separate us from God's love. "Who shall separate us from the love of Christ? Shall tribulation, or distress, or persecution, or famine, or nakedness, or peril, or sword?" (Romans 8:35).

No, if there are difficulties in your life but not in the lives of others, it is not a sign that God does not love you. Rather, in His love He has permitted these things. "Why?" you ask. I do not know; but I do know that these difficulties will serve some purpose, for God is loving, righteous, and just.

When Jesus told Peter the way in which Peter was going to die (by crucifixion), Peter wanted to know how John would die. Would God treat John the same as Peter? To which Jesus, in His love, justice, and righteousness, replied, "If I want him to remain until I come, what is that to you? You follow Me!" (John 21:22).

O precious child of God, do not miss what God has for you by looking at the lives of others and thinking God has favorites or is a respecter of persons. Remember, He is a holy, righteous, just, and loving God. Follow Him.

God's Love Poured Out

FEAR. IT CAN DO AWFUL THINGS to you. Its purpose is to immobilize you. And its source is never God.

I repeat . . . fear *never, never* comes from God.

How could fear come from the One whose name is Jehovah-shalom, "The LORD is Peace" (Judges 6:24)? Have you not heard the words of Jesus: "Peace I leave with you; My peace I give to you . . . . Let not your heart be troubled, nor let it be fearful" (John 14:27)?

Yet hearts are troubled; Christians are fearful. And that fear comes when we believe the father of lies rather than God. Satan would have us doubt God. Doubt breeds insecurity; insecurity breeds fear.

People who know without a shadow of a doubt that they are loved are rarely insecure. Therefore, if you are ever going to know rest from fear, you must first understand that God loves you unconditionally. That will be harder for some of you because you have not known much love here on earth. Yet if you will believe God, your grain-of-mustard-seed faith will remove mountains—of rejection, bitterness, fear, anger, and rebellion (Matthew 17:20)!

God loves you, unconditionally and sacrificially. He loved you before you ever loved Him.

> But God demonstrates His own love toward us, in that
> while we were yet sinners, Christ died for us (Romans
> 5:8).

Read that again, Beloved. It is not just so many words that you nod your head to and say "uh-huh . . . sure, sure." It's *truth, life, fulfillment, peace, security.*

And so that you will never ever be alone, He has sent His blessed Holy Spirit to live within your very own body.

Believing that God loves you, and receiving His love, will cast out fear, for "perfect love casts out fear" (1 John 4:18).

Today, if you in any way doubt God's love for you, why don't you tell Him? "Father, oh, how I need a loving Father. Father, I will choose to believe that You love me . . . help, Thou, my unbelief."

His Love Casts Out Fear

"FEAR HATH TORMENT" (1 John 4:18 KJV). No argument there! If you have ever been fearful, you know the torment it brings.

If you are ever going to learn how to deal with fear, there are a number of facts you need to know. Some I have already mentioned; however, they are worth repeating, so bear with me.

First, recognize that fear is never from God (2 Timothy 1:7 KJV).

Second, believe that God loves you with a perfect love.

Third, true acknowledgment of this love will cast out fear.

> There is no fear in love; but perfect love casteth out fear: because fear hath torment. He that feareth is not made perfect in love (1 John 4:18 KJV).

The last part of that verse means that when I am fearful it is because I am failing in some way to comprehend God's love for me.

Now, let's take a deeper look at what it means to be loved by God.

Because God loves you and because you have received the gift of His love, the Lord Jesus Christ, "there is therefore now no condemnation" (Romans 8:1). This means you never need to fear that God will ever pass sentence or judgment against you.

Because God loves you, "He Himself has said, 'I WILL NEVER DESERT YOU, NOR WILL I EVER FORSAKE YOU,' so that we confidently say, 'THE LORD IS MY HELPER, I WILL NOT BE AFRAID. WHAT SHALL MAN DO TO ME?' " (Hebrews 13:5b,6). The Sovereign God of love will never abandon you nor leave you in the lurch. Therefore, you need not fear.

Because God loves you, and because His Son prays for you according to His will, He will keep you out of the power of the evil one (John 17:15). Satan cannot do a thing to you without God's permission. And if God should grant Satan permission to touch you (as He did with Job), you need not fear, for it will all work together for good (Romans 8:28), it will be used to make you more like Jesus (Romans 8:29), and it will never be more than you can bear (1 Corinthians 10:13).

I have another "because" for you, but I will share it with you tomorrow. You have enough to think upon today.

"When I Am Afraid"

FEAR IS A NATURAL RESPONSE to something we feel is going to hurt us. Although it is natural, still its root cause lies in unbelief.

When we fear, we are afraid we will find ourselves in a situation we cannot handle. We forget that God is always there (Hebrews 13:5), constantly infusing His strength into us (Philippians 4:13).

When we fear, we feel as if things have gotten out of control. Yet God said that "He does according to His will in the host of heaven and among the inhabitants of earth" (Daniel 4:35), "for the LORD of hosts has planned, and who can frustrate it?" (Isaiah 14:27a).

When we fear, we are allowing something that God did not send, for "God hath not given us the spirit of fear" (2 Timothy 1:7 KJV). We are failing to appropriate *the power* that is ours through His resurrection, *the love* that guarantees our highest good, and *the sound mind* that we can have by bringing every thought captive to the obedience of Jesus Christ (2 Corinthians 10:5).

At the root of all this is a fear for our life. Remember, yesterday I told you that I had one more "because" for you? Well, this is it: Because fear in some way involves a threat against life, you need to know that God says that no man has the power of death, nor does Satan. Jesus Christ through His own death rendered "powerless him who had the power of death, that is, the devil" so that He "might deliver those who through fear of death were subject to slavery all their lives" (Hebrews 2:14,15). Therefore, you are to be "in nothing terrified by your adversaries, which is to them an evident token of perdition, but to you of salvation, and that of God" (Philippians 1:28 KJV). Jesus says, "I have the keys of death and of Hades" (Revelation 1:18); therefore, "do not fear those who kill the body, but are unable to kill the soul; but rather fear Him who is able to destroy both soul and body in hell" (Matthew 10:28). To fear for your life or for the lives of your loved ones is to deny God's control over death.

Fear locks us up in a prison of impotence, and that is just what Satan wants!

You must say, with the psalmist, "When I am afraid, I will put my trust in Thee" (Psalm 56:3). Can't you see how liberating this is?

"Be Anxious for Nothing"

HOW DO WE LIVE OUT the character and sovereignty of God? Let me share with you one incident from my own life when I had to put practically everything I knew into faith's action.

A horrible storm was brewing, the kind that makes you pray for protection. The heavens seemed angry. The wind was violent, screaming and beating the trees. Heaven and earth were going to have it out.

In the midst of this, the dinner bell rang, and Jack and I scurried to the shelter of the dining hall, which is part of the conference center called Precept Ministries. I scanned the hall for our son, David, who was only nine years old at the time. Not finding him, I went out and called his name, bellowing over the storm. Then I returned, picked up my plate, and sat down.

Being a typical mother of a typical nine-year-old, I was telling Jack how David needed to learn to be on time for meals. However, when rain began pelting the tin roof above us, concern took hold.

"Where is he?" I asked.

"Don't worry," Jack replied casually. "I'm sure he will be here in a minute." Having been raised on a farm, Jack understood the preoccupations of a nine-year-old boy. But after two more bites my "mother alarm" was making an awful noise in my breast, for by now the heavens were crying with hysterical torrents of wrath. I had to find David.

"Let's take the car and go look for him," I said.

Jack and I were drenched by the time we got to the car. We drove down the road—honking, trying to out-yell the wind, frantically looking for him.

Then the Holy Spirit brought Philippians 4:5-7 to mind:

> The Lord is near. Be anxious for nothing, but in everything by prayer and supplication with thanksgiving let your requests be made known to God. And the peace of God, which surpasses all comprehension, shall guard your hearts and your minds in Christ Jesus.

Meditate on those verses in light of what we have learned this week. How do they fit?

Always Near

BE ANXIOUS FOR NOTHING when your child is missing in a horrible storm? Suddenly I found myself thinking of an acquaintance in our city whose son had just been murdered. What if...?

"What ifs" always come; the enemy will see to it! That is his business—to do anything to keep our minds off the truth of God.

Not finding David along the road, we returned to the dining hall to see if he had come home by now. I anxiously waited in the car until Jack returned, shaking his head.

As we and now others started back out, I wanted to blame Jack. Surely he should have checked on David that afternoon! But there was God's Word again: "Let your forbearing spirit [or sweet reasonableness] be known to all men. The Lord is near [at hand]" (Philippians 4:5). It wasn't fair to make Jack the scapegoat. And the Lord was there for me to lean on. I was to stop being anxious; I was to pray.

I knew that the word for prayer in Philippians 4:6 meant general prayer—prayer encompassing the character of God and the promises of God that fit the particular situation. So I prayed accordingly.

"Father, You are omniscient, and although we don't know where David is, You do. And, Father, You are omnipresent, so if he is frightened, alone, or if someone is hurting him, let him be aware of Your presence." Now supplication (specific requests) merged with general prayer. "Father, bring to his remembrance the Scriptures and truths we have taught him. I know, Lord, that nothing can happen without Your permission, and I submit to You."

Peace and calm came. I no longer wanted to blame Jack. I still wanted to find David, of course, but I was resting in God's sovereignty and love. Every time an anxious thought came to my mind I rejected it and turned instead to all that I knew about my God.

We hunted, searched, called, and came home without him.

And there was David! He had been playing with a friend and had temporarily lost his way.

O Beloved, this is the practicality of knowing God—clinging to what you know and living according to every word that proceeds out of the mouth of God.

Choose Life!

THEY STOOD THERE WEEPING. As Ezra read and explained the book of the Law, they saw the truth of God's Word, and grief overwhelmed their hearts (Nehemiah 8:4-9).

Israel had either forgotten God's words or had not believed Him when He told them He was a faithful God "who keeps His covenant and His lovingkindness to a thousandth generation with those who love Him and keep His commandments; but repays those who hate Him to their faces, to destroy them" (Deuteronomy 7:9,10).

They thought they could walk their own way. They assumed that being a chosen nation gave them special privileges—and it did; but they forgot that with those privileges went grave and awesome responsibility. (Aren't we much the same?)

Before they entered Canaan, the land of covenant, God had gone over His precepts of life a second time. Moses recorded it all in the book of Deuteronomy as a permanent testimony. They had this in their hands; they heard it read and proclaimed by prophets, priests, and kings; yet, for the most part, they ignored it. Like so many today, they wanted God's blessings without obedience.

God had set before Israel "life and death, the blessing and the curse." He told them to "choose life in order that you may live, you and your descendants, by loving the LORD your God, by obeying His voice, and by holding fast to Him" (Deuteronomy 30:19,20).

Because they had not loved God and kept His commandments, Israel had known destruction and captivity. Just as He promised. Seventy years of captivity!

Now only a handful of Israelites lived in the land. Gone were the days of blessing under David and Solomon. Gone was the glory of the temple. Things were not the same, nor would they ever be, and as they heard Ezra read God's Word, they knew why. They had failed to count on God's faithfulness—not only to bless, but to chasten!

O Beloved, do not do as they did. Heed God's Word; believe it; live by it. Because God is faithful, every word shall come to pass . . . the blessings *and* the cursings!

Merciful God

HOW BITTER ARE THE TEARS of what-might-have-been! They seem as if they will surely drown us.

Now we see where we have failed. Now we realize how wrong we were—foolishly wrong. "The LORD is righteous; for I have rebelled against His command; hear now, all peoples, and behold my pain" (Lamentations 1:18). God has chastened us, and we know the chastening is right and just—for He is holy, righteous, and just.

So what do we do? Give up? Weep bitter tears of regret for the remainder of our days?

No, Beloved, no. Read Lamentations and look for your God.

Lamentations was written by Jeremiah during the Babylonian captivity. It is a record of the sorrows of Israel due to God's just judgment. Yet Lamentations is more than just a bitter lament. It is another glimpse into the character of our God.

Our just, holy, righteous, faithful God is also long-suffering and merciful. His righteous anger is slow to kindle against those who fail to listen to His warnings or obey His instructions. His eternal longing for the *highest* good for His creation holds back His holy justice.

God had sent Israel prophet after prophet, waiting for their repentance; but Israel would not repent. They did not see that God's long-suffering and goodness were intended to lead them to repentance (Romans 2:4). So He took them into captivity. But He did not abandon them. God is merciful.

> The LORD's lovingkindnesses indeed never cease, for His compassions never fail. . . . For if He causes grief, then He will have compassion according to His abundant lovingkindness. For He does not afflict willingly, or grieve the sons of men (Lamentations 3:22,23,32,33).

So dry your tears. If you have repented, acknowledging your wrong and turning from your disobedient ways, He stands there in His mercy, reaching out with open arms, saying, "Do not be grieved, for the joy of the LORD is your strength" (Nehemiah 8:10b).

That You May Know Him

During the last two months we have explored some of the facets of God's character—commonly referred to as the attributes of God. I challenge you to study and meditate further on the following list of His attributes. Ask God to reveal Himself to you in new and deeper ways.

Omniscient: God knows all. He has a perfect knowledge of everything that is past, present, or future (Job 37:16; Psalm 139:1-6).

Omnipotent: God possesses all power. He is able to bring into being anything that He has decided to do, with or without the use of any means (Genesis 18:14; Job 42:2; Jeremiah 32:27).

Omnipresent: God is present everywhere, in all the universe, at all times, in the totality of His character (Proverbs 15:3; Jeremiah 23:23,24).

Eternal: God has no beginning and He has no end. He is not confined to the finiteness of time or of man's reckoning of time. He is, in fact, the cause of time (Deuteronomy 32:40; Isaiah 57:15).

Immutable: God is always the same in His nature, His character, and His will. He never changes, and He can never be made to change (Psalm 102:25-27; Malachi 3:6; Hebrews 13:8).

Incomprehensible: Because God is God, He is beyond the understanding of man. His ways, character, and acts are higher than ours. We only understand as He chooses to reveal (Job 11:7; Isaiah 55:8,9; Romans 11:33).

Self-existent: There is nothing upon which God depends for His existence except Himself. The whole basis of His existence is within Himself. There was a time when there was nothing but God Himself. He added nothing to Himself by creation (Exodus 3:14; John 5:26).

Self-sufficient: Within Himself, God is able to act—to bring about His will without any assistance. Although He may choose to use assistance, it is His choice, not His need (Psalm 50:7-12; Acts 17:24,25).

Infinite: The realm of God has no limits or bounds whatsoever (1 Kings 8:27; Psalm 145:3).

Transcendent: God is above His creation, and He would exist if there were no creation. His existence is totally apart from His creatures or creation (Isaiah 43:10; 55:8,9).

Sovereign: God is totally, supremely, and preeminently over all His creation. There is not a person or thing that is not under His control and foreknown plan (Daniel 4:35)!

Holy: God is a morally excellent, perfect being. His is purity of being in every aspect (Leviticus 19:2; Job 34:10; Isaiah 47:4; 57:15).

Righteous: God is always good. It is essential to His character. He always does the right thing. Ultimately, since He is God, whatever He does is right. He is the absolute. His actions are always consistent with His character, which is love (Deuteronomy 32:4; Psalm 119:142).

Just: In all of His actions, God acts with fairness. Whether He deals with man, angels, or demons, He acts in total equity by rewarding righteousness and punishing sin. Since He knows all, every decree is absolutely just (Numbers 14:18; 23:19; Psalm 89:14).

Merciful: God is an actively compassionate being. In His actions, He responds in a compassionate way toward those who have opposed His will in their pursuit of their own way (Psalm 62:12; 89:14; 116:5; Romans 9:14-16).

Long-suffering: God's righteous anger is slow to be kindled against those who fail to listen to His warnings or to obey His instructions. The eternal longing for the highest good for His creatures holds back His holy justice (Numbers 14:18; 2 Peter 3:9).

Wise: God's actions are based on His character which allows Him to choose righteous ends and to make fitting plans to achieve those ends (Isaiah 40:28; Daniel 2:20).

Loving: This is the attribute of God which causes Him to give Himself for another, even to the laying down of His own life. God's love causes Him to desire the other's highest good without any thought for Himself, and this love is not based upon the worth, response, or merit of the object being loved (Jeremiah 31:3; Romans 5:8; 1 John 4:8).

Good: This attribute of God causes Him to give to others in a way which has no motive and is not limited by what the recipients deserve (2 Chronicles 5:13; Psalm 106:1).

Wrathful: There is within God a hatred for all that is unrighteous and an unquenchable desire to punish all unrighteousness. Whatever is inconsistent with Him must ultimately be consumed (Exodus 34:6,7; 2 Chronicles 19:2; Romans 1:18).

Truthful: All that God says is reality. Whether believed by man or not, whether seen as reality or not, if it is spoken by God, it is reality. Whatever He speaks becomes truth (Psalm 31:5; Titus 1:2).

Faithful: God is always true to His promises. He can never draw back from His promises of blessing or of judgment. Since He cannot lie, He is totally steadfast to what He has spoken (Deuteronomy 7:9; 2 Timothy 2:13).

Jealous: God is unwilling to share His glory with any other creature or give up His redeemed people (Exodus 20:5; 34:14).

This is what the Lord says:

"Let not the wise man boast of his wisdom or the strong man boast of his strength or the rich man boast of his riches, but let him who boasts boast about this: that he understands and knows me, that I am the LORD, who exercises kindness, justice and righteousness on earth, for in these I delight," declares the LORD (Jeremiah 9:23,24 NIV).

MARCH

―――――

The Lord Is My Shepherd

Do you long for contentment? Do you crave peace? Are you afraid of what the future holds? If the Lord is your Shepherd, you shall not want! This month as we direct our thoughts toward Psalm 23, you will understand more of what it truly means to be a sheep of the Great Shepherd! You will come to the end of our time together with a new peace, a new perspective, and a greater appreciation for your place at His side!

―――――

Always With You

DO YOU EVER GET LONELY, my friend? I do. I think everyone gets lonely sometimes, and for each of us, loneliness is triggered by something different, something personal.

As I sit down to write this, I am all alone . . . and I feel a little weepy. I wish Jack were home, but he is on his way to Australia. In a few days I will be joining him, and for four packed weeks we will minister in six major cities. Our days will be occupied with people and ministry—and we will experience fulfillment. And yet, I know the loneliness will come back. I won't want it to, but something will trigger a thought, and once again I'll have to deal with it.

How? I will remember the truths of Psalm 23, and there I will find the precepts, which—though they do not remove the loneliness and the pain—enable me to live.

The words are so familiar: "The LORD is my shepherd; I shall not want" (Psalm 23:1 KJV). Familiar . . . like seeing an old friend . . . because we have heard them over and over again.

Maybe you memorized them in Sunday school. Maybe the words seem like an old friend because Psalm 23 is often read at funerals. Maybe the familiar words brought you comfort and assuaged your fear of death: "Yea, though I walk through the valley of the shadow of death I shall fear no evil; for Thou art with me."

When you heard Psalm 23 as a child, you learned that God would always be with you. When you hear it as an adult, you are reminded that even in death God will be there. But meanwhile, what does one do for the day-by-day experiences which are bound to bring loneliness, apprehension, and anxiety?

The same psalm memorized in childhood and heard in the hour of death has the answers, for each day has enough trouble of its own (Matthew 6:34).

Psalm 23 is not merely a charming allegory for children or a memorial for the dead. It is a psalm for living. It is a psalm of comfort for life, no matter what life brings, and its truths are summed up in the first and glorious verse: "The Lord is my shepherd; I shall not want."

A Psalm for You

YESTERDAY I SAID that the Twenty-third Psalm is a psalm for life.

It is a psalm for the forty-year-old man whose letter broke my heart when he told, for the first time, what his parents had done to him when he was a child. When he was only nine years old, he had walked into his parents' room one day while they were looking at child pornography. As I read what they had done to him, I groaned in sorrow. His words came haltingly, even on paper. Some words were missing, replaced with dashes, for they were too perverted, too obscene, too twisted even to be written down. They did to him what they saw on the videotapes and in the magazines . . . and it went on for three years until, at age twelve, he finally ran away. He ran away from the perversion, but he could not escape the anguish of memories which lately had become even more frequent.

It is a psalm for my friend Martha, younger than I, who has a brain tumor.

It is a psalm for another friend who seeks to live moment-by-moment above the rejection of her family, the weariness of earning a living, and the loneliness of her singleness.

It is a psalm of promise for my brothers and sisters who once lived under the atheistic tyranny of communism and to whom we now minister as they seek to know their Shepherd even better.

It is my psalm of assurance that when my days come to an end, I will turn around and see that even the small pain I experienced and the great pain my friends have experienced will be called "goodness and mercy."

I know the words may be familiar, but read them again . . . thoughtfully.

Notice that the pronoun referring to the Lord changes from "He" to "Thou" in verse 4.

Read the psalm again and note what the Shepherd does for His sheep and the benefits which come to the sheep as a result of the Shepherd's care.

Now, then, what does the sheep have to do?

Is this a psalm for you, Beloved?

You Need a Shepherd

IF YOU ARE EVER GOING to know the Shepherd's care, you must first realize your great need for a shepherd. And I truly believe that God created sheep so that we could see that need . . . to see what we are like. For if any animal ever needed a shepherd, it is sheep!

Sheep are helpless, timid, feeble creatures that have little means of self-defense. They are the dumbest of all animals, and because of this they require constant attention and meticulous care. If sheep do not have the constant care of a shepherd, they will go the wrong way, unaware of the dangers at hand. They have been known to nibble themselves right off a mountainside! They will overgraze the same land and run out of food unless the shepherd leads them to new pastures, and if they are not led to proper pastures, they will obliviously eat or drink things that are disastrous to them.

Sheep easily fall prey to predators, and when they do, they are virtually defenseless. Sheep can also become cast down and, in that state, panic and die. And so, because sheep are sheep, they need shepherds to protect and care for them.

If you belong to the Lord, you, Beloved, are the sheep of His pasture. It was for you that God "brought up from the dead the great Shepherd of the sheep through the blood of the eternal covenant, even Jesus our Lord" (Hebrews 13:20). Jesus is there for you, and because He is, although your life might be difficult or fraught with testings, you shall not want.

The question then becomes, where do you turn? To whom do you run?

Hebrews 7:24,25 says: "But He, on the other hand, because He abides forever, holds His priesthood permanently. Hence, also, He is able to save forever those who draw near to God through Him, since He always lives to make intercession for them."

Your Good Shepherd is there at the right hand of the Father. He lives within . . . "Christ in you, the hope of glory" (Colossians 1:27). And He holds you in His hand . . . underneath are the everlasting arms.

O precious sheep, take a good look at your life. Are you trying to make it on your own? Can you see your need for a Shepherd?

Your Shepherd . . . All-Sufficient

THE WELFARE OF SHEEP depends solely upon the care they get from their shepherd. The better the shepherd, the healthier the sheep. When you see weak, sickly, or pest-infested sheep, you can be sure that their shepherd really does not care well for them.

What is our Great Shepherd like? Learn that, and you will understand why you can confidently say, "The Lord is my shepherd; I shall not want" (Psalm 23:1 KJV). Believe it, and you will know a life of perfect rest.

Psalm 23, which shows us the ministry of our *Great* Shepherd, is surrounded by two psalms that show us two other aspects of our Shepherd. Psalm 22 shows us the *Good* Shepherd who lays down His life for His sheep, and Psalm 24 shows us our *Chief* Shepherd, the King of Glory, who is to come again (1 Peter 5:4).

Before the Lord can ever function as your Great Shepherd, however, you must first know Him as your Good Shepherd, because it is here that you meet Him as your precious Savior. Listen to His words: "Truly, truly, I say to you, I am the door of the sheep" (John 10:7).

There is no other door, there is no other way to enter in and become God's sheep, except by Jesus: "All who came before Me are thieves and robbers; but the sheep did not hear them" (John 10:8).

His sheep hear His voice; that is, they know truth when they hear it. And once they hear truth, they recognize it for what it is: reality!

Jesus said, "I am the door; if anyone enters through Me, he shall be saved [perfect security], and shall go in and out [perfect liberty], and find pasture [perfect sustenance]" (John 10:9).

A shepherd who knew nothing of God's Word was describing his sheepfold to a curious inquirer. As he pointed to the sheepfold, the inquirer said, "But where is the door?"

"I am the door," the shepherd replied. "At night, when the sheep enter the sheepfold, I lie down in the opening. Nothing can enter or leave without going over me, because I am the door."

When did you hear His voice? When did you enter into God's family through Jesus the Christ? When did you begin to follow Him?

You Shall Not Want

HE WALKED INTO a nine-foot cell and was immediately imprisoned in darkness. As the bolt slid smoothly across the bars and the padlock was fastened on the door, he found himself caught in a night of steel, bound in bands of iron. It was October 1950. Geoffrey Bull was a prisoner in China.

"I had no Bible in my hand, no watch on my wrist, no pencil or paper in my pocket. There was no real hope of release. There was no real hope of life. There was no real possibility of reunion with those I loved. The only reality was my Lord and Savior Jesus Christ. Divested of all, He was to become everything to me. He was to break my bars and enlarge my coasts in the narrow room. He was to be my fullest nourishment amidst the meager food. My meat which my captors 'knew not of.' He would make me glad with His countenance. He would let me hear His voice. As in the days of His nativity, Herod may reign and imagine slaughter against the innocent, but let me only see His star and I would come to worship Him."[1]

What if that had been you instead, Beloved, imprisoned in that cell? Would you know your Shepherd well enough to be able to say in confident faith, "The Lord is my Shepherd; I shall not want"? In the darkness of the night of imprisonment would you know enough to look for His star so that you might worship Him?

Or maybe I should say, in your prison—whatever the bars are made of—have you looked beyond them to the One who is above, beneath, and within? Are you worshiping Him?

What does it take to be able to worship God and confidently proclaim Him as your all-sufficient Shepherd? Worship is based on knowledge . . . a knowledge that I pray will be wonderfully deepened in the days to come. To worship God is to recognize His worth and to bow before Him.

Suppose someone were to ask you, "What is your Shepherd like that He could so provide for you that you would not want . . . no matter what . . . even if you found yourself in a prison cell?"

How would you answer, Beloved?

All You Need

WHEN MOSES MET GOD at the burning bush, God commissioned Moses to stand before Pharaoh and say, "God says, 'Let My people go that they may serve Me.'" Moses responded by asking, "Who am I, that I should go to Pharaoh, and that I should bring the sons of Israel out of Egypt?" (Exodus 3:11). Interestingly enough, God never answers Moses' question about his personal qualifications for such a task. Rather, we find God saying to him, "Certainly I will be with you" (Exodus 3:12). Moses would not want; the Shepherd was his for the task. All Moses had to do was follow.

However, to do this, Moses did need to know who his God was. He needed to know who was going to separate the children of Israel out of Pharaoh's sheepfold. So Moses asked God His name. "Whom shall I say sent me?" Oh, how I love God's answer: "I AM WHO I AM. . . . Thus you shall say to the sons of Israel, 'I AM has sent me to you.' . . . This is My name forever, and this is My memorial-name to all generations" (Exodus 3:14,15).

I AM! I AM what? I AM all that you will ever need. I AM all that you will ever need at any time, in any place, in any situation.

O Beloved, our Shepherd is our El Shaddai. This name for God, El Shaddai, comes from the word "breast"—the place for succoring one's child. God is our All-Sufficient One whose grace is sufficient for us so that we can be "content with weaknesses, with insults, with distresses, with persecutions, with difficulties, for Christ's sake; for when I am weak, then I am strong" (2 Corinthians 12:10).

What has God asked you to do? Where has your Shepherd led you? Does it seem too hard, too difficult . . . impossible because of who you are?

O Beloved, look to your Shepherd, and you shall not want, for He is your El Shaddai, your "I AM." He is all you will ever need. That is His memorial-name forever, even to you, to your generation.

Where do you feel insufficient? Meditate on how God can meet those needs.

Your Sovereign Shepherd

OUR SHEPHERD IS the Sovereign God. He rules over all.

> His dominion is an eternal dominion; his kingdom endures from generation to generation. All the peoples of the earth are regarded as nothing. He does as he pleases with the powers of heaven and the peoples of the earth. No one can hold back his hand or say to him: "What have You done?" (Daniel 4:34,35 NIV).

If you are going to live a life of peace, a life of rest and contentment no matter what your circumstances, you must be aware of the sovereignty of your Shepherd. When you entered into the sheepfold, you saw that the One who laid down His life for you was truly God incarnate, God in the flesh. Now you must know that, as God, your Shepherd is sovereign. To recognize His sovereignty is to worship Him aright.

When we say that God is sovereign, we mean that nothing can happen in this universe without God's permission. Oh, man retains his free will and responsibility, but they cannot be executed unless God concurs. Neither necessity, nor chance, nor malice of Satan controls the sequence of events or their causes. God is the supreme Ruler over all, and no one nor any circumstance of life can thwart His desire or His plan. Your Shepherd is the sovereign Ruler of all the universe, Beloved, and that is why you shall not want.

Why don't you take a few minutes and meditate upon this truth? You may want to write out exactly what God's sovereignty means to you, listing the particular things in your life over which He has control.

Your Shepherd Loves You

THE BABY WAS CHOKING. Frantic with fear, the young mother picked her up and ran to the car. She had to get to the hospital. Hurriedly she backed out of the garage, not noticing that her older daughter was playing in the driveway. She ran over her and killed her.

As this beautiful young mother shared her story with me, my heart wrenched with the horror of it all. I thought, "O Father, how could she handle it if she did not understand Your sovereignty?" But she did know the sovereignty of God.

What had happened was horrible. It was painful. But it did not destroy her. She was not a demented soul locked in a padded cell of what ifs, whys, and if onlys. She did not bitterly harangue God, asking Him why He had permitted this. Nor did she refuse the open arms that drew her to her El Shaddai and His all-sufficient breast. And I, along with others, saw her peace and realized once again what it means to have the Lord as our Shepherd.

When I have a difficult time understanding how a sovereign God can permit all the pain and suffering that permeates and invades every level of our society, I have to turn and run to what I know of His character. And the first place I run is into my knowledge of the fact that God is love.

The One who sits upon His throne ruling over all the universe is a God of love (1 John 4:8). Love is the very essence of His being; He can never act apart from love. He loves us with an everlasting love, a love that will not fail, a love that continually seeks our highest good.

His sheep are in His hands, and those hands are hands of love. Nothing . . . not any situation or any person . . . can snatch us out of His hands.

Listen to His words: "My sheep hear My voice, and I know them, and they follow Me; and I give eternal life to them, and they shall never perish; and no one shall snatch them out of My hand" (John 10:27).

Has anything ever happened to you that made you doubt His love? Put it away. Look at Calvary where the Shepherd laid down His life for you.

Your Alpha and Omega

HAVE YOU EVER FELT caught or trapped in a situation that seems absolutely insane, horrid, unbelievable, inconceivable? All of a sudden your plans, dreams, hopes are shattered.

It's like a nightmare. *This can't be happening to me,* you think. *It will alter the course of my life. It will ruin everything!* You wonder how you'll survive. Gloom settles like a fog over your heart and mind, and dire forecasts of danger loom through the night of your imagination.

Suddenly you panic. What should you do? You have to do something . . . but what?

The clap of thunder causes the little sheep to stop his grazing and look up. The sudden noise and the pelting of the rain have his attention. Panic sets in. Where is his shepherd?

Fear not, little flock . . . your Shepherd is watching over you.

> "Remember this, and be assured; recall it to mind . . . for I am God, and there is no other; I am God, and there is no one like Me, declaring the end from the beginning and from ancient times things which have not been done, saying, 'My purpose will be established, and I will accomplish all My good pleasure' . . . Truly I have spoken; truly I will bring it to pass. I have planned it, surely I will do it" (Isaiah 46:8-11).

O beloved sheep, whatever happens, you can know that His will shall be accomplished in your life . . . because you are His. He is the Alpha and the Omega, the Beginning and the End. Your Shepherd has not left you; He is there to complete that which He has begun—to make you into His image. His plan for you will not be thwarted. All that God inaugurates, He completes. He is the God of the finished work.

So rest, little sheep, your Shepherd is there. He is in control. Whatever comes to you has been filtered through His fingers of love, and it will serve to accomplish His purpose.

Your Times . . . in His Hands

HAVE YOU EVER BECOME frustrated because suddenly you have been held up or kept from carrying out your plans? You have become agitated, impatient, angry.

O little sheep, why do you get all upset? The Shepherd is there. Did He not lead you this far? The steps of a righteous man are ordered by the Lord (Psalm 37:23). "Man's goings are of the LORD; how can a man then understand his own way?" (Proverbs 20:24 KJV).

You do not need to understand. Quit your frustration. Walk by faith, knowing that goodness and mercy are following you because the Lord is your Shepherd. Your times are in His hands (Psalm 31:15).

The eternal God is the Author of time, and every moment counts to Him. He will not squander your time. He has a precious blessing . . . a precious lesson for you at every turn. Rest and "in everything give thanks; for *this is* God's will in Christ Jesus" . . . otherwise it could not happen.

A pastor was headed for a speaking engagement in another part of the United States. He rushed through the airport to make his connection, only to find that the plane was to be delayed for at least an hour. The pastor's smile was refreshing to the airline agent, quite unlike the angry complaints he had been receiving from other irate travelers. The pastor simply said, "My times are in God's hands, so I don't sweat it!"

With an hour to spare and a promise that they would not leave without him, the pastor went to eat. Fifty minutes later when the pastor returned, the agent turned ashen.

"You got on the plane ten minutes ago. I saw you. How could you be standing here?"

The pastor smiled. "Obviously that wasn't me. I'm here."

Now a deathly white, the agent said, "But I saw you. I know it was you. I saw your ticket and boarding pass."

The pastor just shook his head. "But I'm here."

Later the news came. The plane had crashed. All were killed.

Your times are in the hands of the sovereign God, dear sheep, so do not fret. Rest. If God makes you stand and wait, see it as gain, not loss. It all has a purpose . . . His.

Your Shepherd . . . Your Rest

HAVE YOU EVER WONDERED, *Where is this life of peace that is supposed to belong to the child of God?* Do you ever toss and turn because your mind will not allow your body to rest? Pressures, fears, unhappy relationships tramp up and down the corridors of your mind, forbidding sleep. The night grows long; you grow weary . . . and in your weariness you wonder if this is all there is.

No, Beloved . . . not if the Lord is your Shepherd. He will make you lie down in green pastures (Psalm 23:2). This is the Great Shepherd's promise to His sheep . . . a promise of rest.

Why, then, is there no rest? Why? Because, Beloved, in some way you have failed to appropriate the grace of God, which He says is sufficient for all of your needs (2 Corinthians 12:9). For sheep, true rest is to lie down in green pastures. But before they can do that, they must be free from four things. Today I want to make you aware of what these four things are, and then in the days to come we will take them one by one and discuss them in a practical way. So follow closely, precious sheep, as we pasture at Psalm 23:2 for a while, gleaning all that we can.

First, sheep must be free from hunger. They cannot lie down as long as they are hungry. Yet, in this second verse of the Twenty-third Psalm we find that the Shepherd has so satisfied the sheep's hunger that they can lie down right in the midst of green pastures.

Second, if sheep are to rest, they must be free from fear. Are you, Beloved, beset with fears?

Third, sheep cannot rest unless they are free from friction. Tension with others of their kind keeps them on their feet . . . they feel they must defend themselves!

And fourth, sheep cannot rest unless they are free from pests. Sheep can be greatly aggravated, even driven to distraction, by flies, parasites, or other pests that seek to torment them.

Which of these things holds you prisoner? What hungers, what fears, what frictions, what aggravations?

Write them down and think about them. In the days to come we will take them before the Great Shepherd.

Food That Satisfies

HOURS ARE SPENT in our ministry not only in teaching, but in listening . . . weeping . . . praying . . . and then instructing.

Often we shake our heads in disbelief—not that we think what we are hearing is a lie; rather, in disbelief that people should suffer such trauma at the hands of others or get themselves in such painful predicaments.

Oh, the awful, awful wages of sin! Self-inflicted or afflicted! Have you ever wondered how people get so messed up? Or why are they so restless . . . so tormented . . . so anxious about life? It's because they do not know the Shepherd of the sheep. Or, having known of Him, they have refused to follow Him.

They have not known nor fed upon the green pastures of His Word. And because of hunger they have been constantly foraging for something to satisfy their inner craving.

Sheep that are hungry won't lie down. They can't. They lack vigor and vitality, yet they are driven, because they are not satisfied. So, untended by the shepherd, they eat anything and everything, ofttimes to their own destruction.

This is what has happened to so many with whom we have shared. They have not fed upon the Word of God; they have not desired the sincere milk of the Word that they might grow thereby (1 Peter 2:2). Nor have they gone on to strong meat that they might be mature in the faith, able to discern good and evil doctrine (Hebrews 5:14).

O Beloved, what has hunger caused you to do? Where has it led you? Will you not allow your Shepherd to feed you that you might know rest?

The whole purpose of Precept Ministries is to establish God's people in God's Word as that which produces reverence for Him (Psalm 119:38). Everything we do has this as its goal, from our monthly letters, to our tapes and videos, to our conferences, to the books that I write, and most of all to our inductive Bible study courses.

If you are not already involved in our Precept Bible Studies, contact us so that you can feed in His pastures.

His Pastures . . . His Word

"THE LORD HAS TOLD ME I must talk with you. When can we get together?" Oh, how I admired this chaplain. Pride would not keep him from humbling obedience. God had shown him that he had gotten caught up in the "busyness" of being a chaplain and in the vanity of psychology, all to the neglect of the Word of God. And so he had come to find out how to really dig into God's Word, to study it precept upon precept. He saw that a ministry without the Word of God as its pivotal point is not a life-giving or a life-changing ministry.

Our Shepherd said: "The words that I have spoken to you are spirit and are life" (John 6:63). "Man shall not live by bread alone, but by every word that proceedeth out of the mouth of God" (Matthew 4:4 KJV). And so the Shepherd prayed for His sheep, "Sanctify them [make them holy] in the truth; Thy word is truth" (John 17:17).

But because man thinks he can live by bread alone, because man has been taken captive "through philosophy and empty deception, according to the tradition of men, according to the elementary principles of the world, rather than according to Christ" (Colossians 2:8), man is anything but holy. Man is all messed up.

Sometimes as people sit under the teaching of God's Word, they burst out sobbing. Suddenly confronted with how they have transgressed God's Holy Word, their hearts break in remorse. They have done those things they ought not to have done, and there is no health in them. They are riddled with the seeping sores of sin . . . immorality, incest, abortion, divorce (once, twice, more), wounded children, dominated husbands. They are governed by destructive tongues and hardened hearts that have to be broken with the hammer of God's Word.

O Beloved, are you wandering about, foraging, searching, unable to rest, getting all messed up because you won't spend time feeding in the pastures the Shepherd has prepared for you?

What will it take to make you get into His Word?

> Before I was afflicted, I went astray, but now I keep Thy word. . . . May Thy compassion come to me that I may live, for Thy law is my delight (Psalm 119:67,77).

"When I Am Afraid"

AFTER FIFTEEN YEARS, suddenly it was back. It came after she had boarded the plane. "It was like something was going to happen, and I had no control over it. I wanted to run, to get away, but I was caught on the plane. Before I was saved, when fear would hit me, I would run . . . I would get out of the house or wherever I was."

But this time she could not run. The fear that came over my dear friend that day was not the fear of flying, but a sudden fear for her child whom she had left behind. However, because it happened on a plane, the fear was transferred to flying. What a problem this presented, for every week she had to fly to another state to teach a Bible class.

Have there been times, Beloved, when you have suddenly been struck by fear? What did you do?

Sheep have a tendency to run when frightened. A sudden noise or disturbance can cause panic in the sheepfold. And when fear strikes, the sheep take off frantically in every direction . . . often into danger.

There is only one cure for fear as far as sheep are concerned. And it was the only cure for my friend. When sheep are suddenly struck by fear, the shepherd senses it immediately and quietly moves among them, reassuring them of his presence. As soon as the sheep become aware that the shepherd is with them, the desire to run vanishes; fear has been replaced by trust. *The Lord is my Shepherd; I shall not want.* He makes me to lie down—to rest, not to panic.

My friend soon realized that this fear was a fiery dart from the enemy and that to run would only cause Satan great delight. She learned that she must turn and gaze upon her Shepherd the moment fear struck. "When I am afraid, I will put my trust in Thee. In God, whose word I praise, in God I have put my trust; I shall not be afraid. What can mere man do to me?" (Psalm 56:3,4). And so she would be kept in perfect peace by keeping her mind stayed upon her Shepherd . . . she would trust in Him (Isaiah 26:3).

Was she ever again bothered by fear? Yes. We'll talk about it more tomorrow. But for today, Beloved, why don't you talk to the Shepherd about your own fears? Remember, to lie down in His green pastures, you must deal with fear!

Run to Your Shepherd

WHEN FEAR BEGINS to grip your heart, you must stop at that very moment and remember that fear is not from God. The Lord is your Shepherd, and you shall not want.

God has not given us the spirit of fear, but of power and of love and of a sound mind (2 Timothy 1:7). Therefore, when you find yourself the target of the enemy's fiery darts of fear, you must raise your shield of faith. With this spiritual armor you will be able to extinguish all of the fiery darts of the evil one (Ephesians 6:16).

A sound mind is a mind under control . . . a disciplined mind that does not panic, does not lose touch with reality, does not give way to imagination, does not lose consciousness or fall into depression. When fear would catch you in its viselike grip, you must consciously rehearse the love of God and remember His sovereignty. Remember, whatever comes your way has to be filtered through God's sovereign fingers of love. Perfect love casts out every torment of fear (1 John 4:18).

Recognizing all of this, and knowing that fear comes from the father of lies—that thief who would kill and destroy—you must then appropriate that power which is given to you by God. Remember that God has not given you the spirit of fear . . . but of power.

How do you appropriate this power? First, you must recognize that one of the enemy's favorite weapons of warfare is fear. So look to your Shepherd-God. Submit to Him. Tell Him you are His; He can do anything with you that He wants. This really discombobulates the enemy! Then "resist the devil and he will flee from you" (James 4:7).

Still, periodically, a sudden dart of fear will take aim at my friend. But now she does not panic. The moment that fear comes, she consciously recognizes that it is from the enemy. She says it is almost as if the enemy cries, "Here comes that fear again. You aren't going to be able to handle it. You are going to go into a panic."

"But," she says, "I know it is him, and I do not entertain the thought for a moment. I refuse it and go on with whatever I was doing."

O Beloved . . . this is how you, too, must handle fear. Look to the Shepherd; listen to His words.

Resting in His Pasture

ARE YOU TENSE? Edgy? Discontented? Restless? Irritable? When sheep get this way, they cannot lie down. Rest is impossible! These are sure signs there is rivalry, so the shepherd looks for friction within his flock. People aren't the only ones who compete for status or go about asserting themselves. These attitudes are also common among sheep, and when they are, oh, how the tension builds!

Authority within the sheepfold is established by a butting order. In Ezekiel 34:20-22, God says to His wayward people:

> "Behold, I, even I, will judge between the fat sheep and the lean sheep. Because you push with side and with shoulder, and thrust at all the weak with your horns, until you have scattered them abroad, therefore, I will deliver My flock, and they will no longer be a prey; and I will judge between one sheep and another."

O Beloved, how it must hurt our Shepherd's heart to see us butt, shove, and push one another just so we can be recognized, elevated, or established in authority over others.

The Good Shepherd came not to be ministered unto, but to minister, "to give His life a ransom for many" (Matthew 20:28). Jesus, who is God, did not exalt Himself; instead, He made Himself a servant (Philippians 2:5-7). How can we help but take this form also?

Did He not tell us that to become great in the kingdom of God we must become servants?

Are you missing that life of rest which is yours as His child, the sheep of His pasture, because you are trying to assert yourself . . . or because others are butting you out of the way?

When you sit in church next Sunday, look around you at the flock. What is your attitude toward them? And what is your attitude toward other groups of Christians who seem to be more successful or as successful as your group? Is there jealousy in your heart, or a spirit of rivalry? If so, you will not be able to lie down in the green pastures your Shepherd has prepared for you. If you have been "butting," confess it in your prayer right now.

Oil . . . for Your Irritations

HAVE YOU EVER gotten a bug up your nose? I have! Don't ask me how! But you can be sure that neither of us planned it . . . neither me nor the bug! Somehow either that bug got off course or my sniff just had too much power to it. At any rate, I felt like I had inhaled a Mexican jumping bean. The poor thing was darting back and forth, up and down, apparently panicked by my violent shaking, snorting, and blowing. (It was found dead in my handkerchief.)

When I read Phillip Keller's excellent book, *A Shepherd Looks at Psalm 23*, I discovered just how much we have in common with sheep. Bugs up their noses drive them to distraction! They certainly can't rest in that condition!

Sheep can suffer greatly because of the nose fly. This insect seeks to deposit its eggs on the mucous membrane of the sheep's nose. There the eggs hatch into small wormlike larvae that eventually work their way up the nose into the sheep's head. As these larvae burrow into the sheep's flesh, they cause a tremendous irritation which in turn causes the sheep to thrash and beat its head against anything it can find. A sheep can become so driven to distraction by the irritation that it will actually kill itself trying to get rid of the aggravation.

As I learned this truth, I could not help but think of how men and women can be tormented by the thoughts that burrow their way into their flesh. The eggs of torment are laid by the enemy and hatch into repulsive, destructive worms that work their way into our minds. Thoughts of fear, rejection, bitterness, hatred, failure, incompetency, sensuality, and greed plague God's sheep, tormenting them, even driving some to suicide.

But is this to be the fate of God's sheep? No! Just as there is an oil the shepherd can prepare to protect his sheep from nose flies and their destructive work, so our Shepherd has a way to keep His sheep from such torment. As the psalmist says, "Thou anointest my head with oil" (Psalm 23:5 KJV).

How does it work? We'll see, Beloved, in the days ahead. But for today, let me ask you a question. Is there a bug tormenting you? What is it? Write it down. Then ask your Shepherd for His oil.

Oil...for Your Peace

SATAN IS THE CHRISTIAN'S nose fly. His target is your mind. He wants to deposit thoughts in your mind which will hatch lies that will burrow their way into your flesh and drive you to distraction. Satan will do anything he can to destroy you, for "he is a liar, and the father of lies" (John 8:44).

"I hate my little boy, but I don't know why. I know it's wrong. I try to love him, but I can't." The woman who said this had come to my friend for counseling.

As my friend shared the situation with me, she said, "There's only one thing I learned that might give us a clue to her problem. One day when she picked her little son up from the sitter's house, the sitter's neighbor commented that she hated screaming children. Ever since then this precious girl has been panicked about her child making a fuss in public."

As we prayed about the situation, both of us felt this was our clue from the Lord. Satan had planted a lie in that woman's head through the neighbor's comment. In light of this, my friend advised the dear mother to take captive the lie through warfare praying, resisting the enemy, and refusing his lies.

The woman prayed something like this: "O Father, I refuse this lie from the enemy. Satan, you are a liar and destroyer, and I will have nothing to do with you. I command you to depart with this lie. Father, You love my son just as he is. He is a gift from You. You designed him in my womb (Psalm 139) and I love him and thank You for him."

Satan's destructive lie had caused her great torment, but she now knew where this hatred had come from—from the father of lies. For her Shepherd had already anointed her head with His protective oil through that dream.

Beloved, has Satan deposited a lie in your mind? Do not despair. We will seek the Shepherd's care in the days to come.

Oil . . . for Your Victory

DURING THE SEASON for nose flies or other pests that torment sheep, a good shepherd will prepare a special protective oil and smear it over the head and nostrils of each of his sheep.

So now, Beloved, since it is always the season for Satan's nose flies, let's get our heads duly treated with the Shepherd's oil. Remember, Satan's target is the mind, so God tells us in 2 Corinthians 10:5 that we are to destroy speculations and every lofty thing raised up against the knowledge of God. We are to take every thought captive to the obedience of Christ. This is the Shepherd's oil.

But how is it applied? By raw, naked obedience of faith.

When a thought comes to your mind, before you grant it entrance you are to Philippians 4:8 it: "Whatever is true, whatever is honorable, whatever is right, whatever is pure, whatever is lovely, whatever is of good repute, if there is any excellence and if anything worthy of praise, let your mind dwell on these things."

Every thought is to be frisked at the door of your mind before you let it in. Is it true? Honorable? Right? Pure? If the answer to *any* of the above is no, then you are not to think or dwell upon it.

But what do you do if the lying larvae have already dug into your flesh and set up their irritation? Then you need to perform some radical surgery. First, ask God to search your mind and reveal where the enemy has erected his stronghold. Then find the truth in the Word of God that refutes what Satan has said. When you find that truth, command Satan to leave you, and order the stronghold or fortress torn down by God's Holy Spirit. Tell God that you purposefully, willfully choose to believe His Word.

Ask the Lord Jesus Christ to stand there with you against the enemy's stronghold and, by your God's authority, destroy it, knowing that "the weapons of our warfare are not of the flesh, but divinely powerful for the destruction of fortresses" (2 Corinthians 10:4).

Then, in faith, praise God, for you are more than a conqueror through Him. Should the thought try to come back again, refuse it . . . over and over again . . . until it gets weary and flies away exhausted. Then, Beloved, your cup will overflow (Psalm 23:5)!

Satisfied by Living Water

SHEEP CANNOT LIVE without water. Yet they can go for months without actually drinking. How? By absorbing the dew on the grass. This moisture can satisfy their need until their grazing takes them to streams, springs, or wells where they can drink deeply.

The secret is to catch the grass or vegetation while it is still wet, and to do this, the sheep must be up and about early in the morning, before the sun dries up that clean, pure dew! Thus, the shepherd will make sure his sheep are out and grazing early. Then, when the heat of the day comes, the sheep will have already satisfied their hunger and thirst and can retire to the shade of a tree and lie down to rest.

This is just the way our Shepherd seeks to lead us to the Water of Life. He knows the heat of our day, the pressures that come as things get hot and busy, and so He bids us arise in the early hours and come graze with Him:

> The Lord GOD has given Me the tongue of disciples, that I may know how to sustain the weary one with a word. He awakens Me morning by morning, he wakens My ear to listen as a disciple (Isaiah 50:4).

Now, Beloved, there is no law that says you must meet with God every morning or He will not bless you. Please do not think that! What I am suggesting is that if you want to remain serene, confident, and able to cope, you need to drink of Jesus, the Fountain of Living Water. And it is easier to do this, in all probability, if you meet with your Shepherd before the distractions of the day pull you away.

Unless you are getting good Bible study at church or with a group in your community, it can be a long time between springs, streams, or wells. So you must be sustained by your daily dew. I have found that once my day starts, the heat is on. Then it is difficult to get pure, clean dew . . . and without it my tongue is thick with thirst and certainly is not the tongue of a disciple!

Why not try it faithfully for just *one* month and see if that morning dew doesn't make a difference? Will you?

Safety with the Shepherd

"HE LEADS ME beside quiet waters" (Psalm 23:2). That's important, because sheep are frightened by swiftly moving streams. If they fall into the water, they can easily be carried downstream by the current. Also, if they have not been shorn and are thick with coats of wool, they can easily become waterlogged and sink. So sheep and rapid water do not mix. And sheep know it! Whenever they have to cross water of any depth at all, they know there is only one safe place, and that is next to the shepherd.

For this reason, our Shepherd says to us: "Do not fear, for I have redeemed you; I have called you by name; you are Mine! When you pass through the waters, I will be with you; and through the rivers, they will not overflow you" (Isaiah 43:1,2). The Lord is your Shepherd; you shall not want.

O precious one, have you tried to cross the waters alone? Have you been swept away by some sudden, swift current of events? Are you being pulled under, absorbing your problems rather than casting them off? Are you weighed down in the waters of trouble? Are you overwhelmed? Do you fear for your sanity of mind? Do you feel that you might not make it, that you might drown? Sheep who do not stay close to the Shepherd get into trouble.

But do not despair. Your Sovereign Shepherd is there. Draw near to Him and listen to His words, for He has said, "I WILL NEVER DESERT YOU, NOR WILL I EVER FORSAKE YOU" (Hebrews 13:5b).

The waters will not overflow you. They cannot overflow you when you are close to Him. When the three Hebrew children were thrown into the furnace of fire, they saw a fourth there, the Son of God (Daniel 3:25). When all deserted the apostle Paul, the Lord stood with him and strengthened him (2 Timothy 4:16,17).

God has never forsaken His sheep. Would He forsake you?

Write out a prayer to your Shepherd. Tell Him about the waters you are crossing.[2]

The Restorer of Your Soul

"HE LEADS ME beside quiet waters. He restores my soul" (Psalm 23:2,3). What does the psalmist mean when he says that the Shepherd "restores my soul"? To understand that, we need to understand sheep. For when a sheep becomes "cast down," it needs to be restored.[3]

A cast sheep is one that has rolled onto its back and is unable to get up. Sometimes a sheep will lie down to rest; then, deciding to have a good stretch on its side, it will suddenly get off balance. It may get caught on uneven ground, or it may be heavy with fat or wool or with lamb. Suddenly its center of gravity shifts, and the poor thing finds itself on its back. As the sheep flails its legs frantically in the air, trying to right itself, gases begin to build up in the animal's stomach. As these gases build, circulation to its legs is cut off. On its back, unable to get up, the sheep is utterly cast down.

If the day is sunny and hot, the sheep will only last a few hours. Also, a cast sheep is easy prey for all sorts of predators. The shepherd is the only hope for a cast sheep, and when he spots one, he wastes no time. He hurries to rescue—to restore—his sheep.

Have you ever felt so "down" that you wondered if you would ever get up? Maybe depression has settled around you like a morning fog so that you have forgotten what it was like to awaken to days of expectation, bright with clear blue skies and white cotton-puff clouds. Or perhaps you feel abandoned by God. You know God's Word says that He will not forsake you, but for some reason you feel He has.

If this describes you, it may be that you are "cast down."

But fear not, little sheep. The omniscient, omnipresent Lord is your Shepherd! If you are cast down and unable to get up, He knows where you are. He knows that the enemy's predators are all around, seeking to devour you (1 Peter 5:8). He will rescue you. He will restore your soul.

> The Lord sustains all who fall, and raises up all who are bowed down (Psalm 145:14).

Those, Beloved, are the words of your Shepherd.

If You Are Cast Down

ARE YOU LOCKED in a situation of despair? Have your tears been your food day and night? Have others said to you, "Where is your God?" (Psalm 42:3). Do you wonder why you are where you are or if you will ever change? Or if the depression will ever go away? If so, precious sheep, you are cast down and need to be restored.

Sheep usually become cast down for one of four reasons. Today we will look at two of these reasons, and tomorrow we will examine the other two.

First, many sheep become cast while looking for a soft spot—a cozy, rounded hollow in the ground. They want it easy. But it is in these soft hollows that they are more apt to end up on their back.

People are much the same. People with time on their hands, or people with no outreach, or people who tend to be preoccupied with their own problems are susceptible to depression. Because things are easy or soft, they have time to think, to focus on the negatives in their lives. And ofttimes it rolls them right over on their backs.

The *second* reason many sheep become cast is that they are fat. Overweight sheep are not only the quickest to become caught off-balance, but they are also the least productive and the least healthy. They simply have too much abundance.

How like us! Once we have it made, once we get fat with the over-abundances of life, we see little need to depend upon our Shepherd. Our "busyness," our preoccupation with getting ahead or with keeping up a certain lifestyle, lands us flat on our backs. We forget what it is like to walk in dependence upon our Shepherd, and so we are caught, fat and empty.

Let's stop and take a good honest look at ourselves. Could we become cast sheep? Any sheep can . . . the largest, the strongest, the fattest, the healthiest.

Are you looking for an easy, soft life? Are you getting fat, living luxuriously on the things of the world? Are you entangling yourself in the affairs of this life rather than pleasing Him who has called you to be a soldier (2 Timothy 2:4)?

Take time to think upon these things, Beloved.

Let Your Shepherd Lead You

WHEN A SHEEP has too much wool, its fleece becomes clogged with mud, sticks, burrs, ticks, and manure. The wool, laden with all of this, puts so much weight on the sheep that it just cannot get up. And that's the *third* reason a sheep can become cast down and needs restoring.

If a sheep has become cast because of its wool, the shepherd knows that it is time to shear his sheep. This clogged fleece has to go! His sheep must be stripped down to keep from being cast down!

Not unlike us, Beloved. Did you know that God did not allow His priests who were ministering in the tabernacle to wear wool because wool was a picture of the self-life? We must all be careful of that self-life that can become clogged with sins and encumbrances that would so easily weigh us down. Every encumbrance and the sin which does so easily entangle has got to be laid aside (Hebrews 12:1).

You would think the shepherd of such a sheep would just let it go. After all, it was the sheep who made such a repulsive mess of itself . . . just let it stay on its back. But this is impossible for the Great Shepherd, who gave His very life for this sheep. He came to seek and to save the lost. And so when He finds that one, flat on its back, legs stiff and paralyzed, there is great rejoicing.

Tender words of loving rebuke, of admonition, and of instruction spill from the Shepherd's mouth as He reaches down to this sheep He knows so well. Turning it upon its side, the Shepherd massages its legs, restoring the circulation so that it can again walk at His side.

Finally, a ewe heavy with lambs can become cast. Sometimes, Beloved, those who are bearing the care of others or those burdened with a ministry can suddenly find themselves on their backs, weighted down . . . unable to get up on their feet. How vital it is that such a one walk continuously at the Shepherd's side, being careful to rest on solid ground, wary of hollows that would throw him or her off balance.

May we remember that He "shall gently lead those that are with young" (Isaiah 40:11 KJV). And may we allow ourselves to be led.

The Shepherd never drives His sheep. He always leads them.

If You Go Astray

"ALL OF US LIKE SHEEP have gone astray, each of us has turned to his own way" (Isaiah 53:6).

"Before I was afflicted I went astray" (Psalm 119:67).

It is sad when dependent sheep try to live in an independent manner. But some sheep can be so stubborn! They just don't want to stay with the flock. They want to graze where they want to graze. They don't want to follow the shepherd; they want the shepherd to follow them . . . or to at least be there should they need him. And need him they will if they keep wandering off. You see, sheep are so dumb that they can eat their way right off a cliff!

When a shepherd has a sheep with an independent streak, he often has to take radical action to keep the sheep from "self-destructing." The shepherd will break the sheep's leg. He'll catch that wandering, independent sheep, lay it down, and break its leg with a rock. But his purpose is not to hurt or cripple the sheep. For after breaking the sheep's leg, he tenderly binds it in a splint. Then he lifts the helpless creature to his bosom and enfolds it in his robe.

Brokenness has brought the sheep to the bosom of the shepherd. There it will feel the tender caresses of the shepherd. There it will feel the beat of the shepherd's heart. There it will hear the shepherd's every word. There it will be fed by the shepherd's hand. There . . . because of brokenness . . . the sheep will get to know the shepherd as it has never known him. Then, when the leg is mended, the sheep, having become accustomed to intimacy with its shepherd, will follow closely at his side.

"The LORD is near to the brokenhearted" (Psalm 34:18).

"The sacrifices of God are a broken spirit; a broken and a contrite heart, O God, Thou wilt not despise" (Psalm 51:17).

O Beloved, have you been prone to wander? Have you been broken? Can you not see the love of the Shepherd in that brokenness?

He has broken your independent spirit so that you might dwell near Him in safety. Do not be bitter; He moved in love with your highest good in mind. Will you not thank Him for breaking you?

Live . . . for His Name's Sake

ARE YOU IN A RUT? Has your life become a boring, meaningless existence? Do you feel that were you to die tomorrow, you would have lived a life that never really had any significant effect upon others? If you can answer yes to any of these questions, then it is time to follow the Shepherd who will lead you "in the paths of righteousness for His name's sake" (Psalm 23:3). For, Beloved, you were chosen by Him that you might go and bear fruit (John 15:16).

Sheep are creatures of habit. Left to themselves, they will graze the same ground over and over again until the land becomes wasteland and their paths erode into gullies. Ground overgrazed by sheep often becomes polluted with parasites and disease. That is why sheep so desperately need a shepherd. They must be managed; they must be led on to new pastures, to prepared tables of land where they can be properly fed.

Our Shepherd has prepared abundant pastures for us. But, alas, how many prefer the contaminated ruts to the new and greener grazing grounds He would lead us to if we were only willing to follow.

If you are in a rut or feel that life is meaningless, let me ask you:

—When was the last time you diligently sought His face in prayer, asking Him to reveal His will to you?

—When was the last time you prostrated yourself in prayer and said, "Use me, God, or I'll die! I must worship You by serving You"?

—When was the last time you took the opportunity to counsel a needy one, visit the sick or those abandoned in nursing homes, cook a meal for someone, babysit for a young mother? When was the last time you encouraged younger women to become better wives and mothers or counseled younger men to become better husbands and fathers, prepared yourself in God's Word, encouraged some fainthearted Christian, worked at being a better partner or a better parent or a better child, cared for the orphans and the widows, or shared the precious truths of His Word with others?

Are you being led in paths of righteousness for His name's sake, or are you living in the rut of self-centeredness?

Ask your Shepherd where He would lead you.

Your Valleys ... Chosen for You

EVERY NOW AND THEN it happens, and yesterday was such a day. It was unseasonably warm, bright, and exquisitely beautiful, and I couldn't bear to drive my car down the hill to our office. I had to walk. As I came down through the grass, I felt like doing a Julie Andrews . . . running, twirling, and singing, "The hills are alive with the sound of music." I couldn't thank my Father enough for the beauty and warmth of it all.

Yet every day cannot be sunny, and night must always follow day. If there are to be mountains, there must of necessity be valleys.

"Yea, though I walk through the valley of the shadow of death, I will fear no evil," says the psalmist, "for thou art with me" (Psalm 23:4 KJV).

It is at this point in the Twenty-third Psalm that the pronouns change . . . from "He" to "Thou." And with the change of pronouns comes a change in atmosphere. All of a sudden we become acutely aware of the intimacy of the two walking together. Why? Because they are in a valley of deep darkness. The light of the sun has been blocked out by a looming mountain.

The path that the Shepherd has *chosen* for His sheep passes through a valley. It is dark in the valley; shadows cast frightening images; wild winds and storms can whip down suddenly and violently from the mountain. Why come this way?

Why? Because in the valleys can be found more abundant sources of water, where the sheep can drink long and deep. Also, the valleys are the way to the mountaintop's luscious vegetation!

Jesus stood and cried out, "If any man is thirsty, let him come to Me and drink. He who believes in Me, as the Scripture said, 'From his innermost being shall flow rivers of living water'" (John 7:37,38).

Valleys are not meant to depress or to irritate you, Beloved. They are not there to make you tremble. Valleys are passageways that will bring you into hitherto unexperienced intimacy with your Shepherd.

If you are in a valley . . . if the sun is shut out . . . do not fear, precious sheep. Your Shepherd, God's Son, is there with you. It is all in His plan. He has an eternal purpose. Drink deeply.

His Staff . . . Your Comfort

SHE HAD LIVED FOR ten years in a dark underground dungeon. Her only light came at mealtimes when she was provided with a candle. Although Louis XIV had condemned her to prison, Madame Guyon knew that, like Paul, she was the Lord's prisoner, not the king's. In her tenth year of imprisonment, she wrote these words:

> A little bird I am, shut from the fields of air;
> Yet in my cage I sit and sing to Him who placed me there;
> Well pleased a prisoner to be,
> Because, my God, it pleases Thee.[4]

O Beloved, have you ever wondered how people can be imprisoned and still sing? Have they been given an extra portion of God, of His grace? Do they have something we could never even dream of attaining?

Remember yesterday, when we talked about walking through the valley of the shadow of death and fearing no evil because our Shepherd is with us? Well, I didn't finish the fourth verse, which goes on to say, "I will fear no evil: for thou art with me; thy rod and thy staff, they comfort me" (Psalm 23:4 KJV).

As the sheep pass through the valley, they are not afraid, because the Shepherd is there. And they experience the comfort of His presence through the touch of His staff.

The shepherd's staff is the extension of the shepherd's hand. It is used to rescue sheep, to draw the sheep together, to restore lambs to their ewes, and to guide the sheep. And last, but most precious, the shepherd uses his staff to touch his sheep so that he can have intimate contact with them while he walks beside them and towers above them.

Isn't this just like the Holy Spirit? The Spirit is the staff of comfort and guidance, the extension between our Shepherd's hand and us.

"I will not leave you as orphans; I will come to you" (John 14:18).

"And I will pray the Father, and he shall give you another Comforter, that he may abide with you for ever" (John 14:16 KJV).

So remember, Beloved, wherever you are, His staff . . . His Spirit . . . is your Comforter.

His Rod . . . Your Protection

WHY DO SOME CHRISTIANS seem to have a much more intimate relationship with the Father? One of the major reasons, I believe, is that they have come to know the purpose and, thus, the power of their Shepherd's rod.

The shepherd's rod is an extension of his right arm, the arm of power and authority. And what is our power and authority? The Word of God! By it we live; by it we rule. The shepherd's rod, like God's Word, is a weapon of power and protection.

The shepherd uses his rod to examine his sheep. As the sheep pass under his rod, the shepherd examines each one intimately to determine its needs and to discover any hidden problems that might cause the creature to be weak or infirm.

"I shall make you pass under the rod," says our Great Shepherd (Ezekiel 20:37). And so He watches over us, carefully examining us in the light of His Word, revealing any infirmities, and cleansing us with the water of the Word.

The shepherd also uses his rod as a weapon to ward off predators.

How intimate are you with your Shepherd's rod, Beloved? Do you know its power, authority, and protection against the attacks of the enemy? Do you know the cleansing and, thus, the protection that the Word of God brings? Are you examined by its authority daily?

Remember when I shared with you at the beginning of this month that I was having to deal with loneliness and feelings of rejection? That is like a valley of the shadow of death—death to what I want, what I would like to be true, but isn't. Remember the young man who had been so horribly abused by his parents? Remember the friends who are having to deal with a cancerous brain tumor? For all of us, even in the midst of such dark valleys, because we are the sheep of His pasture, there is comfort, succor, and sustenance through the Word of God. His Word meets our every need; it holds the answer to our every question.

Spend time today looking up the following verses: 2 Timothy 3:16,17; Hebrews 4:12; Ephesians 5:26; Ephesians 5:16,17. Next to each reference write down what you learn about the Word.

Let His rod comfort you, Beloved.

His Table . . .
Prepared for You

"THOU PREPAREST A TABLE before me in the presence of mine enemies" (Psalm 23:5a KJV).

Through the years, many a range war has raged between cattlemen and sheepherders. Why? Because sheep can ruin the land. They will eat the very root of a plant, thus leaving the land barren. For this reason, sheep must be kept on the move.

Many times the shepherd will scout ahead to prepare a mesa for the sheep's grazing, carefully removing certain plants that can poison sheep. The shepherd must also make sure there is adequate water, and he seeks to discover any predators that occupy the land.

When I think of how the Shepherd prepares "a place of feeding" for His sheep, even in the midst of their enemies, I cannot help but think of the story of John Sung.

John was a brilliant young Chinese man who came to America to study. While in seminary, he came under conviction from God that he was not truly saved. Because of this, he fell into a severe depression. The faculty of the school were greatly concerned and were debating what to do with John when his depression suddenly gave way to an unrestrained exuberance! Not realizing that the change in John was the result of his salvation, they committed him to a mental institution.

John tried to escape but failed. Dark thoughts of ending his life took form in his mind . . . until the Lord rebuked him.

"If you can endure this trial patiently for 193 days," God said, "you will have learned how to . . . walk the Calvary road of unswerving obedience."[5] Little did John realize that his Shepherd had gone before and prepared a table for him in the presence of his enemies.

Seeing his ordeal in a new light, John moved under his Shepherd's rod. He devoted his waking hours to reading the Bible. He read it through forty times, each time using a different scheme of study.

As a result of this time shut up with God and His Word, John Sung was to become a brilliant flame for God in the Far East.

What table has God prepared for you, dear sheep? May you sit at it peacefully as you realize your Shepherd prepared it.

Known . . . Loved . . . by the Shepherd

BELOVED, DO YOU EVER feel lost in the crowd . . . like you are not important or significant? You look at other Christians and feel that they are the superstars . . . the greats . . . the ones who are really being used by God. And then there is you!

Of course you would never let anyone know that you feel this way, but it would be kind of nice to hear your own name mentioned now and then. It would feel good, at least, to be recognized . . . at least just once. But, then, it will probably never happen, because you are not *important* . . . so who would remember your name?

O Beloved . . . *NO, NO, NO!* You are wrong. You *are* precious. You *are* important. You *are* special. You are *His* sheep. Turn around and look. Goodness and mercy are following you. You are so special that you will dwell in the house of the Lord forever. You are His . . . He has called you by your name. Oh, how I wish I could put my arms around you and tell you this truth in person.

"I am the good shepherd; and I know My own, and My own know Me" (John 10:14). God knows you, precious one, by name (John 10:3). You are not just one of a flock, but an individual who is very precious to your Shepherd. You are so special to Him that if He had ninety-nine other sheep and you were lost, He would know that you were the one missing. And He would not stop looking for you, calling you by name, until He had found you (Luke 15:3-6).

Your name is important to Him. To Him you are very significant . . . very precious. Don't ever forget it, Beloved.

Oh, you may not be known by multitudes, but what does that matter, for you are known to your Shepherd, the King of kings. And He is coming again to "receive you to Myself; that where I am, there you may be also" (John 14:3).

You will dwell in the house of the Lord forever (Psalm 23:6). Hallelujah! The Lord is your Shepherd, you shall not want.

Write a love note to your Shepherd. Thank Him for His tender care, and tell Him that you will follow wherever He leads.

APRIL

Why Are You in Despair, O My Soul?

The church is lulled into apathy because we have become caught in the things of this world. My concern is for those who are not rooted and grounded in the Word of God, for we know that faith comes by hearing and hearing by the Word of God! What will we do in the days ahead? How will the just live by faith then, when we are not living by faith now? This month will be a time when we consider the challenge of living by faith, of getting prepared so that no matter the future, we will be secure because our hope, our trust, is in the One who never changes!

You Can Walk on Heights

SOME PEOPLE LIVE in utter dread of the future, consumed with fear of the unknown. Wanting to be prepared, they imagine the worst and make provision for it.

Others live with no thought of tomorrow. They are either too frightened to think about it, so they blot out the future entirely by throwing themselves into today—or, they are seemingly so blasé about life that they never consider what the future might hold! Their approach is to eat, drink, and be merry (if you can), for tomorrow you die (Ecclesiastes 8:15). Both are determined to get all they can when they can.

But not all people fall into one of these two categories. I know I don't. Certainly I think about the future, but not with terror, dread, or panic. I know that what our near future holds is not good; difficult times are on their way. Iniquity, crime, graft, deception, and gross immorality crawl over our land like kudzu, an insidious, encroaching vine that can literally cover everything in sight. Fed by a giant taproot, kudzu is virtually impossible to control—and so it is with evil.

Many of us realize that our immediate future holds inevitable judgment; yet this knowledge does not consume or control us. However, neither are we grabbing all that we can while we can. Instead, we look at today as a day to be lived in the light of eternity for our God and Father, a day to be lived in faith as He would have us live it—righteously.

Some of us have chosen to live each day according to the words of Habakkuk: "The Sovereign LORD is my strength; he makes my feet like the feet of a deer, he enables me to go on the heights" (Habakkuk 3:19 NIV).

In other words, no matter what life brings—the valleys, the ups, the downs, present or future—I can walk the heights because of the strength of my God.

Wouldn't you, too, like to walk through the rest of your life on the heights? There is a way, as we will learn in the days to come.

"How Long Will I Call for Help?"

SEVERAL YEARS AGO I was walking rapidly down the corridor as Jan was making a beeline into one of our offices. It had been a busy morning at Precept Ministries, and without the slightest break in speed, she flipped a casual, "How are you doin'?"

I had been caught! There was no disguising it; I couldn't speak without tears, so I said, "I'm crying." Just having to say I was crying produced even more tears. By the time I stepped into my secretary's office, I was a mess!

Billie, Charlotte, and Carolyn all asked at the same time, "What's the matter?" Before I could answer, Jan had made a U-turn and suddenly appeared in our midst. Connie, hearing the commotion, left her layout table and joined us. Pretty soon, we all had tears in our eyes. And when I told them why I was crying, the others confessed that they felt the same way I did.

How was I feeling? I felt like I just couldn't do the job! No matter how much I prayed, no matter how much I searched my heart, no matter how much I studied, I still felt I was falling short. I felt I had failed as a teacher. All I could do was throw up my hands and say, "I don't know what more to do. All I can do is keep on."

How good it was to cry, and to cry together. And how comforting it was to learn that others understood. I didn't get sympathy; I got empathy. We had all been there! Yet until that shared moment we had all thought we were the only ones going through that particular trial!

When we left that office, it was with great resolve, for we realized we were under attack. Satan had sought to put out the fire of consecration with the extinguishing fluid of discouragement and defeat. We had called for help, but God hadn't rescued us—or so it seemed.

And so it seemed to the prophet Habakkuk when he cried, "How long, O LORD, will I call for help, and Thou wilt not hear?" (Habakkuk 1:2).

You understand, don't you, Beloved, for you too have cried. You may be crying now. You have been there—discouraged, defeated, and maybe wondering about abandoning the ship! I understand. We'll talk about it more tomorrow.

Recognize the Enemy!

REMEMBER WHEN SATAN approached Eve in the Garden of Eden? His first words were, "Indeed, has God said . . . ?" (Genesis 3:1).

If you and I are to live by faith, if we are to live by every word that proceeds out of the mouth of God, then we must understand Satan's approach. His tactic is to make us doubt the veracity or the power of God's words. How subtly the enemy sows his seeds of doubt, and what rich harvests he reaps if we are not aware of his methods. So God warns us not to be ignorant of Satan's schemes "in order that no advantage be taken of us by Satan" (2 Corinthians 2:11). But what are the enemy's schemes? How does he work?

Years ago God allowed me to hear a message from Joseph Carroll, a dear brother in the Lord. It was a message on "The Five Deadly D's." Since then I have shared it time and time again, and it has helped so many. Now I want to share it with you, with the prayer that God might use it in your life in the days to come. May it become that by which He strengthens you in your walk of faith with hinds' feet on high places (Habakkuk 3:19).

One of the main principles of warfare is concentration, the massing of one's forces at a critical time and place for decisive action. The objective is to break through the opposing army's front line at a single point and then penetrate its line of defense and secure a stronghold in its territory. Once that penetration occurs, it is easier to forge on ahead.

The enemy was trying to break through the lines at Precept Ministries; the ministry of God's Word had to be thwarted. Doubt cannot abide with faith; therefore, faith had to be destroyed. And since faith comes by hearing and hearing by the Word of God, it would only be logical for Satan to try to convince us to abandon ship as teachers of the Word. If he could bring *disappointment, discouragement, dejection,* and *despair,* then perhaps he could *demoralize* us totally.

But we were not ignorant of Satan's devices! And neither will you be, Beloved, for with your shield of faith you will "be able to extinguish all the flaming missiles of the evil one" (Ephesians 6:16).

Disappointment . . . Satan's Spearhead

SATAN USUALLY SPEARHEADS his attack with disappointment. His target is your mind; his goal—to break down your line of defense.

When an army plans to break through its enemy's line of defense, the first step is to amass all the available weaponry at one particular point. Say the line of defense is 30 miles long. The goal may be to break through that line with a tip of steel (perhaps 500 tanks) a half-mile wide. Behind those 500 tanks there will be another thousand, behind that an armored division of 10,000, and behind that 20,000 soldiers. Once the penetration is made by that tip of steel, the rest will move forward in an ever-widening expanse, taking over more and more of the opposition's line.

So it is with Satan. He spearheads his tip of steel with disappointment, a seemingly common and impotent weapon! Notice I said *seemingly*, for on the heels of disappointment comes a whole armored division of discouragement!

Here was where I had made my mistake. I let Satan's fiery missile of disappointment break through the threshold of my mind.

My service to the Lord had been done as unto the Lord. I had prayed about my lessons; I had studied diligently. Being responsible in my preparation, did not the effects belong to God "who works all things in all persons" (1 Corinthians 12:6)? Yet, for over a year, I continually struggled with thoughts as I stood teaching—thoughts like *they are so bored . . . you're not reaching them . . . they know all this already . . . God's not speaking through you . . . you should have taught something else,* and on and on.

When these thoughts came, instead of throwing up my shield of defense, I let them enter the camp. I failed to walk in the Spirit! Instead of exploding the missiles of disappointment with missiles of praise, I tried to figure out how I could have done a better job!

What about you? Do you ever get disappointed? If you are walking in obedience, seeking His guidance, then the cure for disappointment is to accept it all by faith as His appointment and to rest in His faithfulness.

Discouragement . . . Disappointment's Twin

DISCOURAGEMENT AND DISAPPOINTMENT are like twins. Open the door to disappointment, and you will find discouragement dashing in right behind. Satan's goal is to weaken you, to dishearten you, to make you lose courage. And once discouragement enters your camp, it seems to be downhill all the way.

That is why God was so careful in His instructions to Joshua as the Israelites prepared to occupy the land that God had given them. They had missed occupying Canaan forty years earlier because of unbelief at Kadesh-barnea. Yes, the land was as God had said, a land flowing with milk and honey. *But* there were giants in the land! What disappointment fell upon the children of Israel as they heard the discouraging report of the spies: "The people who live in the land are strong, and the cities are fortified and very large; and moreover, we saw the descendants of Anak there" (Numbers 13:27,28). In total discouragement and disappointment, they lifted up their voices and wept all night (Numbers 14:1). All of a sudden their God had become too small to handle human giants.

Some forty years later, they were preparing to enter the same land and meet the same giants and so God said, not once but three times, "Be strong and courageous!" (Joshua 1:6,7,9). They were not to "tremble or be dismayed," for the Lord their God was with them.

Joshua knew the results of discouragement. He had been one of those original twelve spies. He and Caleb had torn their clothes, beseeching the children of Israel to walk in faith, to believe God (Numbers 13:30). Yet they would not listen. Word of the giants and the fortified cities had penetrated their line of defense, and discouragement followed, bringing dejection and despair, until they were totally demoralized.

And so what is God's word to you today? It is to be strong and courageous, for your Father, the Lord God Omnipotent, reigns. So stop weeping and rejoice in the God of your salvation, for He is your strength and He will enable you to stand (Habakkuk 3:18,19).

The cure for discouragement is encouragement. Encourage your heart by looking at your God and His promises.

Dejection . . . Satan's Deadly Weapon

THE THIRD "DEADLY D" is dejection. Dejection is a lowness of spirit—when you feel tired, emotionally fatigued, and your ability to cope with difficult situations is at a dangerous low. This is a precarious position to be in, and if you are at that point, you need to be aware that this is not the time to make significant decisions. If you do, they will, in all probability, be wrong.

Dejection unchecked gives way to despair, our fourth "Deadly D."

One who is in a state of despair has lost or abandoned hope; his or her mind has become apathetic or numb. Thinking, decision-making, or just getting through the day all seem to be impossible.

Several precious ones have written me recently sharing that they can only make it through each day by rote, one motion at a time. The thought of coping with even the basic routines of living is overwhelming. So they consider only the immediate and force themselves to go through the motions.

Those who find themselves in despair usually feel abandoned by God. At such times the enemy will whisper unbelievable things in the mind. And Satan's schemes are so clever. He always makes them seem to be your thoughts rather than his!

Often, in times of dejection and despair, it seems easier to quit than to face life. At that point, one's thoughts begin to turn to death. *"Why fight it any longer? There's no way out."* You have called and called for help until you are too tired to call anymore. You have tried and tried until you are too tired to try anymore. In your numbness and emotional fatigue, death seems the only cure. At least then you could rest; your struggle would cease. It is too hard to believe you could ever again be happy, out from under these circumstances and filled with joy. No, you have numbly considered the future, and it is hopeless. Time to abandon ship.

This is dejection, this is despair, and it is deadly.

Is there any cure? Yes! For when the psalmist asked, "Why are you in despair, O my soul?" (Psalm 42:5), he was given a cure.

Despair . . . From Satan's Horror Chambers

I USED TO THINK of Psalm 42 as the longing of a consecrated heart for an even deeper communion with God. Then, after reading it carefully in its context, I saw that, instead, it is the inaudible longing from the depths of a soul overcome with despair. Listen carefully:

> As the deer pants for the water brooks, so my soul pants for Thee, O God. My soul thirsts for God, for the living God; when shall I come and appear before God? My tears have been my food day and night, While they say to me all day long, "Where is your God?" (Psalm 42:1-3).

Here is a soul in desperate need of hearing from God. Ever feel this way? The gates are closed; the King is in His chambers. He is too busy or too full of displeasure to be concerned with one so disappointing as you. Even others are saying to you, "Where is your God? . . . Certainly if He were with you, you wouldn't be going through this."

Then you remember: "I used to go along with the throng and lead them . . . to the house of God, with the voice of joy" (Psalm 42:4), and again you feel discouraged. Satan speaks up—in the first person singular and with a voice just like your own—"I have been abandoned by God. And if God has abandoned me, what hope is there?"

These are thoughts of despair. They come not from the counsel chambers of heaven but from the horror chambers of the father of lies.

You must not listen to them. Has not God Himself said, "I will never desert you, nor will I ever forsake you" (Hebrews 13:5)?

In the Greek there are five negatives in that verse. Add two to the first "never" and read, "I will never, never, never desert you." Then add one more to "nor" and read it "nor never will I ever forsake you." . . . "I will never, never, never desert you, nor never will I ever forsake you."

You may *feel* abandoned, but faith answers, "THE LORD IS MY HELPER, I WILL NOT BE AFRAID. WHAT SHALL MAN DO TO ME?" (Hebrews 13:6).

Are *you* in despair? Will you walk in faith or live by feeling?

Demoralized . . .
Denying the God of Hope

THREE TIMES IN Psalm 42 the psalmist reiterates the despair of his soul. And since the mind, will, and emotions all serve as component parts of man's soul, they are all affected.

Despair first touches the mind; we think we are alone, abandoned by God. We cannot reason. The emotions also are disturbed, for not only do we imagine ourselves alone and abandoned, but every cell of our being cries out, "It's true! I feel it! I feel it in my bones!" And the will is taken in tow, dragged along by the mind and emotions.

Are these three to be held captive forever in the prison of despair? Where is the way of escape promised by the One who said:

> No temptation [trial or testing] has overtaken you but such as is common to man; and God is faithful, who will not allow you to be tempted beyond what you are able, but with the temptation will provide the way of escape also, that you may be able to endure it (1 Corinthians 10:13).

And what form does this temptation take when it comes to despair? Is it not the temptation to cease resisting, to be flushed helplessly, like some captured insect, down into the sewage system of demoralization?

Demoralization, this fifth and final "Deadly D," is a state that renders us untrustworthy in discipline of body and soul. It is to be cast into disorder, to run in circles, to be caught in cycles that throw us totally off-balance so we cannot walk as God would have us walk. It is to have a mind that cannot think clearly or bring a thought to completion, when in truth it could be a sound mind, a mind controlled by His Spirit (2 Timothy 1:7). It is to refuse to listen to God's Spirit as He calls to us through the bars and bids us get up and at least try the cell door to see if it's locked.

Demoralization is to deny the God of all hope because our mind just cannot reason, our emotions are numb, and our will is mesmerized by apathy.

"Why are you in despair, O my soul?" (Psalm 42:5). It is because we *will* not hope in God and praise Him in faith.

Remember God . . . Hope in Him

DESPAIR CAN TAKE another form—desperation. Desperation is energized despair which causes a frenzy of activity, often reckless activity with no thought of the consequences. Desperation agitates the soul. It has to move; it cannot be still. Something must be done, but it does not know what.

And what should we do when we find ourselves engaged in the driven, senseless activity of desperation? There is only one thing to do and that is to willfully cry out to God, to tell Him all about it, and trust Him for deliverance. Read Psalm 42:5-8 and see how the psalmist dealt with his despair:

> Why are you in despair, O my soul?
> And why have you become disturbed within me?
> Hope in God, for I shall again praise Him
> For the help of His presence.
> O my God, my soul is in despair within me;
> Therefore I remember Thee from the land of the Jordan,
> And the peaks of Hermon, from Mount Mizar.
> Deep calls to deep at the sound of Thy waterfalls;
> All Thy breakers and Thy waves have rolled over me.
> The LORD will command His lovingkindness in the daytime;
> And His song will be with me in the night,
> A prayer to the God of my life.

As you may have noticed, verse 5 begins with a very needful question for one caught in the throes of despair or desperation. What is the cause of this despair? How did I get here? What brought me to this point? Many refuse to ask these questions, however, or even admit that there is a problem. In Psalm 42, not only does the psalmist ask the question, but he also confesses his state to his God: "O my God, my soul is in despair within me."

And what about your soul, Beloved? Is it in despair? Is it headed that way? Has there been a penetration of disappointment? If so, ask yourself *why*.

His Truth . . . Your Freedom

WHAT STRANGE CREATURES we human beings are! How often we think we can change or alter things simply by refusing to acknowledge them. We find truth so hard to deal with!

Yet did God not say, "You shall know the truth, and the truth shall make you free" (John 8:32)?

Somehow we think it is easier to live a lie. If we can ignore the problem, maybe it will go away. And so, with this twisted reasoning, we try to find our own way of coping rather than standing before the God of all truth, naked in His sight, and crying, "Help!"

And what keeps us away from Him? Is it not our own fantasizing, our own imperfect reasoning, our own concept of what this awesome and terrible God is like? Are we not really victims of the world's old wives' tales or the vain religious traditions of men? Is He a God who is too busy to care about the finite, minuscule problems of someone whose life span will be approximately threescore and ten? Is He out of reach, unattainable, unapproachable? Have we "come to a mountain . . . that is burning with fire; to darkness, gloom and storm; to a trumpet blast or to such a voice speaking words that those who heard it begged that no further word be spoken to them, because they could not bear what was commanded" (Hebrews 12:18-20 NIV)? Is this the One to whom we come when we are in despair?

Oh, no, Beloved. We come to the One who will freely give us all things. We stand before Him without condemnation if we are in Christ. Or, if we come before Him without Christ, we behold His Son at His right hand standing with outstretched, nail-pierced hands saying, "Will you not come to Me that you might have life, and have it abundantly?"

So why, then, do we stop up our ears and say, "He doesn't care," or, "It won't do any good"?

Why will we not come before Him and say, "Help! Examine me, my God. Tell me what my problem is. Why am I in this state? What is the answer? Tell me, God, tell me, and I will be quick to hear Your words. I'll trust You, God. Speak, Lord, for Your servant hears"?

O Beloved, what will your response be?

Your Faith . . . His Cure

BEFORE YOU BEGIN TODAY, read Psalm 42:5-11 one more time. As you see by now, faith is the only cure for despair, or for any of the "Deadly D's." Whether you are disappointed, discouraged, dejected, despairing, or demoralized, there is only one place to run, and that is to your God, your Rock. Cry out to Him. Say a prayer to the God of *your* life (Psalm 42:8).

If you feel as if He has forgotten you, then ask Him if He has. If you feel as if your enemies—be they physical, emotional, or spiritual—have overwhelmed you, ask Him why. Pour out your soul to your God.

Don't let your mind, your emotions, and your will cower in the corner of an unlocked cell. Rise up, O Will. Grab Mind and Emotions. Burst through that iron door and go talk to your Rock. Hope in Him, O Mind, and know, Emotions, you will again praise Him for the help of His presence. Rehearse what you remember of your God and know that the LORD will command His lovingkindness in the daytime; and His song will be with *you* in the night (Psalm 42:8).

Remember, the just shall live by faith. You are not abandoned. You will not live forever in this despair, for as you hope in Him, you will yet praise Him.

> But we have this treasure in earthen vessels, that the surpassing greatness of the power may be of God and not from ourselves; we are afflicted in every way, but not crushed; perplexed, but not despairing (2 Corinthians 4:7,8).

There it is. His Word. Will you believe it?

Faith consists of three things: knowledge, surrender to that knowledge, and obedience to walk in the light of that knowledge.

Will you live by faith?

Saving Faith Perseveres

JESUS KNEW HIS DISCIPLES were going to face difficult times when their faith would be tested to the hilt. Thus, at every opportunity, He sought to prepare them. "These things I have spoken to you, that in Me you may have peace. In the world you have tribulation, but take courage; I have overcome the world" (John 16:33).

Testing was inevitable; yet they were to persevere. And perseverance meant being faithful unto death (Revelation 2:10). Jesus' concern was that "when the Son of Man comes, will He find faith on the earth?" (Luke 18:8). He asked this after "telling them a parable to show that at all times they ought to pray and not to lose heart" (Luke 18:1).

Today we hear a great deal about "saving faith," which is good and vital, for it is the very beginning of life eternal (Ephesians 2:8). Yet sometimes I wonder if that is all we hear. Do we not also need to hear of the faith that perseveres—the faith that not only begins life, but also is the very sustenance of this new life?

God's Word teaches us that saving faith perseveres. It does not shrivel up or shrink away when confronted with the difficulties, the trials, the testings, the challenges, the lusts, and the worries of this age. True faith is not some vague belief that we flirt with or casually embrace; faith is an "until death us do part" commitment. Faith is that for which we earnestly contend, no matter what the cost (Jude 3).

What is involved in saving faith?

Can I just believe, get the assurance of a home in heaven, and then live as I please?

Can I ask the Good Master for eternal life and receive it—with no intention of forsaking all, taking up my cross, and following Him (Mark 8:34)?

Can I call my soul my own and let my mind, emotions, and will go unaffected, uncommitted to the truths of God's Word?

Can I embrace His words for my salvation from hell and yet be ashamed of my God and His Word in this sinful generation (Mark 8:38)? Can I do this and still think I have really believed and been saved?

Can you?

Saving Faith Abides

PERILOUS TIMES ARE not coming; they are here. Like fugitives, they have surreptitiously crossed the borders of our nation, our age. A day of judgment is coming. God's Word tells us so.

Some of you may say, "People have been talking about this day of judgment for almost two thousand years now, and it still hasn't happened." That, Beloved, is the world's mentality; it cannot be the mentality of those "of saving faith." For we are to have an alertness that results in holy conduct, godliness, and perseverance, "looking for and hastening the coming of the day of God" (2 Peter 3:12).

Saving faith doesn't just save us and send us back to our old way of life until it's time to enter heaven's pearly gates. No, saving faith changes our life. Oh, it may not change our occupation or the ordinary routines of day-to-day living; but it does change our perspective on these things. It changes our affections and the way we respond to others. Why? Because when a person is truly saved, he or she becomes a new creature in Christ; old things pass away and all things become new (2 Corinthians 5:17). Suddenly we become aware of the two categories of mankind: those who belong to God and those who belong to the devil.

> By this the children of God and the children of the devil
> are obvious: anyone who does not practice righteousness
> is not of God, nor the one who does not love his brother
> (1 John 3:10).

Saving faith doesn't begin with a bang and then just fizzle out. Nor is it a "plop, plop, fizz, fizz, oh-what-a-relief-it-is" type of Christianity that takes care of the temporary distress of thoughts of hellfire and damnation and then dissolves away.

No, saving faith continues. It abides. It perseveres. It may falter sometimes. It may even get perplexed, confused, and shaky. But, in the end, despite everything this world sends against it, it does persevere.

Look up Colossians 1:22,23 and meditate on it. Pray that God will show you clearly whether yours is a saving faith.

APRIL 14

Your Faith . . . Tested by God!

SOMEDAY YOUR FAITH will be challenged to the core. If God tested Abraham by asking him for Isaac . . . if He tested Joseph by letting him go into Egypt and bondage . . . if He tested Moses with the wrath of Pharaoh . . . and if He let His saints be stoned, sawn in two, tempted, and put to death with the sword, do you think your faith will go untested (Hebrews 11:37,38)? If it does, then you might wonder if you are truly a child of God, for faith is not faith until it is tested!

And so, precious one, I believe God would have us spend yet another day naked in His sight, following His admonition in 2 Corinthians 13:5: "Test yourselves [not others, but yourselves] to see if you are in the faith; examine yourselves!"

Look at 1 John 2:3-5:

> And by this we know that we have come to know Him, if we keep His commandments. The one who says, "I have come to know Him," and does not keep His commandments, is a liar, and the truth is not in him; but whoever keeps His word, in him the love of God has truly been perfected. By this we know that we are in Him.

According to these verses, what will be true if you are saved?

The verbs *keep* and *keeps* are in the present tense, which implies continuous action or an ongoing way of life. This does not imply perfection, but it does suggest continuance and perseverance. These verbs are also in the active voice, which means the subject (in this case, the believer) performs the action of the verb. In other words, the believer is responsible for the obedience. Believers cannot excuse themselves by saying, "The devil made me do it."

O Beloved, do you keep His commandments? Are they your way of life?

Living as God's Child

DO YOU UNDERSTAND God's Word when you read it, or does it seem like there is a veil over it—a veil that lets you see the facts clearly yet dims the spiritual meaning? Do you find God's Word hard to believe and understand? Look at 1 Corinthians 2:12-14.

If you cannot understand God's Word or if it is unacceptable or even foolish to you, then, Beloved, God is showing you that you do not have His Holy Spirit living within you. And "if anyone does not have the Spirit of Christ, he does not belong to Him" (Romans 8:9).

Is your body the Holy Spirit's temple, and do you realize that you *are not* your own (1 Corinthians 6:19,20)?

Does His Spirit bear (present tense) witness with your spirit that you are a child of God (Romans 8:16)? (Remember what we said about the present tense yesterday? It implies continuous action or an ongoing way of life.)

And finally, is your life a life of righteousness?

Before you answer that, let me explain righteousness, for I do not want you to confuse it with morality.

A righteous man will be moral, but being moral does not make a man righteous. Righteousness is living according to God's leadership. Righteousness is the opposite of sin. Sin is lawlessness (1 John 3:4). Sin is acting apart from faith (Romans 14:23). Sin is walking your own way (Isaiah 53:6).

Now then, 1 John 3:9 says: "No one who is born of God practices [present tense] sin, because His seed abides [present tense] in him; and he cannot sin [present tense], because he is born of God."

In other words, a child of God can commit singular acts of sin or be disobedient in one particular area of his life, but he cannot habitually do his own thing or walk his own way (1 John 2:1-6). He must live habitually, more and more, according to God's standard.

Are you a child of God? How do you live?

Finding Rest for Your Soul

A FEW YEARS AGO I stood sharing with a young woman after our Monday night Bible study on marriage. When I asked her where her husband was, her whole countenance changed. He was at home watching Monday night football. His attendance at our course on marriage ended when football got into full swing. The week before, not wanting to come alone, she, too, had stayed home. But when she started to fuss at him for putting football before learning God's Word, he told her she needed to get back to Precept. Her disposition was better when she was studying God's Word, he said. And it was.

So is mine. When I stay in the Word, I stay in touch with reality. I keep life in its proper perspective. But let me go on vacation and ease up on the disciplines, or let me get too busy, and I find myself more easily drawn away by other things.

Does this mean I am weak? Yes, it does. That is why I so desperately need to be careful about how I walk, being wise, making the most of my time for the days are evil (Ephesians 5:15,16).

Have you ever evaluated how you spend your time? What do you do with the 168 hours that are in every week? If you tithed your time like you do your income, how much time would that give you for communal worship, private devotions, and study?

But people need rest and recreation, too, don't they? Yes, they do. And thus Jesus Christ says, "Come to Me, all who are weary and heavy-laden, and I will give you rest. Take My yoke upon you, and learn from Me, for I am gentle and humble in heart; and YOU SHALL FIND REST FOR YOUR SOULS" (Matthew 11:28,29).

Have you ever wondered if so many feel so burdened, so pressured, and in such desperate need because they have *not* taken the time to come to Him, to learn of Him, and to cast all their care upon Him? Should not times of intimate fellowship with our God be our primary means of rest and recreation? Or should television, sports, newspapers, books, and hobbies be our primary means?

When do we fit God in? Is this where He should be if He is truly our God?

Rest for Your Soul . . . His Yoke

"REST FOR YOUR SOULS." That is the promise for those who take His yoke and learn of Him (Matthew 11:28-30).

Remember what constitutes the soul: the mind, the will, the emotions. And what is it like in your mind? What kind of thoughts plague you? What do you think about others? What are your concepts of God, of life, of Christianity, of eternity? Could you possibly be wrong? How can you tell? What is your plumb line for testing what you think, or what you think you know? Let me remind you: As a man thinks in his heart so he is (Proverbs 23:7).

And your will. Is it on target? Do you want to do the will of Him who bought you? Or is your will governed by an unrenewed mind so that you are choosing the good and missing the best? Do you have a Lord, a King, a God, and does He reign over your will? Or are you your own master, governing your own will? Are you like those in the days of the Judges when, because there was no king in Israel, every man did what was right in his own eyes (Judges 21:25)? What they did was wrong, horribly, destructively wrong, yet they thought they were right!

Then there are your emotions. Rest for your emotions? Peace instead of fear. Love instead of hate. Forgiveness instead of bitterness. Trust instead of anger. Joy instead of depression. Quietness . . . confidence . . . gentleness . . . kindness . . . self-control. Can you imagine how much strife would end, how many relationships would be healed, if our anxieties were cared for? Just think of the release that would come if guilt were gone. When our emotions are not under God's control, we do so many things that bring such guilt upon us. Of course we rationalize away our wrong behavior or blame others, but even that does not remove the guilt, does it?

Rest for your souls. Can you imagine it? I pray you can, so that you will long for it.

And where is it to be found? By bearing His yoke, united to His will . . . by learning of Him and being transformed by the renewing of your mind. It will be found in discipline, in selection and rejection (choosing the best over the good), and then in concentration on the things of paramount importance . . . eternal things.

A Crown . . . Without a Cross?

"ALL THESE THINGS will I give You, if You fall down and worship me" (Matthew 4:9). When Satan said this, he was offering Jesus all the kingdoms of the world. *A crown without the cross!* And that is what he continues to offer every single human being—saved or lost. Yet the crown does not come without a cross. You cannot expect to rule and reign when Jesus is King of kings unless you are willing to bear your cross now! To think otherwise, Beloved, is to be deceived.

I am absolutely baffled by the average churchgoer's concept of true spirituality. So many are trusting in a baptism, a confession of faith, a name on the church roll, a confirmation, a life of morality and good deeds, a God who would never let anyone go to hell—yet their lives have never changed; they do not hunger and thirst after righteousness. (Note that I said *righteousness*, not *morality*.)

I wonder about those who claim to possess Him and yet do not carry out to completion their salvation "with fear and trembling" (Philippians 2:12). I am baffled by those who claim Him as Savior, even Lord, and yet love this present world (2 Timothy 4:10). What kind of faith is this?

Remember, we are not to love this "world, nor the things in the world. If anyone loves the world, the love of the Father is not in him. For all that is in the world, the lust of the flesh and the lust of the eyes and the boastful pride of life, is not from the Father, but is from the world. And the world is passing away, and also its lusts; but the one who does the will of God abides forever" (1 John 2:15-17).

Multitudes are saving their lives only to lose them. And many who profess Christ (whether they know Him or not, I do not know—only God knows) are living a pseudo-Christianity, caught up in the things of this world and giving only lip service to Jesus Christ. They use those same lips to justify their behavior with "I am sure God understands," or "He'll forgive me"! There is no cross, no death to the flesh, no giving Christ the preeminence in their lives.

How about you, Beloved? Is the lure of this world more important than His righteousness, or will you bear your cross?

"Who Hindered You?"

"YOU WERE RUNNING WELL; who hindered you from obeying the truth?" (Galatians 5:7). So wrote Paul to the churches in Galatia. Some men had come in and preached another gospel, and the Galatians were in danger of believing it (Galatians 1:6,7). As a result, their faith had been sidetracked. Or, to use the "running" metaphor, as Paul does, they were running a race and got out of their lane.

Sometimes I wonder if that is what is being proclaimed subtly today—the wrong gospel. Some refer to it as "easy believism."

When Jesus and John the Baptist came proclaiming the Kingdom, their first word was "repent." When the people of Thessalonica received the Word in much affliction, they realized that they not only had the privilege of believing on the Lord Jesus Christ, but also of suffering for His sake. The message of the gospel was the good news of God's love for sinful man, but it was also the good news that sinful man would be transformed from sinner to saint by yielding to God's grace.

It was not just a case of receiving a free "giveaway" salvation. Rather, it was a call to walk in newness of life (Romans 6:4) and to persevere in this life until the end (Hebrews 3:14). Simply beginning the Christian life is not enough. It is a race to be finished in God's lane, God's way. And He is the final Judge, the Giver of crowns.

Peter Gillquist says:

> It is remaining faithful to Christ that is essential to true spirituality, and it is of eternal importance in his sight. It is not adequate merely to have a spectacular conversion or a glowing story of deliverance. God calls us to be on our feet and in the fight at the final bell.[6]

Gillquist then illustrates the necessity of perseverance in the Christian life by saying that it is a marathon, not a 100-yard dash.

If Paul were writing to the churches today, would he write, "You were running well; what hindered you?" What is keeping you from total consecration to Christ? Even if it is a career or a ministry, it is an idol. Whether it is television, sports, money, family, or friends—if it comes before Him, it is an idol. Smash it!

Total Commitment

IF YOU DO NOT PLAN to live the Christian life totally committed to knowing your God and to walking in obedience to Him, then don't begin, for this is what Christianity is all about.

It is a change of citizenship, a change of governments, a change of allegiance. If you have no intention of letting Christ rule your life, then forget Christianity; it is not for you.

Now, Beloved, lest you think I am being too hard, remember Mark 8:34-38 and remember that faith is not merely knowledge. True faith includes surrender to and obedience to that knowledge.

Let me share with you Peter Gillquist's illustration of what it means "to live the Christian life."

> I went out for the high school cross-country team—a sport I consider to this day as the worst one in all the world in which to earn an athletic letter! On the first day of practice, the coach took us by bus to a course that ran up and down several hills over four miles. The prospects for those of us who were not in good shape, or who had never run distance races before, were particularly dismal on that late afternoon.
>
> Before he fired the starting gun, that coach said something I have never forgotten: "What I am asking you to do today is to finish the race. If you don't plan to finish, then I do not want you to start. Simply stay where you are when the gun is fired. But if you start, then you *will* finish. You may slow down, or even stop for a bit, but you will not quit. Once you start, I want you to cross this finish line—no matter what."[7]

For today, think about those words. Tomorrow we'll finish this story.

Running the Marathon

PETER GILLQUIST CONTINUES:

The first mile was almost euphoric. The cool, fresh autumn air was a natural boost to my dogged determination to run a good race. But after a mile and a half or so, the joy began to fade. By two miles, whatever pleasure there had been in all of this was totally gone. From then on, it was sheer drudgery.

My legs started to cramp. I did not know thigh muscles could ever be so tired. I felt my breath would leave me forever. My lungs and chest cavity were in almost unbearable pain as I approached an enormous upward hill near the 2½-mile mark.

There is one thing and one thing only that kept me going: *before I started, I had agreed to finish.* My body was spent, my mind screamed, "Quit!" But the choice had been made back when the gun went off. . . . In inexpressible agony, I kept on running.

I can barely remember crossing the finish line. I was told I came in fifth or sixth, but even that was not of first importance. Every ounce of energy I knew had gone into finishing. I really could not believe I had made it.

Over the years, I have thought back to that experience as being an incredible picture of what it is to live the Christian life. In fact, the Scriptures more than once use a race as a metaphor of our life with Christ. And it is not a mere sprint, mind you—it is a marathon.[8]

Yes, the Christian life is a hard and, at times, grueling marathon that will challenge the very core of your faith, Beloved. But what a sense of victory will be yours when you cross that finish line! And what defeat if you do not finish what you began.

Take a few minutes and talk to God about your commitment to Him. Do you intend to finish your course, no matter what?

Passion for God . . . a Choice

WHY DO SOME CHRISTIANS seem to have a greater passion for the things of God than others? Is it because some receive a greater portion of Jesus Christ or of salvation? Do some have an extra blessing or experience with the Holy Spirit? Does God play favorites?

No. According to God's Word, Christ cannot be divided. Each believer is complete in Him. The same Holy Spirit dwells in each one who has been born of water and of the Spirit (John 3:5). So, then, what makes the difference?

I believe the answer is found in the parable of the sower. Jesus told this parable because He wanted to show the people why, when it came to passion for God, some had more than others. As He finished the parable, He said:

> "For whoever has, to him shall more be given, and he shall have an abundance; but whoever does not have, even what he has shall be taken away from him" (Matthew 13:12).

And just before this statement, Jesus said: "He who has ears, let him hear" (Matthew 13:9).

With these words He was telling them that passion for God, intimacy with God, is a matter of choice.

Only *you* will ever limit what you are for God. If you take what you have been given, treasure it, use it for His glory, and cry to God for more, more will be given you and you will have an abundance. However, if you despise or neglect what God has given you, if you do not use it for Him, then even what you have will be taken away.

It all depends on *how* you "hear" what God says to you—and by that God means the type of hearing that makes you a doer of the Word.

Since, Beloved, "nothing is hidden that shall not become evident, nor anything secret that shall not be known and come to light" (Matthew 8:17), why don't you take time to examine yourself? How well do you listen to God's Word? Are you content with the status quo, or do you have a consuming passion for a greater intimacy with Jesus Christ?

A Parable for Spiritual Ears

WHY DID JESUS TELL His followers the parable of the sower as well as the other parables? The answer to that question, in part, is found in understanding the meaning of the word "parable." It comes from the word *parabola* which means "to place alongside for measurement or comparison like you would a yardstick."

Thus, the parable of the sower and the soils was given to show men and women the condition of their hearts. Secondarily, it was given to prepare the disciples for the time when they themselves would be called upon to deliver God's Word.

Jesus knew that His popularity would wane as men and women began to fully understand what it cost to be a true follower of His gospel. When they walked away, when they said it was too much to expect, too hard to do, He wanted His own disciples to understand these different responses. He wanted them to know that it was all a matter of heart. And so He told them this parable:

> "Listen to this! Behold, the sower went out to sow; and it came about that as he was sowing, some seed fell beside the road, and the birds came and ate it up. And other seed fell on the rocky ground where it did not have much soil; and immediately it sprang up because it had no depth of soil. And after the sun had risen, it was scorched; and because it had no root, it withered away. And other seed fell among the thorns, and the thorns came up and choked it, and it yielded no crop. And other seeds fell into the good soil and as they grew up and increased, they yielded a crop and produced thirty, sixty, and a hundredfold." And He was saying, "He who has ears to hear, let him hear" (Mark 4:3-9).

The various soils represent the different heart responses of men and women, which apparently fall into four categories. For the next few days we will look at each of these soils. As we do, pray that God will reveal to you the condition of your own heart.

The Seed Is Sown

"THE SOWER SOWS the word. And these are the ones who are beside the road where the word is sown; and when they hear, immediately Satan comes and takes away the word which has been sown in them" (Mark 4:14,15). Why? Are they helpless victims of Satan? No, they could have heard, but they didn't want to! Remember the times you could have heard but didn't want to? You could not have cared less!

And then there are those "on whom seed was sown on the rocky places, who, when they hear the word, immediately receive it with joy; and they have no firm root in themselves, but are only temporary; then, when affliction or persecution arises because of the word, immediately they fall away" (Mark 4:16,17).

Sixteen-year-old Hugh Makay, a Scottish covenanter, had just been sentenced to death for his faith in Jesus Christ. His trial finished, they thrust him into the street where a curious crowd had gathered. Seeing them, he began to shout, "Good news! Good news! I am within four days' sight of the Kingdom." There was no rocky ground in this young lad's heart!

Have you ever known people who, upon hearing the good news of salvation by grace, embraced it joyfully? For a time, everything went fine—church, Bible study, serving God. They couldn't get enough. The race was on and they were sprinting fast. They didn't know it was a marathon they had entered—a hard and, at times, grueling marathon.

People like this are showy plants with shallow roots. They seemingly receive Christ Jesus the Lord by faith, but they just don't become firmly rooted and built up in Him. They have been instructed to build a strong root system in the faith, but they do not listen (Colossians 2:7). They have their five minutes a day, their daily devotional, their "help me, give me" prayers. Then it hits! Suddenly there is pain, and God seems deaf or away on vacation. The situation only gets worse. "How much can a body take? . . . Why, I'm worse off than I was before I received Christ!" Their faith is only temporary—no marathons for them. And so they never finish.

How is your root system? How well are you getting to know your God?

Sown Among Thorns

"And others are the ones on whom seed was sown among the thorns; these are the ones who have heard the word, and the worries of the world, and the deceitfulness of riches, and the desires for other things enter in and choke the word, and it becomes unfruitful" (Mark 4:18,19).

AFTER JOSHUA DIED, all his "generation also were gathered to their fathers and there arose another generation after them who did not know the LORD, nor yet the work which He had done for Israel" (Judges 2:10). They had not "experienced any of the wars of Canaan" (Judges 3:1). This was a generation, therefore, that did not obey God. Rather than drive out the inhabitants of Canaan as God had commanded, they let them stay. God had said:

"So take diligent heed to yourselves to love the LORD your God. For if you ever go back and cling to the rest of these nations, these which remain among you, and intermarry with them, so that you associate with them and they with you, know with certainty that the LORD your God will not continue to drive these nations out from before you; but they shall be a snare and a trap to you" (Joshua 23:11-13).

Their hearts were filled with thorns, and, as a result, we have the darkest 350 years in the history of Israel! Here was a generation on which the sins of the fathers were truly visited down to the third and fourth generations. Why? Because the fathers compromised the truth. They married whom they pleased. They permitted idols in their land and then in their homes. Even their priests became corrupt.

The days of the Judges were much like our days. Apathy, apostasy, and anarchy reigned because there was no king in Israel. Hearts were filled with thorns—overrun by the worries of the world, the deceitfulness of riches, and the desires for other things. The Word was choked out of these thorny hearts.

Our Worldly Eyesight

THE WORRIES OF THIS WORLD are great, aren't they? The economy, unemployment, broken homes, crime, illness. How are we going to manage? What if Social Security fails? Who will care for us in our old age? And what about the young newlyweds? How will they manage with children if both of them have to work? We had better get it while we can—get as rich as we can as quickly as we can.

And, thus, as we struggle to the top, other things are set aside . . . just for a little while. Until we can slow down and have more time for one another, our families, our God, His Word. Besides, with all we earn, think of how we can help the work of the church!

Yet as we struggle and climb, there are always new allurements ahead, new attainable goals. We think of them as good investments: land, jewelry, homes, stocks, more insurance. Each has its demands, but with careful budgeting, balancing, and a little more work, it'll all pay off . . . somehow . . . sometime.

It's a rat race, isn't it? A maze of possibilities, one of which will surely lead us to the life of our dreams! Yet deep inside, at some point, most of us ask: Is this all life is about? Is this all there is? Or is there more?

There *is* more. But many will never know it—their lives will never bear fruit—because the eternal truths that set men free will be choked out by the worries of this world, the deceitfulness of riches, and the desire for other things. And what will they have when they come to the end of their days? Empty hands and barren lives.

What is the answer? The key is found, I believe, in these verses. Meditate upon them, and then we will discuss them tomorrow.

> "The lamp of the body is the eye; if therefore your eye is clear, your whole body will be full of light. But if your eye is bad, your whole body will be full of darkness. If therefore the light that is in you is darkness, how great is the darkness! No one can serve two masters" (Matthew 6:22-24).

Tell me, honestly, how is your eyesight?

Keep Your Eyes on God!

OUR PROBLEM IS temporal vision. We look at this life as the chief aim of man. And the more we gaze upon it, the more entranced and enmeshed we become, until we are unbelievably obligated to creditors, to professions, to organizations, to increased family activities. Our time is so consumed by all this that we have no time to look anywhere else! We have no time to focus on "the true light which . . . enlightens every man" (John 1:9).

Only when we keep our eyes on God and walk according to His Word, His character, and His will, will we make it through the maze of life. Only then will we find that one Door that leads to perfect security, perfect liberty, and perfect sustenance (John 10:9,10). For everything needful will be added to those who will focus their eyes upon Jesus and seek first His kingdom and His righteousness (Matthew 6:33).

God says: "Do not be anxious then, saying, 'What shall we eat?' or 'What shall we drink?' or 'With what shall we clothe ourselves?' For . . . your heavenly Father knows that you need all these things" (Matthew 6:31,32). Your Father "shall supply all your needs according to His riches in glory in Christ Jesus" (Philippians 4:19).

Therefore, the "thorn killer" must "keep seeking the things above, where Christ is, seated at the right hand of God. Set your mind on the things above, not on the things that are on earth" (Colossians 3:1,2).

As the saying goes, "Easier said than done." The pull of the world is great. Television and advertisements continually set before our eyes the temporal things of life, while catchy little tunes tell us that these are the things that make life worth living. Beautiful homes, beautiful cars, beautiful clothes, beautiful possessions. And almost everyone's conversation is focused on these temporal things.

If we would not be lured by this siren call, we must have "ears to hear." We must constantly measure everything by the plumb line of God's Word. We can only be fruitful by enduring "as seeing Him who is unseen" (Hebrews 11:27).

Do you understand? What will you do about it in your own life?

Don't Be Deceived by Riches

TO BE HOLY is to be godly—set apart unto God. To be holy is to be like Him, filled with the fruit of the Spirit which is His character. Therefore, holiness, or godliness, is to be the goal of your life.

"Godliness actually is a means of great gain, when accompanied by contentment" (1 Timothy 6:6). Yet one of our greatest problems is our lack of contentment. Why? Because we take our focus off of Christ and put it on the world with all its temporal riches.

> But those who want to get rich fall into temptation and a snare and many foolish and harmful desires which plunge men into ruin and destruction. For the love of money is a root of all sorts of evil, and some by longing for it have wandered away from the faith, and pierced themselves with many a pang (1 Timothy 6:9,10).

O Beloved, if there is even one thorn of the deceitfulness of riches in your heart, destroy it, for it could cause you to wander away from the faith. This thorn has kept many a man and woman from holiness.

Fight the good fight of faith, live by every word that proceeds out of the mouth of God. Guard your time alone with your God, for it will keep your life clear and your body full of light (Matthew 6:23).

The fourth kind of soil in the parable of the sower is good ground:

> "And those are the ones on whom seed was sown on the good soil; and they *hear* the word and *accept* it, and *bear* fruit, thirty, sixty, and a hundredfold" (Mark 4:20, emphasis added).

What kind of harvest will you have this year, Beloved, and in the years to come? It all depends on what you want. You determine the harvest by what you will hear and accept and by what you do with it.

Are you listening? What do you hear? Will you accept it all and order your life accordingly? If so, you will have a hundredfold harvest.

Or are you going to settle for less? If so, will it be worth it when you see Him face-to-face?

Wait for God

THE WICKEDNESS OF the people was overwhelming. The burden on Habakkuk was not man-made; it was a load of divinely imposed concern weighing heavily on him. He could not help but cry, "How long, O LORD, will I call for help, and Thou wilt not hear? I cry out to Thee, 'Violence!' Yet Thou dost not save. . . . Strife exists and contention arises. Therefore, the law is ignored and justice is never upheld. For the wicked surround the righteous; therefore, justice comes out perverted" (Habakkuk 1:2-4).

Sin was rife in Israel. The nation was on the brink of catastrophe. Yet instead of repenting, the people multiplied their sins.

Habakkuk knew that God would not let the people of Israel go unpunished. God Himself had told Habakkuk that He was "raising up the Chaldeans [Babylonians], that fierce and impetuous people who march throughout the earth to seize dwelling places which are not theirs" (Habakkuk 1:6). Even so, this was hard for Habakkuk to understand. While he knew that Israel would be judged, deserved to be judged, he did not understand why God would use such a wicked people to do it. Surely Judah was more righteous than the Babylonians (Habakkuk 1:13). All this was a challenge to Habakkuk's faith!

Can you relate? Has your faith ever been challenged? And what do you do when that happens? Let's look at Habakkuk. You can handle anything that challenges your faith in the same way he did.

First, openly discuss your problems and questions with God.

Second, after voicing your problem, you need to keep watch to see what God will speak to you (Habakkuk 2:1).

Third, as you wait to hear from God, you need to realize that you cannot be a man or woman of faith and "live in a day." In other words, faith cannot look at just the immediate situation; faith must look at the eternal outcome. God rules from the perspective of eternity. You must see with the eyes of faith beyond the moment, beyond the situation, to your God. You must say, by faith, "Shall not the Judge of all the earth do right?" (Genesis 18:25 KJV).

In that confidence you will find peace. For today, remember, faith must keep its eyes on God.

One Way to Live— by Faith

WHENEVER I TELL this story, an incredible ache grips the very bowels of my being and I want to cry, "O Lord Jesus, come quickly. Please come . . . please. And let me be, no matter what, faithful unto death." I first read the story in *Jesus to the Communist World, Inc.*, a newsletter published by Richard Wurmbrand in January 1981.

> The Russian Orthodox Priest Dudko, a kind of Soviet Billy Graham, was arrested for his faith. The Communists set before him two alternatives: either to join their evil and lying camp by withdrawing all he had said against them, or to be raped homosexually by several criminals (Welt am Sonntag, West Germany, August 30), to be photographed in this position, to be put to shame through the publication of these pictures, and to be sentenced for sexual perversity. The priest had been prepared to suffer incarceration, beatings, physical torture, or brainwashing for the Lord—he already had ten years of Soviet prison behind him—but this threat was too much. . . . So Dudko recanted publicly on TV and in the press. It was as if Billy Graham had denied on TV everything he had ever preached. A chain reaction followed. Other notable Christian prisoners . . . recanted too and were freed, whereas those who remained faithful . . . were sentenced to long years of prison.

On our final day together for this month, why would I tell you such a story? Because, precious ones, I believe the day is coming when your faith will be challenged to the core. And what will you do on that day? "If you have run with footmen and they have tired you out, then how can you compete with horses? If you fall down in a land of peace, how will you do in the thicket of the Jordan?" (Jeremiah 12:5).

This is the time to determine that the ground of your heart will be good soil: that you will have ears to hear it and live by it with the intention of bringing forth a hundredfold harvest.

M A Y

Listen to Me!

God's message for this month's meditations in
Malachi is not an easy one, but it is very
necessary! Look around you at those who profess
Christ. How many do you see who are totally sold
out to Him, committed to His will no matter what
the cost? I pray that you will listen. If I speak
truth, follow it . . . live it . . . preach it. Our time is
short. He is coming.

God's Plea . . . Return!

"LISTEN TO ME. Listen, please listen." The words seemed wrung from a heart filled with agony. "I love you."

"Love me? How . . . how have You loved me?" Her high-pitched retort was haughty, indignant. It came from pouting lips. Her scowling words caused thunderclaps in the atmosphere. The warm front of His unending love had suddenly collided with the chilling winds of her insolence. It was inevitable. A storm was certain, a storm that would last 400 years. These were to be His last words if she would not listen, if she would not return and be the wife she was supposed to be. And she did not listen. Thus silence reigned for 400 years, and Israel did her own thing—living her own life, yet bearing His name.

Then, in the fullness of time, God broke the silence. Again He said, "I love you," and to prove it He offered His only Son. Still she was haughty. Who needed Him on His terms?

She would not listen to God.

> "O Jerusalem, Jerusalem, who kills the prophets and stones those who are sent to her! How often I wanted to gather your children together, the way a hen gathers her chicks under her wings, and you were unwilling. Behold, your house is being left to you desolate! For I say to you, from now on you shall not see Me until you say, 'BLESSED IS HE WHO COMES IN THE NAME OF THE LORD!'" (Matthew 23:37-39).

Have you ever loved someone who would only love you on his or her terms? Because you knew those terms were wrong, you could not go on accepting them. So you talked, or rather you tried to talk. But there was no reasoning! The one you loved just could not see, would not see, would not admit that he or she was wrong.

If you have ever experienced anything like this, you have had just a glimpse of what God had to deal with in His love for Israel.

In the same way, God loves His church, Christ's bride. Yet too often we only want His love on our terms. He loves us, but we have wandered. He wants us to return. Will we listen?

A Loving Warning

O PRECIOUS ONES, the word that God has given me for you this month is not an easy word; yet it is a word of love. How I pray that you will receive it as such. So many times we think that love is expressed only with words of praise, kindness, comfort, appreciation. We forget what God said through the writer of Hebrews: "MY SON, DO NOT REGARD LIGHTLY THE DISCIPLINE OF THE LORD, NOR FAINT WHEN YOU ARE REPROVED BY HIM; FOR THOSE WHOM THE LORD LOVES HE DISCIPLINES, AND HE SCOURGES EVERY SON WHOM HE RECEIVES" (Hebrews 12:5,6).

Love and discipline go together, for love desires another's highest good. Love never seeks its own (1 Corinthians 13:5).

The message God has laid upon my heart is God's message of love which He sent to Israel through the last of the Old Testament prophets, Malachi: "I am not pleased with you. . . . Return to Me, and I will return to you" (Malachi 1:10; 3:7).

Now granted, I know that some of you have not strayed from God like Israel did in the days of Malachi. Your Christianity does not weary Him; rather, it brings Him great joy. Yet, precious ones, we are members of a body—the church. We have joined hands with others who profess to know Him and who are caught up in the formality of worship; who think they are doctrinally sound and yet who do not esteem His words more precious than their necessary food; who have a form of godliness yet know nothing of His power; who despise other Christians because they are too zealous, too extreme, too holy, too consecrated. To those, God would speak in loving rebuke and warning.

And yet, just as there was a faithful remnant in the days of Malachi of "those who fear the LORD and who esteem His name" (Malachi 3:16), so there is today, and God has a word for you also. Thus we must all listen carefully.

May we hear the words that He would speak to us. And may we then arise and speak His truth from the housetops so that others might listen and return to Him.

Assess and Confess

BEFORE WE LOOK at God's word to us from Malachi, we need to stop and assess where we are with Him personally. If you are using this book for family devotions, do this honestly and openly before one another. Confession is good for the soul. However, as others bare their souls before you, you must be careful not to criticize or condemn. Rather, you should intercede on one another's behalf.

Now, then, what are you going to assess? You are going to honestly assess your walk with the Lord. Why? Because if your walk with the Lord is not what it ought to be, then you are on the road of indifference and, eventually, disobedience. To continue walking that way will only lead you farther away, and if you do not return to Him, you will experience the just judgment of God. Remember, whom the Lord loves, He disciplines. You are also going to assess your walk because God keeps books. He has a book of remembrance "written before Him for those who fear the LORD and who esteem His name" (Malachi 3:16). These are the ones whom God will spare "as a man spares his own son who serves him" (Malachi 3:17).

Notice, precious one, what we are doing is *self-examination*. You can never see a mote in your brother's eye until you have taken the beam from your own (Matthew 7:5).

Today, we are going to look at two questions. First, do you honor God as a child is to honor his parents and as a servant is to honor his master?

Now, before you answer that, stop and think about what it means to honor God in this way. Doesn't it mean to give Him first place in your life and to obey all that He says, to love Him supremely before all others and all else—sports, television, job, everything? Now answer that first question honestly, noting exactly where and how you fail.

Second, are you giving God the very best of your life?

By that I mean, do you spend quality time with Him, or do you just give Him your leftovers—the last few tired minutes of the day? And what do you give Him of yourself, your possessions?

Are You Hearing God?

ONE MORE DAY of self-examination and then we will be prepared to receive God's word to us from Malachi.

Is it tiresome for you to serve God, to walk the Christian walk? Is it difficult and boring for you to study your Bible consistently in order to learn His Word? Is it a drag for you to have a daily time of worship and prayer and to be in His Word? Does going to church or serving God seem a burden to you?

Are you robbing God? Do you hoard your money and possessions, or do you generously give to the Lord's work?

When you give others advice or instruct your children, do you speak the truths of God's Word uncompromisingly, without wavering, regardless of who the person is or the particulars of the situation? In other words, do you advise and instruct people the way God would have you do so?

If you are married, what is your marriage like?

Men, are you fulfilling your role as a husband should? Are you assuming the responsibilities of headship and ruling in the attitude of Christ as the sacrificial lover of your wife (Ephesians 5:25-33)? Are you providing for your household? Are you bringing your children up in the discipline and instruction of the Lord (Ephesians 6:4)?

Women, are you submitting to your husband as to the Lord (Ephesians 5:22) even if he is in rebellion against God's Word (1 Peter 3:1-6)? And are you a sensible and pure woman who is a faithful keeper of her home (Titus 2:5)? Do you seek to be strong in all moral qualities, doing your husband good and not evil so that he can safely trust you (Proverbs 31:10-12)?

To do all these things as a husband or wife means that you are faithful to the covenant of marriage and are not seeking to deal treacherously with one another.

And last but, as the saying goes, not least, do you speak against God? Do you murmur and complain, saying that it does not pay to serve Him? Do you profess to be doing what He says and yet say you are not honored by God, that there's no profit in serving Him? If your answer is *yes*, are you serving God His way? Are you hearing Him?

Are You Weary of Waiting?

BEFORE WE HEAR the Word of the Lord through the prophet Malachi, let's put the book into its historical context.

For years God had warned His people through His prophets that He would judge them with the sword and with captivity if they did not repent. But God's people would not listen. Then in 722 B.C. the Northern Kingdom of Israel was taken captive by the Assyrians, and in 586 B.C. the last of the Southern Kingdom went into Babylonian captivity.

But, oh, the grace and mercy of God! In the midst of all this turmoil came the word of the Lord through Jeremiah: The Babylonian captivity would only last for 70 years (Jeremiah 29:10).

When the Israelites returned to Jerusalem 70 years later, it seemed that the captivity had taught them their lesson. The temple was restored, the sacrifices were reinstituted, and the city walls were rebuilt. However, the sins that Nehemiah addressed and dealt with at that time were the same sins that Malachi cried out against in his prophecy. The corruption of the fathers, rather than being thoroughly dealt with and removed, had spread like a malignant cancer.

> When Malachi wrote . . . the Jews as a nation had been back in the land . . . for about one hundred years. Prophets like Haggai and Zechariah had predicted that God's blessings would be given to the people in the days to come, especially in "the day of the Lord." However, several decades passed and these prophecies of hope were still unfulfilled. It was a period of disappointment, disillusionment, and discouragement . . . of blasted hopes and broken hearts. The Jews' faith and worship were eroding, and their daily lives showed it.[9]

Does this sound familiar, Beloved? Is it not also sin to cause Christ's church to waste away? Have not many grown weary in waiting for the Lord's coming? Are not multitudes in the church so caught up in the formality of their Christianity that they are missing the beat of His heart? And what is God's Word to them . . . to you?

Do You Doubt God's Love?

HAVE THERE BEEN TIMES when you, as a Christian, felt that God did not love you? What caused you to doubt His love?

The opening words of Malachi are God's words: "I have loved you." No sooner are they said than the retort comes back, "How hast Thou loved us?" (Malachi 1:2).

How (or *wherein*, according to KJV) is stated seven different times, each one a rebuttal to God's exposure of their shortcomings. Obviously God and His people are at odds. God is not pleased with them, and they are not pleased with God. The atmosphere is electric, and Israel is murmuring: *Why is He complaining? What's wrong? Certainly there is nothing wrong with us. I tell you, it certainly is vain to serve the Lord. Where has it gotten us?* "What profit is it that we have kept His charge?" (Malachi 3:14). *He says He loves us. How has He loved us?*

Because things were not going their way, Israel (not all individuals, but as a whole) doubted God's love. They apparently never once stopped to consider that maybe there was something wrong in their lives, or that God might be permitting difficulties or disappointments in order to refine them as silver so that they might "present to the LORD offerings in righteousness" (Malachi 3:3).

They were wrong. Wrong and blind. The formality in their worship kept them from examining their hearts and their motives. They were in a state of spiritual decline, but they could not see it because they were still going through the motions of worship!

And so it is with the church at large today. We are only happy with God when things are going *our* way. As long as things are running smoothly and we have no lack of good things, as long as we do not feel we have to toe God's line, then we are willing to believe God loves us. But let God make righteous demands on us, or withhold what we want, and then we pout and with insolent lips say, "How have You loved me?"

God loves you unconditionally, Beloved. The question is: Do you love Him unconditionally? Have you ever thought that maybe you, at times, doubt His love for you because you are not really loving Him as you should?

When God Is Silent

I REMEMBER MANY TIMES standing before my father with a tear-stained face, disappointed, angry, or pouting and hearing him say to me, "Kay, I love you so much that even if you hate me, I am going to do what is right and best for you." His love transcended mine. Yet many times, even after hearing those words, I would run to my room, throw myself down on my bed, and mutter, "You'll be sorry. I'll never love you, kiss you, or hug you again. You'll see."

Try as they may, parents at times cannot convince their children of their love, and it is at those moments that children feel their parents have failed.

Yet, desiring the other's highest good, love bears, believes, hopes, and endures all things. And so it was in the days of Malachi.

In the book of Malachi we hear God's cry of wounded love for His people, a love that was willing to risk being loved for His children's good, just as Daddy was willing to risk my love for my own good. It was a love that could not rejoice in unrighteousness (1 Corinthians 13:6) and therefore had to rebuke, speaking the truth (Ephesians 4:15)—and, if necessary, wound in order to heal. Yet, even if the Israelites would not listen or acknowledge their wrong, forcing Him to chasten them, God would not abandon them. Nor would He ever take "into account a wrong suffered" (1 Corinthians 13:5).

Oh, it is true, God shut up the heavens . . . for 400 years He retreated into silence because they would not listen. Yet He did not retreat into silence without leaving them hope—a promise to cling to!

"Behold, I am going to send My messenger, and he will clear the way before Me. And the Lord, whom you seek, will suddenly come to His temple" (Malachi 3:1).

Jesus, the Messenger of God's unfailing covenant, the ultimate expression of God's love, would come. Whether they believed it or not, whether they recognized it or not, God loved them. And, Beloved, He loves you. Maybe He has been silent for a while, but He is still there. Cling to His promise: "I will never leave thee, nor forsake thee" (Hebrews 13:5 KJV).

Have You Lost Your Love?

THE PROBLEM WITH God's people in Malachi's day was the same as the problem with the church today. Irving Jensen expressed it this way: "The Jews' faith and worship were eroding, and their daily lives showed it." The question is: Why does faith erode? Erosion is a gradual eating or wearing away. What causes it?

Let me ask you, Beloved, was there a time when you were more zealous for the things of God—a time of first love with all its newness, joy, discovery, anticipation, a time when you would have gone anywhere, done anything God asked of you? Was there a time when you longed to serve Him without distraction? Notice, I said *was there*. What happened? You still worship Him, go to church, give of your money, and are active in some work for Him; but things are different, aren't they? And it's not because you have settled down into maturity, but because you have lost something.

Malachi's message shows us where God's people had failed. They still went through the motions of worship, bringing their sacrifices to the temple (Malachi 1:7,8,11). Yet it was all done by rote. What mattered was what was in their hearts, and in their hearts they had strayed from God. They had lost their passion and their zeal. Israel, like the church today, suffered from heart failure.

> "Wherein hast thou loved us?" the people asked. The prophet said, "You have lost your love for God; and now you are questioning God's love for you." That is always so; callousness results from the death of love.[10]

If you have strayed from God, if your Christianity is mere formality, if the zeal and the passion are gone, something is wrong in your heart. The love of God is not there, and only love can maintain true fellowship with God!

O Beloved, have you lost your first love? Or do you feel its very life ebbing away? Do not let it go. Rather, put to death that which is causing your love to die! Nothing, Beloved, is of more value than a heart aflame with love for God. Nothing.

Do You Please God?

BELOVED, BEFORE WE GO any further, you need to carefully read Malachi 1:6-14, written out for you below. In verse 10 (in bold type), notice the phrase, "I am not pleased with you." Then, as you read, note why God was not pleased with them, marking each reason with a pen in some distinctive way so it will stand out on the page.

" 'A son honors his father, and a servant his master. Then if I am a father, where is My honor? And if I am a master, where is My respect?' says the LORD of hosts to you, O priests who despise My name. . . . When you present the blind for sacrifice, is it not evil? And when you present the lame and sick, is it not evil? Why not offer it to your governor? Would he be pleased with you?" . . . says the LORD of hosts. "But now will you not entreat God's favor, that He may be gracious to us? With such an offering on your part, will He receive any of you kindly?" says the LORD of hosts. . . . **"I am not pleased with you," says the LORD of hosts, "nor will I accept an offering from you.** For from the rising of the sun, even to its setting, My name will be great among the nations, and in every place incense is going to be offered to My name, and a grain offering that is pure; for My name will be great among the nations," says the LORD of hosts. "But you are profaning it, in that you say, 'The table of the Lord is defiled, and as for its fruit, its food is to be despised.' You also say, 'My, how tiresome it is!' And you disdainfully sniff at it," says the LORD of hosts, "and you bring what was taken by robbery, and what is lame or sick; so you bring the offering! Should I receive that from your hand?" says the LORD. "But cursed be the swindler who has a male in his flock, and vows it, but sacrifices a blemished animal to the Lord, for I am a great King," says the LORD of hosts.

Now, meditate on what you have observed, asking God to show you how your life compares with what God is saying in this passage. Give yourself time, Beloved. I promise it will be worth it.

Do You Honor God?

YESTERDAY, AS YOU MEDITATED upon Malachi 1:6-14, I'm sure you noticed that one of God's complaints against His people was their improper attitude toward Him. They were treating Him with contempt! They called Him "Father," but did not give Him the honor due a father. They called Him "Master," but did not respect Him as a servant should. They were despising His name. They were filled with disdain, for they looked down upon His altar. What they were offering to God was less than the best! And they could not see or would not admit that they were wrong.

It was a case of, "I'll give God what I want to give Him, and if He doesn't like it, then that's His tough luck." They were calling the shots, so to speak. They wanted all the privileges that went with being children of God, but none of the responsibilities. They didn't mind calling Him "Master" as long as they could do what they wanted.

Does any of this sound familiar? Look around you at church. Take a good look at the people with whom you worship every Sunday. (And while you look at them, look also at yourself.) Don't most of them claim to know God as Father? Do they not profess Jesus Christ as Lord (Master) and Savior? And if you asked them where they will spend eternity, would not most of them say, "In heaven"? Yet, do they, do you, give God *all* the honor that is due Him as Father? To honor Him is to treat Him with great respect, high regard. It is to realize that because of who He is, He is to be reverenced.

Israel would not give God the honor due His Fatherhood, nor would they give Him respect as a Master; they would not listen or obey. They only wanted God with all His benefits and blessings on their terms.

What about you, Beloved? You are loved by God, but do you embrace His love with a loving heart that longs to honor Him as Father and respect Him as Master? Honestly, who calls the shots in your life?

Choose Life . . . Love God!

THE WONDER OF WONDERS is that the eternal God gives man a free will! God sets before him blessing or cursing, life or death, and then leaves the choice to him. These words that were spoken to Israel are for the church also (Romans 15:4). Listen carefully:

> "I call heaven and earth to witness against you today, that I have set before you life and death, the blessing and the curse. So choose life in order that you may live, you and your descendants, by loving the LORD your God, by obeying His voice, and by holding fast to Him; for this is your life and the length of your days" (Deuteronomy 30:19,20).

There it is again . . . the way to succeed, the motive for all behavior and all service, the way to maintain a true and vital relationship with God: "Choose life . . . by loving the LORD your God."

This is where Israel failed. Israel loved only in word, not in deed. They did not honor and respect God.

God is God; He must be obeyed. His people cannot alter His just requirements and laws according to their own desires and then expect God to compromise. Yet this is exactly what Israel did. And although God sent prophet after prophet to warn them, they did not listen (Isaiah 1:3-5). Instead, Israel trampled underfoot the love of God. So God sent them into captivity—the curse of disobedience. Then Malachi, bearing God's burden, came to them after their restoration and spoke the same message again. And again they did not listen. Thus another captivity awaited them: the iron vise of the Roman Empire.

There it is, set before you also. Life or death, blessing or cursing. You can choose your way, but you cannot choose the consequences. Choose life . . . by loving your God, by obeying His voice.

Give Your Best . . . Honor God

HAVE YOU EVER HELPED pack a missionary barrel? What *is* a missionary barrel? some of you may ask. Usually it is a collection of things that people do not need or want anymore. *Leftovers!* It is less than better or best, because better and best are kept in the closet at home. To the naked or poor, the things in a missionary barrel are better than nothing. Yet much of what is in there often ends up on the rubbish heap because it is unusable.

Now, suppose we had the opportunity to appear at the White House to present our president with a gift. What would we take him? Something from the missionary barrel? Absolutely not! We would take him something we treasured, something we hoped he would prize. Yet the gift for the mission field is, in essence, a gift for the Lord, a gift for the furtherance of His Kingdom. And the gift for our president? Well, it's a gift for the president. The latter gift gets the praise and recognition of men; the former, the praise and recognition of God. And there are so many who love the praise of men more than the praise of God!

> "But when you present the blind for sacrifice, is it not evil? And when you present the lame and sick, is it not evil? Why not offer it to your governor? Would he be pleased with you? Or would he receive you kindly?" says the LORD of hosts (Malachi 1:8).

And what do you, Beloved, give to God: *Of your time?* Does He get the first hour or hours of the day or the last few sleepy moments? *Of your talents, gifts, abilities?* Are they all spent in your pursuit of the pride of life or on the things that have no eternal value whatsoever? *Of your possessions?* Does your gift come off the top or do you give whatever is left over after your desires are met? *Of your service?* Do you work as unto Him or for personal praise and recognition?

What are you packing in God's missionary barrel, Beloved? What are you giving to Him? Your leftovers or your best?

Does Your Offering Please God?

A FEW YEARS AGO I asked my Sunday school class why they came to Sunday school. Was it out of a sense of duty or moral obligation, or were they coming to really learn God's Word? And, if they were coming to learn, were they willing to pay the price of disciplined study? Or did they simply want to be fed predigested food?

Now don't get me wrong; there were many dedicated people in my Sunday school class. Yet I cannot help but wonder as I see our lack of zeal, our lack of discipline, how many go to Sunday school and church because of a burning desire to worship God and to grow in the knowledge of Him that they might be equipped for the work of the ministry (Ephesians 4:11-13).

What difference would it make in the lives of churchgoers if the doors of our Sunday schools and churches were barred shut? Would it simply give us two more hours a week to do our own thing without a guilty conscience, or would we beg and plead for the doors to be opened again that we might worship our God and learn more of Him?

The Jews in Malachi's day, for the most part, wouldn't have minded at all if the doors to the temple had been shut and barred. To them it was "tiresome" to serve the Lord. They looked on the whole system of worship as a mere formality, and they sniffed at it with contempt! How soon they had forgotten the pain of their deserved captivity. Now that the fetters of captivity were gone and all was at ease in Zion, who needed God?

Prayerfully read Isaiah 1:10-14 in your Bible.

It is hypocrisy, Beloved, to go through the motions of worship and sacrifice when you are not motivated by love. It is futile to give God the "worthless offerings" of your life and keep the best for yourself or expend yourself for the things of this life.

And so God cries: " 'Oh that there were one among you who would shut the gates, that you might not uselessly kindle fire on My altar! I am not pleased with you,' says the LORD of hosts, 'nor will I accept an offering from you' " (Malachi 1:10).

Does Your Life Reverence God?

" 'I AM A GREAT KING,' says the LORD of hosts, 'and My name is feared among the nations' " (Malachi 1:14). Yet Israel was swindling Him!

Can you imagine cheating God? That is exactly what they were doing. "But cursed be the swindler who has a male in his flock, and vows it, but sacrifices a blemished animal to the Lord" (Malachi 1:14).

The nations feared His name, yet His people would not!

Years ago I was introduced to a remarkable woman. She was a Muslim, a very unusual one. As we talked, she kept shaking her head and saying, "You know, if you really believe what you are saying, Kay, you couldn't do anything else but live the way you're teaching."

How right she is! She does not know our God or His Son. She does not believe that the Bible is God's infallible Word. And yet she, a Muslim, realizes that if I believe what I say I believe, I must live a life that is in total accord with what I profess. I cannot swindle God by professing my total allegiance to Him and then live a life that is a sham.

Beloved, to truly believe on Jesus is to acknowledge His name, the Lord Jesus Christ, and live according to that confession.

The word "lord" is *kurios* in the Greek, which means "master," signifying power or authority. *Kurios* in the Greek translation of the Old Testament and in the New Testament is representative of the Hebrew *Jehovah*, the word used for God.[11] God tells us in Romans 10:9, "that if you confess with your mouth Jesus as Lord, and believe in your heart that God raised Him from the dead, you shall be saved." *Jesus* means "God my Savior." *Christ* is the Koine Greek rendering of the word "Messiah" or "Promised One." Therefore, to believe on His name is to acknowledge that Jesus is God, my Savior, my Master, the Promised One, and to live in obedience to what I profess.

To despise His name, as God said they were doing in Malachi's day, is to claim one thing and do another! They were swindlers, cheating God in their sacrifices and worship, giving God less than best.

And you, Beloved, does your life, your sacrifice for Him, give the reverence due to His name? God wants a pure offering that is totally committed (Romans 12:1)!

Awake! The Time Is Short

IT'S A HEAVY MONTH, isn't it? These messages are not easy. I'm sorry, precious one. I cannot help it. It must be said. Someone must love the church enough to wear the shoes of Isaiah, Jeremiah, Ezekiel, and Malachi. Before God, I have covenanted to be among the ranks of those who will speak the truth in love. How I pray that you will be among those who will listen.

Our time is short, Beloved! I do not set days or hours, because that is not scriptural; yet I do believe from my understanding of prophecy that our time is short. It is later than we think! The day is far spent; the night is coming.

And what about the church in these days? We who profess to be sons of light and of the day consort with those of the night. It is hard to tell one from the other. Percentage-wise, few are alert and sober, donned in battle array, wearing the breastplate of faith and love and the helmet of the hope of salvation (1 Thessalonians 5:5-8).

The onslaught against believers has become more obvious and will only accelerate in the coming years. The church is ridiculed increasingly in the media. Television shows and movies portray us either as impotent and totally ineffective or as a dangerous radical element preying upon the mindless.

If we are honest, we must admit that much of the "bad press" is justly deserved, for we have conformed to the world's thinking and philosophies. We have not been salt and light. We have not repented before our God. The very things that the enemy has planned to destroy us are the very things God will use to prepare, purify, strengthen, and establish us. The choice is ours.

Can you say with a full heart, "Lord, bring me to that point of readiness no matter the cost"? If you are not ready, you'll be buried under it all. And the church in general is not ready. We must awaken others. We must pray. Our time is so short. If only we knew!

You Are God's Messenger

AND WHERE WERE the shepherds of God's flock in Malachi's time? Why hadn't the priests put a stop to their contemptible sacrifices? The priests knew God's Word: "But if it has any defect, such as lameness or blindness, or any serious defect, you shall not sacrifice it to the LORD your God" (Deuteronomy 15:21).

The shepherds were as guilty as the sheep. It was the priests whom God kept taking to task. Why? Because with leadership go responsibility and accountability.

The Great Shepherd—the Great High Priest—knows the needs of His sheep. However, in our case it is one priest speaking to another, for if you are a believer then you are part of a kingdom of priests unto God (Revelation 5:9,10). Therefore, I speak to you, priest to priest. And in doing so, I ask you to listen carefully to the responsibility of priests: "For the lips of a priest should preserve knowledge, and men should seek instruction from his mouth; for he is the messenger of the LORD of hosts" (Malachi 2:7).

But, Beloved, how can we call others to consecration when we will not consecrate ourselves?

> " 'And now, this commandment is for you, O priests. If you do not listen, and if you do not take it to heart to give honor to My name,' says the LORD of hosts, 'then I will send the curse upon you, and I will curse your blessings; and indeed, I have cursed them already, because you are not taking it to heart. Behold, I am going to rebuke your offspring' " (Malachi 2:1-3).

Do you sometimes feel as if your blessings are a curse—that things were better when you were struggling? You were closer to God then. And are your offspring rebuked by God because they are a product of your hypocritical lifestyle?

O precious one, this is not the inheritance of those who love their God and pursue holiness. God's plan for us is life and peace (Malachi 2:5), but these cannot be ours unless our hearts are fully His.

Peace Through Pleasing Him

PEACE IS OURS for the believing, the obeying. Regardless of what is happening to us or around us—small inconveniences or major disasters—we have His promise of peace. We can become upset and cry, "Why this, Lord?" or we can believe God, give thanks (Ephesians 5:20), and walk in perfect peace by keeping our minds and hearts stayed upon Him (Isaiah 26:3). We must choose to give thanks.

God's covenant with Levi (the priests) "was one of life and peace, and I gave them to him as an object of reverence" (Malachi 2:5), and God's covenant with His church is the same. Did not the angels proclaim it when they proclaimed the Messiah's birth, saying, "Glory to God in the highest, and on earth peace among men with whom He is pleased" (Luke 2:14)?

If you read that verse carefully, you will notice it is different from the King James Version, which we so often quote, "And on earth peace, good will toward men." The New American Standard's translation is truer to the Greek. It is not peace on earth, but rather peace among men with whom God is pleased!

Peace comes through knowledge, and through obedience to that knowledge! "Grace and peace be multiplied to you in the knowledge of God and of Jesus our Lord" (2 Peter 1:2). "These things I have spoken to you, that in Me you may have peace. In the world you have tribulation, but take courage; I have overcome the world" (John 16:33).

Our peace is wrapped up in Him, and if we are not wrapped up in Him, we will not know peace. We can't. For He is the Prince of Peace. Outside of His will, separated from a knowledge of Him, or living in hypocrisy, there can be no peace. Instead, there must be chastening, and "all discipline for the moment seems not to be joyful, but sorrowful; yet to those who have been trained by it, afterwards it yields the peaceful fruit of righteousness" (Hebrews 12:11).

O Beloved, if we will only listen and reverence God, fear Him and His Word, then we will know His life and His peace. It's His covenant with us!

Living by Your Convictions

OH, HOW DESPERATELY we need people who have determined in their hearts that they will stand for what is right, people who will live for absolutes that transcend their own personal desires, people who are willing to die for something rather than live for just anything. We need men, women, teens, and children of character, of principle, of conviction.

My husband, Jack, is just such a person. He is a man of great conviction who will do what is right because it is right. It does not matter the cost or the discipline. I have seen people, women especially, try to push him into something, and I have thought, "Now you've had it, honey. He is not going to do it. You can't push him when he is convinced he is right." Not that Jack is bullheaded; he is not. He is reasonable and a peacemaker. Yet he is a man with absolutes, a man who would not hesitate to lay down his life rather than compromise his God.

Now, I know all this about Jack because I live with him. But because he is not as verbal as I am, others might not know it until they see him in a confrontation where truth or principle is involved.

And, Beloved, it may be the same with you. Although you may be a quiet, reserved, even-keeled type, under that personality is a hero or a heroine, a brave and noble person who lives intrepidly according to your convictions and the need of the hour.

Deborah was like this. I love her song in Judges 5 where she says: "The peasantry ceased, they ceased in Israel, until I, Deborah, arose, until I arose, a mother in Israel" (Judges 5:7). Godless Jabin and his army with their mighty iron chariots had oppressed them too long. Even the farmers (peasants) could no longer live on their land. The people were holed up behind the city gates without shields or spears to defend themselves. And Deborah had had it. That was no way for children of the Almighty God to live. So she arose, "a mother in Israel."

O Beloved, it is time for us to awake and arise, even as did Deborah, the sons of Levi, and others in the days of old. I will tell you about it tomorrow. I love you, my heroes and heroines.

A Covenant of
Life and Peace

REMEMBER THE COVENANT of life and peace in Malachi 2? Well, God made this covenant with Levi because He saw that the Levites were zealous for His glory and His righteousness. Thus, God warned the Levites to continue to listen to Him.

As you read these verses from Malachi, give special attention to verse 4 (in bold type). God is saying that life and peace cannot continue if He is disobeyed and dishonored!

> "And now, this commandment is for you, O priests. If you do not listen, and if you do not take it to heart to give honor to My name," says the LORD of hosts, "then I will send the curse upon you, and I will curse your blessings; and indeed, I have cursed them already, because you are not taking it to heart. Behold, I am going to rebuke your offspring, and I will spread refuse on your faces, the refuse of your feasts; and you will be taken away with it. **Then you will know that I have sent this commandment to you, that My covenant may continue with Levi," says the LORD of hosts.** "My covenant with him was one of life and peace, and I gave them to him as an object of reverence; so he revered Me, and stood in awe of My name. True instruction was in his mouth, and unrighteousness was not found on his lips; he walked with Me in peace and uprightness, and he turned many back from iniquity (Malachi 2:1-6, emphasis added).

There are two different places in God's Word that speak of a time when Levi reverenced God and stood in awe of His name. We will look at them for the next three days. Although the primary cross-reference to Malachi 2:4 is Numbers 25, we will look at that after we have looked at Exodus 32:25-29.

Read the Exodus passage and note how Levi played the hero; we'll talk about it tomorrow.

Living Without Compromise

MOSES HAD BEEN on Mount Sinai too long for the children of Israel. Being impatient and fickle, they assembled around Aaron. "Come, make us a god who will go before us," they said. "As for this Moses, the man who brought us up from the land of Egypt, we do not know what has become of him" (Exodus 32:1).

Oh, how like so many of us! If God isn't going to run by our timetable, then we will run without Him; we'll get us another god. And that is exactly what we do! When we want something, rather than pray and wait for God, we decide that if God won't give it to us then we will get it ourselves! And if it takes giving ourselves to other gods—idols of money, position, sensuality, whatever—we will do it.

We can't shake our heads at the Israelites and wonder how they could be so senseless after they had seen God's mighty hand in the plagues on Egypt and the parting of the Red Sea! Look at us! We have seen One far greater than Moses, One who healed the lepers, raised the dead, gave sight to the blind, calmed the stormy sea, and then died on Calvary's tree, was buried and resurrected! We have bowed before Him, cried out for His eternal life so that we might not perish in hell, and then, relieved, gotten to our feet and walked after other gods. And in doing so, like the Israelites, we have corrupted ourselves.

And that makes God angry (Exodus 32:10)! Can you blame Him? Of course not. Yet we do.

The people in Malachi's day could not understand how God could be so upset. But, Beloved, because God is God, He cannot look on sin, nor can He bless it. His holiness, righteousness, and justice demand that it be dealt with!

Moses understood that, because Moses was a man of conviction. There is a right and a wrong, and right cannot be compromised. Moses' heart burned with a righteous, holy anger! And he cried out, "Whoever is for the LORD, come to me!" (Exodus 32:26). And all the sons of Levi gathered together to him. And then they judged sin without partiality, whether the sinner was a brother, friend, or neighbor.

Dear one, are you for the Lord? Then come to Him and put to death that sin which so easily besets you.

Becoming Like What You Worship

SHOW ME THE GOD or gods a man worships, and I will tell you the character of that man. You see, Beloved, we become like that which we worship. The Gentile gods were sensual and so, too, were their worshipers. Immorality inevitably follows idolatry, as you will see as you look at Numbers 25:1-13, the direct cross-reference for Malachi 2:4,5.

> While Israel remained at Shittim, the people began to play the harlot with the daughters of Moab. For they invited the people to the sacrifices of their gods, and the people ate and bowed down to their gods. So Israel joined themselves to Baal of Peor, and the LORD was angry against Israel. . . . Moses said to the judges of Israel, "Each of you slay his men who have joined themselves to Baal of Peor." Then behold, one of the sons of Israel came and brought to his relatives a Midianite woman, in the sight of Moses and in the sight of all the congregation of the sons of Israel. . . . When Phinehas the son of Eleazar, the son of Aaron the priest, saw it, he arose from the midst of the congregation, and took a spear in his hand; and he went after the man of Israel into the tent, and pierced both of them through, the man of Israel and the woman, through the body. So the plague on the sons of Israel was checked. And those who died by the plague were 24,000. Then the LORD spoke to Moses, saying, "Phinehas the son of Eleazar, the son of Aaron the priest, has turned away My wrath from the sons of Israel, in that he was jealous with My jealousy among them. . . . Therefore say, 'Behold, I give him My covenant of peace; and it shall be for him and his descendants after him, a covenant of a perpetual priesthood.'"

Are there any idols in your life, anything that you give yourself to, that have changed your character?

Be Jealous for God!

HOW JEALOUS ARE YOU for the holiness of God? How ready are you to stand for righteousness? How far would you go to keep others from iniquity?

Yesterday you read of Phinehas, the son of Eleazar, the son of Aaron. Jealous with God's jealousy, he put to death the sin within the camp and in doing so checked the plague that had already taken 24,000 lives. And what does God say about Phinehas, as representative of the tribe of Levi? "True instruction was in his mouth, and unrighteousness was not found on his lips; he walked with Me in peace and uprightness, and he turned many back from iniquity" (Malachi 2:6).

How do we measure up as priests today? We are to be as jealous with God's jealousy as Phinehas and the Levites were. I hope you know that godly jealousy. Paul talked of it in 2 Corinthians 11:2: "For I am jealous for you with a godly jealousy; for I betrothed you to one husband, that to Christ I might present you as a pure virgin." And what provoked this jealousy? It was his concern that the Corinthians might be "led astray from the simplicity and purity of devotion to Christ" (2 Corinthians 11:3). Wasn't this what happened to the children of Israel?

It also happened at Corinth, taking the same manifestation of immorality. A young man was committing incest with his father's wife (1 Corinthians 5)! But was the church jealous with a godly jealousy for God's name? No, they had let the sin go unchecked.

When Paul wrote regarding the situation, his admonition to the church was, "Do you not know that a little leaven leavens the whole lump of dough?" (1 Corinthians 5:6). In other words, unchecked sin spreads.

So Paul took the same action the Levites did. He stood against the sin. The offender was to be put out of fellowship and delivered unto "Satan for the destruction of his flesh, that his spirit may be saved in the day of the Lord Jesus" (1 Corinthians 5:5).

And yet, what do so many do when they see sin in the church? Is it dealt with, or merely whispered about and ignored? And how do we check sin in our own lives? We'll talk about that tomorrow.

Choose God's Way

SIN IS AN INSIDIOUS THING. It usually begins in small ways and spreads until finally you are caught in its viselike grip, wondering how you got there and if there is really any way to be set free.

Several days ago I was struck anew and afresh with Genesis 4 and God's dealings with Cain after He rejected his offering. Cain wanted to worship God his own way, on his own terms, and God would not have it! And thus we find Cain angry and pouting!

How typical. We are happy as long as everything is going our way, but let God make any demands on us, and it is another story!

Cain refused to bring a blood sacrifice; if God didn't like the fruit of his labor, He could forget it! "So Cain became very angry and his countenance fell. Then the LORD said to Cain, 'Why are you angry? And why has your countenance fallen? If you do well, will not your countenance be lifted up?'" (Genesis 4:5-7).

In other words, you do not have to be unhappy. The misery you are experiencing is of your own choosing. Isn't that also typical? We long for love, joy, and peace, yet refuse to do what is necessary to have them. All we must do is walk by His Spirit rather than after the desires of our flesh (Galatians 5:16-25). Yet we, in stubbornness, choose not to believe, not to obey! And thus God continues, "And if you do not do well, sin is crouching at the door; and its desire is for you, but you must master it" (Genesis 4:7).

Recently I heard about a young man who has attended several of our teen boot camps at Precept Ministries. He's living in sin, running with the wrong crowd, and he said to his mother, "If God doesn't stop me, then I'll go on living the way I am."

And what has God got to do with it? It is this young man's responsibility, not God's. God has told us what is right and wrong. He has given us His Spirit to be our Comforter, our Guide, our Enabler. However, the choice is still ours. We must master sin. And the minute we choose God's way, then God will meet us.

But let a little sin in, and you have a monster on your hands. Just look at what Cain did. He got up and killed his brother, Abel!

Are You Hiding God?

SIN. WE COVER IT UP. We excuse it. We rationalize it. We do everything but confront it and deal with it honestly and openly. And what does God say? Listen to His Word: "He that covereth his sins shall not prosper: but whoso confesseth and forsaketh them shall have mercy" (Proverbs 28:13 KJV).

If only we realized that sin is never a private affair. When we sin, someone else is always affected. Sin causes repercussions that extend far beyond ourselves, sometimes affecting second, third, and fourth generations. How? Why? Let me explain.

When we sin we are living lives that are ungodly and unrighteous. By unrighteous, I mean a life that is not lived according to what God says is right. When we live like this, we suppress or hold down the truth through our unrighteousness (Romans 1:18). To do so is to eclipse God—in other words, to keep men from seeing Him. Therefore, when we sin it hurts others because they cannot see real godliness or righteousness.

When we cover our transgressions and do not openly acknowledge and confess them as sin, then our sin affects others because they excuse their sin by looking at ours. "After all, nobody's perfect! What can you expect? Don't be so hard on yourself. We're human, aren't we? We're trying, but we just can't be perfect!"

Are we? Are we really trying not to sin? Well, if we were trying, then we wouldn't sin. If you are a Christian, it is a matter of yielding. Remember, you have the choice. You can master sin if you will!

Who is going to run your life? The Spirit of God or your fleshly appetites? Since the Garden of Eden, man has sought to cover his sin. Instead of running to God and confessing his sin, Adam took fig leaves and covered himself. (He now knew good and evil!) So God sought him out, and when He confronted Adam, Adam blamed Eve; then Eve blamed the serpent. They looked for an excuse.

O Beloved, can't you see that when you sin, you cannot cover it! God knows it. Others see it, and it gives them their excuse!

Sin Encourages Sin

THE PRIESTS IN Malachi's day were covering their sins, and the repercussions spread to the whole nation. The Jews looked at their religious leaders and followed suit. Among those who claimed to be God's chosen people, there was great sin.

Listen to God's indictment against the people at that time: " 'Then I will draw near to you for judgment; and I will be a swift witness against the sorcerers and against the adulterers and against those who swear falsely, and against those who oppress the wage earner in his wages, the widow and the orphan, and those who turn aside the alien, and do not fear Me,' says the LORD of hosts" (Malachi 3:5).

Neither the people nor the priests were distinguishing "between the righteous and the wicked, between one who serves God and one who does not serve Him" (Malachi 3:18).

And so it is today. There is sin in the camp. Grievous sin. Divorce abounds not only in the ranks but among the leadership. I know pastors, authors, and leaders who are guilty of immorality and divorce (without biblical grounds). Yet no disciplinary action has been taken, and they have moved to other churches or continued writing Christian books or holding leadership positions in Christian organizations.

O Beloved, we are to pursue "holiness, without which no man shall see the Lord" (Hebrews 12:14 KJV). And leaders cannot call us to holiness if they will not be holy themselves.

When we cover our sin, God calls it "dealing treacherously" (Malachi 2:10). The Hebrew word is *bagad*, and it means to cover (as with a garment), to act covertly, deal deceitfully, treacherously, to depart, offend, transgress.

Sin *does* affect your brother or sister. It affects them in a horrible, insidious, deceitful way. Your sin encourages them to sin as well. And sin is transgression of the law, whereas love is fulfillment of the law. " 'YOU SHALL LOVE YOUR NEIGHBOR AS YOURSELF.' Love does no wrong to a neighbor; love therefore is the fulfillment of the law" (Romans 13:9,10).

God loves you. The question is: Do you love Him?

And you say you love others. Do you? If you do—if I do—then we will pursue holiness instead of excusing and covering our sin.

A Holy Perspective

DIVORCE. IT IS ONE of the things that God literally hates. It destroys the home, the bedrock of any nation.

Still we hear so many say, in whimpering tones of self-indulgence, "Surely God doesn't want people to be unhappy, does He?"

My precious ones, God is not concerned about your happiness. He is concerned about your holiness. Be holy and you will be happy.

True happiness is experienced through a right relationship with God. Such a person can live in the meanest of circumstances with the meanest of people and still know the joy of the Lord which is his strength and the source of his right relationship with others.

Yet what are we doing in our nation and in the church? We are putting away our wives, our husbands. And what does divorce do to a man or woman? It defiles them. And what does it do to the land? It pollutes the land, for it stops or hinders our having godly offspring.

Listen to the Word of the Lord:

> "The LORD has been a witness between you and the wife of your youth, against whom you have dealt treacherously, though she is your companion and your wife by covenant. But not one has done so who has a remnant of the Spirit. And what did that one do while he was seeking a godly offspring? Take heed then, to your spirit, and let no one deal treacherously against the wife of your youth. For I hate divorce," says the LORD (Malachi 2:14).

The priests and the people were dealing treacherously. They were divorcing their wives and not calling it sin. They divorced them and never blinked an eye or missed a beat as they marched to the destroyer's cadence right into God's temple without the slightest shame.

They divorced their wives and sought God at the altar. Yet at the altar they wept. "You cover the altar of the LORD with tears, with weeping and with groaning, because He no longer regards the offering or accepts it with favor from your hand" (Malachi 2:13).

He can't. You can weep all you want, but He can't. He is God. And you either march to His cadence, or you don't march at all!

Justice . . . or Mercy?

ISN'T IT STRANGE that when we get hurt we cry for justice? We insist on justice because we have been wronged. But what do we want when *we* are the guilty party? Mercy, of course!

Iniquity abounded in Israel, yet the people cried, "Where is the God of justice?" (Malachi 2:17). They wanted justice from God because they had been hurt, yet they did not want the God of justice. In other words, give me God to meet my demands and plead my case, but don't put the demands of the holy God on *me*. I want the gifts but not the Giver, the redemption for my sins but not the Redeemer.

And how about you, Beloved? Do you want all the benefits of God without the obligations of godliness?

The Israelites had asked the question, "Where is the God of justice?" They would get their answer. He was coming!

" 'Behold, I am going to send My messenger, and he will clear the way before Me. And the Lord, whom you seek, will suddenly come to His temple; and the messenger of the covenant, in whom you delight, behold, He is coming,' says the LORD of hosts" (Malachi 3:1).

And yet, when He came, it would not be to bring the unjust justice, to lift them out of the rebellious, willful, self-dug pits, but rather to execute judgment upon the earth: "But who can endure the day of His coming? . . . For He is like a refiner's fire and like fullers' soap" (Malachi 3:2).

He would come as the Lamb of God to take away the sin of the world, but only those who knew they needed a lamb would recognize His coming. And so, for all those who were arrogant doers of wickedness (Malachi 3:13-15), as well as for those who feared the Lord (Malachi 3:16), there would be a forerunner who would clear the way of the Lord. John the Baptist. And what would be his message? "Repent, for the kingdom of heaven is at hand" (Matthew 3:2).

There it was . . . the offer of a kingdom in which justice would reign. And the key that would grant entrance into that kingdom hung on a ring of repentance!

Do you really want justice, or would you prefer mercy? Have you ever repented?

God's Message . . . Repent!

"A VOICE IS CALLING, 'Clear the way for the LORD in the wilderness; make smooth in the desert a highway for our God. . . . Then the glory of the LORD will be revealed, and all flesh will see it together; for the mouth of the LORD has spoken'" (Isaiah 40:3,5).

This was to be the ministry of John the Baptist. It was the custom of eastern kings to send men before them to remove every barrier and obstacle in their path. "In this instance, it meant removal of opposition to the Lord by the preaching of repentance and the conversion of sinners to Him."[12]

So, in spite of the blindness of their eyes and the hardness of their hearts, God would reach out to the sons of Jacob once more. This time it would not be through prophets, but through His Son and His Son's messenger, and the message of both would be the same: "Repent."

And what does it mean to repent? The Hebrew word *shubh* used for repentance carries the idea of a radical change in one's attitude toward sin and good. It implies a conscious moral separation and personal decision to forsake sin and to enter into fellowship with God.

There is no fellowship with God, Beloved, if you insist on continuing in sin (1 John 1:6). Repentance is a turning to God from sin, a change of mind resulting in a change of direction.

Before any man, woman, or child can truly be saved, he or she must see the need of salvation and of a Savior. It is one thing to know you need salvation and another to know you cannot save yourself. When you see your total inability to make yourself right with God, then you recognize your desperate need for a Savior.

Yet how many there are who have never seen their need! There are so many sitting in church pews who are typical of the Old Testament Jews . . . sacrificing in the temple . . . involved in religion . . . calling upon the one true Jehovah God . . . going through the rituals of worship . . . having a zeal for God, but not in accordance with knowledge (Romans 10:2). They have not repented; they have seen no need to do so. They are religious . . . but lost.

What about you?

God Loves You . . . Repent!

JOHN THE BAPTIST'S message was very clear, very direct. It needed to be. The people were set and comfortable in their ways. Caught up in their sects, convinced they were right, they did not know it was a case of the blind leading the blind. They boasted in a law they broke, and thus they dishonored God. Their praise came from men, certainly not from God (Romans 2:17-29).

Speaking of the One to come, John said, "His winnowing fork is in His hand, and He will thoroughly clean His threshing floor; and He will gather His wheat into the barn, but He will burn up the chaff with unquenchable fire" (Matthew 3:12). John was letting them know that when the Christ came, He would winnow the grain to expose what was wheat and what was chaff.

Do you like preaching that winnows the grain? I believe we need more of it, much more. And I do believe that if we love God and people we will preach a message that will separate wheat from chaff, even as Malachi did. But as you preach, remember that this message was preached from the foundational truth: "I have loved you."

Tell people of God's love: "For God so loved the world, that he gave his only begotten Son, that whosoever believeth in him should not perish, but have everlasting life" (John 3:16 KJV).

But also tell them that "except ye repent, ye shall all likewise perish" (Luke 13:3 KJV).

"Not every one that saith unto me, Lord, Lord, shall enter into the kingdom of heaven, but he that doeth the will of my Father which is in heaven" (Matthew 7:21 KJV).

And when you preach, ask them if they are doing the will of God or if they are calling the shots, walking the way they want to walk, yet saying, "Lord, Lord."

"Therefore bring forth fruit in keeping with your repentance . . . the axe is already laid at the root of the trees; every tree therefore that does not bear good fruit is cut down and thrown into the fire" (Matthew 3:8,10).

Walk through the vineyards of your life, Beloved, and inspect your fruit. Record your findings.

God Knows Your Heart

A GOOD WAY to inspect your fruit is to look at your walk. I say "walk" because some of us are so introspective and so full of self-condemnation that we cannot trust ourselves to objectively look at our hearts.

"Little children, let us not love with word or with tongue, but in deed and truth. We shall know by this [deed and truth] that we are of the truth, and shall assure our heart before Him, *in whatever our heart condemns us*; for God is greater than our heart, and knows all things" (1 John 3:18-20, emphasis added).

So many dear ones have a hard time accepting the fact of God's unconditional love and commitment that I feel I must say what I am saying for their benefit. Perhaps this is a problem for you. Messages like this month's devotionals sometimes bring condemnation to sensitive souls who long to please God, yet never feel they can measure up!

Many of those in this category have never known unconditional love from their parents. They have received condemnation instead. It is hard for them to relate to God as One who loves unconditionally, and this gives them difficulty with their faith. They heap condemnation upon themselves and thus put themselves into "the pits."

However, even though there is a risk that some might have difficulty in this area, messages like Malachi's must be delivered.

To all those who fear the Lord, and especially to those of you who too quickly condemn yourselves, let me give you a blessed word from Malachi.

God knows those who fear Him. He knows the hearts of all men, and there is "a book of remembrance . . . written before Him for those who fear the LORD and who esteem His name. 'And they will be Mine,' says the LORD of hosts, 'on the day that I prepare My own possession, and I will spare them as a man spares his own son who serves him. . . . For you who fear My name the sun of righteousness will rise with healing in its wings; and you will go forth and skip about like calves from the stall' " (Malachi 3:16,17; 4:2).

O Beloved, never fear. The Lord knows His own and will lose none of them (John 10:27-29). Hallelujah!

Do You Rob God?

THE WAY PEOPLE handle money tells you a lot about their relationship with God.

When the Lord said, "Return to Me, and I will return to you" (Malachi 3:7), the Israelites asked, "How shall we return?"

God's reply was quite interesting, for He dealt with them in the area of their pocketbooks! "Will a man rob God? Yet you are robbing Me! But you say, 'How have we robbed Thee?' In tithes and offerings. You are cursed with a curse, for you are robbing Me, the whole nation of you!" (Malachi 3:8,9).

Can you imagine robbing God, from whom comes every good and perfect gift? God, who has promised to supply all our needs?

It was God who gave the increase, and He only asked them for a tenth—the firstfruits—leaving the entire rest of the harvest for their very own. And here they were begrudging God a tithe of all He had given them.

When the whole tithe was brought to the storehouse (the temple or the place of God's designation), did they not partake of it themselves after it had been offered to God (Deuteronomy 12:1-19)? And if they did not partake of every tithe, did not the rest go to the Levites who labored at the temple and to the widows and the poor (Deuteronomy 26:12-15)? Yet they would not release what belonged to God, the tithes and contributions He had asked for!

No, as they held back their own lives, so they held back their possessions. Their token giving matched their token living.

Find a man who is totally surrendered to God and you will find that everything he has is held in an open hand. What God has commanded, a tenth, does not even trouble him, for a tenth isn't enough to give back to his God.

How do you give? What is your motive? Are you robbing God? Maybe that is why the devourer is destroying your "crops" and you cannot seem to manage or get ahead (Malachi 3:10,11).

JUNE

———

Confidence to Enter Through the Veil
Covenant, Part 1

The next two months we will spend together
focus on one of the most stabilizing, freeing truths
I've ever studied! Understanding covenant will give
a whole new dimension to your relationship with
your Lord. You will never be the same! This is the
testimony of many who have heard this teaching as
I have shared it across the United States. As we
walk through these days together, my prayer is that
you will catch a new glimpse of the love that
motivated God to make a covenant for you—and
that you will see clearly all that is yours as a result!

———

The Covenant Comes

FOR 400 YEARS God had been silent. For years upon years all Israel had to cling to were the promises of a Messiah. The final words had been those of the prophet Malachi.

> "Behold, I am going to send My messenger, and he will clear the way before Me. And the Lord, whom you seek, will suddenly come to His temple; and the messenger of the covenant, in whom you delight, behold, He is coming," says the LORD of hosts (Malachi 3:1).

The promise of the New Covenant, the Covenant of Grace, which would supersede the Old Covenant, the Covenant of Law, had first come through the prophet Jeremiah. It was then confirmed and amplified by Ezekiel. Finally, Malachi recorded his last and wonderful promise, the promise of the coming of the Messenger of the Covenant.

This Messenger would instate a covenant that would literally change the hearts of men—both Jews and Gentiles. The Law, which had been written on tables of stone, would now be written on the fleshly tables of their hearts (Jeremiah 31:33). The Covenant of Law, from which men continually departed, would be replaced by a covenant that would cause them to fear God in such a way that they would not turn away from Him (Jeremiah 31:3,4). He would be their God, and they would be His people, forever and ever. He would put His Spirit within them and cause them to walk in His statutes and keep His commandments (Ezekiel 36:26-28).

Now, there He was. It was the night of the Passover, "And . . . Jesus took some bread, and after a blessing, He broke it and gave it to the disciples, and said, 'Take, eat; this is My body.' And when He had taken a cup and given thanks, He gave it to them, saying, 'Drink from it, all of you; for this is My blood of the covenant, which is poured out for many for forgiveness of sins' " (Matthew 26:26-28).

And they thought back to that day in the synagogue at Capernaum when so many of His disciples had withdrawn, to walk with Him no more. They had not wanted any part of being a covenant partner with this Jesus of Galilee. Little did they know that this was Malachi's Messenger of the Covenant!

A Covenant With Jesus

"THIS IS A DIFFICULT STATEMENT; who can listen to it?" (John 6:60). And so they grumbled and walked out of the synagogue in Capernaum.

Jesus, the Bread of Life! The bread from heaven! Eat His flesh! Drink His blood! Likening Himself to God's manna! Eat and not die! "How can this man give us His flesh to eat?" (John 6:52). It was too difficult, and so "many of His disciples withdrew, and were not walking with Him anymore" (John 6:66).

Did they not understand that Jesus was calling them into a covenant relationship with Himself? In all probability, they understood, for He was talking in covenant terms. But eat His flesh—they couldn't quite understand that. At any rate, to enter into covenant with this One who was held in great skepticism by the religious leaders was too costly. Total commitment was just too much to ask when they weren't really sure who He was. What if He wasn't what He said He was! Working miracles, multiplying loaves and fish was fine; following Jesus that way was great, even exciting. But the binding commitment of covenant? They just weren't ready for that!

I wonder how many of us are ready for it. I wonder how many fully realize what it means to enter into the New Covenant, to become a covenant partner with the Lord Jesus Christ.

O Beloved, how I have longed to put this teaching into print, to share with you what God has taught me about covenant. It is one of the most precious of all the truths I have ever learned. It is a teaching that, once comprehended, lifts the veil off so many Scriptures which at one time were hidden under a cloud of mystery. You have read them, accepted them, quoted them, but still you have felt there had to be more.

Well, here it is, Beloved, the "more" of that covenant which was "cut" for you.

New Testament . . . New Covenant

ANDREW MURRAY, in his book *The Two Covenants*, says, "If we were to but grasp the full knowledge of what God desires to do for us and understood the nature of His promise, it would make Covenant the very gate of heaven."

How true his statement is. And by the end of these next two months, by His grace—and through the blessed Spirit's ministry of leading us into His truth—we shall see what it truly means to eat His flesh and drink His blood, to enter into covenant with Him. It's going to be so good you're hardly going to be able to stand it! But we must take it step by step. So be patient as, under His direction, I lay it down for you, precept upon precept.

The word *covenant* is used approximately 298 times in the Word of God. And if you are going to appreciate its meaning fully, you must know the Hebrew and Greek words used for covenant.

The Old Testament word for covenant is the Hebrew word *bereeth*, which means "in a sense of cutting, a compact or agreement made by passing through pieces of flesh, a confederacy, a league." Now, hang on to this meaning because, in the days to come, it will throw you into a state of awesome wonder as you walk through the pieces!

The New Testament word for covenant is the Greek word *diatheke*, which means "a contract, a testament."

Thus we see the Word of God divided into the Old Testament or Old Covenant and the New Testament or New Covenant.

Everything that God does for you and me as His children is based on covenant. In biblical times a covenant was the most solemn, binding agreement that could ever be made. But because most of us today are unfamiliar with covenant agreements, I am going to share with you, step by step, how men cut covenant. My information comes from a book, *The Blood Covenant*, by Clay Trumbull. As I studied and meditated upon it and upon Andrew Murray's book, *The Two Covenants*, God, by His precious Spirit, led me step by step, showing me what it meant to me as His child.

And then came the verse, "The secret of the LORD is for those who fear Him, and He will make them know His covenant" (Psalm 25:14).

Taking on His Likeness

"NOW IT CAME ABOUT when he had finished speaking to Saul, that the soul of Jonathan was knit to the soul of David, and Jonathan loved him as himself. . . . Then Jonathan made a covenant with David because he loved him as himself. And Jonathan stripped himself of the robe that was on him and gave it to David, with his armor, including his sword and his bow and his belt" (1 Samuel 18:1,3,4).

When two men entered into a covenant with one another, the first thing they did was to exchange robes. The exchanging of robes symbolized the "putting on of one another."

Has anyone ever said to you, "I saw an outfit the other day that looked just like you"? Our clothes are an expression of us. This changing of robes was an act that said, "I am so becoming one with you that I will take on your likeness." This, Beloved, is what the New Covenant is all about—our taking on His likeness.

In Romans 13:14 Paul writes, "But put on the Lord Jesus Christ, and make no provision for the flesh in regard to its lusts." To those in Ephesus he wrote, "And put on the new self, which in the likeness of God has been created in righteousness and holiness of the truth" (Ephesians 4:24). Those who would enter into covenant with God must know that they are to bear the image of the heavenly . . . to be holy even as He is holy (1 Peter 1:16).

I'll never forget that day in July 1963 when I fell to my knees and cried out, "O God, You can do anything to me that You want, if You'll only give me Your peace." And He did; He gave me the Prince of Peace. Oh, I didn't understand it all at the time, but that day I partook of the blood of the covenant. The change was instantaneous. When I arose from my knees, I knew I could no longer dress the way I had dressed. No longer was I to wear the attire of a harlot, for I belonged to Him!

That was over 30 years ago, and since that time, day by day, year by year, as I have beheld His glory, He has been transforming me "into the same image from glory to glory" (2 Corinthians 3:18).

What about you, Beloved? Have you put on His robe? It is part of the New Covenant.

The Robe of Humanity

WHEN A COVENANT was cut between two parties, as we saw, the two exchanged robes. And so we see our Covenant Partner, Jesus Christ, putting on our robe of humanity.

"Since then the children share in flesh and blood, He Himself likewise also partook of the same" (Hebrews 2:14). "Although He existed in the form of God [although Jesus Christ was the perfect expression of the perfect character of God], [He] did not regard equality with God a thing to be grasped [to clutch and hold on to at all costs], but emptied Himself, taking the form of a bond-servant, and being made in the likeness of men . . . He humbled Himself by becoming obedient to the point of death" (Philippians 2:6-8).

What would cause Jesus, the Son of the Sovereign God, the Ruler of all the universe, to leave the ivory palaces, where the heavenly host constantly sang His praises? What would cause Him to come to earth only to confine Himself to our fleshly image and to be despised and rejected of men?

Love. Unconditional, unqualified love. Love for you. Because God loved you as Himself, He wanted to enter into a covenant with you. Therefore, He exchanged robes with you—God put on your humanity.

O Beloved, do you realize the practicality of it all? You have a Covenant Partner who can be touched with the feeling of your infirmities, who can sympathize with the weaknesses of your flesh, because He was tempted in all things, just as you are, yet He was without sin (Hebrews 4:15,16). He understands your weaknesses, so why try to hide them or cover them up? Your Covenant Partner is your High Priest, so run to Him for help in time of trouble, of need, of failure, of weakness, of temptation. Run! That is what He is there for! He was without sin, so He handled the flesh correctly. He will give you His solution.

Remember, you put on His robe, the Holy Spirit. Jesus, as a man, lived by the Holy Spirit, so walk in His likeness by His Spirit, moment by moment, and you shall not fulfill the lust of the flesh! And never forget that because He is your Covenant Partner there is no condemnation, ever (Romans 8:1)!

The Strength Exchange

WHEN JONATHAN AND DAVID made a covenant with one another, they not only exchanged robes, they also exchanged belts or girdles (1 Samuel 18:4). The belt or girdle represented a man's strength. Thus the exchange symbolized the fact that now, as covenant partners, they would compensate for each other's weaknesses. Should one run out of strength, then the other would become his strength.

What a beautiful picture this is for us, for if you are like me, you are so aware of your total inadequacy, your lack of power, of ability when it comes to living life God's way or ministering to others.

One of my most frequent cries to my Lord is, "O Father . . . I can't. You will have to do it. If You do not do it, Father, it will only be flesh, and the flesh profits nothing, and I don't want to waste Your time doing 'nothings.' "

I will never forget hearing Stuart Briscoe say, years ago, "God doesn't need your ability; all He needs is your availability."

So it's, "I can't. You can. Let's go!"

Oh, Beloved, this is what your Covenant Partner is for—your weakness, your "I can'ts." So many times we say that we can't serve God because we aren't whatever is needed. We're not talented enough or smart enough or whatever. But if you are in covenant with Jesus Christ, He is responsible for covering your weaknesses, for being your strength. He will give you *His* abilities for your disabilities!

Really, then, our problem is not weakness, but independence! And in covenant, you die to independent living.

Listen to what Jesus said to Paul: "My grace is sufficient for you, for power is perfected in weakness" (2 Corinthians 12:9). And God's word to us is the same, because Jesus Christ is also our Covenant Partner.

Therefore, we must say with Paul: "Most gladly, therefore, I will rather boast about my weaknesses, that the power of Christ may dwell in me. Therefore I am well content with weaknesses, with insults, with distresses, with persecutions, with difficulties, for Christ's sake; for when I am weak, then I am strong" (2 Corinthians 12:9,10).

We will talk more about this tomorrow. For today, why don't you list ways in which you have failed to appropriate His strength.

His Strength for Your Weakness

ARE THERE TIMES when you think you just cannot go on, you cannot take any more? You feel like fainting, just checking out into peaceful oblivion, going to sleep, maybe to wake, maybe not to! Or you feel like walking away or throwing up your hands—it's impossible! You will never win! What's the use? Or is there so much pressure on you that you wonder how you will ever get it done? Why not give up? (This last one is where I'm hit the most!) Or have you fought and fought—in prayer, in fasting, in labor—and not won yet? Are you about ready to quit, to go AWOL?

Beloved, whatever, whichever, wherever, whenever you have hit the point where you are out of strength and about ready to quit, have you appropriated your Covenant Partner's belt? Are you girded with His strength? Listen to His words to you today.

"Hast thou not known? hast thou not heard, that the everlasting God, the LORD, the Creator of the ends of the earth, fainteth not, neither is weary?" (Isaiah 40:28 KJV).

Hallelujah! That is your Covenant Partner! "He giveth power to the faint [fatigued]; and to them that have no might he increaseth strength" (Isaiah 40:29 KJV).

Those who have no might, Beloved, are those who are tired and weary from the fight! "Even the youths shall faint and be weary, and the young men shall utterly fall, but they that wait upon the LORD shall renew [exchange] their strength; they shall mount up with wings as eagles; they shall run, and not be weary; and they shall walk, and not faint" (Isaiah 40:30,31 KJV).

Our society is filled with runaways, dropouts, and quitters. The epidemic of walking away has hit our land with effects as devastating as the bubonic plague, and it has destroyed millions of effective lives and relationships. We are so self-centered that we have ceased to lay down our lives for others. We have seen others faint or walk away and we have followed in their weakness. We have fainted when we could have persevered by exchanging our strength for His! With His strength, not only could we have kept on walking, we could have run!

Tell your Father where you have fainted. Then talk to Him about it.

The Weapons Exchange

THE THIRD CEREMONIAL ACT that covenant partners performed was the exchanging of their weapons. This act symbolized the taking on of one another's enemies. "And Jonathan stripped himself of the robe that was on him and gave it to David, with his armor, including his sword and his bow and his belt" (1 Samuel 18:4).

When two entered into covenant, they understood that now all they had, they held in common—even each other's enemies. Whenever one was under attack, it was the duty of the other to come to his aid!

Oh, what light this brought when I discovered it! Now I could understand why I did not have to worry about defending myself against my enemies! My Covenant Partner was my defense. I was to give love. He would deal in justice.

"Never take your own revenge, beloved, but leave room for the wrath of God, for it is written, 'VENGEANCE IS MINE, I WILL REPAY,' says the Lord. 'BUT IF YOUR ENEMY IS HUNGRY, FEED HIM, AND IF HE IS THIRSTY, GIVE HIM A DRINK; FOR IN SO DOING YOU WILL HEAP BURNING COALS UPON HIS HEAD.' Do not be overcome by evil, but overcome evil with good" (Romans 12:19-21).

As I meditated upon this, I remembered the apostle Paul's first face-to-face encounter with the Lord. Paul, then Saul, was on his way to Damascus to root out Christians in order to take them prisoner and thus stamp out Christianity. He had already consented to Stephen's stoning. "Suddenly a light from heaven flashed around him; and he fell to the ground, and heard a voice saying to him, 'Saul, Saul, why are you persecuting Me?" (Acts 9:3,4). Because Christians were in covenant with Christ, when Paul persecuted them, he was persecuting Jesus!

How we need to see this truth. When you wound, harm, or persecute another Christian, you are doing it to Christ! In Psalm 105:8-15 God reminds His people of the covenant He had made with them and that He had permitted no man to oppress them and had even reproved kings for their sake, saying, "Do not touch My anointed ones, and do My prophets no harm" (Psalm 105:15).

Has someone come against you? Call to your Covenant Partner. In His perfect timing and in His perfect way, He will come to your defense.

Standing With the Lord

WHEN WE ENTER into covenant with Jesus Christ, not only does He take on our enemies, but we are to take on His! It is a mutual agreement to be honored by both parties.

Oh, how our hearts thrill when we hear wonderful stories of the Lord's protection of His people. But what about stories of how Christians have stood with the Lord against His enemies?

Jehoshaphat, king of Judah, had to be reproved by Jehu for not doing that very thing: "Should you help the wicked and love those who hate the LORD and so bring wrath on yourself from the LORD?" (2 Chronicles 19:2).

How can we, who say we love God, side with those who hate Him? How can we love God and walk in the world's ways, join in its activities, and espouse its philosophies when they go against all for which God and His kingdom stands? Yet so many side with the world, don't they? John 13–15 records a conversation Jesus had with His disciples right after they partook of their covenant meal.

It was during this time of instruction that Jesus warned them of His enemy, the world. "If the world hates you, you know that it has hated Me before it hated you. If you were of the world, the world would love its own; but because you are not of the world, but I chose you out of the world, therefore the world hates you" (John 15:18,19).

The world hates Jesus because He took away every excuse for sin. As a man of like passions, He lived and served God as man was created to do. And in so doing, He took away man's cloak, man's excuse for sin. And so men hated Him because of His righteous life—a life lived according to God's standards, according to God's wisdom.

The world does not like righteousness! Why? Because the world has set its own standards, it has adopted its own philosophies— standards and philosophies opposed to God.

What about you? Does the world love you or does it hate you? Does your righteous life expose its sin, or have you so adopted the world's philosophies that it has opened up its arms to you in loving welcome? And if so, where does that leave your Covenant Partner? Take time to meditate on this.

Adultery . . . in Covenant?

IT HAPPENED YEARS AGO when I stood in Grace Kinser's home in Atlanta, preparing to teach our class. Approximately 250 women came to an instant silence when I took the microphone and said, "I am so horribly grieved, for I have just heard that someone in this class today is guilty of committing adultery." No one moved a muscle. There was a horrible, deathly silence. Each wondered who it was. Would I dare say her name aloud? They waited, and I paused. Adultery—it was too horrible an offense to be named among Christians, and I felt God would have them feel the awfulness of such a sin.

I had prayed much about that class that day when I would be teaching the book of James. "Father, O Father, how can I teach it in such a way as to make them see what an abomination it is to be spiritual adulteresses. How can we be friends with the world, Father, when the world hates You and Your Son?" And this was the way that God had given me to get their attention. And it did!

Physical adultery among Christians causes many a head to wag and many a heart to grieve. But what effect does spiritual adultery have upon us when we see it or hear it named among the saints?

James wrote: "You adulteresses, do you not know that friendship with the world is hostility toward God? Therefore whoever wishes to be a friend of the world makes himself an enemy of God" (James 4:4).

And who is the prince of this world system that sets itself against God and against His righteous standards? Is it not Satan? So for you to love the world and adopt its standards, its code of living, its philosophies, is to say to Jesus, "Jesus, I know I belong to You, but before the wedding I want to have an affair with Your archenemy." And so we crawl into the world—the devil's bed! And our Covenant Partner weeps. His "pure virgin" has been deceived, beguiled, "led astray from the simplicity and purity of devotion to Christ" (2 Corinthians 11:3). She has not taken on the enemies of her Covenant Partner, but rather has chosen them above the Lover of her soul.

Are you guilty of adultery? Confess it. Then "go your way. From now on sin no more" (John 8:11).

Siding With Sin . . . in Covenant?

AT THE RISK of belaboring a point, precious one, I feel that God would have us spend one more day looking at our covenant agreement to stand with our Partner against His enemies.

Spiritual adultery is rampant in our churches. And spiritual adultery takes an awful toll upon the next generation of Christians. "A spirit of harlotry has led them astray, and they have played the harlot, departing from their God. . . . Therefore your daughters play the harlot, and your brides commit adultery" (Hosea 4:12,13).

Spiritual adultery gives birth to physical adultery! This is why, Beloved, we are seeing so much immorality among those who claim the name of Christ. And they are sinning! They are walking out of marriages! They think they are remarrying without impunity! There is no fear of God before their eyes! Why? Because so many have played the harlot with the world that rather than expose sin, the church has given men an excuse to sin!

We (and I use the term because I am a member of the church) have tolerated sin within the camp. We have overlooked it, rather than judging those within the church by not associating "with any so-called brother if he should be an immoral person, or covetous, or an idolater, or a reviler, or a drunkard, or a swindler." We have not removed the wicked man from among *ourselves* (1 Corinthians 5:11,13).

Recently I heard of a music director who asked his pastor for prayer because he had to confront a member of the choir who was committing adultery. It was a known fact, yet the pastor forbade him to confront the adulterer. "Let it go. Maybe it will pass over."

Not to deal with sin in the church is to choose man's reasoning and ways above God's orders. This, then, is to side against God.

O Beloved, can you not see that this compromise, this adoption of worldly philosophies, is spiritual adultery? And in our spiritual adultery, we have bred physical adultery.

What are you tolerating or loving that is of the world and thus against Christ? Deal with it thoroughly before it destroys you and others.

Breaking the Covenant

A COVENANT WAS NOT entered into lightly. Breaking a covenant commitment was punishable by death.

Now, dear one, what I am about to share with you for the next few days may be hard, very hard, for some of you to handle. But, Beloved, I must teach the whole counsel of God's Word. I cannot, before God, leave out that which you may find distasteful, hard to believe, or incompatible with your understanding of God. And I'm sure you appreciate this, knowing that "if I were still trying to please men, I would not be a bond-servant of Christ" (Galatians 1:10). I fully realize that as a teacher of God's Word I "shall incur a stricter judgment" and that I am to be careful how I build upon the foundation of Jesus Christ in your life (James 3:1; 1 Corinthians 3:10,11). And so in godly reverence I share the following.

After robes, belts, and weapons were exchanged, the covenant partners would then take an animal and split it down the middle, down its back. They would lay the two pieces of the animal on the ground opposite each other. Then the two individuals would stand between these two walls of blood and point to heaven, calling out to God. Pointing their fingers to the dead animal, they would say, "God, do so to me and more if I break this covenant." In other words, they were saying that this covenant was so binding that to break it would warrant the transgressor's death!

What does this mean to you and to me? Very simply, it means that if you are not faithful to your covenant with Jesus Christ, He has a right to kill you prematurely (early, before your time) and take you home. If you are His and you break covenant, you will not die and go to hell; you will simply go home early—in embarrassment!

Now there are a number of passages that deal with dying before one's time. We will deal with those in the days to come. But for today, meditate upon Ecclesiastes 7:17: "Do not be a fool. Why should you die before your time?"

Priorities

WHEN DAVID AND JONATHAN entered into a covenant with one another, that covenant agreement superseded all other relationships, even those of birth. Therefore, when King Saul, Jonathan's father, became jealous of David and sought to take David's life, Jonathan was obligated by virtue of covenant to protect David from his father. Jonathan's love for David was to have preeminence over his love for his father.

In 1 Samuel 20:8, we see David reminding Jonathan of that fact: "Therefore deal kindly with your servant, for you have brought your servant into a covenant of the LORD with you." And so Jonathan, having called upon God to deal with him if he did not keep this covenant, swore to protect David. "If it please my father to do you harm, may the LORD do so to Jonathan and more also, if I do not make it known to you and send you away, that you may go in safety" (1 Samuel 20:13).

But then Jonathan, too, was concerned, for I'm sure he knew that Samuel had anointed David as the next king of Israel. And so Jonathan reminded David of the solemn commitment of covenant: " 'And if I am still alive, will you not show me the lovingkindness of the LORD, that I may not die? And you shall not cut off your lovingkindness from my house forever....' So Jonathan made a covenant with the house of David, saying, 'May the LORD require it at the hands of David's enemies' " (1 Samuel 20:14-16). In doing this, Jonathan was calling upon the Lord to kill David by the hands of his enemies if David failed to care for Jonathan's descendants.

Understanding that a covenant relationship supersedes all other relationships helps you to understand our Lord's call to those who would enter into covenant with Him. "If anyone comes to Me, and does not hate his own father and mother and wife and children and brothers and sisters, yes, and even his own life, he cannot be My disciple" (Luke 14:26).

Let me ask you a question. Does Jesus Christ have the preeminence in your life above all other relationships? If the answer is no, then something is very wrong. Deal with it today. Write your excuse in black and white so you _can_ deal with it.

Search Your Heart

IT IS KIND OF HARD to believe that God would cause someone to die prematurely, isn't it? And yet it is true, and we will see that it is because of a failure to keep our side of the covenant. This is clearly taught in the eleventh chapter of 1 Corinthians. However, Beloved, before we go there, let me briefly share some Scriptures with you.

James 5:19,20 says, "My brethren, if any among you strays from the truth, and one turns him back, let him know that he who turns a sinner from the error of his way will save his soul from death, and will cover a multitude of sins." First John 5:16 says, "If anyone sees his brother committing a sin not leading to death, he shall ask and God will for him give life to those who commit sin not leading to death. There is a sin leading to death."

Now, let's look at 1 Corinthians. This passage concerns the Lord's Supper, and this meal symbolized entering into a covenant.

> And when He had given thanks, He broke it, and said, "This is My body, which is for you. . . . This cup is the new covenant in My blood; do this, as often as you drink it, in remembrance of Me." For as often as you eat this bread and drink the cup, you proclaim the Lord's death until He comes. Therefore whoever eats the bread or drinks the cup of the Lord in an unworthy manner, shall be guilty of the body and the blood of the Lord. But let a man examine himself, and so let him eat of the bread and drink of the cup. For he who eats and drinks, eats and drinks judgment to himself, if he does not judge the body rightly (1 Corinthians 11:24-29).

What happens when you partake of the Lord's Supper in your church? Do you take it casually, wishing secretly that they would hurry and get it over with? Or do you spend time searching your heart?

You may say, what difference does it make? Well, Beloved, it could be the difference between strength and weakness, sickness and health, or life and death. We'll look at it tomorrow.

Honoring the Covenant

WHAT IS THE PURPOSE of the Lord's Supper or, as some call it, Holy Communion? As Paul tells us in 1 Corinthians 11:25,26, it is done in remembrance of Christ. We are remembering the covenant that was instituted by Jesus, the Messenger of the Covenant.

This New Covenant is an agreement, a confederacy by which God and man become one. Wonder of wonders! But it is even more than that; it is also a proclamation of the Lord's death until He comes again.

Now then, since you, in taking the Lord's Supper, are acknowledging the necessity of Christ's death for your sins, how can you partake without examining yourself and seeing if there be any wicked way in you? What happens if we do not judge ourselves and just lightly, routinely, take communion? God says, "For this reason many among you are weak and sick, and a number sleep" (1 Corinthians 11:30).

Because the Corinthians would not judge themselves rightly, God had to discipline them (1 Corinthians 11:31,32). Some experienced a bodily weakness. Are you weak, and yet do not know why? Or are you sick, and doctors cannot find out why?

Now listen carefully, Beloved, so you do not misquote me. I am *not* saying that *all* weaknesses and *all* sicknesses are due to unconfessed, unjudged sin when taking communion. But I am saying that weakness or sickness may be due to that! Sin can take an awful toll upon our bodies! As a matter of fact, sin unchecked, sin undealt with, can bring premature death. This is what Paul means when he says, "and a number sleep."

Now, let me clarify one more point. If a person dies at a young age, it does not necessarily mean that God has taken him home early because he has broken covenant. Who can determine, then, the reason for a person's early death? Only God or the believer who dies. But for all of us, these words are a warning of the seriousness of entering into covenant with the Lord.

Beloved, why not take a few minutes alone with your Lord Jesus Christ and ask Him to reveal to you any ways in which you are failing to honor Him as your Covenant Partner. Write down His thoughts to you that they might be kept as a reminder of His will and His way for you.

Commit to Being Faithful

I WILL NEVER FORGET that day in a chapel service when we were told about a man of God who had gotten involved in an adulterous affair. I was sick and I was afraid. As soon as the service ended, I ran to the prayer room and locked the door. I opened my Bible to 1 John 5:14: "This is the confidence which we have before Him, that, if we ask anything according to His will, He hears us."

Then I stretched out on the floor of that prayer room, flat on my face, and cried out to God, "O Father, You know that I am capable of doing the same thing that man did. You know the weakness of my flesh. O Father, You have to promise now that if I ever walk away from You, if I ever say 'Leave me alone, I don't care anymore,' that You will kill me and take me home early rather than let me bring shame to Your name. O Father, do You see the fourteenth verse . . . well, I have asked according to Your will, so You must answer me."

At that time I knew nothing about covenant; I was but a babe in Christ. But God knew my heart, and I knew His holiness.

I think sometimes, Beloved, many Christians have a warped understanding of God's love. They don't know how to balance or reconcile it with His holiness, justice, and righteousness or with the rest of His character. It is hard for them to conceive of God taking a life prematurely; yet Deuteronomy 32:39 says, "It is I who put to death and give life."

God is a holy God, and His will for His people is holiness. When you came to Him, Beloved, it was to make Him Lord of your life, to be conformed into His image. Is there anything stopping you? If there is, forsake it, give it to Him. Whatever it is, it's not worth missing His blessing, His "Well done, My good and faithful servant."

Or possibly you, like me, have a fear of slipping, of falling, of getting caught in a sin. If so, then fall on your face and tell Him all about it.

Turn to God

ONE DAY AFTER I had been studying covenant for some time, I nearly came unglued. I was reading through the Old Testament and came upon Jeremiah 34. But before we look at what thrilled me so, let me refresh your memory about the Old Testament word for covenant so you can appreciate my excitement. It is the word *bereeth*, and it means "a compact or an agreement made by passing through pieces of flesh." Now don't forget that definition because in the next few days it is absolutely going to give you spiritual goose bumps. At least it will if I can capture the thrill and awesomeness of it all on paper!

Jeremiah 34 tells how the word of the Lord had come to Jeremiah for His people. Remember, Jeremiah prophesied and warned the Southern Kingdom of Judah right up through the time of their captivity. Judah had already seen Israel go into Assyrian captivity because of breaking God's covenant, but that did not seem to deter her from her own wicked ways. Oh, why is it that we will not listen to God?

Judah had profaned God's name, and thus the word of the Lord came: " 'Behold, I am proclaiming a release to you,' declares the LORD, 'to the sword, to the pestilence, and to the famine; and I will make you a terror to all the kingdoms of the earth. And I will give the men who have transgressed My covenant, who have not fulfilled the words of the covenant which they made before Me, when they cut the calf in two and passed between its parts—the officials of Judah, and the officials of Jerusalem, the court officers, and the priests, and all the people of the land, who passed between the parts of the calf—and I will give them into the hand of their enemies and into the hand of those who seek their life' " (Jeremiah 34:17-20).

I wonder what God will do to America if she does not turn from her wicked ways? Did we not, in a sense, enter into an agreement with God when we promised religious freedom in our constitution and when we put on our coins, "In God we trust"?

How long will it be before we repent or before God brings sword, pestilence, famine, and enemies upon our land? And remember, when or if judgment comes, it must begin at the house of God (1 Peter 4:17)!

Living in Covenant

AFTER ROBE, BELT, and girdle had been exchanged, and those entering into covenant had cut an animal in two, laid its parts on the ground, stood between the parts and vowed, "God do so and more to me if I break this covenant," the next thing they did was to walk through the pieces in the form of a figure eight. This was called a "walk into death," and it signified that they were dying to their rights, to independent living. Now they would no longer live for themselves, for their own pleasure, but they would live for their covenant partner.

Was this not what Christ was calling His disciples to, and was this not why so many walked away? "And He summoned the multitude with His disciples, and said to them, 'If anyone wishes to come after Me, let him deny himself, and take up his cross, and follow Me' " (Mark 8:34).

I believe that what we call the "call to discipleship" is really . . . equally . . . inseparably a call to salvation, a call to enter into the New Covenant. When I deny myself, am I not dying to my rights? And when I take up my cross, am I not walking into death? And when I follow Him, am I not walking His way and not mine? Can you see the parallel?

O Beloved, do you ever wonder if we are really presenting the gospel as Jesus, our Lord, would have it presented? I think sometimes we are so eager to get decisions, head counts, names on the roll, or baptisms for our church records that we present a watered-down gospel which in essence is not really the gospel! For when the gospel is truly believed, it is unto salvation, not only from sin's penalty but also from sin's power and, someday, from sin's presence.

True salvation is a walk into death—we are crucified with Christ so that old things pass away and all things become new! It is saying, "I turn from my old way of life to your way, God . . . to serve You, the true and living God, and to wait for Your Son from heaven" (1 Thessalonians 1:9,10).

Beloved, when did you walk into death? Have you ever told God that you were willing to deny yourself, to take up your cross, to follow Him, to lose your life for His sake and the gospel's? When?

God's Covenant With Abraham

UNTIL I UNDERSTOOD the customs of covenant, I never fully appreciated what happened to Abraham on the day of his salvation.

Remember how, in Genesis 12, God called Abraham out of Ur of the Chaldees and promised to bless him and make him a great nation? Abraham was 75 at the time, and his wife Sarah (then called Sarai) was only ten years younger. Well, time passed, year after year, and this man who was to be the father of many was still without a son. Then one day Abraham asked God about his apparent sterility. Would God have Abraham's servant Eliezer be his heir since Abraham was childless?

> Then behold, the word of the LORD came to him, saying, "This man will not be your heir; but one who shall come forth from your own body, he shall be your heir." And He took him outside and said, "Now look toward the heavens, and count the stars, if you are able to count them." And He said to him, "So shall your descendants [seed] be." Then he believed in the LORD; and He reckoned it to him as righteousness (Genesis 15:4-6).

This was the day of Abraham's salvation, the day according to Romans 4 and Galatians 3 that righteousness was imputed to Abraham's account by faith. When God made the promise of the seed, then Abraham *believed* God.

The word for believe in Genesis 15:6 carries the idea of an unqualified committal of oneself to another. This is the belief that saves. It is not just a mental assent, but rather a belief by which a person surrenders himself completely to a truth that he has heard.

And what truth had God shown Abraham? It was the promise of a seed. "Now the promises were spoken to Abraham and to his seed. He does not say, 'And to seeds,' as referring to many, but rather to one, 'And to your seed,' that is, Christ" (Galatians 3:16).

Christ was the seed. It was about Christ that Abraham believed. And so God reckoned him righteous, and that very day God made a covenant with Abraham. We'll look at it tomorrow.

God's Covenant Stands

WITH THE PROMISE of a seed to Abraham also went the promise of a land. So, after God reckoned Abraham as righteous, Abraham had another question for God. (What a neat relationship they had! It's the kind you and I are supposed to have, where we talk out everything with God. God loves it!)

Abraham said: " 'O Lord GOD, how may I know that I shall possess it?' So He said to him, 'Bring Me a three year old heifer, and a three year old female goat, and a three year old ram, and a turtledove, and a young pigeon.' Then he brought all these to Him and cut them in two, and laid each half opposite the other; but he did not cut the birds. [Now don't ask me why he didn't cut the birds because I don't know.] . . . And it came about when the sun had set, that it was very dark, and behold, there appeared a smoking oven and a flaming torch which passed between these pieces. On that day the LORD made a covenant with Abram" (Genesis 15:8-10,17,18).

Do you know who that smoking oven and flaming torch was? It was the Lord. God came down in a theophany (a visible manifestation) and by Himself passed through the pieces of flesh.

He was making an unconditional covenant with Abraham . . . a covenant that would stand no matter what, a covenant that could not—would not—be broken because God had walked through the pieces Himself! It was a covenant that guaranteed that one day the Messiah, the Messenger of the Covenant, would come, and, with His coming, all the nations of the earth would be blessed, including the Gentiles. "And if you belong to Christ, then you are Abraham's offspring [seed], heirs according to promise" (Galatians 3:29).

What a day that was when God passed through the pieces!

But if it was a covenant, didn't two have to pass through the pieces? Was man not also to walk through the pieces?

O Beloved, I can hardly wait to share with you tomorrow what God showed me—all by Himself!

Outside the Veil

WHAT I WANT to share with you for the next three days, Beloved, is a most thrilling insight on the teaching of the covenant. As I sat and meditated upon this ceremonial custom of cutting covenant, I kept asking, "But, Father, in covenant *both* parties had to walk through the pieces of flesh. You walked through the pieces, but—" and then the answer came! It was so beautiful I could hardly contain myself! I saw it all, and then "the Lamb of God" took on even a deeper meaning.

The mysteries of the New Covenant were laid out for us thousands of years ago when Moses, by God's command, erected the tabernacle. To appreciate covenant, you must be aware of how the tabernacle was constructed. The book of Hebrews tells us that the earthly tabernacle was patterned after God's throne in heaven. Just as the priests were to serve as "a copy and shadow of the heavenly things," so "Moses was warned by God when he was about to erect the tabernacle; for, 'SEE,' He says, 'THAT YOU MAKE all things ACCORDING TO THE PATTERN WHICH WAS SHOWN YOU ON THE MOUNTAIN'" (Hebrews 8:5).

"Now when these things have been thus prepared, the priests are continually entering the outer tabernacle, performing the divine worship, but into the second [the Holy of Holies] only the high priest enters, once a year, not without taking blood, which he offers for himself and for the sins of the people committed in ignorance. The Holy Spirit is signifying this, that *the way into the holy place* [Holy of Holies] *has not yet been disclosed*" (Hebrews 9:6-8, emphasis added).

The veil in the temple was that which separated the Ark of the Covenant (a picture of God's throne) from the people. Only once a year, on the Day of Atonement, could the high priest enter beyond the veil to appear in the presence of God for the people. The people themselves could not enter into God's presence. A priest had to go for them. They were shut out by the veil. And what a veil it was! Josephus, the Jewish historian, said it would take two teams of oxen pulling from opposite directions to tear the almost four-inch thick veil apart.

The only way into God's presence was through the veil. But man could not enter. He was shut out from direct communion with God!

JUNE 22

Entering Through the Veil

NOW, WHAT DOES ALL this mean to us as regards covenant—walking through the pieces of the flesh of an animal cut in two, the tabernacle, the veil that separated the Holy Place from the Holy of Holies?

"It was now about the sixth hour, and darkness fell over the whole land until the ninth hour" (Luke 23:44). As Jesus hung on the cross, the Judean Jews filled the temple area. It was the Passover. Family after family were slaying their Passover lambs. Suddenly there was a cry—a cry from Golgotha that reached the portals of heaven and then reverberated through Jerusalem's man-made tabernacle as "the veil of the temple was torn in two from top to bottom, and the earth shook; and the rocks were split" (Matthew 27:51).

There it stood, open to all who would look, never to be hidden from man's sight again—the Ark of the Covenant! The veil hung limp, ripped in two by some unseen, supernatural hands. What had once been shut to man was now open, for the veil that kept man out had been torn in two.

"Therefore, brethren, we have confidence to enter the holy place [the Holy of Holies] by the blood of Jesus, by a new and living way which He inaugurated for us *through the veil, that is, His flesh*" (Hebrews 10:19,20, emphasis added).

Now can you understand the cry of John the Baptist? "Behold, the Lamb of God who takes away the sin of the world!" (John 1:29). God had a Passover Lamb—a Lamb without spot or blemish. Now it was the fourteenth day of Nisan, the day to slay the Lamb, and the Lamb was slain. There He hung, the covenant sacrifice, the veil of His flesh ripped in two for you and me.

God has laid out the pieces. We are no longer separated from the Holy of Holies. Behold the Lamb and walk through the pieces into the very presence of the Almighty God Himself! And cry out, "My Lord and my God!"

True Surrender

THERE HE HUNG, Jesus, the Christ, the Lamb of God, the veil rent in two. Truly He is the Way, and the Truth, and the Life, and no one comes to the Father but *through* Him (John 14:6). There is no other way to enter into God's presence except through the rent veil of His flesh. Now, through His death, the way into the Holy of Holies has been disclosed (Hebrews 9:8). Now, by the blood of Jesus, man can enter that place with confidence and without fear of judgment (Hebrews 10:10).

The Way has been made. Now it is up to man to say to God, "By faith I walk into death—death to my old way of life, death to my independent way of life, death to my rights." This, Beloved, is the true repentance, the true surrender, that brings genuine salvation. Have you ever walked this way, through the pieces of the Lamb of God?

Not only was Jesus the Way, but He was also the Truth. He spoke the truth, but many did not believe. Instead they believed the devil, the father of lies, who does not stand in the truth because there is no truth in him. When you walk into a whole new realm, the realm of truth, of reality, you leave the darkness of his lies and deception behind because finally you know what is right—what God says in His Word.

Jesus, the Covenant Lamb of God, the Way, the Truth, and the Life. He is life, for "unless you eat the flesh of the Son of Man and drink His blood, you have no life in yourselves" (John 6:53). For His flesh is true food and His blood is true drink; he who eats the bread of life shall live because of Him (John 6:55,57).

Yes, there He hung—the Way, the Truth, the Life. The Way you should walk; the Truth you should believe; the Life by which you should live.

Have you gone His way, believed His truth, lived His life? When did you walk into covenant?

JUNE 24

Becoming One With Jesus

AFTER HAVING WALKED into death by passing through the parts of the animal, the two cutting covenant would stand opposite one another and make a cut in their own flesh. Usually they would cut their wrists and then, clasping hands, would mingle their blood to signify that two had become one. No longer were they to live or act independently of one another. What affected one would now affect the other.

Remember the day when a man's word was his bond, when what was vowed with the lips was as binding as any written contract? Remember when you could ask, "Will you shake on it?" and seal an agreement with a handshake? Many feel that the handshake had its origins in the cutting of the wrists and the mingling of the blood.

It was after the Passover that Jesus, having inaugurated the New Covenant, prayed to the Father before He went to the cross. At Calvary the cut of covenant would take place as His executioners pierced His hands and His feet—and two would become one. Our Lord's prayer to His Father that night was on behalf of those whom God had given Him out of the world. His prayer was that "they may be one, even as We are . . . that they may all be one; even as Thou, Father, art in Me, and I in Thee, that they also may be in Us . . . that the love wherewith Thou didst love Me may be in them, and I in them" (John 17:11,21,26).

What bearing would it have on the body of Jesus Christ if every member were to realize the full implication of what it means to be one with Christ, to fully realize the import of Paul's words: "Or do you not know that your body is a temple of the Holy Spirit who is in you, whom you have from God, and that you are not your own?" (1 Corinthians 6:19.)

Do you know, Beloved, that if you are His by covenant, you are no longer your own? And knowing that you are not your own, how do you live? What do you do with the members of your body which are now the members of Christ?

The Blessings of Covenant

HOW COMPLETE WAS this oneness between covenant partners? How far did it extend? To what extent am I now one with my Covenant Partner? What, besides myself, is now His? And what, besides Himself, is mine? *All*—all that we both possess.

After they had passed through the pieces and mingled their blood, the covenant partners would give each other "the blessings." Each would give to the other an accounting of all his resources, for these resources were now at the disposal of the covenant partner should they be needed!

And so when we enter into covenant with our Lord and our God, all that is His becomes ours. Thus comes the sure promise of Philippians 4:19: "And my God shall supply all your needs according to His riches in glory in Christ Jesus." Because we are in covenant with Him, we are now "heirs; heirs of God, and joint-heirs with Christ" (Romans 8:17 KJV).

This is why, after the inauguration of the New Covenant at the Last Passover, Jesus told His beloved disciples: "Truly, truly, I say to you, if you shall ask the Father for anything, He will give it to you in My name. Until now you have asked for nothing in My name; ask, and you will receive, that your joy may be made full" (John 16:23,24).

If you are His, Beloved, then this is your right, your privilege of covenant, a blessing to be appropriated by faith. What do you need? What do you lack? It is yours for the believing, for the asking, for all that is His is now yours.

If you have not (and you are not asking just to gratify your own lusts), then it is only because you ask not (James 4:2,3). What is His is yours, because you are His.

Members of a New Family

HOW WELL THOSE of Jesus' day understood the principles of covenant! With them it was a full commitment that penetrated every area of their lives. A covenant entered into was a covenant to be kept!

This commitment is clearly seen as we look at the days of the early church. Being in covenant put the believer into a covenant relationship not only with God, but also with the whole family of God! It was a relationship that took on deeper ties than those of flesh and blood.

One day when Jesus was told that His mother and brothers had arrived, "He said, 'Who are My mother and My brothers? . . . Whoever does the will of God, he is My brother and sister and mother'" (Mark 3:33,35).

When we enter into covenant with God, we come into a new family where we are members one of another. It is to be a relationship of such depth that if one member suffers, we all suffer—and if one rejoices, we all rejoice—for it is a relationship that puts away independent living (1 Corinthians 12:12-26).

The book of Acts tells us how well the early church understood and lived by this principle. "And all those who had believed were together, and had all things in common; and they began selling their property and possessions, and were sharing them with all, as anyone might have need. And day by day continuing with one mind in the temple, and breaking bread from house to house, they were taking their meals together with gladness and sincerity of heart, praising God, and having favor with all the people. And the Lord was adding to their number day by day those who were being saved" (Acts 2:44-47).

Some have said this was communism; others have called it communal living. But neither is right. It was simply covenant!

Let me give you something to meditate upon, Beloved, and as you meditate, write down your insights for future reference. If you were to live this way, how would it change your relationship with other Christians?

Meeting the Needs of Others

HOW COMMITTED SHOULD we be in our relationship with other members of Christ's body? As we have seen, those in covenant held all things in common so that if one had any need, whatever his covenant partner possessed was at his disposal without questions and without reservation.

In Acts 4:32-34 we see this attitude being lived out in the early church: "And the congregation of those who believed were of one heart and soul; and not one of them claimed that anything belonging to him was his own; but all things were common property to them. And with great power the apostles were giving witness to the resurrection of the Lord Jesus, and abundant grace was upon them all. For there was not a needy person among them."

When Paul wrote to the believers in Corinth, he had to remind them that they were to abound in the gracious work of giving. "But just as you abound in everything, in faith and utterance and knowledge and in all earnestness and in the love we inspired in you, see that you abound in this gracious work also. . . . For this is not for the ease of others and for your affliction, but by way of equality—at this present time your abundance being a supply for their want, that their abundance also may become a supply for your want" (2 Corinthians 8:7, 13-14).

Is it right for us to store our funds for emergencies and, in doing so, ignore the immediate needs of our brothers and sisters in Christ? If Christ has promised to supply all our needs because we are in covenant with Him, then do we need to fear that if we meet another's needs, we will have nothing left for ourselves in a day of want? Should any member of the body of Christ ever have to seek financial aid outside the church? For what are we given an abundance? For our own pleasures or so that we might supply another's want? Which do you think it is?

Think of what it would mean to the body of Jesus Christ, and to the work of Jesus Christ, if we were to live in the fullness of covenant!

J U N E   2 8

Engraved on His Hands!

HAVE THERE EVER been times when you have wondered if God had forgotten you or abandoned you?

After the covenant parties had made a cut upon their bodies and mingled their blood, and after they had shared the blessings with each other, they would then seek a way to seal that covenant cut. They would rub something into the wound in order to cause a permanent scar that would be a constant reminder of the fact that they were now responsible to one another. If the cut had been in the wrist, every movement of the hand—dressing, eating, working—would remind them of their covenant partner and of their obligation to care for him forever.

I am sure there have been times of difficulty, stress, loneliness, and testing in many of your lives when you may have wondered if the Lord had forsaken you. Possibly you have cried out in need and have not seen help forthcoming immediately. Or maybe you have felt desperately alone, confused, and helpless because the arm of flesh upon which you leaned has been taken away in death. The loving arms of protection are gone, the counsel of another has been silenced, and you feel horribly alone.

"But Zion said, 'The LORD has forsaken me, and the Lord has forgotten me.' Can a woman forget her nursing child, and have no compassion on the son of her womb? Even these may forget, but I will not forget you. Behold, I have inscribed you on the palms of My hands" (Isaiah 49:14-16).

So the next time you feel forsaken or horribly alone, "Reach here your finger, and see My hands; and reach here your hand, and put it into My side; and be not unbelieving, but believing" (John 20:27).

Remember, He has engraved you on His palms, and "He Himself has said, 'I will never DESERT YOU, NOR WILL I EVER FORSAKE YOU,' so that we confidently say, 'THE LORD IS MY HELPER, I WILL NOT BE AFRAID. WHAT SHALL MAN DO TO ME?'" (Hebrews 13:5,6).

Endure "as seeing Him who is unseen." Overwhelmingly conquer through Him who loved *you.* For nothing shall be able to separate you from the love of God, which is in Christ Jesus our Lord (Hebrews 11:27; Romans 8:37,39).

You Have His Name!

THE NEXT THING that took place in the covenant was the changing of names. To call another's name or to bear his name gave you both the authority that went with that name and authority over the one whom you named. In covenant you would take on, in addition to your own name, the name of your covenant partner. We see a picture of this in the covenant of marriage where the bride takes the name of her husband.

After God cut covenant with Abram, the Lord appeared to him and said, "As for Me, behold, My covenant is with you, and you shall be the father of a multitude of nations. No longer shall your name be called Abram, But your name shall be Abraham; for I will make you the father of a multitude of nations" (Genesis 17:4,5).

When God changed Abram's name, He put the breath sound of His own name ("the heth," as it is called) into Abram's name—Abram became Abraham. He did the same to Sarai's name. "Then God said to Abraham, 'As for Sarai your wife, you shall not call her name Sarai, but Sarah shall be her name'" (Genesis 17:15).

And thus to all Christians comes the promise of a new name, as John records the words of the Lord in Revelation 2:17: "To him who overcomes [1 John 5:5], to him will I give some of the hidden manna, and I will give him a white stone, and a new name written on the stone which no one knows but he who receives it."

And even now, do we not bear a new name, the name Christian? Christian means "little Christ." How well do we carry that name? Can the world see His authority *over* us and *in* us? Has He not breathed into us also the breath of life and thus the authority of His name?

" 'As the Father has sent Me, I also send you.' And when He had said this, He breathed on them, and said to them, 'Receive the Holy Spirit. If you forgive the sins of any, their sins have been forgiven them; if you retain the sins of any, they have been retained'" (John 20:21-23).

"Peter said, 'I do not possess silver and gold, but what I do have I give to you: In the name of Jesus Christ the Nazarene—walk!'" (Acts 3:6).

You have His name—live like it!

The Covenant Meal

AFTER ALL THESE THINGS had taken place, those cutting covenant sat down to partake of a covenant meal. At this meal they took bread, broke it, and then placed it into the mouth of their covenant partner with these words, "You are eating me." Then a cup of wine was offered to the covenant partner along with the words, "This is my blood; you are drinking me." Often, unless they were Jews, the covenant partners mingled drops of their own blood in with the wine.

Does all this have a faintly familiar ring? Remember the little ceremony at the wedding reception? Remember wondering if you should order the photographer's ridiculous shot of you with your mouth wide open while your mate fed you a piece of wedding cake? Did you ever wonder where that custom came from? Now you know. Isn't it beautiful! It is a picture of giving yourself to another—unconditionally, totally, eternally.

An unqualified committal of oneself to another—this, Beloved, is covenant. This is salvation. They are one and the same. This is what God means when He says, "Believe in the Lord Jesus, and you shall be saved" (Acts 16:31). It means to give yourself to Christ unconditionally, without qualification; to cease from your independent living; to become one with Christ, bone of His bone and flesh of His flesh.

Oh, there is so much more to share with you on covenant. There are so many rich, precious gems that will so graciously adorn your salvation as their facets brilliantly reflect the light of truth. How I look forward to sharing them with you in the coming month.

But for today, Beloved, let me ask you: Have you drunk of His cup? Have you partaken of the Bread of Heaven? Or will you, like so many others, walk away? Many have. Many have walked away after realizing that salvation is a denial of self, a taking up of the cross, and a life to be spent following Him. Many have walked away because His words are difficult sayings—too hard for them to believe.

Have you believed?

JULY

I Call You Friend

Covenant, Part 2

Do you feel lame in both feet when it comes to being what you should be for God? Does it seem that you are destined to be nothing, nobody? Well, this month together we will see why this thinking is not to be! I can't wait to walk through these truths with you!

Becoming Friends With God

DARE HE SPEAK to God? Did he have any right to be so bold, so presumptuous? Was he not but dust and ashes? Abraham had no trouble in challenging men, but to challenge God?

He felt sick. How could a righteous God do this? It didn't seem fair. What was he to do? Keep silent? Just submit? Suddenly it hurt. This was his Covenant Partner, and he questioned His justice. Should he speak his mind and risk God's anger or keep silent and be disillusioned? Was he just to be a "yes-man" to God? Was this what God wanted from their relationship?

As Abraham walked with his three unexpected guests, he reasoned that these three men had sought him out. He did not seek them. Hadn't the Lord even broached the subject when He said, "Shall I hide from Abraham what I am about to do?" (Genesis 18:17).

Now they stood alone, face-to-face. The other two had gone. Abraham continued to reason within himself, "Surely the Lord did not mean for me to be a mere pawn, otherwise why would He even bother to tell me what He was going to do to Sodom and Gomorrah?"

Suddenly it was too much. This was not the God Abraham had worshiped. Something was wrong. He had to speak. Abraham had to know how his God could do such a thing!

"Wilt Thou indeed sweep away the righteous with the wicked? Suppose there are fifty righteous within the city? Far be it from Thee to do such a thing, to slay the righteous with the wicked" (Genesis 18:23-25).

Later, as Abraham rehearsed all that followed after he challenged God with his "Far be it from Thee," he smiled. So this was what it meant to be the friend of God, instead of being just His slave! "No longer do I call you slaves; for the slave does not know what his master is doing; but I have called you friends" (John 15:15).

Those chosen by God—those in covenant with God—had recourse with God. They did not have to fear God's anger or suppress their questions about the justice of His ways. They could talk to God. They could reason with Him. They were God's friends!

The Strength of True Friendship

FRIEND—WE SAY IT so casually, so loosely. How far we have digressed from the original meaning of the word! "Friend" was the term used to describe those who had become partners through a blood covenant, and it was really quite a costly title.

As we saw during our study last month, the final step in entering into covenant was to partake of a covenant meal. During this meal the partners would feed each other a piece of bread and say, "This is my flesh. You are eating me." Then, as they offered each other a cup, they said, "This is my blood. You are drinking me." After having performed the rites of the covenant ceremony, they were known as "blood brothers" and from then on they would call each other "friend." The word "friend" was synonymous with "blood brother." There was no other relationship in the East stronger or more binding than that of friend/blood brother.

In the East today, Abraham is known as Ibraheen el Khaleel, Abraham the friend, or as Khaleel Allah, the friend of God. And so he was! For in the Old Testament Abraham is the only one called "the friend of God."

Exodus 33:11 tells us that God spoke "to Moses face to face, just as a man speaks to his friend," but the word for "friend" in this verse means companion or neighbor. It is not the same word for "friend" used to describe God's relationship with Abraham. Why? Because God had entered into a covenant with Abraham, as we saw in Genesis 15, when He appeared as "a smoking oven and a flaming torch which passed between" the pieces of the flesh of the animals. "On that day the LORD made a covenant with Abram" (Genesis 15:17,18).

Throughout the world and the ages, men who were friends because of a blood covenant were to be ready to give their very lives for one another or even to give that which was dearer than life itself—their sons.

Can you see now how far we have departed from the true meaning of the word "friend"?

The Scars of Covenant

FRIEND—THE TERM OF COVENANT. Remember what I said about this friendship? Those who were in covenant with one another were to be ready to lay down their very lives for each other. They had cut their flesh, mingled the blood from their wounds, and then rubbed a substance into their cuts in order to leave permanent scars to serve as a constant reminder of their commitment and obligations to their covenant partner.

For all eternity our Christ shall bear in His body the brand marks of covenant, marks made that day when they pierced His hands and His feet and put a spear into His side. His resurrected body will eternally bear those marks of covenant. Did not Thomas testify to this when, doubting the Lord's resurrection, he said, "Unless I shall see in His hands the imprint of the nails, and put my finger into the place of the nails, and put my hand into His side, I will not believe" (John 20:25)? Then one day, there Jesus stood before him saying, "Reach here your finger, and see My hands; and reach here your hand, and put it into My side; and be not unbelieving, but believing." And Thomas answered, "My Lord and my God!" (John 20:27,28).

I wonder, in a way, if Thomas's doubt was not sort of a picture of Israel's! How awesome are the words of Zechariah's prophecy regarding the second coming of the Messiah, Jesus the Christ.

"And I will pour out on the house of David and on the inhabitants of Jerusalem, the Spirit of grace and of supplication, so that they will look on Me whom they have pierced" (Zechariah 12:10).

"And one will say to him, 'What are these wounds between your arms [literally, hands]?' Then he will say, 'Those with which I was wounded in the house of my friends'" (Zechariah 13:6).

God's covenant with Abraham was a covenant with Israel. He was wounded by His friends for His friends! What love! What a Blood Brother! Someday Israel will realize it and weep!

Have you realized it yet? Stretch forth your hand and put it into His wounds, before it's too late and you weep in the shame of doubt!

JULY 4

The Test

COVENANT COMMITMENT was unconditional. It was so deep that a friend would lay down his life for his blood brother or give that which was even dearer than his own life; he would give his own son. To a man of the East, there was nothing more precious than his seed, his son, the one who would carry his name and his life into the next generation.

God had cut covenant with Abraham and passed through the pieces. They had taken on one another's name. Abram became Abraham as God put the "heth" from His name into Abra-h-am. And then God had taken on Abraham's name by calling Himself "the God of Abraham."

Then the day came. The day when God tested the strength of Abraham's covenant commitment to Him! God said:

> "Abraham!" And he said, "Here I am." And He said, "Take now your son, your only son, whom you love, Isaac, and go to the land of Moriah; and offer him there as a burnt offering on one of the mountains of which I will tell you." So Abraham rose early in the morning and saddled his donkey, and took two of his young men with him and Isaac his son; and he split wood for the burnt offering, and arose, and went to the place of which God had told him. . . . And Abraham built the altar there, and arranged the wood, and bound his son Isaac, and laid him on the altar on top of the wood. And Abraham stretched out his hand, and took the knife to slay his son. And the angel of the LORD called to him from heaven, and said, "Abraham, Abraham!" And he said, "Here I am." *And he said, "Do not stretch out your hand against the lad, and do nothing to him; for now I know that you fear God, since you have not withheld your son, your only son, from Me"* (Genesis 22:1-3,9-12, emphasis added).

Beloved, has God ever tested you to see if you were willing to put on the altar that which is as dear to you as life itself?

How did you respond? Were you willing? If not, why not?

Lovingkindness . . .
Covenant's Promise

MANY TIMES COVENANT agreements extended beyond individuals to their families. This was the type of covenant that God made with Abraham. God would become not only the God of Abraham, but also of Isaac and of Jacob. Abraham's descendants would know the benefits of God's covenant with Abraham.

Have you ever thought about that term used so often throughout God's Word, the term "lovingkindness"? It is a covenant term. Listen to these precious words of David:

> But the lovingkindness of the LORD is from everlasting to everlasting on those who fear Him, and His righteousness to children's children, to those who keep His covenant, and who remember His precepts to do them (Psalm 103:17,18).

Lovingkindness—the pledge of the promises and benefits of covenant not only to Abraham, but just as surely to Abraham's seed.

Jehoshaphat, king of Judah, knew that because of God's covenant with Abraham and his seed, lovingkindness was also his. And how he needed it! Word had just come that the sons of Moab and of Ammon had massed together to war against him. So Jehoshaphat called the people of Judah together to seek help from the Lord. And when they were all gathered, what did Jehoshaphat do but remind God of His covenant relationship with Abraham and, thus, with him because he was part of Abraham's seed.

Listen to his words of covenant faith: "Didst Thou not, O *our* God, drive out the inhabitants of this land before Thy people Israel, and give it to the descendants of Abraham Thy *friend* forever?" (2 Chronicles 20:7, emphasis added).

God loves to extend the lovingkindness of His covenant promises to Abraham's descendants. "And if you belong to Christ, then you are Abraham's offspring, heirs according to promise" (Galatians 3:29).

Where do you run in your time of need? Why not cry out to your covenant-keeping God? He heard Jehoshaphat. Will He not hear you?

The Sign

HAVE YOU EVER WONDERED why on earth God chose circumcision to be a sign of His covenant with Abraham? I know that to some it has been a matter of embarrassment. I have even had precious women come to me and ask in a whisper, "What did Jewish women do? They couldn't be circumcised! How, then, could they be included in the covenant promise? Or weren't they included?"

The word of God to Abraham had been, " 'This is My covenant, which you shall keep, between Me and you and your descendants after you: every male among you shall be circumcised. And you shall be circumcised in the flesh of your foreskin; and it shall be the sign of the covenant between Me and you' " (Genesis 17:10,11).

There it was, ordered by God—every male to be circumcised in the flesh of his foreskin. But why there? And why did God make it such a cut that women could not participate in it? These are probably questions that many have had in their heart but have never verbalized. Well, I can relate to those questions, dear one, because I wondered the same thing.

How beautiful it was for me to see God's answer. Let me share it with you, for I know it will thrill you. But first let's talk a moment about these bodies that God created for us. You know, when God made man, He said, "And it was good." He made every part of us—body, soul, and spirit. So I wonder why we often look upon them with disgust or shame. Surely that is not from God, nor is it spiritual, even though some would prudishly consider it to be.

Why circumcision? Well, when men wanted to show that they were extending their covenant to their descendants, to their seed, they made a cut on their bodies *closest to the site of paternity*. And so God required a cut in the foreskin as a reminder that when a man's seed came forth, be it a sperm that would produce a male or a female, that child was under the protection and bonds of covenant.

Isn't that beautiful? It was God's good, perfect, beautiful, and holy design.

Where Do Your Loyalties Lie?

ONE OF THE MOST beautiful illustrations regarding covenants between families is found in the story of Jonathan's son, Mephibosheth. Oh, how it will minister security to your soul. I can hardly wait to share it with you in the days to come!

In 1 Samuel 18 we have the first account of the covenant made between David and Jonathan. After that covenant was made, King Saul, Jonathan's father, would not permit David to return to his home. David now became one of Saul's men of war.

David's victories at war brought him great acclaim from the people, and jealousy reared its ugly head. "Now Saul was afraid of David, for the LORD was with him but had departed from Saul" (1 Samuel 18:12). From that time on Saul could not rest. "Now Saul told Jonathan his son and all his servants to put David to death. But Jonathan, Saul's son, greatly delighted in David" (1 Samuel 19:1).

Now remember, David and Jonathan were in covenant together. They had made an agreement to protect one another, to take on one another's enemies. Where would Jonathan's loyalty lie? It had to be with David, even above his natural loyalty to his father. This was covenant—a relationship that superseded all others.

> So Jonathan told David, saying "Saul my father is seeking to put you to death. Now therefore, please be on guard in the morning, and stay in a secret place and hide yourself. And I will go out and stand beside my father in the field where you are, and I will speak with my father about you; if I find out anything, then I shall tell you" (1 Samuel 19:2,3).

Before we go any further, Beloved, let me ask you, does your covenant with Christ have preeminence over all other relationships (Matthew 10:37)? You are to live "so that He Himself might come to have first place in everything" (Colossians 1:18). Anything less is disloyalty, disobedience, and idolatry.

The Promises Stand

TENSION HOVERS IN THE AIR like fog, giving a haziness to the covenant made in days gone by. David, fully aware of Saul's intentions and knowing "there is hardly a step between me and death" (1 Samuel 20:3), pleads the promises of the covenant made with Jonathan. "Therefore deal kindly with your servant, for you have brought your servant into a covenant of the LORD with you" (1 Samuel 20:8).

But if David is apprehensive, so also is Jonathan! Jonathan knows God has left his father. He knows that Israel is David's, not Saul's. Will David, as the king, remember his covenant with Jonathan? And what will happen to Jonathan's descendants? Jonathan reassures David, but, needing assurance himself, he also pleads for another covenant—a covenant between the two houses of David and Jonathan.

> " 'And you shall not cut off your lovingkindness from my house forever, not even when the LORD cuts off every one of the enemies of David from the face of the earth.' So Jonathan made a covenant with the house of David. . . . And Jonathan made David vow again because of his love for him" (1 Samuel 20:15-17).

That night Saul's anger at Jonathan's allegiance to David throws him into a rage. When "Saul hurled his spear at him to strike him down . . . Jonathan knew that his father had decided to put David to death" (1 Samuel 20:33).

Jonathan went out to warn David. As they kissed each other and wept, Jonathan said to David, "Go in safety, inasmuch as we have sworn to each other in the name of the LORD, saying, 'The LORD will be between me and you, and between my descendants and your descendants forever' " (1 Samuel 20:42).

And so they parted, in grief but in assurance. The covenant promises stood no matter what the future held.

No matter what your trials, Beloved, the covenant holds for you as well, because when "you belong to Christ, then you are Abraham's offspring, heirs according to promise" (Galatians 3:29).

Waiting on God

THE DAYS TURN INTO WEEKS, the weeks into months as David continues to flee and Saul pursues, determined to destroy him. Saul also continues to belch out his bitterness, lashing out at those around him: "For all of you have conspired against me so that there is no one who discloses to me when my son makes a covenant with the son of Jesse [David], and there is none of you who is sorry for me or discloses to me that my son has stirred up my servant against me to lie in ambush" (1 Samuel 22:8). And even though "Saul sought him every day . . . God did not deliver him into his hand" (1 Samuel 23:14).

And what about David? How did he handle it all?

When opportunity came for David to kill Saul, he knew that he could not stretch out his hand against the man because Saul was the *Lord's anointed* (1 Samuel 24:6,10). David rested in God's sovereignty. He knew that God had anointed him rather than Saul to be king over Israel. But he also knew that he had to wait for God's timing. So when an opportunity came to kill Saul, David refused to do so (1 Samuel 24:12).

Oh, there were days of doubt as well as days of trust. The clouds of circumstances at times obliterated the reality of the presence of God's promises. David even said to himself, "Now I will perish one day by the hand of Saul" (1 Samuel 27:1). And yet the promise of God stood sure whether David *felt* the reality of it or not (2 Timothy 2:13).

The days of testing would come to an end; it was just that David did not know when! But God did!

What about you, Beloved? As I write this, I cannot help but feel that we all need this message. Too often the clouds of circumstances or feelings obscure the reality of the sun. The warmth, brightness, and resultant joy of clear sunny days are replaced by a dismal dreariness that seems to have moved in to stay.

At such times, may we remember that beyond the clouds the promises of God still shine, and those clouds will eventually be lifted. So let us daily put on "the oil of gladness instead of mourning, the mantle of praise instead of a spirit of fainting" (Isaiah 61:3).

If Only

"SAUL AND JONATHAN are dead." The words, delivered in breathless excitement, did not have the effect that the Amalekite expected. Would this not give David the throne? Saul was dead, as well as all of his sons but one!

Why his words had struck a chord of grief that began a wait of mourning rather than a chord of joy resounding an anthem of praise, he did not know. Why did David tear his clothes and weep?

The Amalekite did not understand. He did not know the heart of David. Saul had been his king before he was his enemy. Saul had been God's anointed. And his son Jonathan was David's blood brother!

Instead of being the hero who had delivered the final deathblow to the already wounded body of Saul, the Amalekite became the enemy. Suddenly he was made aware of the grievousness of his act as David asked, "How is it you were not afraid to stretch out your hand to destroy the LORD's anointed?" (2 Samuel 1:14).

It was over just like that! "David called a young man and said, 'Go, cut him down.' So he struck him and he died" (2 Samuel 1:15). Then David chanted a lament over Saul and Jonathan and told the people to teach the sons of Judah this "song of the bow" (2 Samuel 1:18).

The song was sung in Judah, but apparently never reached the ears of the one who so desperately needed to hear it—Mephibosheth, Jonathan's son. Or if he did hear it over the next bitter years of his life, he did not believe it. Part of the lament went this way: "How have the mighty fallen in the midst of battle! . . . I am distressed for you, my brother Jonathan; you have been very pleasant to me. Your love to me was more wonderful than the love of women" (2 Samuel 1:25,26).

Oh, what a difference it would have made if only Mephibosheth, Jonathan's seed, had known of the covenant cut for him when he was still in the loins of his father! But ignorance crippled him.

And it is the same today, Beloved. Multitudes have been crippled because of ignorance of the New Covenant, cut for us in the body of Jesus Christ.

"Crippled, you say? I don't understand." You will in the days ahead. Bow today and ask God to prepare your heart for His message.

Is There Hope?

CAN YOU IMAGINE what it must have been like for Saul's household when that report came?

"Saul is dead."

"Jonathan . . . what about Jonathan?"

"Jonathan is dead. And so are Abinadab and Malchishua. You must flee!"

Flee! Why would they have to flee? Possibly because only one of Saul's sons, Ish-bosheth, was left. That meant Mephibosheth was now second in line for the throne. What if David found out? Would he not kill Mephibosheth so he could have the throne of Israel?

It was enough. Mephibosheth's nurse "took him up and fled. And it happened that in her hurry to flee, he fell and became lame . . . crippled in his feet" (2 Samuel 4:4).

Mephibosheth was five years old. Old enough to remember. Old enough to grow up in bitterness. He was a prince without hope of a throne, living in Lo-debar! He belonged in a palace with servants, not in these mountains of Gilead being raised by Machir, son of Ammiel.

As the years lengthened, so, I imagine, did his bitterness as he watched the other children run and play. Sometimes it must have seemed unbearable. Crippled! Nothing but a piece of garbage. And what if David ever found out about his existence? Would David's men kill him as they had killed his uncle, Ish-bosheth (2 Samuel 4:5-12)?

Even his inheritance was gone! David was ruling Israel when *he* should have been! And so the years passed in bitterness, in fear, in disgust, in disappointment. All because Mephibosheth was ignorant of the covenant cut for him. He was crippled because of ignorance, because he fled when he did not have to!

What about you, precious one? Are you crippled because you have run away from God in fear, ignorant of the covenant cut for you? Have you been living in the poverty of Lo-debar rather than in the riches of the inheritance that belongs to those of covenant? Do you sometimes feel worthless? Is there any hope for you?

Oh, yes, you'll see in the days to come.

Are You Anxious?

WHEN MEPHIBOSHETH WAS finally summoned by King David, he apparently knew nothing of the conversation between David and Ziba, Saul's former servant. Nor did he really understand David's heart. Instead, he was overcome by a fear and a bitterness born of prejudice and of rumor—rumor which spreads like dandelion seeds, caught and carried by the winds of "have you heard," taking root wherever they land, marring the beautiful meadows of truth.

David had been thirty years old when he was anointed king over Israel at Hebron (2 Samuel 5:3,4). When he captured the stronghold of Zion, the City of David, he had said, " 'Whoever would strike the Jebusites, let him reach the lame and the blind, who are hated by David's soul, through the water tunnel.' Therefore they say, 'The blind or the lame shall not come into the house' " (2 Samuel 5:8). The word apparently spread among the people that their king despised the lame and the blind and therefore they would never be allowed in the City of David. In all probability this rumor only added to Mephibosheth's bitterness and fear.

Now that the long war between the house of Saul and the house of David had ended, "David reigned over all Israel; and David administered justice and righteousness for all his people" (2 Samuel 8:15); "and the LORD helped David wherever he went" (2 Samuel 8:14).

Ziba had been a servant in Saul's house, "and they called him to David. . . . And the king said, 'Is there not yet anyone of the house of Saul to whom I may show the kindness of God?' And Ziba said to the king, 'There is still a son of Jonathan who is crippled in both feet.' " After learning his whereabouts, "King David sent and brought him . . . from Lo-debar" (2 Samuel 9:2-5).

And so Mephibosheth came to the City of David lame in both feet.

Let me ask you a few questions for your meditation: How well do you know the One who sits upon the throne? Are you fully aware that He administers justice for all His people, or are you the victim of rumors about God? Do you feel that God would never find you acceptable, fit to enter His city, because you are lame?

Are You Fearful?

MEPHIBOSHETH LIMPED INTO David's presence. His body shook. The fear that had begun to seethe and foam in the very core of his being was about to erupt. Just as gases build in a volcano until the magma blasts its way to the surface, venting itself in the weakened rock, so Mephibosheth's fear could no longer be contained. Maybe relief would come when he prostrated himself on the floor before David's throne. Maybe that would silence the tremors.

Suddenly it was as if he were five again. He could hear the frantic shouts. "Saul and Jonathan are dead!" His five-year-old mind was confused. And then it came, that awful, excruciating pain. His feet dangled uselessly. He wanted his daddy. "Hush, child. Daddy's gone, and so is Granddaddy. Hush!" The events of that day caused magma to form, and the pressure had built with time, as Mephibosheth was warned over and over again that David would surely kill him if he ever found him. Over and over he heard about the inheritance that was rightly his as Saul's grandson. Over and over he had to deal with the shame of being lame in both feet. Now he was prostrating himself before a throne that was seemingly occupied by an usurper.

It was too much. At least Mephibosheth thought it was. The fear showed. And David saw it.

Compassion and lovingkindness flowed from the throne, but Mephibosheth was totally ignorant of it. Why? *Because he did not have the facts straight.* He knew only what people who had Saul's point of view told him. Mephibosheth had lived in utter ignorance of the covenant that his father, Jonathan, had cut for him, cut for just this occasion.

And so Mephibosheth trembled in fear before the throne.

And what about you, precious one? Have you lived in ignorance and in fear of God? Have you been taught that you were heir to the throne of your life? Have you feared that if you ever gave your life to God, He would do something terrible to you like send you to Africa, or give you cancer, or kill your loved ones?

Quit shaking. You have heard lies. Those who told you such things knew nothing about the covenant cut for you when you were yet to be brought forth by incorruptible seed (1 Peter 1:23)!

Come and Dine!

And Mephibosheth, the son of Jonathan . . . came to David and fell on his face and prostrated himself. And David said, "Mephibosheth." And he said, "Here is your servant!" And David said to him, "Do not fear, for I will surely show kindness to you for the sake of your father Jonathan, and will restore to you all the land of your grandfather Saul; and you shall eat at my table regularly." Again he prostrated himself and said, "What is your servant, that you should regard a dead dog like me?" Then the king called Saul's servant Ziba, and said to him, "All that belonged to Saul and to all his house I have given to your master's grandson. . . . nevertheless Mephibosheth your master's grandson shall eat at my table regularly." . . . So Mephibosheth ate at David's table as one of the king's sons" (2 Samuel 9:6-11).

COME AND DINE at the king's table? Incredible! A dead dog eating at the king's table regularly?

The term "dead dog" was a Hebraism for an embarrassing piece of garbage. And yet here was Mephibosheth—an enemy of David's by his own choosing—a man lame in both feet, crippled from fleeing from David, a man worthless and embarrassing in his own eyes being bidden by the king to come and dine! Why?

Because of Jonathan: "I will surely show kindness to you for the sake of your father Jonathan" (2 Samuel 9:7).

Because of covenant. Mephibosheth was set apart, sanctified, because of covenant.

And so are we. "For both he that sanctifieth and they who are sanctified are all of one: for which cause he is not ashamed to call them brethren" (Hebrews 2:11 KJV). He is not ashamed to call us brethren. Can't you hear Him?

" 'Come and dine,' the Master calleth, 'Come and dine.' You can feast at Jesus' table anytime."

Oh, Beloved, have you entered into covenant with Him?

Chosen by the King

MOST OF US LIVE the better part of our lives with the subconscious dread that someday we will be caught . . . found out . . . exposed for what we *really* are. The mask will be taken off! All that we have hidden behind, all we have covered ourselves with—be it a certain personality, an image, power, success, obscurity, illness, whatever—will suddenly be taken away. We will be exposed! And we tremble at the thought. What will be the verdict?

I believe that many times these things—wisdom, might, affluence, and influence—are what keep us from being all that we were created to be. They keep us from the inheritance we have in Christ Jesus. They keep us, perhaps, from acknowledging that apart from Him we are nothing—that we are "dead dogs, crippled in both feet."

Mephibosheth, having been summoned to the king, could not help but notice the difference between David's house and Machir's of Lodebar! And it is the same when you come into the King's presence. Suddenly all you thought was so great fades into pale insignificance. As you prostrate yourself before the throne, under the King's gaze, everything is stripped away. You see yourself as nothing but a piece of garbage, a dead dog. Crippled! Crippled because you ran away!

But when the King looks at you, He sees you from an entirely different perspective—the perspective of the throne! Compassion pours from His heart of love. Dead dog? Nonsense! You are Jonathan's seed! Don't you know that a covenant was cut for you? I have searched for you, found you, and chosen you to dine with Me!

With God it does not matter what the "real you" is like: "For consider your calling, brethren, that there were not many wise according to the flesh, not many mighty, not many noble; but God has chosen the foolish things of the world to shame the wise. . . . But by His doing you are in Christ Jesus, who became to us wisdom from God, and righteousness and sanctification, and redemption" (1 Corinthians 1:26-30).

You are not a piece of garbage. You are precious in His sight. God cut a covenant for you with His Son.

"And if you belong to Christ, then you are Abraham's offspring [seed], heirs according to promise" (Galatians 3:29).

An Heir . . . Because of Covenant!

DINING AT THE KING'S TABLE was not the only privilege David gave to Mephibosheth! He was also to receive an inheritance—an inheritance that had been lost through his grandfather's death. Everything that had belonged to Saul and his family had been restored to Mephibosheth. And with that inheritance came Saul's servant Ziba, along with his sons and his servants.

Thirty-six people would serve Mephibosheth (2 Samuel 9:9,10). They would cultivate his land and harvest its fruit. How good this was for, even with his inheritance, Mephibosheth still remained lame.

As I meditated upon all of this, I began to see even more parallels between Mephibosheth and me, and I would like to share these with you for the next couple of days.

Trace my bloodline way back, and you will find that my very great-grandfather was Adam. He had an inheritance of land—the earth. He lost that inheritance and eventually died because he turned from the King's way. Thus, because of Adam's sin, I lost my inheritance.

As I grew up, my concept of the King of kings became more and more twisted. One day, in the heat of disappointment, pain, and frustration, I ran away, leaving behind the little bit of truth I possessed. I thought, "I should be sitting on the throne calling the shots." However, in the process of running downhill, I became crippled.

Thereafter, I hobbled along in darkness, growing more disillusioned, more dissatisfied. Fear began to nibble at what was hidden in the dirty alleys of my life. What if I were to die? What if I were to stand before the King? Surely He would have to condemn me to hell.

Oh, I tried to clean up my act, to wear masks of respectability. The apron of motherhood was tied around my waist regularly, many times out of guilt and to cover my Dr. Jekyll-and-Mr. Hyde transformations as I desperately sought for love. I became whatever the occasion required just so someone would want me.

Yet underneath it all, it began to hit me: "You aren't what you thought you were. This is the real you. You can't change; you can't walk straight anymore; you are deformed for life."

Do you in any way relate to this?

Receiving the Inheritance

WAS THERE NO HOPE? Was this to be my character for life? The fear grew. The fear of being found out. The fear of it all catching up with me. The fear of self-destructing. The fear of the King's just judgment (somehow, even then, I knew it would be just).

Then one day the summons came to appear before the King. Someone said, "Kay, why don't you quit telling God what *you* want and tell Him that Christ is *all* you need?"

But Christ was not all I needed. I needed a husband. I had divorced mine. And I needed other things. So I replied curtly to this rude, inappropriate challenge, *"Christ is not all I need."* And I went home.

The next morning when I awoke, I needed peace. I was sick. Sick with a sickness no doctor could cure. I was a nurse. I knew. That day I just couldn't go to work. I couldn't handle it.

The summons came within several hours. I turned to my son, Mark, and said, "Mommy has to be alone for a few minutes. I'll be right back."

I ran up the stairs and prostrated myself beside my bed and cried, "O God, I don't care if I never see another man as long as I live, I don't care if You paralyze me from the neck down—if You'll just give me peace." And He gave me peace, the Prince of Peace, the Lord Jesus Christ. "Come now, and let us reason together. . . . Though your sins are as scarlet, they will be as white as snow" (Isaiah 1:18).

"THIS IS THE COVENANT THAT I WILL MAKE WITH THEM AFTER THOSE DAYS, SAYS THE LORD: I will put My laws upon their heart . . . and their sins and their lawless deeds I will remember no more" (Hebrews 10:16,17).

The fear and condemnation were gone. I had lain there, naked in His sight with naught to cover my sin, and He had called me "Beloved" when there was nothing lovely about me (Romans 9:25).

When I got up, I only knew that now I belonged to Him and that He was by my side. For me it was enough. Little did I realize the inheritance that was mine—the inheritance that I would begin to hear about the next day! All I knew then was that everything was all right.

The fear was gone. But the lameness wasn't.

Restored

"COME AND DINE," the Master called. "I have food to eat that you know nothing about" (John 4:32 NIV). God sent a young man for me to date, and he brought the food—a Phillips' translation of the New Testament. I devoured it. I saw things I had never seen before. How could I ever have thought this Book was boring? It was alive!

One night, as I lay on the living room floor reading Philippians 4:19, it suddenly dawned on me: "I'm wealthy! I'm wealthy! My God shall supply all my needs according to His riches in glory through Christ Jesus my Lord." I just rolled over onto my back and grinned at the ceiling. The King had begun to reveal to me the inheritance that had been lost through Grandfather Adam but restored through covenant. I was an heir of God, a joint heir with Jesus, the last Adam!

As I dined at the King's table regularly, I learned more about my inheritance. And yet, transformed though I was, I was still lame in both feet! Lame but changed! How could it be?

Let me show it to you in the story of Mephibosheth. But as I do, I want you to know that I am simply using this story as an illustration. It is not to be carried any further theologically. It is simply that I saw myself in Mephibosheth as God emphasized his lameness by repeatedly referring to it.

Apart from Jesus I am nothing, I can do nothing. I need a helper, a servant, because I am lame in my flesh. And so, just as Ziba and company served Mephibosheth, I have the Holy Spirit to give me the aid, the help I so desperately need. "By His doing [through the Holy Spirit] you are in Christ Jesus [baptized into His body], who became to us wisdom from God, and righteousness and sanctification, and redemption" (1 Corinthians 1:30,31).

When our Grandfather Adam sinned and died, he lost the Spirit of God. But when God saves us, there is a renewing of the Holy Spirit, and He then becomes our enabler and overrides the lameness of our flesh.

This, Beloved, is what the New Covenant is all about, as we will see in the wonderful days to come.

Know Your Inheritance

DO YOU KNOW what I find as I speak in various parts of our country? Ignorance. And apathy. The apathy excuses the ignorance. People do not really know their God. Nor do they know His Word. As a matter of fact, if you were to ask the majority of those who *profess* Christ to explain to you what is theirs by virtue of the blood of the New Covenant, many could not tell you. Yet their whole life in Christ is based on the truths of this covenant.

To prove it, let's do a little experiment today. Today, right now, I want you to list all that you know about the New Covenant. (Now don't squirm or put this devotional down or read on. Be a good trooper, even if it hurts. It will do you good!) Do not consult any books, not even your Bible. Pretend that you have been caught without your Bible and that you have to explain to someone what God promised His people through the New Covenant.

Oh, precious one, listen to me. This is not to embarrass you, but rather to help rescue you from any apathy or complaining that has mired you down into the quicksand of God's disapproval. It is to keep you from being ashamed when you see Him face-to-face and have to give an account at His judgment seat (2 Timothy 2:15; 2 Corinthians 5:10). This is to help you gird up the loins of your mind so you might run the race that is set before you.

Get out of the grandstands of criticism and get on the track and run where you belong. Sweat—go ahead, it is all right. It's natural for those who run! And it is good. It gets rid of the impurities, the body wastes.

Don't let this be said of you: "For though by this time you ought to be teachers, you have need again for someone to teach you the elementary principles of the oracles of God, and you have come to need milk and not solid food" (Hebrews 5:12).

Three Covenants of Salvation

NOW, DURING THE NEXT few days let's learn all we can about what I call "The Three Covenants of Salvation." This knowledge will enrich your life immeasurably and enable you to share His gospel more effectively.

By the way, have I told you that there burns within my heart a love for you, though many of you are unseen and, thus, unknown to me? It's the love of the Lord, and this is why I discipline myself to write. I write for you, at His bidding, because you truly are precious, Beloved of God, and He and I want you to know that!

There are three covenants that God uses to bring a person to Christ: the Abrahamic Covenant, the Old Covenant, and the New Covenant.

Let me give you a brief synopsis of each, and then tomorrow we will begin looking at each one separately. Now, Beloved, what I am going to do is give you some good solid teaching, so "hangeth thou in there"! It will get very practical, very livable, but *first* you must have an understanding of the truth of it all. Duty is always based on doctrine. Share with me how you live, and I will tell you what you really believe.

The Abrahamic Covenant is the covenant that gives us the promise of the seed, the Lord Jesus Christ.

The Old Covenant is the Law which came by Moses, and, believe it or not, it plays a vital role in bringing a man or woman to Christ. If we would use it more, we would probably not have so many *false* professions of salvation!

The New Covenant is the Covenant of Grace which comes by Jesus Christ and makes us children of God. "For the Law was given through Moses; grace and truth were realized through Jesus Christ" (John 1:17).

As you learn more about each covenant in the days to come, record the essentials about each on a separate sheet of paper. God is going to give you truth by which you not only can live, but also disciple others!

A Covenant with Abraham

THE FUTURE SEEMED so dark, so final. Why hadn't they listened! How could she have been so deceived? Now everything was ruined. "It was that serpent's fault. He lied to me! Who wants to be as gods knowing good and evil if it means this? What if God sees us?"

Frantically they wove their fig leaves. But their hiding was in vain. Suddenly they were face-to-face with God. They were afraid. They should have been. They had sinned.

Then the word of the Lord came. Hope dawned, like the brilliance of the morning sun as it pushes away the burden of darkness from earth's shoulders. Eve would have a seed, a seed that would bruise Satan's head! Hallelujah! That old deceiver, that horrible serpent, would not triumph after all.

There it was, the first promise of the coming of the Messiah through the seed of the woman.

Hundreds of years would pass and then the promise of the seed would be spoken again, this time to a man named Abram (see Galatians 3:16). The Messiah, the Christ, would come forth from the loins of Abraham. "In hope against hope he believed, in order that he might become a father of many nations, according to that which had been spoken, 'So shall your descendants [seed] be'" (Romans 4:18).

"On that day the LORD made a covenant with Abram," and God, in the form of a smoking oven and a flaming torch, passed through the pieces of the sacrifice (Genesis 15:17,18). Because God *alone* passed through the pieces of flesh, it was a covenant that depended on the faithfulness of God alone.

The Abrahamic Covenant was made and ratified by God: The seed as promised to Eve and then to Abraham would come and take away our sins.

And what, with regard to the Abrahamic Covenant, is God's promise to you and to me? It is this, recorded for us in Galatians 3:29: "And if you belong to Christ, then you are Abraham's offspring [seed], heirs according to promise."

Do you belong to Christ? How do you know?

Is God Pleased With You?

HAVE YOU EVER TAKEN a good, honest look at your life? I mean, have you ever really sat down and evaluated the way you are living in the light of what you know or what you have heard is right and wrong?

Has there ever been a time when you realized that your life did not measure up to God's commandments? A time when you realized that, were you to stand before God, you would stand guilty because you had not obeyed His commandments?

Maybe you lingered around some married friends, looking, wondering what it would be like to be married to him or her, even flirting a little—coveting.

Maybe, because you were hurt or jealous, you implied, said, or led others to believe wrong things about another person—bearing false witness.

Maybe you did not give your parents the obedience, the respect due them—not honoring father and mother.

Maybe on a test you copied an answer that was not yours, or took too much change at the store, or even took some things that did not belong to you—stealing.

Maybe you satisfied your physical desires outside of marriage or thought about seducing someone—adultery.

Let me ask you: How do you really feel about your life? Are you pleased with it? And how do you think God would evaluate your life? Do you think He would be pleased with it?

Why don't you meditate on this for a few minutes and then jot down your thoughts on a sheet of paper.

Now, what do you think you could do that would make your life more acceptable to God? Think about it, write it down, and we'll talk more tomorrow.

A Covenant With Moses

OVER 430 YEARS had passed since God had cut covenant with Abraham. Now Moses stood at Mount Sinai bearing the message of another covenant as he "recounted to the people all the words of the LORD and all the ordinances" (Exodus 24:3).

As the people stood to hear these laws of God, they knew that they were good. The Law was right! Man should abide by it! After all, God should be first. Idolatry was wrong. Parents should be honored. Coveting and stealing were bad. And murder—God forbid! And who would want his wife to lie with another? Yes, these were fine laws—laws that would benefit them as a people—for surely those who would abide by these would live righteous lives, pleasing to God and to man.

There it was, a covenant acceptable to both parties. The order was given; sacrifices were offered. Then Moses "took the book of the covenant and read it in the hearing of the people; and they said, 'All that the LORD has spoken we will do, and we will be obedient!'" (Exodus 24:7). The Covenant of Law was made. So Moses, Aaron, Nadab, Abihu, and seventy of the elders of Israel went up on Mount Sinai to partake of the covenant meal, and they beheld God, and they ate and drank (Exodus 24:9-11).

The Law was established. Now it was to be obeyed to the letter, without fail (James 2:10). It was right. It was good. It was holy. They were to keep it . . . but they didn't! They thought they could, but they couldn't because they were sinners.

Sin . . . indwelling sin! They had not recognized it, and, try as hard as they could, they still broke the Law. That old man, that old self born of Adam's sin, ruled their flesh, causing the members of their bodies to be slaves to sin (Romans 6:6).

The Law that they thought would bring righteousness and life brought only death. Why had God given the Law if it couldn't make a man righteous? Good question, isn't it?

Have you ever tried to do what was right and found out that, no matter how hard you tried, you failed? What's the answer? We'll see in the days to come. How precious and liberating it will be!

Why the Law?

IF THE LAW can't shape us up, if it can't change us and make us righteous, then why on earth did God give it?

The Law was given by God for two reasons. First, it was given to show us our sin; and second, it was given to keep us in custody until the day when we would believe in the Lord Jesus Christ.

Now, Beloved, let me urge you not to rush through this next part, because what I have to share with you is absolutely essential, even though it may seem a little heavy. You see, many of our problems come because of our ignorance of God's Word and His ways. And if it is not ignorance, then it is disobedience.

God gave the Law because man needed to see his sin. He needed to see that in his flesh dwelt no good thing . . . and thus by the works of the Law no flesh would be justified in God's sight (Romans 3:20). The only way man would ever recognize his sin was through seeing God's holy, righteous, just Law, "for through the Law comes the knowledge of sin" (Romans 3:20). That is why the apostle Paul wrote: "I would not have come to know sin except through the Law; for I would not have known about coveting if the Law had not said, 'YOU SHALL NOT COVET' " (Romans 7:7).

How my heart aches for our world today, for we live in a society that has heard so little of God's Law, God's Word, God's way. As a result, multitudes have sown an awful crop of corruption in their flesh. Their lives, along with relationships that were designed to sustain them as whole persons, have become as bitter as gall, so that they can hardly speak for the retching nausea of their sin.

How I hurt when I hear them say, "Why didn't I hear these truths before? Maybe I wouldn't have gotten so messed up. Oh, if only I had heard!"

Where were those who were supposed to proclaim God's Law so that men and women, boys and girls, might at least have recognized sin for what it was?

As I write this tonight, my heart is so filled with love for you that it spills over into my eyes!

Preparing the Way for Grace

"I WOULD NOT HAVE COME to know sin except through the Law; for I would not have known about coveting if the Law had not said, 'YOU SHALL NOT COVET'" (Romans 7:7).

What part has God's holy Law played in your life? Have you realized just exactly what sin is? When you sin, do you know that you are going directly and willfully against His holy commandments?

As I grew up, I was raised with clear-cut absolutes—most of life was either black or white, with very little gray. And these absolutes kept me in check as far as my external behavior was concerned. Consequently, I considered myself to be a pretty good girl. I really did not see myself as an awful sinner. For although I knew the commandments, I do not remember sitting under any really convicting teaching or preaching that pointed out the exceeding sinfulness of my flesh. Thus, I did not see my desperate need for change, my desperate need for Jesus Christ to rescue me by His Spirit from my sinful old nature of self.

As a child I had to work in our World War II Victory Gardens and help dig flower beds. Sometimes, when the ground was particularly hard from lack of rain, I would have to jump up on the spade with both feet in order to get it to penetrate that hard earth. That was the kind of teaching and preaching I needed. I needed to hear a word from the Lord that dug in and broke up the hard soil of my heart!

It takes the Law to show us our sin and God's just displeasure with those who transgress His holy commandments. It is the preaching of the Law that prepares the way for the message of grace. It is the proclamation of the Law that brings men to repentance, and except we repent, we will all likewise perish (Luke 13:3).

How does your life measure up to the Law?

"But," you may say, "I'm not under the Old Covenant. I've been saved!"

Good. How does your life measure up to the Law? Does grace make you lawless? No, for the righteousness of the Law is fulfilled in us who walk not after the flesh, but after the Spirit (Romans 8:4).

The Law . . .
Your Tutor

YOU . . . CHURCH . . . LAY DOWN that wedding garment. It is not time yet for the bride to put on white. Rather, clothe yourself in black sackcloth. Put a cloth to your nose and mouth and step out into the neighborhoods of the world. Don't stop up your ears. Listen to their wailing, to the cry of mourners. Families weeping for their dead.

As you walk through the streets, doesn't the stench of death seep through that cloth you hold over your nose and mouth? No, don't run back to the security of your sanctuaries and sing your hymns. Quit shutting your eyes. Open them. Look for a minute at the children of those who have never heard the gospel, let alone the just commandments of God's holy Law. For a moment gaze fully on the awful wages of sin, and then you will see more clearly why God gave men the Law even when He knew they could never keep it. Even when He knew it could never make them righteous. Even when He knew it would only expose their sin for what it was—sin—a very real condition of their hearts because they were born of Adam.

God's second purpose in giving the Law was to restrain men from drinking the dregs of sin's chalice, from tasting in full the bitter gall that would convulse their beings until they withered up into cold, twisted forms of human beings. The Law was given to keep men in custody from sin's awful wages until they could come to faith in the Lord Jesus Christ.

Listen carefully, Beloved, to God's Word: "But before faith came, we were kept in custody under the law, being shut up to the faith which was later to be revealed. Therefore, the Law has become our tutor to lead us to Christ, that we may be justified by faith" (Galatians 3:23,24).

Today, Beloved, let me leave you with a question: How would the Law be an asset rather than a detriment in the life of an unbeliever?

Write out your answer. Put it in black and white, for there are many humanistic voices that say hearing God's commandments only causes men to go on an awful guilt trip and therefore messes them up psychologically for life.

The Covenant of Grace

COULD KNOWLEDGE OF GOD'S holy Law mess us up psychologically and produce guilt and a sense of condemnation that would damage us for life?

Yes, I think it could in a way, if all we ever heard was the Law, and we never heard of Jesus Christ who was the fulfillment of that Law.

So as we reason together today, it is important for you to remember that, ever since the day sin entered into the world through Adam and Eve, there has *always* been the promise of the seed, the One who would come and crush Satan's head and set men free from sin. Before God ever gave the Law, the Old Covenant, He gave the Abrahamic Covenant promising a Savior for man's sin, the Lord Jesus Christ.

Thus, when we share the Law, when we tell men of its holy and just requirements, we must *always* tell them of the way of escape, the grace of God that is every man's through belief in the Lord Jesus Christ.

Now, then, let's take one last look at the Law before we proceed to the New Covenant. The Law, as we have seen, served two purposes. First, it was given to reveal man's sin so that man, having seen his sin clearly, might then see his need of a Savior. Second, it was given to restrain men from sin. It served to keep the Jews—and us—from the contamination of the world's vices; to keep men locked up within its restrictions and thus out of trouble.

This is why, Beloved, I wanted you to take a walk through the world's streets of death, to smell its stench, to see its awful wages. I wanted you to be convinced of the place of the Law so you will teach it to your children and thus keep them from the world's contamination. I want you to see it so you won't be taken "captive through philosophy and empty deception, according to the tradition of men, according to the elementary principles of the world" (Colossians 2:8).

I want you to see it so that you might go into the world and preach the *whole* counsel of God—which includes all three covenants. Don't leave out the Law!

Your Heart . . . God's Tablet

AS THE ARMIES of Babylon laid siege to Jerusalem—as the word of the Lord warning of famine, of fighting, of fire, of destruction was about to come to pass—there came a new word from God. A word of promise. A word of hope. A New Covenant. It was a promise to remember, to cling to, to believe in, to wait for!

What was this New Covenant like? What did it promise? What would it do for man?

> "Behold, days are coming," declares the LORD, "when I will make a new covenant with the house of Israel and with the house of Judah. . . . I will put My law within them, and on their heart I will write it; and I will be their God, and they shall be My people. And they shall not teach again, each man his neighbor and each man his brother saying, 'Know the LORD,' for they shall all know Me, from the least of them to the greatest of them," declares the LORD, "for I will forgive their iniquity, and their sin I will remember no more" (Jeremiah 31:31-34).

Whereas the Old Covenant was God's law written on tablets of stone, the New Covenant was God's law written within, upon the tablet of man's heart.

There would now be an inner knowing of what was righteous and what was unrighteous, of that which pleased God and that which offended Him. This New Covenant would not kill a man, slay him in his sin, but would bring life—life from the Spirit. It would not be like the Law, a ministry of condemnation, but its ministry would be to produce the righteousness that the Law could not produce, "weak as it was through the flesh" (Romans 8:3).

Tomorrow, I will explain Jeremiah 31:33,34 to you. For now, read—really read—2 Corinthians 3:5-9 and then meditate upon its words.

Comparing the Covenants

WHEN YOU TRULY BELIEVE on the Lord Jesus Christ and are saved, God causes certain definite changes to take place within you. This is the difference between the Old and the New Covenants. In the Old Covenant the responsibility for keeping the Law rested totally upon man, and, because of his flesh, he just couldn't handle it! However, in the New Covenant the Spirit of God comes in and does what the flesh cannot do; He changes man!

In the New Covenant God not only writes His law upon the fleshly tablets of a man's heart, as we saw yesterday, but He also says that He becomes your God and you become His people. Can you imagine? You become His. What a privilege! "See how great a love the Father has bestowed upon us, that we should be called children of God; and such we are" (1 John 3:1).

In the New Covenant God says that "they shall not teach again, each man his neighbor and each man his brother, saying, 'Know the LORD,' for they shall all know Me" (Jeremiah 31:34).

When you have really entered into the New Covenant, you know God from an inner experience, witness, or teaching by His Spirit rather than only knowing about God from what you hear from others! You get a new "resident" Teacher: "Now we have received, not the spirit of the world, but the Spirit who is from God, that we might know the things freely given to us by God" (1 Corinthians 2:12).

While the Old Covenant could only expose our sin, the New Covenant takes our sin away, for under this covenant the Lord declares, "I will forgive their iniquity, and their sin I will remember no more" (Jeremiah 31:34).

You become His; He becomes yours. You know Him now, not because of the external witness of others, but by revelation. Your sins are gone forever, never to be remembered by God.

But is this all? Oh, no, there is more. There is the Enabler who transforms you so that you can live the life God requires. We'll see more about that truth tomorrow.

The Keeping Power of Covenant

HAVE YOU EVER BEEN afraid that you might turn your back on God and walk away, never to return? It's a devastating thought, isn't it? Could that happen to you as a child of God?

Beloved, I know that many have been taught differing theologies on the eternal security of a believer, but what does God's Word say about the New Covenant, the Covenant of Grace?

Listen to His Word in Jeremiah 32:39,40 as we look at still another aspect of the New or Everlasting Covenant: "And I will give them one heart and one way, that they may fear Me always, for their own good, and for the good of their children after them. And I will make an everlasting covenant with them that I will not turn away from them, to do them good; and I will put the fear of Me in their hearts so that they will not turn away from Me."

God promises that *He will put the fear of Himself into our hearts.* God Himself will do it *so that* we will not turn away from Him!

This, Beloved, is the keeping power of God that causes us to fear Him always. This, Beloved, is the Father's answer to the prayer of His Son on our behalf: "Holy Father, keep them in Thy name, the name which Thou hast given Me, that they may be one, even as We are" (John 17:11). And so those of the New Covenant, in the confidence of faith in God's Word, can join with Paul as he says, "I know whom I have believed and I am convinced that He is able to guard what I have entrusted to Him until that day" (2 Timothy 1:12).

We are kept by Jesus, held in the hand of God, *never to perish*, for He has said, "I WILL NEVER DESERT YOU, NOR WILL I EVER FORSAKE YOU" (Hebrews 13:5).

> Now to Him who is able to keep you from stumbling, and to make you stand in the presence of His glory blameless with great joy, to the only God our Savior, through Jesus Christ our Lord, be glory, majesty, dominion and authority, before all time and now and forever. Amen (Jude 24,25).

Stop, Beloved. Meditate upon this lesson, and then ask God to speak a word to your heart. What are His thoughts toward you?

The Holy Spirit . . . Your Helper

HOW CAN YOU LIVE the Christian life? How can you serve your God? Only one way—by the Spirit. Only the Spirit of God can endue you with power for service. This is what the New Covenant brings—holiness and power by the indwelling of the Holy Spirit.

"Moreover, I will give you a new heart and put a new spirit within you; and I will remove the heart of stone from your flesh and give you a heart of flesh. And I will put My Spirit within you and cause you to walk in My statutes, and you will be careful to observe My ordinances" (Ezekiel 36:26,27).

In the New Covenant you are given the Holy Spirit of promise, "another Helper, that He may be with you forever." He "will be in you" (John 14:16,17). And when the Spirit comes to live in you, what will He do? According to Ezekiel 36:27, He will cause you to walk in His statutes and you will be careful to observe His ordinances.

O Beloved, do you not see that what the Old Covenant, the Law, justly demanded, the New Covenant, Grace, provided!

How could His disciples ever live the life? How could they ever carry on His work? How could they ever convince the world that Jesus had come in the flesh? It would not be by might, nor by power, but by His Spirit (Zechariah 4:6). This was His promise to those of the New Covenant, to those whom He would send into the world—to be in the world but not of the world, so that the world might believe in Him through their Word (John 17:16,18,20).

Jesus has left us here, but He has not left us without a Comforter, without a Guide, without an Enabler, because He is our Friend.

"And I will ask the Father, and He will give you another Helper, that He may be with you *forever*; that is the Spirit of truth, whom the world cannot receive, because it does not behold Him or know Him, but you know Him because He abides with you, and will be in you" (John 14:16,17, emphasis added).

This is the New Covenant! Live in the light of it!

AUGUST

————

Taking the Bitter, Making It Sweet

This month we will focus on the cross and the powerful, freeing work it accomplishes for us. The cross is the identification mark of a Christian, first because of what it effects in our lives . . . and second because of our constant identification with its work. The cross works deliverance from sin's dominion, sin's penalty, and Satan's power as we learn to allow its work to take effect in us. We will learn to take the cross and place it in the bitter places of life, and we will see how, because of the reality of the cross, those situations can be made sweet!

————

Blessed Are the Meek

HAVE YOU EVER STOOD in line for a long time, patiently waiting your turn, only to have someone walk up and cut right in front of you? To use an old expression, "It gets your goat," doesn't it? How can people be so rude? They don't apologize! They don't excuse themselves! And, if you call their hand, they either stand there unapologetically and say nothing or they get angry! I have to admit it, such behavior gets to me. When it happens in traffic, I pray the police will get them. But when it happens when I'm standing in line, then I want to straighten them out myself.

Several years ago we went on a family outing to Opryland. It was David's fifteenth birthday, and he got to choose how we would celebrate it. Mark, our middle son, and his wife, Leslie, joined us for the weekend.

Opryland is entertaining for all ages. Besides exciting amusement rides like the Wabash Cannonball, there are many musical stage shows. In fact, it was at one of those musicals that it happened. We had already stood in line for one show, only to be turned away at the door. Now, after a long wait in another line, we had dashed across the park to the Roy Acuff Theatre, where the lobby was so filled with waiting patrons that the line spilled outside. We waited with anticipation, wondering if we would again be turned away at the last minute.

Finally the line began to move; we were eager and hopeful. This was supposed to be the best of the musicals, one we couldn't miss! Then it happened. A couple from somewhere back in the line had walked up and sat down on a nearby wall, supposedly to wait in comfort. Then, when the line started to move, they glibly, with nary a pardon-me-please, walked up in front of us and got in line.

We had been waiting there thirty minutes, and they just moved right in front of us! Something had to be done! It was more than I could take—or was it?

Later, when I got quiet, the Lord would say, "Blessed are the meek: for they shall inherit the earth" (Matthew 5:5 KJV). And I would have to confess my sin, for sin I did.

Handling the Bitter

I DON'T KNOW WHAT your temperament is, but mine is the type that just cannot stand injustice. There is nothing naturally meek about me. If something is wrong, I want to straighten it out. If it's unjust, let's go to war! If I recall correctly, there was a battalion during the Revolutionary War that carried a flag with the slogan, "Don't Tread on Me." It bore the symbol of a snake. Well, that summarizes my personality apart from the Spirit of God—"Don't Tread on Me."

Like that serpent of old, the "I" is very strong in my flesh. If you're the same way, then you understand exactly how I felt that day at Opryland. If you are the peace-at-any-price type, then a shrug of the shoulders would have suited you. Yet, for either type, there was only one Christlike thing to do in that situation. Obviously I didn't do it, because later I had to confess! What I did do was tell the couple how wrong they were.

The line kept moving, and soon the intruders were out of my sight. The crush got tighter as we entered the door. Whew! We had made it! My chicks in front of me, the mother hen in me wanted to cackle—until suddenly I missed the closeness of the protective wings of my rooster. As I turned around, what should I see but the guide at the door holding out her arm forbidding entrance to any more.

Jack was outside! And who was standing in line *in front of him* but that same foxy couple! That was it! Scratching the ground, feathers ruffled, wattle shaking, I turned back to the door. There I complained to the establishment, pointing out the offenders, while Mr. Peace-at-Any-Price just shook his patient head and silently mouthed words that told me not to fret. Finally the arm came down, and my beloved husband, along with others, was admitted—after the couple that had cut in. Oh, I didn't say a word to them, but if looks could kill, they would have been dead. I glared at them the way I used to look at people before I came to know Jesus Christ!

Why did I act just like I used to in such bitter situations? Why? Because I forgot how to take the bitter and make it sweet. I forgot about God's tree. I forgot that, like the apostle Paul, I, too, had been "crucified with Christ." Can you relate?

Be Angry but Don't Sin

HOW MY HEART was smitten by the Lord the next morning, as, in my quiet time, He brought that Opryland situation to mind. I had reacted just like a lost person with my type of temperament would have reacted! How sad! How would I ever make it in the face of *real* injustice?

Have you ever heard that verse that says, "*It's the little foxes that spoil the vines*" (Song of Solomon 2:15 KJV)? Sometimes it's the little things that mess us up, and I think that's what happened to me. I was caught off guard because of the inaneness of it all. I wasn't walking "circumspectly," as the King James Version puts it in Ephesians 5:15.

But whether our situations are grave or inane, we need to learn how to take the bitter and make it sweet. The world needs to see Jesus living in these temples made of flesh. That is why we have Jesus Christ, "this treasure in earthen vessels, that the surpassing greatness of the power may be of God and not from ourselves" (2 Corinthians 4:7).

There's a little chorus that goes, "You're a pot, you're a vessel, made to hold Someone special." Well, my pot sure got in the way, didn't it? There was nothing special about my behavior at all. Jesus' longsuffering love certainly was not radiating through my mean eyes. They say that the eyes are the windows of the soul. Whew! What dark things were in my soul. I was angry!

Now, anger is not always wrong. Read the Old and New Testaments and you find God the Father and God the Son both getting angry. Therefore, all anger is not sin. There is a righteous anger. However, God does say, "BE ANGRY, AND yet DO NOT SIN; do not let the sun go down on your anger" (Ephesians 4:26).

I was angry, but I sinned because I did not act in righteousness. My anger, rather than God's Holy Spirit, was controlling me.

"But, Kay," I can hear you say, "how do you handle it?"

As you have already seen above, I am not an expert. I have failed. But I do have the answer, and I intend to learn to live accordingly. You can, too, so hang in there. During the next month we are going to talk about life at the cross, or taking the bitter and making it sweet. We will learn together.

The Waters of Marah

IT HAD BEEN THREE DAYS since their glorious triumph, when the Israelites had found themselves caught between the Red Sea and the Egyptian army, and God had worked a miracle. The first lines of their song of triumph gave God all the credit.

> "I will sing to the LORD, for He is highly exalted; the horse and its rider He has hurled into the sea. The LORD is my strength and song, and He has become my salvation; this is my God, and I will praise Him; my father's God, and I will extol Him" (Exodus 15:1,2).

Now they had come to Marah. And "they could not drink the waters of Marah, for they were bitter; therefore it was named Marah. So the people grumbled at Moses, saying, 'What shall we drink?' Then he cried out to the LORD, and the LORD showed him a tree; and he threw it into the waters, and the waters became sweet. There He made for them a . . . regulation, and there He tested them" (Exodus 15:23-25).

The bitter water was a test, for God wanted to teach them another lesson—how to take the bitter and make it sweet. He did it by using a tree to make the waters drinkable. And what is God's lesson to us in this? Some theologians would say, "There is no lesson for the Christian today. It is merely a historical account of a miraculous event performed by God for the children of Israel."

Yet, in this case, I would disagree. I believe that God has hidden spiritual truths for His church in many events in Israel's history. When God does this, He then uncovers these "hidden treasures" for us by paralleling them in the New Testament. If an Old Testament event is specifically paralleled in the New Testament, there can be no doubt that God has a lesson for us in it. However, if the New Testament does not clearly show us what the Old Testament foreshadowed, then we must be careful not to read in something which is not there.

Tomorrow we will talk more about this. But for now, rest assured that there is no bitter situation that Jesus cannot make sweet.

The Riches of God's Word

FOR YOU TO REALLY appreciate what I want to teach you about the bitter waters of Marah and the tree that made them sweet, I should first give you a little teaching on typology. Now, don't shy away from such terms. Doctrine, which is another word for teaching, is invaluable, because our lifestyles are based upon that which we believe. Unfortunately, we don't know God's Book very well, so we are loose in our living, doing what is right in our own eyes rather than living by every word that proceeds from the mouth of God. As a result, we follow man's traditions, vain philosophies, and worldly wisdom.

In biblical interpretation, a "type" is an Old Testament foreshadowing of a New Testament truth or spiritual reality. The word "type" comes from the Greek word *tupos*, meaning a mark formed by a blow, an impression, or an image. For example, Adam was a type of Christ who was to come. Romans 5:14 says, "Nevertheless death reigned from Adam . . . who is a type of Him who was to come." In 1 Corinthians 15:45, Christ is referred to as "the last Adam." The parallel is clear and specific and cannot be denied.

A beautiful example of a type is given to us in John 3:14,15: "And as Moses lifted up the serpent in the wilderness, even so must the Son of Man be lifted up; that whoever believes may in Him have eternal life."

Here, Jesus likens His death on the cross to Moses lifting up the serpent in the wilderness (Numbers 21). As those in Moses' time were saved from physical death by looking to the brass serpent on the pole, so men would be saved from spiritual death by believing in Him, for He was made sin for us and hung on a tree. The act of faith—looking unto Christ to save you from your deserved death as a sinner—gives you eternal life.

Now that you understand types, can you see how "beginning with Moses [the first five books of the Old Testament] and with all the prophets, He [Jesus] explained to them the things concerning Himself in all the Scriptures" (Luke 24:27)?

Blessed, isn't it? Oh, what riches there are in God's Word! If we would only take the time to discover them, how wealthy we would be!

God's Examples

ONE PASSAGE THAT CLEARLY shows the purpose of types for our lives is 1 Corinthians 10:1-13. As you read it, note the two uses of the word "example" (the Greek word *tupoi*, "types," is here translated "examples"). Then note how God uses the incidents in the lives of the Israelites as a means of instructing us.

> For I do not want you to be unaware, brethren, that our fathers were all under the cloud, and all passed through the sea; and all were baptized into Moses in the cloud and in the sea; and all ate the same spiritual food; and all drank the same spiritual drink, for they were drinking from a spiritual rock which followed them; and the rock was Christ. Nevertheless, with most of them God was not well-pleased; for they were laid low in the wilderness. Now these things happened as examples for us, that we should not crave evil things, as they also craved. And do not be idolaters, as some of them were; as it is written, "THE PEOPLE SAT DOWN TO EAT AND DRINK, AND STOOD UP TO PLAY." Nor let us act immorally, as some of them did, and twenty-three thousand fell in one day. Nor let us try the Lord, as some of them did, and were destroyed by the serpents. Nor grumble, as some of them did, and were destroyed by the destroyer. Now these things happened to them as an example, and they were written for our instruction, upon whom the ends of the ages have come. Therefore let him who thinks he stands take heed lest he fall. No temptation has overtaken you but such as is common to man; and God is faithful, who will not allow you to be tempted beyond what you are able, but with the temptation will provide the way of escape also, that you may be able to endure it.

What was a type of Christ in this passage? And what are God's lessons to you, dear believer?

Lessons From the Wilderness

NOW LET'S RETURN to Exodus 15 and see what lessons God has in this Old Testament event for His church.

> And when they came to Marah, they could not drink the waters of Marah, for they were bitter; therefore it was named Marah. So the people grumbled at Moses, saying, "What shall we drink?" Then he cried out to the LORD, and the LORD showed him a tree; and he threw it into the waters, and the waters became sweet. There He made for them a statute and regulation, and there He tested them. And He said, "If you will give earnest heed to the voice of the LORD your God, and do what is right in His sight, and give ear to His commandments, and keep all His statutes, I will put none of the diseases on you which I have put on the Egyptians; for I, the LORD, am your healer" (Exodus 15:23-26).

It was the tree applied to the waters of Marah that turned the waters from bitter to sweet and made them drinkable. Was the tree a picture of something? I believe so. In Galatians 3:13, Paul writes, "Christ redeemed us from the curse of the Law, having become a curse for us—for it is written, 'CURSED IS EVERY ONE WHO HANGS ON A TREE.' " Paul was quoting from Deuteronomy 21:22,23.

And what tree did Christ hang on? A cross. The Greek word translated "tree" in Galatians 3:13 is the word for wood. The same word is translated "cross" in Acts 5:30: "The God of our fathers raised up Jesus, whom you had put to death by hanging Him on a cross."

Do you think that God intended, by having Moses place the tree in the waters of Marah, to teach us to apply the cross to the bitter situations in our lives?

Tomorrow we will look at the timing of this event in Israel's history. But what is God's lesson for you today? Ask Him, and then write it out in your own words on a separate sheet of paper.

The Sweetness of Obedience

THE BITTER WATERS of Marah followed the Passover, which was truly a symbol of salvation. Under the cruel bondage of Pharaoh, the children of Israel had lived as slaves in Egypt for 400 years. (Egypt serves as a type of the world, Pharaoh as a picture of Satan.) As God's angel of death moved throughout Egypt visiting every home and killing the firstborn male, he passed over every dwelling where he saw the blood of the lamb on the doorpost. And so we have a picture of our salvation: living in the world, in bondage to sin, under the dominion of Satan, we find freedom only through the blood of Jesus Christ applied in faith to the doorpost of our heart. Thus we pass from death to life (John 5:24).

Since the waters of Marah came after the Passover, the tree could not symbolize the cross as it brings salvation. Yet if not salvation, then what? If the tree represented the cross, then we should look at the significance of the cross in the life of a believer. What place does the cross have at that point? The place of preeminence, for it is there that every believer is to live. This is what Jesus meant when He said, "If anyone wishes to come after Me, let him deny himself, and take up his cross daily, and follow Me" (Luke 9:23). The cross must be a place of daily crucifixion so that you do not live independently of Him.

What is the lesson of Marah? Is it not that, even as a child of God, I will face bitter situations? These bitter situations are meant to test me. However, the bitter can be made sweet and palatable through the tree, the place of crucifixion. There I am to let the cross have its effect in my daily life as I die to my way and follow Him.

It was the cross that was needed at Opryland. The bitter could have been sweet had I stopped and said in faith, "Lord, although what they are doing is wrong and hard to take, I will not react in my own way. I choose to take up my cross, to follow You . . . to walk as You would walk."

Oh, the sweetness of obedience! It so outweighs belching the gall of disobedience.

Great Strides . . . Little Difference

A GALLUP POLL in the early 1980s showed that more Americans were attending church now than at any time in history. The percentage is higher than in colonial America. As a result of that poll, George Gallup was impressed with the following:

1. The high percentage of people who claimed that the Bible is the Word of God and authoritative for their lives.

2. The high percentage who believed in a literal heaven and a literal hell.

3. The large percentage who believed that a born-again experience is essential for entrance into heaven.

The results were really quite impressive, until one read Gallup's conclusion: "Never before in the history of the United States has the Gospel of Jesus Christ made such inroads—while at the same time making so little difference in the way people live." And as we are now living in the 1990s, we'd all agree with his conclusions!

When you read things like that, do you ever ask, "Why?"

I believe it all centers around the cross. Believing in it, in its purpose and its work, is far different from embracing it as a way of life. I can acknowledge the cross's existence, agree with its necessity, and yet still not take it up daily and live accordingly.

How many of us can honestly say with Paul: "I have been crucified with Christ; and it is no longer I who live, but Christ lives in me; and the life which I now live in the flesh I live by faith in the Son of God" (Galatians 2:20). Surely if we lived crucified lives, we would have a greater impact on the world!

What is the problem? Let me answer that by asking you how many sermons you have heard or how many books you have read on the cross in the past few years? What is the thrust of the messages you are hearing? Are they centered around man and his needs or around holiness, purity, and denial of self?

What do you want to hear? What do you need to hear?

AUGUST 10

The Call of the Cross

IN THE GOSPELS there are seventeen references to the cross. Of these, six refer to the cross as the identification mark of all who would follow Jesus as disciples. The question that students of God's Word have debated is whether one can be a Christian without taking up his cross and becoming a disciple.

It is interesting to me that, as you read the Gospels, you find Jesus addressing the multitudes with the message of the cross. An example of this is found in Luke 14:27: "Whoever does not carry his own cross and come after Me cannot be My disciple."

From this, one thing is clear and certain. Apart from taking up the cross and following after Him, you *cannot* be His disciple.

Now, then, let me ask this. Do you think it is right or equitable to receive God's free gift of eternal life and yet refuse to love Him above all others or to take up your cross and follow Him? I personally believe that discipleship is synonymous with salvation. If you disagree with me, then tell me how you or anyone could bear to enter heaven's portals and stand before the One who, in doing the will of the Father, denied Himself and took up His cross?

At the end of His discourse on discipleship in Luke 14, Jesus concludes with an analogy to salt: "Therefore, salt is good; but if even salt has become tasteless, with what will it be seasoned? It is useless either for the soil or for the manure pile; it is thrown out. He who has ears to hear, let him hear" (Luke 14:34,35).

Salty salt acts as a preservative to stop the spread of corruption. Used in this way, salt loses its life, disappearing into what it seasons. You only know it has been there because of its effect.

Yet when salt loses its savor, it still retains its identity. In the days of the Bible, when salt lost its savor and was therefore not even good for the soil or manure pile, it was thrown away—men trampled on it. Is this not so with our brand of Christianity today? We have lost our savor because we are not willing to lose our lives, and so we have little impact on a corrupt society.

How salty are you, Beloved? And would you call yourself a disciple of the Lord Jesus Christ?

United With Christ

WHAT PLACE DOES the cross have in our lives? It is twofold. At Calvary's tree we are crucified with Jesus Christ once for all. And at the cross we are to live as we take up our cross daily.

Today we will look at the first aspect of the cross.

> What shall we say then? Are we to continue in sin that grace might increase? May it never be! How shall we who died to sin still live in it? Or do you not know that all of us who have been baptized into Christ Jesus have been baptized into His death? Therefore we have been buried with Him through baptism into death, in order that as Christ was raised from the dead through the glory of the Father, so we too might walk in newness of life. For if we have become united with Him in the likeness of His death, certainly we shall be also in the likeness of His resurrection, knowing this, that our old self was crucified with Him, that [in order that] our body of sin might be done away with, that we should no longer be slaves to sin; for he who has died is freed from sin (Romans 6:1-7).

The "baptism" referred to means "to be united with." If you have been united with Christ, you have died with Him, been buried with Him, and are raised with Him. You are free from sin's power to reign over you!

When you died with Christ, your old *self* (all you were "in Adam" [Romans 5]) was crucified. "Was crucified" means that it happened at one point in time. When that old man died it rendered your body of sin powerless—you were no longer a slave to sin. The phrase "done away with" does not mean "annihilated" but rather "made inoperative" or "powerless."

When the old man was put to death, your body was rendered inoperative as an instrument of sin. Therefore, no true Christian has to sin. A Christian only sins because he or she chooses to sin. The cross of Christ sets you free from sin's dominion by crucifying the old man. Are you living like you've been set free?

A New Creation

IN GOD'S ECONOMY, crucifixion always brings resurrection. We are going to see that over and over in the next few days, and what a blessing it will be! How I pray, precious one, that you are hanging in there with me. I so long to be used of God to root and ground you, always establishing you in the truth, so that you will not be "tossed here and there by waves, and carried about by every wind of doctrine, by the trickery of men, by craftiness in deceitful scheming" (Ephesians 4:14).

In Romans 6 the whole purpose of death is life—death to sin's power "so we too might walk in newness of life" (verse 4). Thus Paul writes to the Corinthians, "Therefore if any man is in Christ, he is a new creature; the old things passed away; behold, new things have come" (2 Corinthians 5:17).

"Passed away" means that it took place at one point in time. The verb "have come" denotes a past completed action with a present or continuous result. This is how effective Calvary was: For all who truly believe, there *is* newness of life.

What makes us new creations? It is the death of the old man and the new indwelling of the Holy Spirit: "For the law [principle] of the Spirit of life in Christ Jesus has set you free from the law [principle] of sin and of death" (Romans 8:2).

But is this the only work of the cross in the life of the believer? No. Yet this work is a sure work in the life of *every single* believer.

Remember I said, in essence, that life always follows death. In Galatians 2:20 Paul wrote: "I have been crucified with Christ; and it is no longer I who live, but Christ lives in me; and the life which I now live in the flesh I live by faith in the Son of God, who loved me, and delivered Himself up for me."

The Crucifixion itself is a thing of the past: "I *have been* crucified." Yet does that mean we have no more need of the cross? Did Christ not talk about taking up our cross daily? What did He mean by that? We will look at it tomorrow.

The question for today is, "Who is living your life—you or Christ?"

Christ in You

ANDREW MURRAY, a mighty man of God, wrote, "The cross leads to the Spirit and the Spirit to the cross."

What did he mean by that? Simply that it is through our identification in the death, burial, and resurrection of Jesus Christ that we are given the gift of God's Holy Spirit. Thus the cross leads us to the Spirit. Yet, when the Holy Spirit comes to indwell us, where does He lead us? To the cross! A personal cross.

Why? Because the cross works death—to self, to our ways, to our desires—death to our own life. And through this death, Christ is manifested in our flesh. That is why, Beloved, God does not redeem our bodies immediately when we are saved. Instead, He puts His Spirit in our mortal bodies of flesh in order that men might see the surpassing greatness of the power of His Holy Spirit.

When other mortals watch us living lives that are different than theirs, although we live in bodies just like theirs and experience the same trials and testings, then they see the reality of "Christ in you, the hope of glory" (Colossians 1:27). It is in difficult situations that the reality of God's presence in us is best seen. "Just as it is written, 'FOR THY SAKE WE ARE BEING PUT TO DEATH ALL DAY LONG; WE WERE CONSIDERED AS SHEEP TO BE SLAUGHTERED' " (Romans 8:36). Slaughter hogs and the screaming is horrible; slaughter sheep and you do not hear a sound. "As a sheep before her shearers is dumb, so he openeth not his mouth" (Isaiah 53:7 KJV). Death worked in our Lord that life might work for us.

Let me repeat Andrew Murray's statement: "The cross leads to the Spirit and the Spirit to the cross." These are two different crosses. The cross that leads to the Spirit is Calvary's cross, which is common to every believer; but the cross that the Spirit leads us to is unique to each believer. Oh, granted, it is the same in that it is a place of death; yet it is unique in that it takes different forms. Thus Jesus said, "If anyone wishes to come after Me, let him deny himself, and take up *his* cross, and follow Me" (Mark 8:34, emphasis added).

Have you, precious one, found yourself in a difficult situation? Have you seen it as an opportunity for His life to be seen in you?

Delivered Over to Death

IT WAS HARD to hold back the tears. Her anguished lips trembled; she wanted to scream. Periodically her eyes would dart down at the wasted form of her mother. As the stretcher moved through the hospital corridors down to the dingy X-ray department, she wondered if her face reflected the anguish of her heart. She tried to smile but couldn't. How could she smile when her mother is suffering so? Why didn't God just take her? Why did He let her linger? What purpose was all this pain? The referred pain from mother to daughter was too much. Tears welled up. Suddenly she squinched her eyes, but it was too late. The tears spilled out, and her lips gave way to a whimper. As she looked down to see if her mother had heard her, their eyes locked. Her mother smiled weakly as she formed a kiss with her lips.

Finally they were alone outside X-ray. Looking away, gazing at nothing, still fighting tears, she suddenly felt her mother's hand in hers. Then her instructions came. Once more she was a little girl, listening to her mother's wonderful words of wisdom. "Smile, darling, smile. God has us on stage and all the world is watching. His grace is sufficient."

Who can smile in the face of death? Or who is willing to live in difficult situations? Only those who are willing to take up their cross and follow Him, saying, "Not my will but Thine be done." Only those, Beloved, who know that "to live is Christ, and to die is gain" (Philippians 1:21). Only those who know that they are considered as sheep to be slaughtered (Romans 8:36).

Only those who "are convinced that neither death, nor life, nor angels, nor principalities, nor things present, nor things to come, nor powers, nor height, nor depth, nor any other created thing, shall be able to separate us from the love of God, which is in Christ Jesus our Lord" (Romans 8:38,39).

In Balance

NOW, BELOVED, IF YOU read yesterday's devotion and are upset because you are a proponent of the doctrine that says that with enough faith and a positive confession you can be healed or never know sickness, please do not write me. I love you, but it grieves me to hear this unbalanced teaching that has wrested God's Word out of context and distorted it to the point of saying that Job and Paul ended up in their respective states because of a lack of faith or a negative confession. I would challenge you to search the Scriptures inductively rather than to base your doctrines on the experiences and interpretations of men. What grave harm this teaching is doing.

Yes, I believe God can and does heal. I have seen Him do it. Yet I know there are times when He does not heal (1 Timothy 5:23; Galatians 4:13-15).

Where, Beloved, is the teaching on holiness, on purity, on suffering for Christ's sake in the arena of His choosing, on a cross of His sovereign design? Much of our current theology lays emphasis on obtaining blessings rather than on attaining holiness, which comes through trials, testings, and sufferings.

"Death works in us, but life in you" (2 Corinthians 4:12). A death situation can take all sorts of forms, but whatever form it takes, it will be a difficult situation, a situation we would not choose nor remain in except for one purpose only—"that the life of Jesus also may be manifested in our body" (2 Corinthians 4:10).

"Therefore we do not lose heart, but though our outer man is decaying, yet our inner man is being renewed day by day. For momentary, light affliction is producing for us an eternal weight of glory far beyond all comparison" (2 Corinthians 4:16,17).

Note that Paul says that the "outer man is decaying." The Greek word for decaying (perish, KJV) is *diaphtheiro* and is in the passive voice, which means "is being destroyed."

Let us look unto God. "See now that I, I am He, and there is no god besides Me; it is I who put to death and give life. I have wounded, and it is I who heal; and there is no one who can deliver from My hand" (Deuteronomy 32:39).

Resurrection Follows Crucifixion

"DEATH WORKS IN US, but life in you" (2 Corinthians 4:12). How imperative it is that we know what this means, for here is the key to the Christlike life! Here is the bitter made sweet!

If men are again to see Jesus, it will only be as we bear the dying of Jesus in our bodies so that the life of Jesus also may be manifested in our bodies (2 Corinthians 4:10). Although I have said it before, let me repeat it: In God's economy, resurrection always follows crucifixion.

Calvary. Calvary! At times we speak of it so lightly, and yet it was a bitter and horrible experience. The flaying, the contortions of pain, the agony of unquenchable thirst. These were nothing compared to the sheer horror of absolute holiness being made sin and then forsaken by the Father (Psalm 22:1,2). All this awaited our Jesus, and He knew it full well, thus His pleading with the Father in Gethsemane.

> And He went a little beyond them, and fell on His face and prayed, saying, "My Father, if it is possible, let this cup pass from Me; yet not as I will, but as Thou wilt." And He came to the disciples and found them sleeping, and said to Peter, "So, you men could not keep watch with Me for one hour? . . . He went away again a *second* time and prayed, saying, "My Father, if this cannot pass away unless I drink it, Thy will be done." And again He came and found them sleeping. . . . And He left them again, and went away and prayed a *third* time, saying the same thing once more (Matthew 26:39-44, emphasis added).

What was the cup Jesus wanted to pass from Him? John 18:11 states clearly: "The cup which the Father has given Me, shall I not drink it?"

After Jesus had wrestled in prayer, they came to arrest Him. When Simon Peter saw this, he drew his sword and cut off the ear of the high priest's slave; his intention was to save Jesus from arrest. But Jesus told Peter to put away his sword. It was a bitter cup He had been given—the cup of death. Yet He would drink it, for it was the Father's will.

Death would work in Him, but life in us. If He did not drink it, we would die. Because He drank it, we live.

"If Any Man Is Thirsty"

THE TREE MADE the waters sweet. God's people could drink . . . and be satisfied.

Life is hard, bitter, cruel. It is marred, distorted, disfigured. Sin has done it. And whether your life is hard or not, you are still a member of the human race which has experienced untold suffering because of man's sin. We reach, grasp, and pursue dreams that somehow never quite satisfy the yearnings deep down inside. Even the pleasures of life sometimes seem to have a hint of bitterness about them. There is a purity missing. Thus our thirst is never quite satisfied.

Jesus knew this. He was man, and as man He knew that only one thing would ever really fill that God-shaped vacuum in everyone, and that is God. Fellowship with the Father. Communion with the Father. Submission to the Father.

Therefore, "on the last day, the great day of the feast, Jesus stood and cried out, saying, 'If any man is thirsty, let him come to Me and drink. He who believes in Me, as the Scripture said, "From his innermost being shall flow rivers of living water." ' But this He spoke of the Spirit, whom those who believed in Him were to receive; for the Spirit was not yet given, because Jesus was not yet glorified" (John 7:37-39).

The sweet water that would satisfy and take away life's bitterness would come from His death on the tree.

"The soldiers therefore came, and broke the legs of the first man, and of the other man who was crucified with Him; but coming to Jesus, when they saw that He was already dead, they did not break His legs; but one of the soldiers pierced His side with a spear, and immediately there came out blood and water" (John 19:32-34).

The disciples looking on mourned, they wept, they grieved, for they did not yet realize that resurrection would follow death, that the death worked in Him would be life for them. It was so then, and it is so today.

The Cost of Following Jesus

IT WOULD HAVE BEEN hard to believe that George Mueller, the handsome Prussian playboy, would become a man totally consecrated to God—a man who would live a life of such dedication that, even after his death in 1898, he would continue to minister clear into the twentieth century.

During his early years, George Mueller's life was entirely devoted to the world. By the time he was 16, his lifestyle was set. Drinking, gambling, lying, forging, stealing, partying were all an integral part of his life, even through his first year at seminary.

When he was 21, the turning point came. George saw a young man bow to his knees in prayer. He had never seen anyone on his knees, nor had he himself ever knelt to pray! Within a few days he was saved; weeks later he decided he ought to be a missionary. It was then that George had his first experience with taking up his cross to fully follow his Lord, for his father was vehemently opposed to his becoming a missionary.

> "Do not think that I came to bring peace on the earth; I did not come to bring peace, but a sword. For I came to SET A MAN AGAINST HIS FATHER, AND A DAUGHTER AGAINST HER MOTHER, AND A DAUGHTER-IN-LAW AGAINST HER MOTHER-IN-LAW; and A MAN'S ENEMIES WILL BE THE MEMBERS OF HIS HOUSEHOLD. He who loves father or mother more than Me is not worthy of Me; and he who loves son or daughter more than Me is not worthy of Me. And he who does not take his cross and follow after Me is not worthy of Me. He who has found his life shall lose it, and he who has lost his life for My sake shall find it" (Matthew 10:34-39).

At 21, George Mueller had a choice to make. It was only one of many that would come in the months and years ahead.

Following Jesus costs. It costs you your life—but then it gives you His!

What do you want? At what cost? You need to decide. This is your month of decision.

Life's Pivotal Point

THE CROSS IS THE pivotal point of history, of man's destiny, of every situation in life. Study the diagram below and you will see what I mean. Look up the Scriptures and meditate on them.

Of History

| B.C. | A.D. |

Of Man's Destiny

Death (Ephesians 2:1)	Life (1 John 5:11,12)
Sin (John 8:34)	Salvation (Forgiveness) (Ephesians 2:8,9)
Old Self (Colossians 3:9)	New Self (Has Holy Spirit) (Colossians 3:10; Ezekiel 36:27)
Heart of Stone (2 Corinthians 3:3)	New Heart of Flesh (Ezekiel 36:26)

Of Every Situation of Life

| Live by Flesh (Galatians 5:16,17) | Live by Spirit (Galatians 5:24,25) |

Not only does all of mankind's history pivot around Jesus Christ, but so does the history of your life. There were those B.C. days—before Christ came into your life; and now you have Anno Domini (A.D.), the years of our Lord.

And what was your destiny, your condition, before you came to Him? Christ's cross was your only way to life, to God.

Yet there is another cross—your cross—the cross that determines the outcome of every situation of your life, that works death in you, that deals with your self life . . . and in doing so manifests His life.

Think about it. Where are you in the history of your life?

Dying to Self

GEORGE MUELLER ONCE MADE this statement about himself:

> There was a day when I died,
>   utterly died,
> died to George Mueller and his opinions,
>   preferences,
>   tastes,
>   and will,
> died to the world, its approval
>   or censure,
> died to the approval
>   or blame of even my brethren,
>   and friends
> and since then
>   I have studied only to
> show myself approved unto God.

In April 1874, when he was almost 69, George Mueller wrote:

> "Delight thyself also in the LORD; and he shall give thee the desires of thine heart" (Psalm 37:4 KJV). I know what a lovely, gracious, bountiful Being God is, from the revelation which He has been pleased to make of Himself in His Holy Word; I believe this revelation; I also know from my own experience the truth of it; and therefore I was satisfied with God, I delighted myself in God; and so it came, that He gave me the desire of my heart. . . . "But may it never be that I should boast, except in the cross of our Lord Jesus Christ, through which the world has been crucified to me, and I to the world" (Galatians 6:14).[13]

Can you imagine the ramifications of such a life? Think upon it, Beloved.

In Dying, You Live

"SAVE YOURSELF, and come down from the cross!" (Mark 15:30). They shouted it at Jesus. They will shout it at you.

Listen to their voices. Close your eyes and imagine what it must have been like. He was hanging there for them, yet they wanted Him to come down from the cross! They didn't understand; they didn't know what they were saying.

And so it will be with you, Beloved. They will taunt you with their words, "Save yourself and come down from the cross." The same words will be said to you that were said to Jesus, but, in a sense, for a different reason. Maybe they won't understand your sacrifice. Maybe it will seem stupid to them, a waste, or a judgment from God.

"Why be a martyr?" they will probably reason. But in all probability their motive for trying to get you off that cross will be more self-centered. For your Christianity convicts them—not by your preaching, but by your eloquent silence in following your Lord's example when He laid down His life for us.

"I am the good shepherd; the good shepherd lays down His life for the sheep . . . even as the Father knows Me and I know the Father; and I lay down My life for the sheep" (John 10:11,15).

We, too, can lay down our lives, following in His footsteps, because we know the Father. And knowing Him, we know His heart for His sheep. And, in love's obedience, we will stay on the cross we have taken up as we have sought to follow Him.

"If You are the Son of God, come down from the cross," they cried. And "in the same way the chief priests, along with the scribes and elders, were mocking Him, and saying, "He saved others; He cannot save Himself" (Matthew 27:40b-42a).

O Beloved, if Christ had come down off that cross, He never could have saved us. He would have lived, and we would have died.

"Death works in us, life in you" if reversed would rightly read, "If life works in us, death will work in you."

It is in dying that we live. Stay on that cross. For His sake and the sake of others do not come down from your cross.

AUGUST 22

What Makes the Difference?

WHAT DISTINGUISHES Christians from non-Christians? The cross!

The cross is the identification mark of a Christian, first because of what it effects in our lives, and second because of our constant identification with its work. Note, I said "effects," not affects. Not that lives and situations of life are not affected; but the essential and fundamental thing is what the cross works (effects) *within* a Christian. That is what we will talk about for the next several days.

The cross works deliverance—from sin's dominion, from sin's penalty, and from Satan's power. Remember when we discussed Romans 6 and how our identification in Christ's death, burial, and resurrection set us free from sin's dominion? "For sin shall not be master over you, for you are not under law, but under grace" (Romans 6:14).[14]

And what about sin's penalty? It is one thing to be free from sin's dominion, but what do we do about the awful wages of sin which is death—eternal separation from God (Romans 6:23)?

Praise God, the cross wrought deliverance from sin's penalty! At Calvary, God "made Him who knew no sin to be sin on our behalf, that we might become the righteousness of God in Him" (2 Corinthians 5:21), causing Jesus to cry out "MY GOD, MY GOD, why hast Thou forsaken Me?" (Mark 15:34).

Because He was forsaken, we will never be (Hebrews 13:5)! Hallelujah! I just had to say it! O Father, thank You for so great a salvation. No longer condemned, no longer a slave, all because of Calvary!

But what about that enemy of our soul who for so long dominated our lives, the prince of the power of the air, that devil Satan who blinded our eyes, desiring our destruction?

Praise God, the cross also delivers us from Satan's power. "Since then the children share in flesh and blood, He Himself [the Lord Jesus Christ] likewise also partook of the same, that through death He might render powerless him who had the power of death" (Hebrews 2:14).

O Beloved, is this deliverance yours? And what will you give back to God for Calvary? Is the cross too much to ask?

Separated by the Cross

WHAT PRESSURES YOU MOST, your self or the world? It's a toss-up, isn't it? For one appeals to the other, and round you go in a vicious circle, first dealing with one and then the other. Is there no relief? Will it continue until you die?

Yes, it will. But you can die early! You can strike a death blow at the root of the problem. You can take up your cross.

The cross works separation—separation from self and separation from the world.

Listen to Paul's words again in Galatians 2:20: "I am crucified with Christ, nevertheless I live; yet not I" (KJV). *I* am not to live; it is no longer *my* life but His, no longer *my* body but His.

But the cross not only separates us unto God; it also separates us from the world. "But may it never be that I should boast, except in the cross of our Lord Jesus Christ, through which the world has been crucified to me, and I to the world" (Galatians 6:14).

Therefore, when self or pride would insist upon its own way, or when the world would try to squeeze us into its mold, we must remember the cross.

> Even so consider yourselves to be dead to sin, but alive to God in Christ Jesus. Therefore do not let sin reign in your mortal body that you should obey its lusts, and do not go on presenting the members of your body to sin as instruments of unrighteousness; but present yourselves to God as those alive from the dead, and your members as instruments of righteousness to God (Romans 6:11-13).

Did we not choose to follow Him? Then follow we must—His way!

> For the love of Christ controls us, having concluded this, that one died for all, therefore all died; and He died for all, that they who live should no longer live for themselves, but for Him who died and rose again on their behalf (2 Corinthians 5:14,15).

Life...
From the Cross

THE CROSS OF CALVARY not only effected our deliverance and our separation—it also brought us life. One can only pass from death to life through the cross of Calvary. Eternal life, the fruit of Calvary, came when that precious and priceless grain of wheat died.

> "Truly, truly, I say to you, unless a grain of wheat falls into the earth and dies, it remains by itself alone; but if it dies, it bears much fruit. He who loves his life loses it; and he who hates his life in this world shall keep it to life eternal. If anyone serves Me, let him follow Me; and where I am, there shall My servant also be; if anyone serves Me, the Father will honor him. Now My soul has become troubled; and what shall I say, 'Father, save Me from this hour'? But for this purpose I came to this hour" (John 12:24-27).

He was born to die that we might live; that was His purpose. Without His death there would be no life for us.

The same truth carries over into our own lives. When we are willing to die, to lose our lives for His sake and the gospel's, it brings life to others. All of life's power radiates from the cross.

Oh, that we would be willing to be poured out for others, even as the apostle Paul: "But even if I am being poured out as a drink offering upon the sacrifice and service of your faith, I rejoice" (Philippians 2:17).

Your Body...
His Temple

ALL THAT YOU and I will ever need, or should ever want, will be found in the fruit of Calvary. Since God gave you His all, His Son; since Jesus gave you His all, His life; since the Holy Spirit gives you His all, His indwelling presence, is it too much for Him to ask your all in return? Where would you be if it were not for Calvary?

How I shudder when I think about it! I look at the women "of this world," scantily clothed, moving from one husband to another or from one affair to another. I see them pushing, shoving, demanding, crying out for fulfillment as they abandon their God-ordained roles. I see their guilt, their frustration, their depression, and I understand. The pleasures of sin only endure for a season; there is always "a morning after the night before" that one must awaken to! I ache as I see them living with the "if onlys" of their past. I see it all, I feel it all, I've known it all, for before Calvary I was there.

But now, because of Calvary, it seems as if I have lived two totally different lives in two different bodies. Because I have become His temple, my body behaves so differently. It has been released from its slavery as an instrument of sin, and, although it still has its fleshly appetites, it has taken on robes and deeds of righteousness. It has become my means of ministering life rather than death. Truly I am a new creation in Christ Jesus. The old things have passed away; all things have become new (2 Corinthians 5:17).

I will never forget the day I discovered 2 Corinthians 5:17. I was a brand-new Christian, so hungry for truth that I couldn't get enough. One day I nearly came unglued. I couldn't believe what I had just read! It said that if any man was in Christ he was a new creature, old things had passed away! Why, that was an exact description of me! I shook my head! In my naïveté I thought God had put it into His Word just to describe what had happened to me! Now I know that it is God's work for all who come to Calvary.

New! Oh, it is so good to be new. And to be free! Free to be what He wants me to be.

Glory in the Cross

FREE! FREE FROM SIN, free from guilt—but most of all, free from me! Oh, how we need the message of Calvary, not just from the lips of men, but from their very lives. Will it not be easier for others to believe in Him who laid down His life for us if they see us lay down our lives also? Oh, that we would learn to glory in the cross.

How true are F. J. Huegel's words in his book, *The Cross of Christ, the Throne of God.*

> A great cry went up from the jeering, reviling Jews . . . "If he be the King of Israel let him now come down from the cross and we will believe on him." . . .
>
> In recent years a great cry, an echo of that ancient clamour, has gone up from the Church. If Christ would only come down from the Cross! We want the Christ of the Mount, we believe on the Christ of the healing ministry, we preach the Christ of the Social Gospel—but the Christ of the Cross is an offense. "Let him now come down from the cross and we will believe on him."
>
> But the King did not come down. His right to Kingship was never more Divine than in that awful Hour. It was from the Accursed Tree that He would reign. It was *here* that He wrought redemption. . . . It was when *here* He tasted death for every man, that the veil of the temple was rent, symbolic of the clearing of the way for immediate access into the Presence of God for all the children of men. . . .
>
> Christians do not enter into the unutterable glories of the Christian Life, in union with Christ, until they learn to glory, as did Paul, in this Cross, offensive as it is to the natural man. The Cross is *still* the only way to God. The Christ of the Cross is *still* humanity's only hope. Calvary's amazing consummation is *still* the Alpha and the Omega of the Church's life and message.[15]

Is this your message?

To Live Is Christ

"TAKE THE WORLD but give me Jesus." Oh, that this were the heart cry of every Christian, so that at every moment, in every place where we find ourselves, He would abide as our everlasting portion. To be satisfied with Him alone! Jesus, our all in all.

And where is such a passion schooled? How can one be so disciplined as to attain such a measure of life? Paul can tell us, for the passion of his life was that Christ would be exalted in his body whether by life or by death. His commitment was such that for him to live was Christ and to die was gain (Philippians 1:20,21).

And now listen as Paul describes that one thing which is of such unequaled value that he was willing to give his all for it:

> That I may gain Christ, and may be found in Him, not having a righteousness of my own derived from the Law, but that which is through faith in Christ, the righteousness which comes from God on the basis of faith, that I may know Him, and the power of His resurrection and the fellowship of His sufferings, being conformed to His death; in order that I may attain to the resurrection from the dead (Philippians 3:8b-11).

Being conformed to His death! There it is again. Death! But death followed by resurrection—"that I might attain to the resurrection from the dead"! What does this mean?

It means that you will lay hold of His life only to the degree that you lay hold of His death. You simply cannot have the world and have Jesus too! The two are incompatible. The world hates Jesus. You cannot cooperate with Jesus in becoming what He wants you to become and simultaneously be what the world desires to make you. If you would say, "Take the world but give me Jesus," then you must deny yourself and take up your cross. The simple truth is that your "self" must be put to death in order for you to get to the point where for you to live is Christ.

What will it be? The world and you, or Jesus and you? You do have a choice to make. God is setting it before you as you read these pages.

Are You Following Jesus?

YESTERDAY I TOLD YOU that you had a decision to make—your way or His cross. When you read that did you think, *Later, I'll decide later*? Or perhaps you said, *I will, but first I must . . .*

> And as they were going along the road, someone said to Him, "I will follow You wherever You go." And Jesus said to him, "The foxes have holes, and the birds of the air have nests, but the Son of Man has nowhere to lay His head" (Luke 9:57,58).

Do you want to follow Him? Then first you must know the path He trod. If it is to have any holding power, your decision to follow Jesus cannot be based on your emotions. It must be based on knowledge and conviction. Therefore, Jesus says, if we want to follow Him, we must be prepared to leave the comforts of home. How hard that is! So we hold on to things and lose the joy of companionship, the deep satisfaction of His "Well done, My good and faithful servant."

Jesus is saying to you, just as He said to another centuries ago, "Follow Me." That man's response was, "Permit me first to go and bury my father." And Jesus replied, "Allow the dead to bury their own dead; but as for you, go and proclaim everywhere the kingdom of God" (Luke 9:59,60). The man's father was not dead. He was really saying that he wanted to follow Jesus at a later time, after his father died.

Are relationships keeping you from following Him? Remember, you cannot love others more than Jesus and be His disciple (Luke 14:26).

Or did you start to follow Him but somehow got waylaid? Do you keep saying, "As soon as I _____, then I'm going to fully serve the Lord"?

> And another also said, "I will follow You, Lord; but first permit me to say good-bye to those at home." But Jesus said to him, "No one, after putting his hand to the plow and looking back, is fit for the kingdom of God" (Luke 9:61,62).

A Voluntary Sacrifice

THE CROSS IS endurance in the face of misunderstanding! Endurance like that of the Lamb of God, "WHO COMMITTED NO SIN, NOR WAS ANY DECEIT FOUND IN HIS MOUTH; and while being reviled, He did not revile in return; while suffering, He uttered no threats, but kept entrusting Himself to Him who judges righteously" (1 Peter 2:22,23).

The cross is a voluntary place of sacrifice. The choice is yours, and you must choose. Be assured that it will be a place of laying down your life for others. You will have to sacrifice yourself, even as your Lord did, in order to be used of God to save others. To live at the cross is to pour out your life for those who have misjudged, scorned, rejected, or deserted you. And then to say, "Father, forgive them; for they do not know what they are doing" (Luke 23:34).

How do you do it? It is not easy, and many times I fail, yet those failures are getting less frequent. Usually when I am tempted to react in my flesh, I stop and remember that others will never see Christ if they see me. And the world is still saying, "We would see Jesus."

If we remember this, then we will say with Paul, "For all things are for your sakes." This is the heart of Calvary.

We are not to lose heart, for "though our outer man is decaying, yet our inner man is being renewed day by day. For momentary, light affliction is producing for us an eternal weight of glory far beyond all comparison" (2 Corinthians 4:16,17).

Let me give you an illustration from the life of Henrich Suso.

> He had suffered much, so much that he was quite at home with the Cross. So at home that he once said to a friend, "I guess the Lord has forgotten me, He has not sent me any great trial for a long time." Then . . . a woman of evil character came to his door and left a babe in his arms, saying, "Here you have the fruits of your sin." Suso was innocent . . . [but he] went back home, took the child and reared it in silent resignation. Years later the woman . . . returned for her child, publishing to the four winds the saint's innocence. Thus was the Lambhood nature of Christ wrought into the great Suso. Verily we are the partakers of the Cross of our Redeemer.[16]

Follow Him

EVERYTHING THAT IS NATURAL in you is repulsed by turning the other cheek, going the extra mile, giving away your cloak, blessing those who curse you, praying for those who despitefully use you! I understand. Yet what did our Lord say?

> "You have heard that it was said, 'AN EYE FOR AN EYE, AND A TOOTH FOR A TOOTH.' But I say to you, do not resist him who is evil; but whoever slaps you on your right cheek, turn to him the other also. And if anyone wants to sue you, and take your shirt, let him have your coat also. And whoever shall force you to go one mile, go with him two. Give to him who asks of you, and do not turn away from him who wants to borrow from you. You have heard that it was said, 'YOU SHALL LOVE YOUR NEIGHBOR, and hate your enemy.' But I say to you, love your enemies, and pray for those who persecute you. . . . For if you love those who love you, what reward have you? Do not even the tax-gatherers do the same? And if you greet your brothers only, what do you do more than others? Do not even the Gentiles do the same? Therefore you are to be perfect, as your heavenly Father is perfect" (Matthew 5:38-48).

As you read this did you notice that Jesus was covering all the insults and misuses of our person, our possessions, and our privileges as members of the human race? Why can't we behave as "the Gentiles"? Why can others react "normally" and yet we cannot?

Because, precious ones, we are not just ordinary human beings. We are soldiers of the cross of Jesus Christ. To turn the other cheek, to give to him who asks, to pray, to love those who are your enemies is not natural. It is divine. It is sacrifice. It is death to the natural and thus resurrection of the supernatural.

Take Up Your Cross

THE CROSS MUST COME before the crown. Christianity is more than "I am saved. I am healed. I am happy!" Beware of any gospel which does not tell you that you are "not only to believe in Him, but also to suffer for His sake" (Philippians 1:29).

Satan offered Jesus the world and its temporal crown without the cross; he will seek you out with the same offer. And if that does not work, then he will seek to strip and afflict you as he did Jesus . . . as he did Job. His desire is to get you to turn back in order to spare your life. "Skin for skin!" Satan said to God. "Yes, all that a man has he will give for his life" (Job 2:4). Yet Satan is wrong, for anyone who has truly taken up his cross to follow his Lord has already died.

The story is told of a man whose life was being threatened because he would not deny Christ. He said, "You cannot take my life, I am already dead"—already dead because his life was hidden with Christ in God!

Yet boldness in the face of adversity does not always come immediately. Sometimes it must be wrestled out at the foot of the cross.

> Dr. J. G. Fleming tells how, in the days of the boxer uprising in China, Boxers captured a Mission school, blocked all gates but one, placed a cross before it, and sent in word that any one who trampled on that cross would go free, but that any one who stepped around it would be killed. The first seven, we are told, trampled on the cross and were allowed to go free. The eighth, a girl, knelt before the cross, and was shot. All the rest in a line of a hundred students followed her example.[17]

As sheep for the slaughter, we are put to death all day long! Beloved, beware of teaching that centers around man and concentrates on the blessings of God rather than on the cross of Christ—that is more concerned with our pleasure than with His! Realize that your Sovereign God permitted the bitter waters and that with the cross they will be made sweet and palatable. So do not run away; take up your cross and follow Him.

SEPTEMBER

Following in His Steps

Unjust suffering is so hard to understand. You wonder where God is and, if He is sovereign, how He can allow it. Sometimes the questions seem almost overwhelming, the suffering unbearable. How do you handle it? It is my prayer that God will use these daily messages to speak to you far beyond the power of these feeble words as you meditate upon them.

Handling the Difficulties of Life

HAVE YOU EVER FOUND yourself in a situation that was so horribly bitter that you wondered how you could bear it, how you could go on? I have. I've been in bitter situations—situations I never dreamed I would ever face. And yet there are moments when I look at the excruciatingly painful lives of others and realize that I have never really tasted bitterness. Not compared to some!

I remember one night when I sat on my bed and, as is my custom many evenings, took out a file folder of correspondence to work on. In that file folder was a transcript of a man's confession to a horrible crime. In words devoid of emotion, he told how he had raped a little girl. As he forced himself on her in the backseat of a car, she quietly said, in essence, "You shouldn't do this. Jesus says it's wrong." With that, in anger, he proceeded to kill her.

My account is brief. His was not. It seemed as if he did not miss one horrible detail. As I read, my body contorted with pain, my lips could not hold back the groans. The words resounded back and forth through the corridors of my mind, *Oh, God! . . . Why? . . . How?* The torment was too great. My mind turned into a chamber of horrors. Mentally I ran out of it and slammed the door.

"Father, I cannot think about it. I cannot understand it. It's too much for me . . . too difficult." And with that I buried my head in the bosom of my El Shaddai. I clung to the One I knew, the God of Calvary.

I would not, I could not permit myself to think of anything else but Him, the One who "was marred more than any man," and yet, in the midst of it all, cried out, "Father, forgive them; for they do not know what they are doing" (Isaiah 52:14; Luke 23:34).

There are many things, many situations, I could not handle if I did not know how to put the tree, the cross, into the bitter waters of life. That, Beloved, is what we will continue to talk about this month—taking the bitter and making it sweet, palatable, drinkable . . . bearable!

Making the Bitter Waters Sweet

WHEN THE CHILDREN OF ISRAEL came to the bitter waters of Marah, the Lord showed Moses a tree, "and he threw it into the waters, and the waters became sweet" (Exodus 15:25). And so the Lord showed us last month that our tree, the cross (Galatians 3:13), when applied to the bitter situations of life, can make them sweet . . . drinkable. As the waters of Marah were a test and the tree was the solution, so are the bitter situations in our lives a test for which we have a cross, His or ours. And you can know, Beloved, with every test that God "will provide the way of escape also, that you may be able to endure it" (1 Corinthians 10:13).

Although we know the truth of 1 Corinthians 10:13, don't we wonder deep in our hearts if life's situations are not sometimes really more than we can bear? That is what caused me such agony when I read the transcript of that little girl's death. I wondered, "How could she bear it, God?"

I do not know how God met that precious girl's need. But I do know God's Word, and so, when I start to wonder, I cling to the God of Calvary, who "causes all things to work together for good to those who love God, to those who are called according to His purpose" (Romans 8:28).

Knowing the God of Calvary will enable you to apply the cross to any bitter situation of life. Therefore, in the next days, we are going to look at the God who conceived and permitted Calvary. Then we will look at how these truths can be applied to any of life's bitter situations. Our devotions this month should then become, Beloved, a manual of how-to's in applying God's precepts.

Give yourself time to meditate each day upon what you read. Examine what I share very carefully in the light of His Word, and, if you find my words to be truth, then live accordingly. We shall move together step by step, precept upon precept, line upon line, trusting God's Spirit to guide us into all truth.

Bitter days are ahead; the last days are coming to a close. We must be prepared.

Living Crucified Lives

WHO IS THE GOD of Calvary? If we are called to live crucified lives, to deny ourselves and take up our cross and follow Him (Mark 8:34,35), then we need to know the character of the One who sanctioned Calvary. Or did He? Did God have anything to do with it, or was His Son nailed to that cross despite all God could do? Was the cross an accident, a whim of ungodly men, or was it part of God's predetermined plan? And, if God permitted Jesus' cross, does He permit mine?

Before Adam and Eve ever sinned and acted independently of God, there was the cross, older than man's sin. Jesus, the Lamb of God, was slain before the foundation of the world (Revelation 13:8). Therefore, when God confronted Adam, Eve, and the serpent in the Garden of Eden, He knew what was to be! There would be a righteous pardon for Adam and Eve's sin. Thus, to the serpent God said, "I will put enmity between you and the woman, and between your seed and her seed; He shall bruise you on the head, and you shall bruise him on the heel" (Genesis 3:15).

Crucifixion is the only death whereby the heel is bruised! God not only knew His Lamb would someday die, He also knew how He would die! Nothing escapes His notice, not even the sparrows sold for mere farthings nor the hairs of your head, which are numbered by Him.

Jesus' apostles knew this. God had announced beforehand through the prophets that His Christ would suffer (Acts 3:18). Thus, when the apostles experienced the suffering that came from taking up that cross and following Jesus, they cried to the God of Calvary, saying, "Truly in this city there were gathered together against Thy holy servant Jesus, whom Thou didst anoint, both Herod and Pontius Pilate, along with the Gentiles and the peoples of Israel, *to do whatever Thy hand and Thy purpose predestined to occur*. And now, Lord, take note of their threats, and grant that Thy bond-servants may speak Thy word with all confidence" (Acts 4:27-29, emphasis added).

The bitterness that came from following Jesus was made sweet because they knew the God of Calvary.

What about you? Do you know your God?

The Sovereign God Is There

HAVE YOU EVER FELT helpless? A victim of circumstances that seemingly could alter the course of your life? Have you wondered what would become of you?

O Beloved, have you not seen your Father, the Sovereign God, standing in the shadows behind the curtain as you have lived out those events? Look! He has been there all along! Look to His cross and drink the sweetness of the waters that flow because of Calvary.

> Pilate therefore said to Him, "You do not speak to me? Do You not know that I have authority to release You, and I have authority to crucify You?" Jesus answered, "*You would have no authority over Me, unless it had been given you from above*; for this reason he who delivered Me up to you has the greater sin." As a result of this Pilate made efforts to release Him, but the Jews cried out . . ." (John 19:10-12, emphasis added).

Jesus was neither in the hands of Pilate nor in the hands of the angry mob of Jews. His Father, the Sovereign God of Calvary, was in control, and Calvary was His plan. It had a purpose: man's redemption.

And so your cross, Beloved, comes from God.

In any trial, in any bitter situation, you are not alone, you are not helpless, you are not a victim. You have a tree, a cross, shown to you by the Sovereign God of Calvary. Whatever the trial or temptation, it is not more than you can bear. It is bearable. It can be handled. You can know as Joseph knew, "You meant evil against me, but God meant it for good in order to bring about this present result, to preserve many people alive" (Genesis 50:20).

Therefore, "consider it all joy, my brethren, when you encounter various trials, knowing that the testing of your faith produces endurance" (James 1:2,3).

You count it all joy by putting the cross into the trial and bringing death to your evaluation, to your expectations.

The God of Grace . . . of Love

LOOK AT CALVARY and what do you see besides a Sovereign God? You see that the One who is in control is a God of grace, a God of love. Only love would cause Him to give His Son to die in our stead, to bear the just judgment for our sins (Romans 5:8).

The God who bids me put the tree into the bitter situations of life is a God of love. He can never act apart from that love—a love that desires my highest good, that never fails, that never ceases no matter how I respond.

God's love is incomprehensible; we can never fully plumb its depths. Yet isn't it in the face of bitter situations that we question that love? Haven't you heard people say, "If God is a God of love, how could He ever permit this?" When people ask questions like this, they forget that the God of Calvary is not only a God of love, but also a God of grace.

Usually when we speak of God's grace we refer to that unmerited favor that is bestowed upon us when we deserve otherwise. And this is true. Yet grace has a more comprehensive definition. The grace of God is all that Christ is and has made available to us. This marvelous grace is available to all who would come to God through the Lord Jesus Christ. When one is justified by faith—put in right standing before God because he has acknowledged that Jesus is the Christ and has surrendered to Him as God and walks in the obedience of faith—then he has access to the grace of God.

Listen to Romans 5:1,2: "Therefore having been justified by faith, we have peace with God through our Lord Jesus Christ, through whom also we have obtained our introduction by faith into this grace in which we stand."

Since as a child of God you stand forever in the grace of God, you can rest secure in the knowledge that everything, including life's bitter situations, comes to you filtered through His fingers of love. And you can face them because His grace is sufficient to cover the bitterness of the past, even those years before you knew Christ, and it is also sufficient for anything the future may hold.

God's Grace Is Sufficient

SOME LIVE WITH the bitter memories of the past. Though the sickness of what happened is long gone, their minds still have periodic attacks of the dry heaves. A sight, a sound, a word, a look, a face—or even a mind with nothing to occupy it—brings on the nausea. There seems to be no cure. It was too horrible, too unfair, too much for any human being to bear! "No wonder I am what I am! Wouldn't you be too if the same thing had happened to you?"

And for many there really is no cure, no solution—at least not one that men could devise. They are victims, and what does it matter who is at fault; a victim is still a victim! The question is, are they to remain victimized for life? Is there never to be a way of escape? A new beginning? A life with purpose? Hope? Peace? Must they drink bitter waters forever, or can the bitter be made sweet, palatable, satisfying?

There is only one real solution. The cross—and the grace of the God of Calvary.

Paul called himself the chief or foremost of all sinners (1 Timothy 1:15). Formerly a blasphemer, a persecutor, a violent aggressor, he could have been distressed forever because he had given consent to Stephen's death and to the death of other Christians. Yet Paul would not waste the grace of God. He knew that where sin abounded, the grace of God abounded far more. There was one cure and only one and that was to choose to believe in the grace of God and say, "But by the grace of God I am what I am, and His grace toward me did not prove vain" (1 Corinthians 15:10). God's grace was not empty, devoid of power, or useless in respect to Paul's situation because Paul appropriated it!

Beloved, where are you? Regretting or resting? You cannot tell me there is no cure, no hope, no way to mend the wounds. To say so is to say that the grace of God is not sufficient, and to say that is to contradict His Word.

Whatever the past, whatever the present, whatever the future, the God who bids you take up your cross and follow Him says, "My grace is sufficient for you" (2 Corinthians 12:9).

Don't Waste God's Grace

HAVE YOU EVER RIDDEN the waves on an ocean beach? I'm not much of a swimmer, yet I enjoy riding the waves if I can stay in control of the situation. Watching for that big wave, catching it at its crest, and allowing it to propel me toward the shore is grand fun.

But have you ever been picked up by a wave, pitched headfirst into the surf, and held there by the relentless force of the water? I have, and I can tell you I was terrified. I tried desperately to regain my footing, and my throat burned from all the salt water I was swallowing. All dignity gone, crawling on all fours, I clawed the sand frantically, only to feel the undertow dragging me farther from the safety of the shore.

Fighting with all my strength, I finally made it to my feet and stumbled toward shore, only to be knocked down again as I was hit by a second wave. Engulfed in the water, I couldn't even cry for help. But I pleaded inwardly, *O God, don't let me drown!* Head over heels I turned until I hit the bottom. Finally getting to my feet, weak and choking, I was caught for a third time and taken under. With all that was in me I fought the waters and cried to God. I didn't give up. I didn't want to surrender to the waters. I wanted to live.

Those who have never been caught so helplessly in an undertow cannot understand my panic and my desperate effort to survive. But those who have been where I was can relate. They understand my struggle to survive and say with empathy, "I know the feeling. You survived because you were determined you weren't going to give up." And it is true: The survivors are those who "fight the good fight," those who persevere. If you do not persevere, you have surrendered!

A life lived for Jesus, a life lived at the cross, a life that follows Him fully will always be a life that is contested on every hand. Waves and undertows may knock the breath out of you, pulling you under, leaving you gasping and choking. Men may not hear your cries, but God will—"O God, don't let me drown!"

> The cords of death encompassed me, and the terrors of Sheol came upon me; I found distress and sorrow. Then I called upon the name of the LORD: "O LORD, I beseech Thee, save my life!" (Psalm 116:3,4).

"We Overwhelmingly Conquer"

THE PSALMIST ASKED: "What shall I render the LORD for all His benefits toward me?" (Psalm 116:12). What is the answer? Is it not to live at the cross, letting the bitter be made sweet?

I read of just such a woman, to me a heroine of the faith, in *The President's Letter*, a publication sent out by Dr. Robertson McQuilkin, former president of Columbia Bible College and Seminary. In April 1982, he told the story of Mae Louise Westervelt. When I read her story, I remembered my experience at the beach, for Mae Louise was a survivor. She knew the God of Calvary, and, because of this, the bitter was palatable.

The child of missionary parents, Mae Louise's dream was to provide a home for missionary children. Her husband shared that dream. "She was carrying her first-born when her husband was crippled in body and spirit in a terrible automobile accident. Partially recovered, he carried on valiantly, but Mae Louise was destined to carry the spiritual thrust of the family."

While recovering from the first wave, they were hit by a second—their newborn son was born helplessly handicapped. The third wave came years later when, at the age of 11, their son drowned. But life went on—without bitterness.

"FOR THY SAKE WE ARE BEING PUT TO DEATH ALL DAY LONG; WE WERE CONSIDERED AS SHEEP TO BE SLAUGHTERED" (Romans 8:36).

A fourth wave was to hit when their daughter, a few weeks away from college graduation, was killed in an automobile accident.

"But in all these things we overwhelmingly conquer through Him who loved us" (Romans 8:37).

Undaunted, Mae Louise kept on leading the missions program in her little Baptist church, teaching the teenage girls, and shepherding the children of the neighborhood.

A fifth wave and a sixth would come, and again she would say, "The LORD preserves the simple; I was brought low, and He saved me" (Psalm 116:6).

You can say the same, if you will. He saves you. He preserves you at Calvary. Don't give up. Fight the good fight of faith.

Fighting the Good Fight

ALTHOUGH MAE LOUISE WESTERVELT and her husband never attained their dream of providing a home for missionary children, God did allow them to secure several low-cost homes near Columbia Bible College. These were rented to students and to missionaries home on furlough.

Then, unexpectedly, she was hit for the fifth time. As her husband was changing a tire by the roadside, he was killed by a drunken driver.

"But we have this treasure in earthen vessels, that the surpassing greatness of the power may be of God and not from ourselves; we are afflicted in every way, but not crushed . . . always carrying about in the body the dying of Jesus, that the life of Jesus also may be manifested in our body" (2 Corinthians 4:7,8,10).

"Undaunted, Mae Louise walked the streets of Denny Terrace, selling Avon products to support her adopted son, and sharing the good news of life in Christ. On Fridays she visited the sick in the hospital. On Thursdays there was an evangelistic home visitation, at other times there were Bible studies with the unsaved."

Then came the sixth wave. "A pacemaker extended her fragile life, but she just kept pressing on. Sunday morning she would gather a load of little boys in her rattly old Plymouth, bring them to Sunday school and sit with them as they wiggled their way through the worship service."

At Christmastime Dr. McQuilkin told her, "You are one of my true heroes!"

A hero she was, a soldier of the cross, and her God had not let her drown. Nor had she let Him down.

Then one day, having been poured out as a drink offering upon the sacrifice and service of others' faith (Philippians 2:17), while sipping tea as she sat on her living room sofa, she heard her Lord say, "Come home, and we'll dine together at My table."

Someday, Beloved, He will call you home. How comfortable will you be when you see Him face-to-face, the God of Calvary? How well have you fought the good fight? How well have you kept the faith?

God Is Merciful

THE GOD OF CALVARY is a merciful God. You can trust His mercy in any bitter situation because at the cross He granted you your own High Priest, the one and only mediator between God and man, the man Christ Jesus (1 Timothy 2:5), that you might always find mercy and grace to help in time of need (Hebrews 4:16).

How quick we are to cry for justice! How slow to realize that what we need is not justice but mercy!

And what is the difference?

Justice is that which is fair or correct in treatment, in reward, or in punishment. When we find ourselves in seemingly unjust circumstances, we need to ask ourselves: "Why should any living mortal, or any man, offer complaint in view of his sins? Let us examine and probe our ways, and let us return to the LORD" (Lamentations 3:39,40). And when we return, what will we find? Justice? Yes, justice, but justice in mercy poured out in righteous wrath, not upon us but upon the One who, voluntarily, was made to be sin for us. At Calvary we see God as "just and the justifier" that we might obtain mercy, for "His mercies are over all His works" (Psalm 145:9).

Mercy goes beyond justice. Mercy is kindness or compassion over and above what can be expected or even claimed. And how does mercy differ from grace? "Grace is concerned for man as he is guilty; mercy, as he is miserable."[18]

In the misery of the bitter situations of life, we need to remember that each situation has been sovereignly permitted by a merciful God. Enthroned at His right hand is our High Priest who can sympathize with our weaknesses because, although without sin, He was "tempted in all things as we are" (Hebrews 4:15). Therefore, we can hold fast to our confession. We need not give in or give up.

> The LORD's lovingkindnesses indeed never cease, for His compassions never fail. They are new every morning; great is Thy faithfulness (Lamentations 3:22,23).

Mercy—it is yours for the appropriation—new every morning. You may not say, "I cannot have it because I don't deserve it." You can only say, "I do not have it because I will not take it."

The Cross... the Supernatural

DOES THE CALL TO TAKE UP your cross and follow Jesus strike terror in your heart? I can understand, but you need not fear. Let me explain.

The cross was an instrument of death, and man is bent on life. Yet, even more than death, the cross was an instrument of inexorable torture. It was the place of the cursed, not only to the Jews but also to the Romans (Galatians 3:13). Cicero wrote, "Let the very name of the cross be far away not only from the body of a Roman citizen, but even from his thoughts, his eyes, his ears" (Cicero, *Pro Rabirio* 5).

Yes, natural men were to shun the cross, to keep it from their thoughts, their eyes, their ears. Yet, to those who would be God's men and women, came the call of Jesus to keep the cross ever before them. Why? Because the cross is where the natural dies and the supernatural takes over (Galatians 2:20).

We who love God are never to fear the cross. Rather we are to fear its absence. Therefore, when you want to run, to escape, to save yourself from the call to forsake all and take up your cross and follow Him, you can be certain that fear is not from God.

Fear would cause you to doubt the character of the God of Calvary, who is a God of love. Fear that would keep you from the cross comes only from the one who would offer you a crown without a cross, the devil himself. Satan fears the cross, for there men are set free from bondage to death.

O Beloved, you can rest secure in His love—be it in taking up your cross daily or in applying the cross to each of life's bitter situations.

We will talk more about this tomorrow, but for today let me leave you with this thought. If you will permit yourself to be secure in God's love, then that security will become the foundation for dealing with all other fears. Never let the cross out of your thoughts, your hearing, or your sight, for it is God's eternal testimony of His immutable love. It is your release from the natural to the supernatural.

Fear Immobilizes . . . Faith Energizes!

WE NEED TO TALK about fear for two more days, dear one, for we live in times when men's hearts will fail them for fear.

In any bitter situation, you need not fear. See that cross? What does it tell you? It tells you that your Sovereign Father God loves you with a perfect love. Remember this. Never forget it.

Fear is to Satan what faith is to God. Satan operates on the basis of fear, and that immobilizes you. He will parade before you the fear of death, the fear of failure, the fear of criticism or rejection, the fear of having your weaknesses exposed for all to see. And where does all this fear find its root? Is it not in pride? And what is the answer to pride? Death. The cross. There all pride is stripped away. When Jesus hung on the cross, He hung there at almost eye level, stark naked, to be gaped upon by dogs and bands of evildoers (Psalm 22:16,17).

Let me say it again: Fear is to Satan what faith is to God.

God never operates on the basis of anything but faith. "Without faith it is impossible to please Him" (Hebrews 11:6). "Be it done to you according to your faith" (Matthew 9:29).

While fear immobilizes, faith energizes. Therefore, in every bitter or difficult situation, if you apply the cross, you will drink the sweetness of power, love, and a sound mind that belongs to every believer. "For God hath not given us the spirit of fear; but of power, and of love, and of a sound mind" (2 Timothy 1:7 KJV). That power is resurrection power.

Last month I shared that, in God's economy, resurrection always follows crucifixion. Thus the apostle Paul prayed that the eyes of our understanding would be enlightened that we might know "the surpassing greatness of His power toward us who believe . . . which He brought about in Christ, when He raised Him from the dead, and seated Him at His right hand in the heavenly places, far above all rule and authority and power and dominion, and every name that is named, not only in this age, but also in the one to come" (Ephesians 1:19-21).

Fear is always held in check by power, love, and a sound mind.

Power, Love, and a Sound Mind

GOD HAS GIVEN YOU power, love, and a sound mind. They are yours for the believing. Faith unlocks the door to God's treasure house. To fear is to forget God and to live like a pauper when you really are a prince.

> "I, even I, am He who comforts you. Who are you that you are afraid of man who dies, and of the son of man who is made like grass; that you have forgotten the LORD your Maker, who stretched out the heavens, and laid the foundations of the earth; that you fear continually all day long because of the fury of the oppressor" (Isaiah 51:12,13).

Fear of man causes us to forget God. Note this carefully. And who is man in comparison with God? Is not the Sovereign God of Calvary in control? Of course!

When fear hits, remember you have been given a sound mind. A sound mind is a mind under control (2 Timothy 1:7). You don't have to be thrown into a tizzy, lose touch with reality, check out, or go bananas (that's a fruit that does not belong to the Spirit)! The Holy Spirit is there with His fruit basket (Galatians 5:22,23). Partake! There's self-control in there! Bring your thoughts, every one of them, captive to His obedience. Remember, His Word is truth: "When I am afraid, I will put my trust in Thee. In God, whose word I praise, in God I have put my trust; I shall not be afraid" (Psalm 56:3,4). "I will cry to God Most High, to God who accomplishes all things for me" (Psalm 57:2).

That's right, cry to Him and know that love provides all you need (Romans 8:32).

"For I am convinced that neither death, nor life, nor angels, nor principalities, nor things present, nor things to come, nor powers, nor height, nor depth, nor any other created thing, shall be able to separate us from the love of God, which is in Christ Jesus our Lord" (Romans 8:38,39).

Sweet, isn't it? Drink deep and be satisfied. It is all yours because of the cross.

Endure the Cross

WE HAVE LEARNED HOW to take the bitter and make it sweet by looking to the God of Calvary. But is there anything more we can learn about how we are to respond or behave when we are being crucified by another? How do we bear up under sorrows when suffering unjustly? This is what I mean when I say "crucified by another."

Peter and the Gospels have the answer, and I believe that as we examine them together, God is going to give us some invaluable insights.

Some of you are suffering so unjustly, and I ache for you. I hurt with you. There is a mental anguish that can exceed even physical pain, and some of you may suffer more emotionally than you do physically. Yet emotional pain also takes its toll on the body. We are psychosomatic beings. What affects the body affects the soul, and vice versa.

Or maybe you are not hurting right now; maybe all is sweet. Perhaps God has given you a time of rest, a time to prepare, a time to grow in the easy progression of the seasons, rather than in a forced hothouse environment.

The early church had this kind of rest and uncontested time to grow. Then, suddenly, the tide turned with the stoning of Stephen, and they all fled Jerusalem.

Please, let me share a word of admonition. Watch carefully during these times of rest, for it is then that we can become lax in spiritual exercises and drift away, only to be caught in a weakened condition, unprepared for the trials of faith that must come if we are ever to be fully prepared to be glorified with Him—since "indeed we suffer with Him in order that we may also be glorified with Him" (Romans 8:17).

Suffering . . . suffering unjustly . . . teaches us obedience and matures us even as it did Jesus. Listen carefully to Hebrews 5:8,9: "Although He was a Son, He learned obedience from the things which He suffered. And having been made perfect, He became to all those who obey Him the source of eternal salvation."

We have been called to suffer; therefore, let's learn how by looking unto Jesus, "the author and perfecter of faith, who for the joy set before Him endured the cross" (Hebrews 12:2).

The Reality of Suffering

UNJUST SUFFERING IS HARD. It goes against the flesh. And we are all made of flesh!

When He saved us, God crucified the old man, setting us free from slavery to sin. He gave us a new heart and put His Spirit within us. Our bodies became His temple. Yet, with all that, God left us in a body of flesh, for "we have this treasure in earthen vessels" (2 Corinthians 4:7).

Because of this we are going to suffer just as any other human being would suffer. Rejection, abuse, contempt, defamation, or any other cruel thing that man can do to man does not hurt less simply because we are a child of God. Note, now, that I am talking about the reality of pain, *not* the mentality of acceptance which can ease pain's intensity! As Christians we still sorrow, we still grieve, but not as others who have no hope (1 Thessalonians 4:13).

As Christians, we are not of this world. We are strangers and pilgrims whose citizenship is in heaven (Philippians 3:20). As a result, we are not only called upon to suffer the normal distresses of life in a world under bondage to sin, but also to face, as Christ faced, the hostility of sinners (Hebrews 12:3).

And how do Christians deal with all the suffering—much of which will come simply because we are living in a world that cannot understand our righteous lifestyle and even hates us for it? How do we respond in such a way as to let the life of Jesus Christ be manifested in our *mortal* flesh?

We will answer that question step-by-step in the days to come as we look at God's Word precept upon precept. Today, though, precious one, I want you to remember one thing: Being a Christian does not mean you hurt any less.

So, if at times you feel as if your heart will literally break, do not despair. You are not any less "spiritual"! If Jesus cried, shedding tears, shall we not also cry (Hebrews 5:7)?

It is not the pain of suffering that reflects your Christlikeness; it is how you handle that pain!

When You Suffer Unjustly

TODAY I WANT US to concentrate on one passage of Scripture: 1 Peter 2:18–3:2. You will need to turn to this passage in your Bible. To many of you this will be a very familiar portion of God's Word; yet I pray that as you read it, you will ask God for a fresh insight into what He is saying.

Read through the passage first, and then we will do a little digging together with the questions below. Have a piece of paper handy and on it put the heading: "When You Suffer Unjustly."

1. Now that you have read the passage, go back and mark the words "suffer" and "suffering" like this suffer each time they appear.

2. Verse 21 says, "You have been called for this purpose." To whom is Peter speaking? Write it on your paper. Do you think this applies to Christians in general or only to servants (slaves)? Why?

3. The word "example" in verse 21 is translated from the Greek word *hupogrammos*. This is the only place this word is used in the New Testament. It refers to an outline drawing or copybook of letters to be used by a pupil.

Who is to be our example in suffering? What steps did He go through that we are to follow when we suffer unjustly? List them.

4. Mark the word "submissive" with a submissive each time it appears. What role does submission play in unjust suffering? Look at 1 Peter 2:20 in conjunction with this.

5. What does the phrase "In the same way" refer to (1 Peter 3:1)?

6. What is the key in this passage when it comes to suffering: my pain, the equity of it all, my behavior, Christ's toughness in enduring, or God's judgment? Underline one and write out why you chose the answer you did.

Now, Beloved, meditate on all you've read today.

Finding Favor With God

FAVOR WITH GOD. Beloved, there is nothing on this earth, absolutely nothing, greater or more satisfying than knowing that what you have done has found favor with God. Conversely, there is nothing worth the loss of His favor, for when this world and all it contains pass away and you stand naked before God, nothing else will matter except that you have found favor in the eyes of the One who created you for His pleasure.

When "for the sake of conscience toward God a man bears up under sorrows when suffering unjustly" (1 Peter 2:19), then you find favor with God.

Why? Because, you have been called for this purpose.

Precious one, if you can only see it as having a purpose, suffering is so much easier to take. You are not a doormat to be trampled upon by the feet of wicked man; you are a platform to be used to give them a closer glimpse of God.

You are not alone. Jesus has gone before you, suffering unjustly, and becoming to every man and woman either a stepping-stone into heaven or a stone of stumbling into the depths of hell. He did His part. The choice then became man's. God asks no more and no less of you than that you follow in His steps (1 Peter 2:21).

And what is His example? I know you saw it for yourself yesterday, but let me state it again and elaborate on each step just a little so we won't miss what God wants us to know and to do.

The first thing we see is that when Jesus suffered unjustly, He did not sin.

What does God mean when He says that Jesus did not sin? Well, sin has a number of definitions in God's Word, such as being a transgression of the law (1 John 3:4) or knowing to do good and doing it not (James 4:17). However, the root of all sin is independence from God. It is "each one turning to his own way" (Isaiah 53:6). And when Jesus suffered unjustly, He did not act or react independently of God. Instead, He did what pleased the Father.

Therefore, when we are suffering unjustly, we must run to God and say, "O Father, what would You have me do? I will to do Your will."

Your High and Noble Purpose

NEVER FORGET THAT IT was Christ's purpose to suffer—the just suffering for the unjust so that the unjust might be made just before God.

And, Beloved, don't forget your purpose. It is a high and noble one, a godly one, one that the world will scoff at, calling you a fool while they seek to crush out your lifeblood. Oh, do not listen to the taunts of blind, ignorant, deceived sinners who shout, "Come down off that cross." Do not believe them when they say, "If God delighted in you, He would deliver you!" They know not what they say. "For the word of the cross is to those who are perishing foolishness, but to us who are being saved it is the power of God" (1 Corinthians 1:18).

Remember as they crucify you that "the foolishness of God is wiser than men, and the weakness of God is stronger than men" (1 Corinthians 1:25). Therefore, follow Christ's example, "WHO COMMITTED NO SIN, NOR WAS ANY DECEIT FOUND IN HIS MOUTH; and while being reviled, He did not revile in return; while suffering He uttered no threats" (1 Peter 2:22,23).

What was the second thing Christ did in leaving us an example? He kept His mouth shut. No battle with words. No, "You'll be sorry," or "You'll get yours." As a lamb before its shearers is dumb, so He opened not His mouth (Isaiah 53:7).

To me, this is the hardest example of all. All my life I have fought with my tongue. It has been my weapon. I was always too weak to overcome anyone physically, so I fought and defended with my tongue. And my flesh is adept in verbal battles.

Remember how we used to taunt each other as children? "Sticks and stones will break my bones, but names will never hurt me!" How childish we were—and how wrong! It is easier to mend bones than to restore the wounds inflicted by cruel tongues. Many of these wounds never show; yet without God's balm of Gilead they can leave irreparable damage.

What have you said when you've suffered unjustly? What good did it do?

Let God Control Your Tongue

SO FAR WE HAVE SEEN two things that we are to do when someone treats us unjustly. *First*, we are not to sin, not to act independently from God. And *second,* we are to keep our mouths shut. This means no verbal battles; it does not mean, however, that we give our reviler the "silent treatment."

Jesus did talk while they crucified Him, but He did not retaliate in kind or utter threats. His speech was not abusive. Controlled by God's Spirit, He never acted apart from love. Love "does not seek its own, is not provoked, does not take into account a wrong suffered" (1 Corinthians 13:5). That was Love hanging on that tree, remember?

And because you, too, are being crucified, the same God of Calvary is present with you when you take up your cross to follow Him. Please do not carry what I am saying to an extreme that God never intended. The key is Christianity in balance—balance that comes from knowing the whole counsel of God rather than going off on tangents. To help us avoid this, let me cite a time when Jesus did respond.

> Pilate answered, "I am not a Jew, am I? Your own nation and the chief priests delivered You up to me; what have You done?" Jesus answered, "My kingdom is not of this world. If My kingdom were of this world, then My servants would be fighting, that I might not be delivered up to the Jews; but as it is, My kingdom is not of this realm." Pilate therefore said to Him, "So You are a king?" Jesus answered, "You say correctly that I am a king. For this I have been born, and for this I have come into the world, to bear witness to the truth. Everyone who is of the truth hears My voice." Pilate said to Him, "What is truth?" (John 18:35-38).

You might also want to read John 19:9-11.

The example Jesus left us is a tongue under God's control, gracious speech seasoned with salt (Colossians 4:6), wisdom from above which is "pure, then peaceable, gentle, reasonable, full of mercy and good fruits, unwavering, without hypocrisy" (James 3:17).

Pray . . . God Is With You

THE THIRD THING Jesus did that we are also to do was to pray, entrusting Himself to God. We cannot survive in such a way as to find favor with God without communicating with Him. The whole ordeal of the cross was wrestled out in Gethsemane and then sustained on Calvary. God does not expect us to go it alone. To do so is more than we can bear.

The apostle Paul speaks of this in 2 Timothy 4:16,17: "At my first defense no one supported me, but all deserted me; may it not be counted against them. But the Lord stood with me, and strengthened me, in order that through me the proclamation might be fully accomplished, and that all the Gentiles might hear; and I was delivered out of the lion's mouth."

Jesus, as He walked through the Kidron Valley to Gethsemane, said: "Behold, an hour is coming, and has already come, for you to be scattered, each to his own home, and to leave Me alone; and yet I am not alone, because the Father is with Me" (John 16:32).

God's promise to us is as true as He is unchangeable. "For He Himself has said, 'I WILL NEVER DESERT YOU, NOR WILL I EVER FORSAKE YOU,' so that we confidently say, 'THE LORD IS MY HELPER, I WILL NOT BE AFRAID. WHAT SHALL MAN DO TO ME?'" (Hebrews 13:5,6).

His promise is good. You can trust Him. But remember, all that He said is ineffectual if you do not appropriate it by faith. God is waiting for faith's call. His ear is not deaf that it cannot hear, nor is His arm short that it cannot help (Isaiah 59:1), but you must call to Him in the day of trouble (Psalm 50:15).

Peter says that Jesus "kept entrusting Himself to Him who judges righteously" (1 Peter 2:23). He kept on entrusting Himself to God during His unjust suffering. He stayed in constant communion with the Father.

O Beloved, you may not feel like praying, but do not quit. You cannot survive without it!

Entrust Yourself to God

YOU CANNOT PRAY EFFECTIVELY to someone you really do not trust. This is the grabber. This is where the rubber hits the road.

It stirs our soul when we hear the mighty battle cry: We must be soldiers of the cross! But when it gets down to that moment when we are to take up our cross and follow Him, what is our response? Or, to put it bluntly, can we really trust God? Can we really give Him our all and leave the results with Him? Can we handle life's situations God's way, according to His Word, rather than our way?

Our counselors at Precept Ministries and many of our dedicated Precept leaders are finding that, under the guise of Christianity, many today are being counseled to flee from the suffering that obedience would bring. In many counseling situations, human philosophy has usurped the authority of God's Word.

When Jesus suffered unjustly, He "kept entrusting Himself to Him who judges righteously" (1 Peter 2:23). Note the phrase, "who judges righteously." The suffering was unjust. Jesus was the innocent victim. Yet He knew God was in control. He had complete trust in the will and sovereignty of His Father. In God's time and in God's way, He would be vindicated.

You will be too, if you follow Christ's example. Some of you have unjustly lost homes, money, children, land, prestige, possessions, even credibility. It has seemed almost unbearable, hasn't it? You dare not even let your thoughts dwell on it, for to do so would throw you into depression or worse. So how do you handle it? There is only one way. Complete trust and constant communion. It is not over yet. There is a payday someday—a day of retribution.

Just think! Jesus could have called a legion of angels to come to His defense. But He didn't. It wasn't God's time. So instead, He entrusted Himself to Him who judges righteously.

Do you find yourself in the same straits? I know it's hard. I cannot even begin to imagine how hard it is for you. Yet I do know that, because He promised, it is not more than you can bear (1 Corinthians 10:13). Will you follow His example?

Bear Another's Sin

FINALLY, 1 PETER TELLS US of one last thing Jesus did that we, too, must do when we suffer unjustly. It's a hard step, and God is patiently teaching me the reality of it in my own life. *"He Himself bore our sins in His body on the cross"* (1 Peter 2:24).

This, I believe, was the hardest part of Calvary for Jesus, for two reasons. First, He bore the sins of every human being who ever lived. Second, Jesus Himself knew no sin; therefore, sin was much more repulsive to Him than it would ever be to me or to you.

No invisible shield went up to protect Jesus from the full impact of sin's despicable awfulness. I want to say more, to describe it better, but I cannot find words atrocious enough. To me, bearing another's sins in your own body must be the epitome of "turning the other cheek"— being willing to be hurt, if it will heal the one who is hurting you.

We are not talking about the passive reaction of quietly "taking it" because you don't have the courage to do otherwise. We are talking about exercising that amazing kind of strength which is able to receive unjust, personal suffering for the purpose of healing.

Neither are we talking about finding masochistic pleasure at the hands of a sadist. No, the only delight here is in finding favor with God for Christlike suffering. Read 1 Peter 2:24,25 again so you can see the purpose for bearing another's sins in our body. As you read, think about the use of the words "that," "for," and "but now."

> And He Himself bore our sins in His body on the cross, that we might die to sin and live to righteousness; for by His wounds you were healed. For you were continually straying like sheep, but now you have returned to the Shepherd and Guardian of your souls.

Whenever I have been hurt unjustly, my tendency has been to fight back, to hurt back, rather than just take it and keep on loving in return. Now, though, God has opened my eyes, and by His grace I'm learning, opportunity by opportunity, to look beyond my hurt to their healing.

After all, Jesus won me that way! Amazing grace!

Forgive Them ... Love Them

I WANT US TO GO ONE STEP further in looking at the cross so that we might gain an even deeper insight into how we are to behave when we are "being crucified" by another.

Luke 23:34 gives us the first of the seven statements that Jesus made during those dark hours of crucifixion: "Father, forgive them; for they do not know what they are doing."

The cross is a demonstration of love and forgiveness. It is at Calvary that love and forgiveness marry, becoming inseparably one.

Jesus said: "For if you forgive men for their transgressions, your heavenly Father will also forgive you. But if you do not forgive men, then your Father will not forgive your transgressions" (Matthew 6:14,15). Therefore, the work of the cross begins with, "Father, forgive them."

No bitterness. Bitterness is incompatible with the character of God. What about anger? Can you be angry? Yes! There can be righteous anger at sin, but no bitterness. There is a difference! Look at Calvary and you see the wrath of God poured out on sin as you hear Jesus cry, "MY GOD, MY GOD, WHY HAST THOU FORSAKEN ME?" (Matthew 27:46). But, before wrath, did you not first hear His pardon to sinners? Calvary shows you the love of God, the wrath of God, the forgiveness of God, but never do you see bitterness in God, because bitterness contradicts His character.

If you are bitter, Beloved, it is because you have not put the tree into the waters. Forgive them and you will find the situation palatable.

Now don't say, "I can't." If you are a child of God it is not that you cannot, it is that you will not!

Forgive them. It will be the beginning, and from there you can move forward. You must by faith utter those words, "Father, forgive them, for they do not know what they are doing." And believe me, they do not know! They are blind, living in darkness. Yet your light may pierce that darkness. You may be their only human hope.

May they hear the gospel through your words, "Father, forgive them," so that their blood will not be upon your hands.

Look Beyond the Bitter

WHAT FOLLOWS CRUCIFIXION? Paradise! Fellowship with the faithful of God, with those who have believed, who have persevered, who have held "fast the beginning of our assurance firm until the end" (Hebrews 3:14). Jesus' second statement from the cross was the promise of Paradise to one of the malefactors being crucified with Him. "And He said to him, 'Truly I say to you, today you shall be with Me in Paradise'" (Luke 23:43).

All suffering has an end. To those who believe on Jesus, it has a beginning and it has an end. It will not go on forever because it is controlled by the Alpha and the Omega. The end for every believer is Paradise, and Paradise belongs to God. It is the reward of those who overcome: "To him who overcomes, I will grant to eat of the tree of life, which is in the Paradise of God" (Revelation 2:7). Isn't that beautiful?

What do we need in the midst of suffering? Hope! The hope of glory, of life, of fellowship with Jesus! And what do we need to convey to others as we hang there suffering? We need to convey the reality and glory of the sure hope of heaven, "for I consider that the sufferings of this present time are not worthy to be compared with the glory that is to be revealed to us" (Romans 8:18).

And what does such certainty say to those who still persist in crucifying us? When we suffer and are "in no way alarmed by [our] opponents" because Paradise is before us, then our confidence becomes "a sign of destruction for them, but of salvation for you, and that too, from God" (Philippians 1:28).

The bitter is made sweet if we keep looking to the reward, enduring as seeing Him who is invisible, and remembering His promise, "You shall be with Me in Paradise."

This, Beloved, is God's gift to you—the promise of heaven for all those who receive God's gift, the Lord Jesus Christ.

The Cure for Misery

JESUS' FIRST THREE STATEMENTS from the cross reveal our Lord's primary focus, and what a marvelous lesson there is in them for us. If heard with your heart so that this lesson is truly believed and acted upon, it can become one of the most potent cures for the cancer of misery that consumes the lives of many of God's children.

Jesus' third statement, like His first two, dealt with His concern for others.

> When Jesus therefore saw His mother, and the disciple whom He loved standing nearby, He said to His mother, "Woman, behold, your son!" Then He said to the disciple, "Behold, your mother!" And from that hour the disciple took her into his own household (John 19:26,27).

Recently I have read two autobiographies of Jews who became Christians and lived under the terror of Hitler's holocaust. I have tried as best I could to imagine the fellowship of their sufferings that I might not live at ease, with no thought for those who are "filling up that which is lacking in Christ's afflictions" (Colossians 1:24). As I read, over and over I was challenged by those who said, "I will take his beating for him," or those who acted as one Jewish girl did when she gave herself up to be raped in order to spare the lives of the other women hidden behind coal boxes in a cellar.

You see, the cross assumes our death, the surrender of our life that others might live. And yet what do we do? We cling to what is not ours! "Do you not know that . . . you are not your own? For you have been bought with a price: therefore glorify God in your body" (1 Corinthians 6:19,20).

If we would only learn to get our eyes off ourselves and onto others. "Woman, behold, your son. Behold your mother." Many a counselor's office could be cleared, many a depression cured, if we would not merely look out for our own personal interests, but also for the interests of others (Philippians 2:4).

The Agony of Abandonment

ONE OF THE HORRENDOUS THINGS about unjust suffering is the devastating premonition that you have been abandoned, forsaken by God. It happens to the godliest of saints. It happened to Jesus, only His was real. God did forsake Him. But because His was real, yours will never be.

Suddenly, about noon on that day of crucifixion, a darkness came over the whole land, the sun's light failing. "And at the ninth hour Jesus cried out with a loud voice, 'ELOI, ELOI, LAMA SABACHTHANI?' which is translated, 'MY GOD, MY GOD, WHY HAST THOU FORSAKEN ME?'" (Mark 15:34).

God had forsaken Jesus. It was not His imagination! God had actually abandoned His Son, leaving Him in the throes of sin's awful death. Jesus had no recourse; He had no aid. In that one inexplicably horrendous moment, the Father and the Holy Spirit were estranged from the Son. Thus, abandoned by both, He cried twice, "My God, My God," or literally, "God of Me, God of Me, why hast Thou forsaken Me?"

The cry had been recorded a thousand years earlier when His agony was prophetically penned by the psalmist in Psalm 22. Written by the Word and read countless times by the Word who had become flesh! Now it was fulfilled and screamed into the ears of the Holy God who had to punish sin, for He who knew no sin was at that moment made to be sin for us.

Who suffered the greater agony? The Father who was made impotent by His own righteous justice? Or the Son, who foreseeing this had pled, "Father, if thou be willing, remove this cup from me: nevertheless, not my will, but thine, be done" (Luke 22:42 KJV)?

The hour had come, the eternal hour of destiny. Never before, never again would there be a time like it when God the Father and God the Spirit would forsake God the Son for the sake of mankind, who for the most part could care less! Yet He did it that we, who were dead, estranged from God, might live, never to be forsaken by Him.

You Are Never Forsaken

JESUS WAS FORSAKEN by God so that the immutable God could say to you, "I will never, no, never, forsake you nor ever leave you, that you, My child, might not fear what man would do to you" (Hebrews 13:5). Yet at times we wonder, don't we? Deep within we know God cannot lie; yet dazed by pain, tormented by men, and crying to Him but seemingly not being heard, we *feel* forsaken.

Beloved, when you suffer unjustly and you want to cry, "My God, my God, why have You forsaken me?" He understands. He does not want you to feel forsaken because you are not! Silent though He may be at the time, He is an ever-present help in the time of need (Psalm 46:1). Remember the trial is not without purpose, His eternal purpose.

In *Run for the West*, Sandor Berger, a Christian Jew, tells of being on a grueling march toward the Nazi camp where he was to be exterminated. On the way they came across a detachment of Jews working outside a city. Berger stared at them, envy gnawing at his heart.

"Their cheeks were full and their arms strong and muscular. . . . I was more jealous of that group than I had ever been of anyone. . . .

"I cried out to God, but there was no answer. . . .

"As I walked, I began to consider the suffering of Jesus Christ on the cross. . . . He did it for me, Sandor Berger, so I could have victory over death and spend eternity with him. Who was I to expect to be treated differently than any other Jew?"

The day before Sandor Berger was to be killed, the Americans liberated his death camp. Later, he walked back across the land to his home, remembering the large detachment of Jews he had envied so. He stopped to ask a farmer about them.

" 'Them?' the bent, gray-haired farmer echoed, a strange tone in his voice. 'When the Nazis decided to pull out, they shot and killed the whole lot.' . . .

"Tears streamed down my gaunt cheeks as I asked God to forgive me. I had learned again the truth of the Bible verse, 'All things work together for good to them that love the Lord.' God had shown his marvelous lovingkindness and care to me, something I did not deserve."[19]

O Beloved, you can imagine yourself forsaken by God—but it's a lie. He is there in His all-sufficient grace.

Suffering With Others

"REPROACH HAS BROKEN my heart, and I am so sick. And I looked for sympathy, but there was none, and for comforters, but I found none" (Psalm 69:20).

"Jesus...saith, 'I thirst'" (John 19:28 KJV). It was His fifth statement from the cross.

There's an agony of heart and soul that leaves one weak and broken of body. At times like that, when the pain is so intense, it's almost impossible to talk. The hysteria of emotion can bring on hyperventilation that leaves you parched. Your heart aches so that you feel it will burst. You need relief. You thirst. The cup or wet washrag is lifted up to your lips; you choke and turn away. Why can't you just die?

Crucifixion hurts. Don't deny it, and don't make others deny it and play the hero while you, immune to their pain, exclaim: "See, God is sufficient. They didn't even cry! They smiled the whole time. What a testimony! Praise the Lord."

No, Beloved, no! Crucifixion hurts. Let them weep! Let them tell you that they hurt! Weep with them!

After my father's death I have a whole new compassion, an empathy; no more pious platitudes when others are suffering. They thirst. And all I want to do is to be there and minister to their needs. The bitter is bitter. If it were not bitter, it would not be a test.

When a person is taking an exam from God, you don't cheat and give them the answers. God never would have taken them through that exam without first preparing them. No, instead of showing answers, you sit, wait, pray; and when they look up with a face beaded with perspiration, you hand them your handkerchief and say, "I know it's hard, awfully hard, but you'll make it. I'm pulling for you with the Father." You are there to affirm, to confirm, not to lecture. Meet their need.

"I thirst." Of course you do, insufferably. And I will not make you deny it. I will suffer with you.

Your Trial Has an End

"SO THEY PUT A SPONGE full of the sour wine upon a branch of hyssop, and brought it up to His mouth. When Jesus therefore had received the sour wine, He said, 'It is finished!' "(John 19:29,30).

Jesus' purpose was to give His life a ransom for many; that He had done. Now He could say, *Tetelestai.*

Tetelestai comes from the Greek word *teleo,* which means "to bring to an end." *Tetelestai* was also used as a legal term to denote the fact that a debt had been paid in full.

Man's debt of sin had been paid in full by Christ's death on the cross, so He could say, "It is finished!" with full assurance, for there was not a thing He had left undone. Jesus' unjust suffering had come to an end because its purpose was accomplished.

And so it is with you, Beloved. Throughout the Epistles in the New Testament the believer is told, in one form or another, to rejoice in trials. James 1:2-4 puts it this way: "My brethren, count it all joy when ye fall into divers temptations; knowing this, that the trying of your faith worketh patience. But let patience have her perfect work, that ye may be perfect and entire, wanting nothing" (KJV).

The word "perfect" in James 2:4 comes from the same root as "it is finished." What does it mean? It means that all trials, including unjust suffering, are for the purpose of bringing you to a specific end, a specific state of maturity or completion. When that has been accomplished, then the trial or suffering comes to an end.

And how will this help you to endure the cross, although you, like Jesus, despise its shame? Whenever you are suffering unjustly, you can rest assured that the time is coming when you can say, "It is finished."

Yet, Beloved, know this: You are not to bring this suffering to an end yourself—not in any form, including suicide. To do so is to fall short, to fail to persevere, never to be able to say to God, "It is finished." You will not be shut out of Paradise, but I'm sure that, in a way, heaven will not be as joyous at first, for the shame of not enduring.

Persevere. The end will come, and you, too, will say to your Father, "I have glorified Thee on the earth" (John 17:4).

Trust the God of Calvary

JESUS' FINAL WORD from the cross was uttered with a loud cry—a cry of trust, a cry of committal, the cry of a son to a father.

"And Jesus, crying out with a loud voice, said, 'Father, INTO THY HANDS I COMMIT MY SPIRIT.' And having said this, He breathed His last" (Luke 23:46).

It is evident from Jesus' words that the darkness was gone, the light of the Father's face had been restored, the serenity had returned. No longer is it "My God"; it is "Father." It is to His Father that He commits His spirit.

Matthew tells us that Jesus "yielded up His spirit" (Matthew 27:50). His spirit was not taken from Him in death; it was surrendered (John 10:17,18). His last words were a direct quote from Psalm 31, a psalm that shows the security that comes when one knows the character and ways of his God.

Let me share with you a true story that illustrates the reality of this—the bitter being made sweet.

A young traveler was mesmerized by the countenance of a woman sitting across the aisle from him on the train. *How could someone with a hook for a hand be so radiant?* he mused. Finally, he asked her if he might sit beside her. She said yes, and as the train rhythmically clattered along, he learned her story.

The woman had been a missionary when illness forced her to leave her life work. Broken in health, without family, she returned to her homeland and a little plot of ground. As her health improved somewhat, she began to farm the land to eke out her existence. Then one day her hand got caught in a threshing machine. "As I stood in the field, my hand torn from my arm, I looked to heaven and said, 'Father, what is it now You would have me to do since I have lost my hand?' I did not question His ways. I trusted Him. I only wanted to know what was next!"

What was next? Collecting clothing and taking it over the border to Christians in Russia.

O Beloved, you will never be able to take the bitter and make it sweet until you trust the God of Calvary and can say to Him, "Father, I trust You; into Thy hands I commit my spirit."

OCTOBER

The Promises of God Are Yea and Amen

When everything around you is failing, there is one thing that will stand . . . the promises of God. But promises must be claimed! This is the key. First, however, you must know the promises that are meant for you! May this month be used to spur you on to know, in truth and deed, the great and immeasurable promises of our God!

The Key of Obedience

ONE KEY THAT UNLOCKS the door to a life of usefulness, power, and blessing is the key of obedience.

One day as a dear Indian believer was preparing to go to a conference, the Lord spoke these instructions into his ear, "There is a brother who wants to go to the conference also, but he does not have a blanket."

Bahkt Singh was taken aback. "But, Lord," he replied, "this is my only blanket. You know that we must have two things to go to the conference, money for the train and a blanket!"

But the voice persisted, and Bahkt Singh obeyed. The blanketless man's joy knew no bounds. "I have been praying. I knew I was to go to the conference, but I told God that I had no blanket."

Then, upon entering into prayer, another conversation took place within his soul. "There is another man who is to go to the conference, but he has no money. Go and give him your money."

Bahkt Singh went and gave the man his money. It was hard, because now, without a blanket and without money, it seemed he himself could not go to the conference.

Then the word of the Lord came to Bahkt Singh a third time. "Go to the conference."

"But, Lord, I have no money. You had me give it away."

"What would you do if you had the money?"

"I would go buy my train ticket."

"Go."

When Bahkt Singh arrived at the train station, he found the longest line he could stand in so that the Lord would have more time to supply the money. But soon the ticket agent was asking, "Round trip or one way?"

He hesitated. Sensing the man's impatience, he said, "Round trip."

"That will be thirty-seven, twenty-five."

Suddenly there was a great commotion as a man burst into the station. "Oh, Bahkt Singh! I was told to get this to you. I must rush or I'll miss my train."

Bahkt Singh opened the envelope and read the note inside: "The Lord told me to enclose the following and send it to you. I can understand the thirty-seven, yet why the twenty-five...I do not know!"

God's Promise . . . Your Refuge

"SURVIVALISTS" ARE BEING interviewed on television talk shows and are gaining national attention as we seem to be hurtling more and more rapidly toward a chaotic national disaster. Survivalists are people who make elaborate preparation for themselves and their families in order to survive any circumstance, natural or man-made, that would create shortages of food, fuel, and other of life's necessities. Survivalists are trusting in their own capacity to protect themselves.

Christians, however, have the promise of God Himself as the place of refuge. The decision that Christians make regarding preparation for days of famine and national upheaval must be based on individual conviction, but God's promises to His children are worth careful consideration:

> My times are in Thy hand; deliver me from the hand of my enemies, and from those who persecute me (Psalm 31:15).

> Behold, the eye of the LORD is on those who fear Him, on those who hope for His lovingkindness to deliver their soul from death, and to keep them alive in famine (Psalm 33:18,19).

> But the LORD sustains the righteous. . . . They will not be ashamed in the time of evil; and in the days of famine they will have abundance (Psalm 37:17b,19).

> God is our refuge and strength, a very present help in trouble. Therefore we will not fear, though the earth should change, and though the mountains slip into the heart of the sea (Psalm 46:1,2).

And what of the fate of survivalists? They have only themselves. At best, they'll hold on for a few terror-filled days.

But as for the Christian, his refuge is the secret place of the Most High. There he abides, forever, under the shadow of the Almighty. What a difference!

Hide God's Promises!

He that dwelleth in the secret place of the most High shall abide under the shadow of the Almighty. I will say of the LORD, he is my refuge and my fortress: my God; in him will I trust. Surely he shall deliver thee from the snare of the fowler, and from the noisome pestilence. He shall cover thee with his feathers, and under his wings shalt thou trust: his truth shall be thy shield and buckler (Psalm 91:1-4 KJV).

SHE HAD STOPPED at a red light. Before she even realized the car door had opened, a man had a gun stuck in her side. He demanded, "Lady, just drive. Don't do anything dumb!"

She had just heard a message on Psalm 91. This psalm told her that God was her refuge, that He was her fortress, that He would deliver her from the snare of the fowler, that He covered her with His feathers, that He was her shield and buckler. But in this instant, with a gun in her side and her mind in a whirl, she could not think of the exact words of the Scripture.

In desperation, all she could come up with and exclaim was, "Feathers! Feathers! Feathers!"

The hijacker panicked. He shouted, "Lady, you are crazy!" And as quickly as he had appeared, he disappeared!

Oh, how precious to know that when we can't think of a promise word for word, or when we don't have time to quote a promise for the situation in which we find ourselves, God knows His promises and He knows our heart.

How important it is for you to hide His promises in your heart so that you will be ready to claim them at any moment!

Faith That Believes The Promise

WHAT DO YOU DO when you find yourself in need? What is your first impulse? Is it to turn to man or to God?

Sometimes I think we in the United States are plagued by having too much—so much that we see no need to call upon God. We seem to have everything we need and all the answers. Computers. Libraries. Universities. Television. Stores. Factories. Doctors. Psychologists. All are easily accessible. Is it any wonder that we see no need to run to the promise of Jeremiah 33:3: "Call to Me, and I will answer you, and I will tell you great and mighty things, which you do not know"?

Oh, for that childlike faith and trust that would flee to the throne of grace crying, "Abba, Abba, Father, I need you!" Oh, for that faith that would turn to God before it ever turned to man, that would turn to man only because it had been directed to do so.

Let me tell you a true story that will thrill your heart. It's a story of childlike faith among a group of natives who had received the gospel from a young man who vividly opened to them the life and ministry of Jesus Christ. They listened to story after story with rapt attention, believing, receiving, wanting more. Finally, the young missionary had to move on. But he would be back!

Soon after he left, one of the natives fell from a tree and broke his leg. The distortion of the bones could not be hidden beneath the unbroken skin. Immediately, in one accord, the natives began to call upon God: "O Jesus, when You walked upon earth, You healed the lame man. Our brother is lame. He cannot walk. So, Jesus, You heal him, too." The man was healed!

Some time later, a believer suddenly died. Again, they called: "Father! God! Jesus! Jesus, come quickly. This man is dead like that man Lazarus that You brought to life. Bring him to life." The man lived!

O Beloved, that we might have that kind of childlike, mustard-seed faith that would call unto Him so that He might answer us and show us great and mighty things!

What will your prayer be today? I pray that it will be, "Father, teach me to run to You in childlike faith . . . to call for You."

God's Promises Sustain You

"CAST YOUR BURDEN upon the LORD, and He will sustain you; He will never allow the righteous to be shaken" (Psalm 55:22).

Sometimes God gives us promises with conditions, and this is one of them. Holding on to burdens too heavy to bear will only cause us to stumble as we struggle to maintain our stance. Peter narrows down the conditions of the promise when he tells us to cast all our care upon Him, for He cares for us (1 Peter 5:7). There's the problem. Our anxieties throw us off balance. Anxiety . . . care . . . worry is a bump in the road that causes many Christians to stumble. Yet God has promised that He will never allow the righteous to be shaken. The condition of the promise? Cast your burden upon the Lord.

The Greek word for anxiety or care means "to divide or rip or tear apart." That's what worry does to you. When you hold on to your anxiety, when you refuse to cast it on the Lord, the result in your life is a dividing, a ripping, a tearing apart.

The man who says with his mouth, "I am a Christian," says in his heart, "I trust, I rely on, I have confidence in the Lord Jesus Christ." The same man, then, denies this trust, this reliance, this confidence when he confesses worry, care, or anxiety. The circle becomes a vicious one until the reality of God's simple truth sinks in: If you will cast your burden on the Lord, then you will not be shaken.

Jay Adams, in his booklet *What to Do About Worry*, notes three questions that are helpful in getting your worries sorted out, collected in a bag, and ready to be cast on the Lord. These are good to apply when anxiety comes in like a black cloud. Ask yourself the following questions. Then act!

1. What is my problem?
2. What does God want me to do about it?
3. When, where, and how should I begin?

If your desire is to be sustained, to be immovable, the Lord promises that He will sustain you, that He will make you immovable.

God's Angel Camps Around You

ONCE AGAIN VANYA had been summoned. But Vanya loved his God, and he would stand up for Him even in the Russian army!

As he walked to Major Gidenko's office, suddenly "something flashed and glittered in the sky overhead. . . . He lifted his eyes upward at the same instant that he heard a voice, 'Vanya. Vanya.'" There was an angel above him. " 'Do not be afraid. . . . Do not be afraid. Go. I am with you' . . . His joy was like a fire within him."

As the interrogation session ended, Vanya received Major Gidenko's orders. "I am going to order you to stand in the street tonight after taps are played until you are willing to come to me and apologize for the nonsense you have been circulating around the base about yourself and your so-called experiences with God. Since the temperature is likely to be some twenty-five degrees below zero, for your sake, I hope you quickly agree to behave sensibly . . . you will obey my instructions in summer uniform. That is all."

At first the cold wind slamming against him was painful. Then the glory of the morning revisited him. "Do not be afraid. I am with you!" The angel's words! They had been for tonight!

When the officers came out at midnight to check on him, they offered to let him in if he would deny his God. He refused! "By three o'clock in the morning, he was dozing on his feet. . . . He had sung. . . . He had prayed for every officer." Suddenly a voice startled him, "You are to come inside."

Inside the officer asked, "What kind of a person are you that the cold does not bother you?"

Vanya answered quietly, "Oh, comrade, I am a person just like you, but I prayed to God and was warm."[20]

> The angel of the LORD encamps around those who fear
> Him, and rescues them (Psalm 34:7).

Yes, an angel ministered to Vanya! And isn't it a great consolation to know that the angel of the Lord encamps around you to deliver you? This promise, this sure word of God, frees you to go where He calls you to go, to be what He calls you to be, to do what He calls you to do!

God's Promise to the Weary

ARE YOU EXHAUSTED? Is life wearing you out? To use an old expression, do you feel like you are "spinning your wheels"? When you slow down and take stock, do you find life rather routine, rather empty? Have you set certain goals for yourself and then found that when they are attained, they don't seem worth the price?

There is a familiar promise in the Word of God that has taken me through many a "wearying" situation. Before we go any further, let me quote this promise for you.

> He gives strength to the weary, and to him who lacks might He increases power. Though youths grow weary and tired, and vigorous young men stumble badly, yet those who wait for the LORD will gain new strength; they will mount up with wings like eagles, they will run and not get tired, they will walk and not become weary (Isaiah 40:29-31).

Here is God's promise to those who become weary, to those who lack might, to those who would faint. However, before you run with this promise, let me share with you the condition that accompanies it.

Those who gain this new strength are those who *wait for the Lord*, who *hope in the Lord*. In wearying situations, there must be a turning to the Lord, a looking to Him who is the Lord of your life.

Are your tasks, your goals, under His Lordship? Maybe your strength is gone because you have not waited before God nor sought His face or His will in your undertaking. Maybe God can't give you strength because you are expending it on things that are dissipating your energies. So when you are weary and no strength comes, be still, get alone with God, wait upon Him to see what He would say to you.

If you are walking under God's leadership, if you are in the place or task of His appointment and you find yourself weary, needing strength, go to the Father, hope in Him, claim His promise, and soar above all those difficulties with your eagle wings.

OCTOBER 8

Promises for the Fearful

YOU KNOW THE FEELING—your heart races, your chest tightens, and panic paralyzes your mind. It comes on you suddenly and unpredictably. It may take a moment for you to realize what has gripped you in its vise, but soon you know that it is fear!

Fear hits all of us at different times. The phone rings in the middle of the night. The doctor says the lump is malignant. Your child runs away from home. All of these, and a thousand other situations, are fear-producing.

Practically speaking, how do you cope? How do you conquer the paralyzing fear that seems to strike at your most vulnerable point?

The first step is to recognize its source. Second Timothy 1:7 says, "For God has not given us a spirit of timidity, but of power and love and discipline." When fear strikes and you find yourself lacking in power, failing in love, and thinking irrationally, you can be sure this fear is not from God.

The second step in dealing with fear is to rid your life of it. First John 4:18 states, "There is no fear in love; but perfect love casts out fear." How does perfect love act? Perfect love has come to know and has "believed the love which God has for us. God is love, and the one who abides in love abides in God, and God abides in him" (1 John 4:16).

When faced with fear, we must consciously turn from the irrational to the rational. We must say: "I know and believe that God loves me and that He is sovereign. Nothing can happen without His permission. This fear is not from God who abides in me. I will not be overwhelmed by paralyzing thoughts. I will put my trust in God."

The consequence of this choice is the "casting out," the hurling away, of the dread and the torment of fear. This is the sound mind—a mind under control—that God promises us. Then, with our mind under control, we will be able to act, to react, to move in power and in love in every fear-producing situation.

Tomorrow I'll share a fantastic, true account of some people who claimed and acted upon this promise.

"When I Am Afraid"

THE NIGHT THAT the dam broke at Toccoa Falls, Georgia, was a night when fear could have prevailed. The testimony to the world would have been far different had not the Word of God been planted earlier in the hearts of those who would be leading characters in the tragic drama that claimed the lives of 39 people, most of them children. One man's story illustrates it well.

> We had less than five minutes' warning before the water struck our trailer. I ran to help get the children to-gether. . . . We huddled together in the hall and prayed as the water picked up the trailer and started hurtling it and us down the current. The trailer broke apart and as I tried to pull the children out and put them into a clump of trees that we had bumped into, one of the walls collapsed and I knew my wife and two youngest children were gone. My three oldest children and I were finally able to get out of the flood. Later, while I was sitting by a fireplace in a neighbor's house, I thanked God for His grace and His presence for I felt a deep sense of His nearness to me. I remembered that my wife had spent some time telling the kids to be ready to meet Jesus when they were riding the flood out. I knew the children were ready because they did not scream in panic but each time they were scared by some new thing, they yelled, "Jesus, Jesus!"[21]

When you are afraid, what can you do? You can panic, lose control, become paralyzed, or you can say, "When I am afraid, I will put my trust in Thee" (Psalm 56:3).

When fear comes, you can run to the Rock that is higher than you, the One who promised you a refuge in the midst of storms.

Child of God, learn well His promise to you, then run and hide in its folds: "GOD is our refuge and strength, a very present help in trouble" (Psalm 46:1).

Resting in the Promises

IN THE MIDST of great hurt or grievous tragedy, the almost-too-glibly quoted, "And we know that God causes all things to work together for good . . ." becomes a promise that we might tend to deny in our pain. Yet, when thoughtfully compared with the sovereign love that spills out of similar promises, we know that the Word of God is true. His promises are yea and amen!

" 'For I know the plans that I have for you,' declares the LORD, 'plans for welfare and not for calamity to give you a future and a hope' " (Jeremiah 29:11). If we could only see that God does not design our ruin, but our refinement, we could fall back on this great, comforting promise.

Again, let me share a lesson in trust, in reliance on God's promise, learned from Toccoa Falls.

The sounds of the dam breaking awoke the Kemp family from their sleep. Thurman Kemp grabbed his son Morgan, and Dixie, his wife, grabbed Chris. Dixie shares her story.

> In an instant, tons of water came hurtling down on us, shattering the roof. The floor beneath us gave way and something hit Chris under his chin. He was pulled away from me but I grabbed him back by the sleeve. Then there was such a force of water that it ripped him out of my grasp and he was gone. . . . I know I won't see Chris again until I reach heaven, and I will never get over missing him . . . but I will not mourn, because I am content to know that God has a plan and my son was part of that plan. Because of his death, others have already found life in Jesus Christ. This is my comfort.[22]

Painful? Yes. Hard to handle? Yes. But God has promised, "And we know that God causes all things to work together for good to those who love God, to those who are called according to His purpose" (Romans 8:28). And God's Word is true!

You cannot change the circumstances, but you will find rest and refuge in His promises which are yea and amen.

Receiving the Promise

HAVE YOU EVER BEEN in a large house alone at night? Have you ever experienced that sick feeling deep down inside when you believed you heard footsteps in the hall?

Recently, the reality of one of our Father's promises to us really struck me as I listened to a tape of Darlene Rose's testimony. Darlene was the first non-native woman to enter New Guinea, where she lived among the brutal Boogus people.

She tells of a time when the Boogus people stabbed to death four of her near neighbors. Shortly after this event, Darlene was awakened in the middle of the night.

> I moved quickly toward the door. . . . I saw a man pass by . . . one of the Boogus men. He stopped and raised his black robe to pull out his large knife. Although I do not know why, I began to chase this man down our long hall, through the bathroom, off the back porch, and down the mountainside. When he was joined by other Boogus people, I stopped dead still and thought of what a foolish thing I had just done. But the Lord comforted me and assured me of His protection.

> . . . Never again did they try to break into the house!

> After the war was over . . . I talked with one of the boys from the Boogus people. I asked him if he had been with them the night that they robbed our house. He dropped his head and answered, "Yes, and we came back several nights after that, but you always had all those people in white on guard out there."[23]

What is the promise that has taken on new meaning and depth for me? It is Psalm 91:10,11: "No evil will befall you, nor will any plague come near your tent. For He will give His angels charge concerning you, to guard you in all your ways."

How blessed it is to know that He has given His angels charge over me—over you!

How to Receive the Reward

WHAT WILL IT BE LIKE when you see Jesus face-to-face? Suppose God were to take you home today and your labors for Him were ended. Do you know what follows death for the Christian? It is the Judgment Seat of Christ. "For we shall all stand before the judgment seat of God" (Romans 14:10b). There, "each one of us shall give account of himself to God" (Romans 14:12).

Did you know this? I didn't! For several years I lived as a Christian thinking that heaven was heaven and that once you got there, that's all there was to it. I had not yet seen that God in His righteousness had to distinguish faithfulness and reward it . . . for in all ways He is a just God.

His *warning* to us is: "Watch yourselves, that you might not lose what we have accomplished, but that you may receive a full reward" (2 John 8).

On the other hand, God's *promise* is: "Blessed is a man who perseveres under trial; for once he has been approved, he will receive the crown of life, which the Lord has promised to those who love Him" (James 1:12).

God has promised crowns! Crowns for you, crowns for me! Rewards—not loss, not shame, not embarrassment. He has promised: "Well done, My good and faithful servant, enter thou into the joy of the Lord."

It is yours. It is mine. It is a promise for the taking . . . if we will only love Him with a love that will persevere no matter what the trial, the testing, the temptation.

One day I had the privilege of talking with Harlan Popov, the author of *Tortured for His Faith*. This precious saint of God lived in man's hell as a prisoner of the Communists for thirteen years. I asked him that day, "What kept you faithful?" He looked at me in the sweetest way and said, "When you love someone, you'll do anything for Him."

Popov's love for his God will, someday, be rewarded with a crown of life, for he persevered under trial. That is God's promise, His reward.

Will you so love Him—no matter what?

Conquering by Faith

RAVENSBRUCK! When one spoke that word in 1945, it was always in a whisper. The terror, the anguish, the dread it conveyed to so many was just too much to bear. Ravensbruck was the notorious women's extermination camp of World War II. It was in this much-dreaded prison that Corrie and Betsie ten Boom found themselves.

As the two sisters looked about them at their circumstances—the hunger, the cold, the lack of privacy, the brutality of the enemy, the loneliness for home, the sickness—they realized why God had placed them there. Around them were thousands of terrified, tortured women who desperately needed to be ministered to, and God had even preserved their Bible through the inspections!

As the world in which Corrie and Betsie were being engulfed grew stranger and darker, one fact grew increasingly clearer, brighter, truer, and more beautiful, and this fact was the truth of the promise of God:

> Who shall separate us from the love of Christ? Shall tribulation, or distress, or persecution, or famine, or nakedness, or peril, or sword? . . . But in all these things we overwhelmingly conquer through Him who loved us (Romans 8:35,37).

In the book in which she tells about those days, *The Hiding Place*, Corrie says: "Life in Ravensbruck took place on two separate levels, mutually impossible. One, the observable, external life, grew every day more horrible. The other, the life we lived with God, grew daily better, truth upon truth, glory upon glory."

Do you find yourself, even now, in a hard situation, a difficult circumstance? Is your walk with your Father growing better daily, truth upon truth, glory upon glory, as a result of your difficulty?

Have you stopped and considered His love for you, His child? Have you meditated upon His promise to you?

Even in the most difficult of circumstances, you will overwhelmingly conquer! He has promised it! Will you live in the light of it?

A Promise to the Overcomers

> " 'And he who overcomes, and he who keeps My deeds until the end, TO HIM I WILL GIVE AUTHORITY OVER THE NATIONS; AND HE SHALL RULE THEM WITH A ROD OF IRON, AS THE VESSELS OF THE POTTER ARE BROKEN TO PIECES, as I also have received authority from My Father; and I will give him the morning star' " (Revelation 2:26-28).

WE WILL RULE with Christ over this earth when He returns as King of kings and sets up His kingdom here on earth. But this is another promise that must be examined carefully, for it is directed to those who overcome and to those who keep His deeds.

Who are overcomers? The author of Revelation is also the author of 1 John, and it is he who defines overcomers: "Who is the one who overcomes the world, but he who believes that Jesus is the Son of God?" (1 John 5:5).

Overcomers, then, are all believers. They overcome by their faith, by believing God, by taking Him at His Word. Can you imagine someone ruling with Christ who does not believe the Word of God? No! Can you imagine someone ruling apart from the Word of God? Of course you can't! We have seen it in nation after nation! Horrible, isn't it? No absolutes—inconsistencies, vacillation, inequities. Man, in his finite, limited wisdom, ruling according to his own convictions and desires.

The second condition for ruling over the nations is that we must keep His deeds. In other words, we must do His works. Can you imagine God allowing someone to rule in His kingdom who refused to do His deeds, His works? Of course not!

What is God trying to show us? Would we someday rule with Christ? Then we must learn to walk in faith, to take God at His Word, to trust in Him. We must learn to persevere—we must not quit, not faint. We must keep His deeds, do His works, until the end.

God is training us in this life to rule with Him in the next!

Let God Fulfill His Promises

WHEN YOU ARE CAUGHT between a rock and a hard place because of a need in your life, what do you do? Recently I heard a godly, godly man, Dr. P. N. Kurien, tell of how he ran to his Father with a need!

> I was preaching in the Boston area, and there came a call from Los Angeles to come immediately. I went to the airport to purchase my ticket. . . . The ticket's price was one hundred and eighty dollars. I pulled out my wallet. . . . Ninety dollars was all that I had! . . . So I asked for a ticket to get me as close to Los Angeles as possible . . . I was headed to Kansas City. I got on the airplane.
>
> At once the devil began, "You are so foolish! You are in a land that flows with milk and honey. You could have asked someone for your fare!"
>
> I said, "Devil, you are a liar; God is faithful!" I opened my Bible at Genesis, and I began to claim the promises of God. I went all the way to Revelation. While I was in Revelation, the plane landed.
>
> I got my baggage and went to the lobby to wait on God. I said, "God, I don't even have money to buy a Coke, but I have enough food on my body to live for a week." As I closed my eyes to continue in prayer, someone touched my shoulder. She said, "Are you a minister?"
>
> "Yes," I replied.
>
> "What are you doing here?" she continued.
>
> "I am a pilgrim, a traveler for Jesus," I said.
>
> She said that she had watched me on the plane as I opened and closed my Bible, and God had shown her that I had a need. She handed me one hundred and fifty dollars. It was plenty to get to Los Angeles.

The next time you are caught between a rock and a hard place, go to your Father and give Him an opportunity to fulfill His promise: "My God shall supply all your needs according to His riches in glory in Christ Jesus" (Philippians 4:19).

According to His Will

THEIR COMMUNIST PROFESSOR was so late for class that the men decided he wasn't coming. Since they could not leave the classroom without an order from their officer, one of the men proposed a debate. "We shall debate the question: What is the difference between Vanya's God and our god, which he claims is the state?"

The debate was begun by asking Vanya who his God was. His reply came, "My God is almighty and all-powerful—"

Before he could continue, a sergeant in the room interrupted, "If your God is all-powerful and can do anything, prove it. Let Him get me a leave tomorrow to go home. Then I'll believe in Him."

Vanya prayed in his spirit, *"Lord! Can this be from You? Will You be tempted by men? What they ask, is this right, Lord?"* The answer of the Lord to Vanya's heart was *"Tell them I will do this."* So Vanya boldly announced, "Tomorrow the Lord says you will go home on leave."

That night, Vanya found Sergeant Prokhorov lying on his bunk wide awake. It all seemed absurd to him; he half-believed that he might get a leave! Vanya whispered to the sergeant, "There is much to talk to you about. Since you will become a believer tomorrow, there are many things I must tell you." As the morning broke, Sergeant Prokhorov could only say, "My head is so full of ideas, I may never sleep again."

After the bugle had sounded, Vanya learned that the night delivery of bread had not arrived and he had to leave for Kerch right away.

When Vanya pulled back into the camp about an hour later, he noticed a small commotion. As he jumped down from the truck, excited shouts pierced the air. "Comrade Prokhorov has left on leave! Prokhorov has gone! We have been waiting to tell you!"[24]

> And this is the confidence which we have before Him, that, if we ask anything according to His will, He hears us. And if we know that He hears us in whatever we ask, we know that we have the requests which we have asked from Him (1 John 5:14,15).

What a promise! If we ask anything according to His will, He will grant it! May we learn to hear His voice and pray according to His will.

God's Conditions for Forgiveness

DO YOUR PAST SINS stalk the corridors of your mind? Even though you rehearse the promises of God which confirm that you are a new creation (2 Corinthians 5:17) and even though you acknowledge that you know your sins have been removed as far as the east from the west and that God remembers them no more (Psalm 103:12), when night falls and all is quiet, do their creaking memories cause you to toss and turn?

Ezekiel 33:16 says: "None of his sins that he has committed will be remembered against him. He has practiced justice and righteousness; he will surely live."

If your sins are forgiven, if God remembers them no more, then why are they being mentioned to you? That is a good question. Either you are not believing God's promises, or you have not fulfilled the conditions of this promise in Ezekiel 33, or the devil is attacking you. Let's take them one step at a time.

If God says that you are forgiven and tells you what He has done with your sins, then your response must be one of faith, taking God at His Word and walking in the light of it. However, it is possible that you have not fulfilled God's conditions and, therefore, your sins are being mentioned to you so that you will deal with them properly.

Listen to the conditions of Ezekiel 33:14,15: "But when I say to the wicked, 'You will surely die,' and he turns from his sin and practices justice and righteousness, if a wicked man restores a pledge, pays back what he has taken by robbery, walks by the statutes which ensure life without committing iniquity, he will surely live; he shall not die."

If your sins are not to be mentioned to you, then you must make full restitution to the one you have offended, even though your sins are confessed and are under the blood. For how can you expect him to receive you as forgiven by God if you have not made things right with him? Even if you tell him that you are right with God, does that make you right with him whom you have offended? Of course not! This is why God, as He instructs His people about their trespass offerings, also instructs them to make full restitution (Leviticus 6).

When you are right with man and right with God, then your sins will not be mentioned to you. If they are, it will be by the enemy, and you can tell that liar to leave!

Comfort for the Brokenhearted

"THE LORD IS NEAR to the brokenhearted, and saves those who are crushed in spirit" (Psalm 34:18).

What a glorious principle and promise we see repeated over and over throughout Scripture. David, the man after God's own heart, knew the agony of the brokenhearted and the inner pain of the crushed in spirit. Yet David could affirm with his whole being, "It is good for me that I have been afflicted."

A. W. Tozer has said, "It is doubtful whether God can bless a man greatly until He has hurt him deeply."

Abraham could never have known the depths of God's promise and provision until he was asked to slay his only son. Moses, called to lead the Israelites out of Egypt, was usable only after he had been exiled, crushed, and broken on the backside of the desert. In the crushing, in the breaking, there was God.

Saints throughout the ages have repeated the same story: "When I was at my lowest, when I thought my heart would literally break, there was God. I wouldn't take anything for that communion."

Algerius was a young man who lived and died as a Christian during the dark days of the Inquisition. This young man, only a teenager, was imprisoned and eventually burned at the stake for his faith in Jesus Christ. His words from prison indicate that he knew the reality of the promise: "The Lord is near to the brokenhearted, and saves those who are crushed in spirit."

> "In a state of misery I have had very great delight. In a lonely corner I have had most glorious company, and in the severest bond, great rest. All these things, my fellow brethren in Jesus Christ, the gracious hand of God has given me. Behold, he who at first was far from me is now with me, and the one I knew but a little, I now see clearly.... He comforts me, he fills me with joy, he drives from me bitterness and renews within me strength and sweetness."[25]

How is it with you? Is your heart broken? Is your spirit crushed? Do you find reality in the promises of God?

Imprisoned . . . but in Peace

WHAT IS IT THAT WILL hold you, that will keep you, that will sustain you, that will maintain you when you feel like you could literally burst at the seams?

Roger Ingvalson was an American pilot during the Vietnam War. He was flying his plane one day at 500 miles an hour when he had to bail out over Communist-held territory. Two miracles occurred at this point. First, he had no broken bones. Second, he was captured immediately by Vietcong soldiers, which prevented the furious natives from killing him.

Roger was kept in a bamboo-cage prison until he could be taken to a prison camp. Once he arrived at the prison camp, he was put into a four-foot-wide cell for 20 months of solitary confinement. During those months he saw no one except the guard. He was given a toothbrush, and every 45 days he was given a bar of soap. Despite the cold winter, he was not given socks to wear with his sandal-type shoes (made of tire casings). He had mosquito netting to place over his wooden-board bed, but he could have no paper and pen and no books except those containing Communist propaganda.

You might ask, "How could he survive? Who could endure living in a box alone? Is he sane today?"

Roger says, "Actually, I kept from going crazy by knowing that God was with me. I wasn't alone. I had a cellmate named Jesus Christ."[26]

> The steadfast of mind Thou wilt keep in perfect peace, because he trusts in Thee (Isaiah 26:3).

It is a promise, a surety, that you can have His peace no matter what—if you meet His condition. This promise will hold you, will keep you, will sustain you, will maintain you—if you will keep your mind stayed upon Him.

Forgiving and Forgiven

IT WAS 1947, and Corrie ten Boom had just related to a group of desperate, despairing German people the truth that when a man confesses his sins, God removes them as far as the east is from the west and remembers them no more. As she finished her message, she looked up and saw *him* walking toward her.

It all came rushing back! She could see him in uniform standing in the large, stark room where the women's dresses and shoes were in a pile on the floor. In her mind's eye she could see the frail, pain-riddled form of her dear sister, Betsie, ahead of her in the line of naked women.

Then her thoughts were shattered by his voice. "A fine message. How good it is to know that *all* of my sins are forgiven." He could not be saying that to her! Maybe he did not remember that she was at Ravensbruck where he had been her guard.

But he continued. "I was a guard at Ravensbruck, but since then I have become a Christian. I know God has forgiven me, and I want to hear from your own lips that you, too, forgive me." Then he extended his hand to her.

Does he not remember that Betsie died in that place? she thought. *How does he expect me to erase her slow, terrible death simply by his asking me to do so?*

Then, in the midst of her inner battle, the Lord reminded her that every day He had to forgive her of her sin. She knew that for her sins to continually be forgiven by her heavenly Father, she, too, must continually forgive others. Now could she handle the *reality* of the truth which she knew so well, which she had just taught?

She knew that forgiveness was an act of the will, and she knew her will could function regardless of her feelings. Mechanically she held her hand out. Their hands met. "I forgive you, brother, with all of my heart." She could truly say that to this man.

The former guard and the former prisoner stood for a moment, hands clasped. Corrie says of that moment, "I had never known God's love so deeply as I did then."[27]

Is forgiveness a truth you know in your head, or is it a reality in your life? Is there anyone you need to forgive?

When You . . . Then God . . .

"FOR YOU HAVE NEED of endurance, so that when you have done the will of God, you may receive what was promised" (Hebrews 10:36).

It is tempting sometimes to pick a promise out of the Word and run with it, isn't it? We declare it to be "a word from the Lord." Yet we fail to read "the fine print." And when the promise does not come to pass in our life, we feel that God has failed.

What is the problem? Is it the Word of God? No! God who promises is always faithful (2 Timothy 2:13).

The most practical illustration of this truth hits home with all of us when we consider the common problem of dieting! We pray, "Lord, I know that undisciplined eating does not glorify You as Lord of this temple. Just fill me with Your Holy Spirit, and I will have the fruit of the Spirit which is love, joy, peace, patience, gentleness, self-control. Ha! Self-control."

The next day you still weigh more than you are comfortable with, or you still know your eating habits aren't healthy. And it is true the next day, and the next, and the next. And you continue to eat according to your appetite, your desires, your rationalizations. Then you go back to the Lord and cry, "But, Lord, You said I have self-control."

The Lord answers in that still, small, easy-to-recognize voice: "My child, have you done My will? Have you exercised that self-control? Have you worked out that which I have worked in you (Philippians 2:12,13)? Have you dieted or eaten what you know is best for you?"

You see, the Lord is faithful. The promise has not failed. You must do the will of God. Then you will receive the promise!

For the past two weeks I have been on a very restricted diet. For the last three days I have been sorely tempted not to endure. But when I got on the scales today, I received the promise. I had endured. I had done the will of God. I had lost eight pounds!

Our problem is that we do not see that we have need of endurance so that *when we have done the will of God* we may receive the promise.

The Power of Promise

"RESIST THE DEVIL and he will flee from you" (James 4:7). This is such a powerful promise! But you will notice that it involves a direct act of the will on your part. Resist—literally, "stand against"—the devil. It's a call for action on your part.

> The incident happened on a warm Saturday afternoon in a downtown women's dress shop. In the fitting room, Carol was glancing in the mirror at the first dress she had tried on. Suddenly, the curtains opened and a tall man stood in the doorway. "Take off your clothes and lie on the floor," he shouted. Assuming that this meant he intended to rape her, she replied, "No. I will not."
>
> "In that moment," says Carol, "he looked like the personification of Satan. . . . He brandished a pocket knife, saying, "Either you do what I say or I'll kill you." Instantly, Carol was aware that the power within her (Jesus Christ) was far greater than the power of evil which she faced. So . . . she said, "In the name of Jesus Christ, I command that you leave me alone."
>
> Immediately the man's hand, holding the knife, dropped to his side. The look of anger and hatred changed to . . . bewilderment as he backed toward the door. . . .
>
> Thomas Mitchell, the man who had invaded Carol's dressing room that day, in a letter to her, says, ". . . when I was attempting to rob that dress shop, you made a statement to me that literally, physically sent chills down my back. You said, 'In the name of Jesus Christ, I command you to leave me alone.' At that very moment, Mrs. Clark, I felt the presence of something very strong and powerful. My physical being was unable to function temporarily."[28]

Oh, how you should praise your Father for the potency of His promise that will protect you from the evil one—if you will act!

Effective Prayer Accomplishes Much

HAVE YOU EVER BEEN really burdened to pray for someone? You may have prayed for several weeks or maybe even a month. Then, because you have not seen any concrete results, you may have just stopped praying.

God tells us, "The effective prayer of a righteous man can accomplish much" (James 5:16).

After Carol Clark's experience with Thomas Mitchell, she began to pray for him daily. She continued to pray for him until the night I called her. Then the dam gave way. The strain of laboring prayer caused tears of release to burst forth. A few days later, Thomas Mitchell's letter arrived.

In his letter to Carol, which was written after his salvation, Thomas said: "After I escaped from jail last August, my life was so messed up and I had so little hope for the future that I took a loaded pistol and almost took my life. After I was recaptured, I was placed in an isolation cell by myself. Nothing was in that cell except a small New Testament. And once again, Mrs. Clark, I would find myself thinking of you and also the feeling I had at that time. I don't remember what day or night it was, but I started to read that New Testament.

"In the second week of January of this year, I was saved by the Lord, and dedicated the remainder of my life to Jesus Christ to do with as He sees fit. . . . I realize that I may never again be a free man for the rest of my life, in a physical sense, but my soul will forever be free."

Because Carol was willing to fervently pray for Thomas Mitchell, he is, in actuality, a free man! He will never again be driven by the enemy of his soul. He is free to serve Jesus Christ!

Is there someone for whom you have prayed in the past, yet now, because of discouragement, you have stopped?

Oh, you must cling to that promise. Don't faint! It is the *effectual prayer of a righteous man* that can accomplish much!

Remember, Beloved, there is a condition to this promise. It is the righteous man whom God hears. The righteous are those who are walking "rightly," in accordance with the truths of God's Word and in accordance with God's will.

Listening for His Voice

HAVE YOU EVER HEARD someone say, "God told me . . . ?" Did you want to ask them, "But how did God tell you? How did you know it was God speaking to you?" You wanted to ask, but you did not want them to know that you were not familiar with the voice of the Lord. So you kept your mouth shut, all the while longing to know how to have such an intimate relationship with God as to have Him speak to you. I understand! I have been there!

Now here is a promise from God for every child of God: "And your ears will hear a word behind you, 'This is the way, walk in it' " (Isaiah 30:21).

If you are like me, you want to know His will; you long to walk in His way. But how can you know that this is God's way?

Learning to distinguish God's voice takes time and practice.

Elijah wanted to hear what God had to say to him. He was depressed, afraid for his life, and apparently he was exhausted. As he sought to hear God's Word, "a great and powerful wind tore the mountains apart and shattered the rocks before the LORD, but the LORD was not in the wind. After the wind there was an earthquake, but the LORD was not in the earthquake. After the earthquake came a fire, but the LORD was not in the fire. And after the fire came a gentle whisper" (1 Kings 19:11,12 NIV).

God usually speaks in a still, small voice . . . in words not audible, but in conversations of the soul . . . in word-thoughts. The secret of hearing God's voice is getting to know God's voice. Then, when conversations of the soul take place, you will soon learn to distinguish His voice from your own voice or the voice of the enemy.

How can you learn to distinguish God's voice?

First, you need to take time to be still before Him, to know that He is God. Then, tell God that you want to be led by His Spirit, to commune with Him, to hear so that you might obey. And remember, Beloved, when God speaks, He will never speak contrary to His written Word.

"And your ears will hear a word behind you, 'This is the way, walk in it.' "

God Never Forsakes You

The guard shoved me . . . into a six-by-six-foot cell. I dropped to my knees. I was watching the end of the key. I thought, "When that key turns a complete revolution, I am locked in death row." . . . Suddenly, I realized I was singing. It was a song I had learned as a little girl in Sunday school: "Fear not little flock whatever your lot, He enters all rooms the doors being shut. He never forsakes. He's never gone. So count on His presence from darkness to dawn." They locked me in death row, but they could not lock my Lord out! He was there with me! Sometimes, the glory of His presence filled that cell, and I would open my eyes and think I must be in glory.[29]

HOW WOULD YOU REACT if you were locked in death row? Would you panic? Would you cry out to God, "Where are You? Have You forsaken me?"

There were times in Darlene Rose's life when she cried out to God, thinking He had forsaken her. But in all of those times, her Father would gently remind her of His promise to her: "I WILL NEVER DESERT YOU, NOR WILL I EVER FORSAKE YOU," so that we may confidently say, "THE LORD IS MY HELPER, I WILL NOT BE AFRAID. WHAT SHALL MAN DO TO ME?" (Hebrews 13:5,6).

Do you feel that the Lord has forsaken you in your time of need? Would God abandon His child? No! As the perfect Father, He cannot, He will not!

"But Zion said, 'The LORD has forsaken me, and the Lord has forgotten me.' Can a woman forget her nursing child, and have no compassion on the son of her womb? Even these may forget, but I will not forget you. Behold, I have inscribed you on the palms of My hands" (Isaiah 49:14-16).

Quit pouting! Run back to Him. Fling yourself into your Father's arms. Ask to see His hands.

A Sober Promise

SOMETIMES PROMISES OF GOD don't seem like promises at all, for they bring judgment rather than blessing! Listen carefully to the Word of the Lord, those of you who have declared Christ as your Savior and Lord:

"Now it shall be, if you will diligently obey the LORD your God, being careful to do all His commandments which I command you today, the LORD your God will set you high above all the nations of the earth. And all these blessings shall come upon you and overtake you, if you will obey the LORD your God. . . . And the LORD shall make you the head and not the tail, and you only shall be above, and you shall not be underneath, if you will listen to the commandments of the LORD your God, which I charge you today, to observe them carefully, and do not turn aside from any of the words which I command you today, to the right or to the left, to go after other gods to serve them. But it shall come about, if you will not obey the LORD your God, to observe to do all His commandments and His statutes with which I charge you today, that all these curses shall come upon you and overtake you" (Deuteronomy 28:1,2,13-15).

God's promise is nothing short of blessing for obedience, cursing for disobedience.

Somehow, Christians have been greatly deceived. We think that as long as we are saved, it really doesn't matter if we disobey; Christ will forgive us if we just confess our sins. But disobedience has a price!

"It is time for judgment to begin with the household of God" (1 Peter 4:17). "When we are judged, we are disciplined by the Lord in order that we may not be condemned along with the world" (1 Corinthians 11:32).

Why do I stress the "cursing" aspect of this promise rather than the blessing? Look at the typical Christian. Is he holy? Is she careful to keep God's commandments with *all* of her heart and soul?

As you meditate on God's thoughts toward you today, ask Him to show you any way in which you have turned aside from His words.

Promises of Blessing

"AND EVERYONE WHO has left houses or brothers or sisters or father or mother or children or farms for My name's sake, shall receive many times as much, and shall inherit eternal life" (Matthew 19:29).

Rees Howells relates the following story of how he and his wife prayed about taking their small son with them to the mission field:

> The Holy Ghost said to us, "You must prove to me that you love the souls of the Africans who are to live for eternity, more than you love your own son. . . . If you give Samuel up, you can never claim him again." . . .
>
> The morning came when my sister arrived to fetch him. . . . The devil was not quiet. . . . He said I was the hardest man in the world to give my little child up. . . . When I came home that night, I asked my wife, "How did you get through?" She said she went out into the garden and wept, and thought to herself, "I have been singing that hymn many a time: But we never can prove the delights of His love, until all on the altar we lay; and this morning I have to prove it. But then the Lord told me, 'Measure it with Calvary.'" And with those words she came through. In praying together afterwards, the Lord showed me the reward. He said to us, "For everything you give up for Me, there is the hundredfold; and on this you claim 10,000 souls in Africa," and we believed it.[30]

God gave Rees and his wife their ten thousand souls! But God rewarded their obedience in a far greater way. One day Rees met a ship from America that had docked. Off stepped Samuel Rees Howells. He had come to labor with his father in Africa.

Has God called you to forsake your home, your father, your mother, your land? Will you go? Will you prove the delights of His love by laying all on the altar? God has promised you a hundredfold in return.

OCTOBER 28

Living in the Light of Promises

"IF I HAVE TO PUT UP with this another day, I think I'll scream!" Does this sound familiar? You may have phrased it differently, but the sentiment was the same. Self-pity, disbelief, murmuring, and complaining are all reflected in an attitude of, "I'm the only one who has ever had to endure this kind of trial."

When the tension builds and panic rises in your heart, God has a word to cool and to calm. He gently whispers that you are experiencing only those trials and temptations to which mankind is continually subjected. He then reassures that although your temptation may seem heavy, it will not break you; you will be able to cope; there will be a way to escape.

What is your trial? What testing or temptation looms as a specter over your sanity and threatens your peace?

Are you in a marriage that keeps you in a daily hell? Do you have a rebellious child for whom you have despaired? Is your body decaying with an unconquerable disease?

Beloved, these trials are common to man. They are normal. But the sovereign God of the universe has a promise for you in the midst of it all:

> No temptation has overtaken you but such as is common to man; and God is faithful, who will not allow you to be tempted beyond what you are able, but with the temptation will provide the way of escape also, that you may be able to endure it (1 Corinthians 10:13).

Don't defeat yourself by entertaining self-pity and indulging in murmuring and complaining. Instead, take God at His Word. You're in a normal situation. You can endure. You will escape! Act, walk, and speak in the light of this promise!

Abide, Ask, and Receive

"IF YOU ABIDE IN ME, and My words abide in you, ask whatever you wish, and it shall be done for you" (John 15:7).

The Christian life is to be a life of total dependence, a life cast upon God. We should go to Him for *all* that we need. He has told us that "apart from Me you can do nothing" (John 15:5). God must be the supplier of all. We are to ask, and God is to answer. That is His promise.

But this promise is another that is conditional. The condition of asking and receiving is *abiding*. That abiding is twofold: We are to abide in Him, and His words are to abide in us. Ours is to be a life of dwelling in Him, in His presence, in His life, until we become so one with Him that His life fills and permeates every cell of our being. Abiding is not only defined as "dwelling in," but also as "remaining in"—to be "at home in."

If we are to ask with the expectation of receiving, we must abide in Him. When we do abide, we will ask in accordance with God's will, God's desire, and God's character.

The second condition for asking and receiving is that God's Word would abide *in* us, dwell *in* us, remain *in* us, be at home *in* us. God's Word is a revelation of Himself, His ways, His will, and His purpose. To miss part of His Word, to neglect the whole counsel of God, is to be deficient or lacking in a complete knowledge of all that God esteems needful for man. His Word has been inspired (God-breathed), set down on paper, and carefully guarded so that "no jot or tittle" has been altered. These are words of life: "The words that I have spoken to you are spirit and are life" (John 6:63).

Therefore, if we expect to have the blessed privilege of asking and receiving, we must see that His words abide in us. We must esteem His words more precious than our necessary food.

How does the Word of God fare with you, dear child of God? Is it important enough that it takes priority in your life? If not, then how can you expect to run to God and ask for whatever you wish?

Blessings in Disguise

AFTER BEING TRANSPORTED to Ravensbruck, Corrie and Betsie ten Boom slept in an open field for three nights until they were processed. Then they, along with the other prisoners, were herded into barracks.

As Betsie and Corrie were looking over their new surroundings, suddenly something pinched Corrie's leg. "Fleas!" she cried. "Betsie, the place is swarming with them! How can we live in such a place!"

Betsie's calm, quiet reply was not directed to Corrie but to her heavenly Father: "Show us. Show us." Then her voice held excitement as she addressed her sister, "He's given us the answer before we asked, as He always does! In the Bible this morning. Where was it? Read that part again!"

Corrie slipped the Bible from its hiding place and turned to that morning's devotional passage: "Rejoice always, pray constantly, give thanks in all circumstances; for this is the will of God in Christ Jesus."

"That is it, Corrie! That's His answer. 'Give thanks in all circumstances!' That's what we can do. We can start right now to thank God for every single thing about this new barracks."

"Such as?" Corrie questioned.

"Such as being assigned here together. Such as what you're holding in your hands [their Bible]." And on and on Betsie went, enumerating every detail of their circumstances. But, then, Betsie came to the fleas!

Corrie's immediate response escaped her lips, "Betsie, there's no way even God can make me grateful for a flea."

Weeks later, however, they were to discover that the fleas had been the only reason that their barracks was not checked or supervised at night! This lack of supervision had allowed Betsie and Corrie to hold nightly Bible studies and prayer meetings and to minister to the women.

Not only did God use the fleas to keep out the guards, He also used them to conform Corrie into His image. That is why so many loved her—they saw Jesus! Was it worth it?

"When You Pass Through the Waters"

IF YOU HAVE TROUBLE trusting or believing God in the good times, what will it be like for you in the hard times? "If you have run with footmen and they have tired you out, then how can you compete with horses?" (Jeremiah 12:5).

Darlene Rose, missionary to New Guinea for 42 years, was able to stand and to withstand physical and emotional abuse that broke other godly people. Before the age of 26, she had been a missionary, a prisoner of war, and a widow. When her prison ordeal was over, she weighed 60 pounds. Yet she had competed with horsemen, and she had won! The source of her strength was the Word of God she had committed to memory.

In a voice sweetened by suffering and still tender with tears some 40 years after the fact, Darlene tells how she received the news that her pioneer-missionary husband had died three months earlier in a prison camp to the north of where she was held.

"I walked away. I turned to the only One I know to turn to, and I said, 'God.' He answered me immediately, 'My child, did I not tell you that "When you pass through the waters, I will be with you; and through the rivers, they will not overflow you. When you walk through the fire, you will not be scorched, nor will the flame burn you" ' " (Isaiah 43:2)?

Darlene was in prison. She was alone. She had lost the husband she loved so dearly. Yet she had the promise of God that when she passed through the waters, He would be there.

Beloved, are you running with footmen and fainting? Are you passing through waters and drowning?

There is a day coming when the competition will be with horses. The race will be faster. The waters will be deeper. In that time, only the promises of God will hold you. Do you know them?

If your answer is yes, then let God speak to you in the still, small voice of His Word. And when He does, remember that "the promises of God are yea and amen."

I Sought for a Man to Stand in the Gap

Have you ever seen a picture of terribly malnourished children or adults living in squalor? Have you ever felt the flush of anger and righteous indignation as you've heard of the massacre of thousands by ungodly warmongers? Have you felt helpless and thought . . . *but there's nothing I can do!* There is! You can pray around the world as we visit country after country.

Go Into All the World

THERE ARE APPROXIMATELY 5.5 billion people in this world that God created, and at the present growth rate that number will reach 6 billion before A.D. 2000. The majority of these people are without the gospel—and without the gospel, they will perish. Without the gospel, they will spend eternity in the lake of fire where the worm dies not and the fire is not quenched.

This is the truth God's Word teaches. Yet, do we Christians really believe that all men and women without Christ, all who have never heard of Jesus, will really perish without a second chance? Does that not seem too hard, too difficult to believe? So what have we done? In some way or another, we have rationalized it away: "God is a God of love . . . God just wouldn't do that . . . God would never send a man to hell when there has been no way for him to know, to hear . . . Surely . . ."

We want to get rid of our responsibility. Still, there resounds in the chambers of our heart that incessant echo of the voice of God, "Go ye into all the world . . . you shall be witnesses of me."

Look at your feet. They were given to you that you might go. If you cannot go on your feet, go on your knees.

Pray? you say. Intercede on their behalf? But how? How can I speak to God about a world of almost 6 billion people except in vague, boring, insipid prayers?

How? By becoming aware of the needs of others around the globe. One thing that will help you do this is *Operation World,* a book written by Patrick Johnstone. This magnificent piece of work will take you to every country in the world, laying before you the needs of the people in those places.[31]

Beloved, what is God saying to you about this world in which we live, this world of spiritually needy people?

The Ministry of Intercession

GO. THIS IS THE COMMAND of our Lord. Where? To the world, for it is the world that is on God's heart. Out there are multitudes for whom Christ died. And the minute you and I receive the light of the gospel we, at that moment, become responsible for spreading that light to those who are still in darkness.

Granted, we cannot all go physically, but we can go *on our knees*.

Let me tell you a true story that will woo you to your knees. It is a story told by Dr. P. N. Kurien of India.

An American girl by the name of Eleanor was ministering the gospel in a village in Nepal. Suddenly she was taken captive by the wicked chief of the village. He dragged her away and imprisoned her in the dark, empty basement of his house, where only the four walls heard her cry, "O God, help me!" It was 9:00 in the morning.

Hundreds of miles away, Dr. Kurien's sister, Mary, came flying into his room at 9:00 that same morning. "Oh, brother, come and pray. Eleanor is crying in Nepal, and she needs help."

After several hours they rose from their knees, but the burden remained. Mary said, "I am going home and pray some more."

And pray she did until 10:00 that night! Soon after that, Mary joyously returned to her brother's home. "Eleanor is free now. She is safe," she said adamantly.

How did Mary know? The burden was gone!

One week later, a letter came from Eleanor telling Dr. Kurien and Mary the story of God's deliverance. She told how the wicked village chief had kidnapped and imprisoned her, only to return that night, drunk, intent on raping her. But as he entered the basement, he was stopped by a strong man, a man who threatened his life.

The chief turned to Eleanor, "I would show you what I can do to you, but this strong man standing here says he will kill me if I touch you. Get out of here!"

As Eleanor groped her way out of the dark basement, she knew she had been saved by the angel of the Lord.

Go? What if we do not go, at least on our knees? What will happen to the Eleanors who are ministering in such difficult circumstances?

O God, teach us this ministry of intercession.

God Seeks Pray-ers!

HAVE YOU EVER KNELT to pray and had the fleeting thought, *Why should I pray? God is going to do what He wants to do anyway?* Maybe you have never voiced it, but haven't you ever thought about it? Why does God, who is sovereign, who by His very word can speak worlds into being, depend on little, finite, frail humans to release His power in this world? Yet we see all through Scripture that He waits on man; He pleads with man; He urges man to exercise the privilege he has as a believer—the privilege to pray.

When Israel was in as sad a state as America is today, God said: "And I sought for a man among them, that should make up the hedge, and stand in the gap before me for the land, that I should not destroy it: but I found none. Therefore have I poured out mine indignation upon them; I have consumed them with the fire of my wrath: their own way have I recompensed upon their heads" (Ezekiel 22:30,31 KJV).

Picture it, Beloved: God looking, searching, seeking for one man to pray, to intercede, so that He wouldn't have to carry out the just judgment of His wrath on the nation. It boggles the mind, doesn't it? If the principle of this lesson were ever seared upon our hearts, just think of its ramifications for the world today!

Have you ever thought of the great needs of a vast land like India, for instance, and wondered why God doesn't raise up more missionaries and support workers to go in and meet the needs of those people?

To understand this perplexing question, we must consider Matthew 9:38: "Pray ye therefore the Lord of the harvest, that he will send forth labourers into his harvest" (KJV).

What a powerful principle, if we would only believe it, apply it, and do it. If it is important enough that God will not move in His own fields until we ask Him, then it must be important enough for us to take Him at His Word and to pray.

Will you covenant before God this month to pray for His world?

Ask God How to Pray

LOOKING AT THE SPINNING GLOBE of this world doesn't do a great deal to provoke my interest. It's all too big, too massive, too far beyond my comprehension and experience. But introduce me to the people of a country! Tell me how they live, where they hurt, and what their dreams are, and then you have me.

People respond to people. So until we really see the world as people, we will never really have a true burden to pray.

In his book, *The Prayer Ministry of the Church,* Watchman Nee says, "Whenever God wishes to do a thing He will place a burden upon a brother, a sister, or the whole church." The prayer ministry of the church, then, "is God telling the church what He wishes to do so that the church on earth can then pray it out. Such prayer is not asking God to do what we want to do, but asking Him to do what He wants to do. Oh, let us see that the church is to declare on earth the will of God in heaven." The Scripture says in Romans 8:26,27 that "we know not what we should pray for as we ought: but the Spirit itself maketh intercession . . . for the saints according to the will of God" (KJV).

As you pray this month, ask God to show you His will and to lay His burden upon your heart for individuals and countries who desperately need prayer. I'll be sharing with you several individuals' experiences, and I'll give you various needs of countries as I know them. But God is waiting for you to ask Him what you should pray, what you should do. The Spirit is waiting to intercede through you on behalf of those who are perishing and those who are laboring for their salvation.

As you finish reading each day's devotional, ask God to lay His burden upon your heart. How will God speak to you? He will impress upon your mind a certain thought or a certain need. As that thought or need comes to your mind, pray it back to God.

Claim the covering of Jesus' blood that is yours as a believer and ask God to guide you into all truth. Tell God you will do His will. Ask God for His wisdom, then believe that He will give it to you.

Holding Back His Power

WATCHMAN NEE, IN HIS outstanding book *The Prayer Ministry of the Church*, makes a statement that has been rich food for thought for me as I've been learning more about prayer.

> God will not execute anything independently; whatever He does today He does with the cooperation of the church. She is that through which God manifests Himself . . . .
>
> This whole matter can be likened to the flow of water in one's house. Though the water tank of the Water Supply Company is huge, its flow is limited to the diameter of the water pipe in one's house. If a person wishes to have more flow of water, he will need to enlarge his water pipe.

It may well be that we are a constricted water pipe. While God's desire is for His power to come forth like a flood, our fragile, half-faith prayers have been holding back His life-giving power to a mere trickle, insufficient to truly water a parched land.

When I see the bones of a small child protruding through leathery, malnourished skin, and when I see a mother hold that child, rock him, and kiss him as I have my own, my heart is wrenched within me. But for the grace of God, that could be me holding my son, without God, without hope, knowing nothing of the Bread of Heaven, knowing nothing of the God who will care for His own.

Something deep within me says, *Why, Lord? Why are people sitting in darkness?* And if I am honest and if I listen carefully, I'll receive the answer I don't really want to hear: "Because you, the church, have not obeyed My command to go and make disciples. Because you have not interceded; you have not sacrificed your comfort, your money, or yourself to work My work!"

The Lord cannot move through one who will not obey, through one who will not pray. He has made you in His image; He has given you a free will. Therefore, the choice is yours. But the consequence is God's.

NOVEMBER 6

Fuel for Prayer

IF YOU AND I ARE GOING to pray effectively for God's world, we must have fuel for prayer. Lately, my cry has been, "God, show me how to pray. Let me know the burdens of people and their needs."

There was a time when I had never even heard of the Kurds. Then, through *Operation World*, I became aware of them, and they became a focus of my prayers. Now I am more alert to the television accounts of their awful plight, and I feel as though I know them. I have seen their faces, and I understand a little of why they live in darkness. My heart breaks for the homeless families, the starving children, and their feelings of hopelessness. Instead of shaking my head and thinking there is nothing I can do, I pray.

The Kurds are the largest group of people in the world without a land to call home, and for the last 70 years they have fought to survive and maintain their identity as a people and to gain status as a nation. Hundreds of thousands of Kurds live along the Turkish and Iraqi borders. Yet the Turkish government denied that nearly 10 million Kurds even existed.

Now, however, there is new hope for these forgotten people. According to Operation Mobilization, the Prime Minister of Turkey recently proposed legislation to allow the Kurdish language to be used in the production of audio cassettes, and he acknowledged their name, "Kurd," in one of his speeches. We are seeing God work in direct answer to our prayers as He opens doors for ministry to these people.

Pray, Beloved, pray! Pray that the door will remain open, that the medical personnel who are so desperately needed will heed the call for volunteer service in the rural clinics at the border camps. Pray that Christians who can speak their language will come as coworkers, translators, and medical aides.

Ask the Lord to rule in the hearts of the governments in Turkey and Iraq so that Christian workers might be allowed to distribute His Word and share the gospel to those who sit in darkness.

Pray that these desperate people will be led from their crisis to the cross.

Watchmen for the World

THE PROPHET EZEKIEL was commissioned by God to go to the children of Israel, a nation that had rebelled against God, that had transgressed His covenant. But before Ezekiel could go and be an adequate spokesman for God, he had to sit where the Israelites sat. He did not have to partake of their rebellion, but he needed to be fully informed of their state. Thus, Ezekiel says, the Spirit of the Lord "lifted me up, and took me away, and I went in bitterness, in the heat of my spirit; but the hand of the LORD was strong upon me. Then I came to them of the captivity . . . and I sat where they sat, and remained there astonished among them seven days" (Ezekiel 3:14,15 KJV).

It was at this time that God showed Ezekiel his responsibility as a watchman on the tower.

Has God shown you how to be a watchman for the Kurds and other neglected people? Has He given you a glimpse into the eyes of the little children, hungry, sick, in desperate need of attention? Have you felt their parents' hearts breaking for them?

Pray, Beloved, for our omniscient, omnipotent Father hears you.

The people of the Middle East are predominately Muslim, and Christianity has made few inroads into that part of the world—until recently. In fact, God has used the desperate plight of the Kurds, through their mistreatment under various political situations, to bring about an openness to the gospel. The last ten years have been devastating for the Kurdish people as the Iraqis have invaded almost 4,000 Kurdish villages, destroying their local economy, deporting 500,000 to distant camps, and killing an estimated 250,000.

Many Christian groups brought relief to the Kurdish refugees following the Gulf War. These people openly received New Testaments, and many were very receptive to the gospel after they saw the love of these Christians in providing food, clothing, and other practical help. Pray that the seed planted will come to full harvest.

O Beloved, let us pray today for one another. Pray that God will help us sit where others sit and that we will become watchmen on the walls of the world.

Burdened for Humanity

IN EARLY FEBRUARY OF 1973 there was a wave of killings in Kampala. Idi Amin and his advisers had drawn up a list of 2,000 prominent Ugandans and scheduled them for execution.

> The pattern of arrests was almost always the same. The Nubian assassins . . . entered an office or home in broad daylight. They called out the name of their victim and humiliated him in front of employees and family members. The terrified man was then tied up and dragged away to the trunk of a waiting automobile. . . .
>
> Only a few victims were killed immediately. The rest were taken to prison and tortured to death by the most sadistic methods. . . . In one prison, Naguru College, men were tricked into killing each other. A prisoner was given a heavy hammer and promised freedom if he would smash in the head of another. When after many blows his fellow prisoner died, another prisoner was brought to the courtyard, with the same promise of freedom, to kill the "executioner" with the same hammer. The chain went on for hours. Soldiers and Nubians gathered in the courtyard to watch the bloody spectacle. They drank gin, and laughed and joked.[32]

Where was the church in the midst of all this? How many meetings of prayer were called? How many tears were shed in God's stead as those created in His image desecrated that which God had made (Genesis 9:5,6)? How many days and nights were spent in fasting?

I hang my head in shame all these years later, for I heard about Amin's reign of terror, but not once did I talk to God about it.

O Beloved, may we learn to go to our knees with the burdens of others! Whenever we hear of a crisis—wars, uprisings, famines, plagues, diseases, accidents—whether on a worldwide level or affecting one individual, we can know, Beloved, that God wants to use it to bring people to the cross. May we be alert to His ways!

Breaking the Enemy's Power

WHAT BREAKS THE POWER of the enemy in lands where men are caught in the web of fear, waiting to be devoured piecemeal by Satan and all his demonic host? Kefa Sempangi, in his book *A Distant Grief,* speaks to this question so well. As we read his insights, we gain a powerful new perspective on prayer for those in darkness.

> Africans make no distinction between the spiritual and the physical. The spiritual is not a category among categories but the lens through which all of life is viewed. A tribesman from my village knows that cutting a tree, climbing a mountain, making a fire, planting a garden and bowing before the gods are all religious acts. He lives in the presence of the gods, and he knows that without intervention from them, without baraka, a blessing, there is nothing. There is no coffee harvest, no wood for the fire, no wife, no children.

> For such people, people who live their lives in daily hardship at the edge of nothingness, witchcraft is not a set of beliefs. It is a way of life. I have never heard a poor or needy person discuss the philosophy of witchcraft. Their only concern is what it does, that it works. . . . They were not looking for a world view but for a power to transform their lives. If Christianity could not help them, the witch doctor could.[33]

O Beloved, let us pray diligently for those who know Christ, that their lives would be constant testimonies to the power of the gospel so that those in darkness might see that "greater is He [Christ] who is in you [Christian] than he [Satan] who is in the world" (1 John 4:4).

The Persecuted Need Prayer

AFTER THE EASTER SERVICE, Kefa Sempangi pushed his way through the crowd to the vestry. He was too tired to notice that five of Idi Amin's Nubian Assassins had followed him, until he heard the door close behind him.

> For a long moment no one said anything. Then the tallest man, obviously the leader, spoke, "We are going to kill you." . . .
>
> From far away I heard a voice, and I was astonished to realize that it was my own. "I do not need to plead my own cause," I heard myself saying. "I am a dead man already. My life is dead and hidden in Christ. It is your lives that are in danger, you are dead in your sins. I will pray to God that after you have killed me, He will spare you from eternal destruction."

The tall one took a step toward Kefa and then stepped back. His face was changed. "Will you pray for us now?"

Kefa asked the men to bow their heads and close their eyes. Then, in deep fear and with great simplicity, he prayed that the men would be forgiven and would not perish in their sin.

As the prayer ended, the tall one said, "You have helped us. . . . We will speak to the rest of our company and they will leave you alone."

The five men started to leave, but then the tall one turned and said, "I saw widows and orphans in your congregation . . . singing and giving praise. Why are they happy when death is so near?"

"Because they are loved by God," said Kefa. "He has given them life, and will give life to those they loved, because they died in Him." The tall one shook his head in perplexity and walked out the door.[34]

O Beloved, let us pray that all those under persecution in the world will stand firm in one spirit, with one mind, striving together for the faith of the gospel, and that they will in no way be alarmed by their opponents (Philippians 1:27,28).

Reaching the World's People

NEEDS AROUND THE WORLD are so different and yet so similar. If you flew from country to country, you would find people in every imaginable state of need. And their physical needs are of as much importance to the Father as their spiritual needs.

Consider the believers in Guatemala for example. While they have freedom to worship, they must struggle to obtain every morsel of food their family eats. I learned this from a tremendous little book recently published in Guatemala, *Unto the Least of These*, written by two missionaries who work in different sections of that country, David Beam and Frank Waggoner. I want to share just one of their stories with you, for I know it will draw you to your knees, as it did me. . . .

His world was an apple box in a doorway. His name was Rene, and he was only two years old. Rene lived in Guatemala with his poor, illiterate, 19-year-old mother who tried desperately to earn enough money to feed him. Little Rene was so quiet, so weak, that no one ever noticed him. No one seemed to know that the baby in the box was starving to death.

A young missionary finally saw Rene and tried to help him and his mother. The day he arrived with a check for them, the mother met him at the door with tear-stained cheeks, "You came too late," she said. "We buried Rene yesterday."[35]

As I was reading about Rene, my spirit groaned within me; tears welled up in my eyes. Then I was stopped short by the words: "Rene was born in Guatemala. He lived in darkness. He died in despairing hunger. Will he meet you at the judgment?"

"O God," I prayed in that moment, "move on our fattened, sluggish hearts to reach out to people in the world. But, Father, please don't give us the burden without showing us the way. Teach us to pray for these people, but may we never fall into the 'bless-you-brother-and-be-warmed' syndrome. Show us, burden us, break us until we give, until we go, until their children become as our children in our compassion and in our love. O God, forgive us, teach us, touch us—for Jesus' sake."

Breaking Barriers Through Prayer

IF YOU ARE LIKE ME, when you think of mission fields, you immediately envision huts and savages. Or perhaps you see people bowing down to strange carved gods with extra arms or legs or a big, fat tummy, or maybe you see people walking on fire, casting spells, or climbing a tower of sharp swords.

When we think of the more Christian countries, however, our minds usually take us to Europe, that civilized continent which multitudes long to visit and there gaze on the magnificent altars and majestic domes of great cathedrals bearing images of the Christian saints.

But is Europe really as Christian as it seems? Actually, Europe is a continent, for the most part, bereft of true Christianity. For instance, the country of France is one of the world's more important mission fields. Over 43 million French people have no real understanding of the gospel and no connection with a church, though most are baptized in the Roman Catholic tradition. In France, there are many barriers to the gospel, among them intellectualism, rationalism, and widespread involvement in the occult. Only about 1,500 of France's 38,000 villages, towns, and cities have a permanent evangelical witness, and it is estimated that there is currently only one Christian worker for every 46,000 people.

O Beloved, pray especially for those in France who think they are all right because of their church membership, for those who have a showing of zeal for God but who know nothing of the power of His presence. Surely these are stumbling blocks to those who have shed any covering of a religious nature and who openly and blatantly deny the existence of God, heaven, and hell. Pray for those who "in vain . . . worship me, teaching for doctrines the commandments of men. For laying aside the commandment of God, ye hold the tradition of men" (Mark 7:7,8 KJV).

Pray for Awakening

GERMANY'S SPIRITUAL DECLINE has been one of the great tragedies of modern history. Humanism and destructive criticism of the Bible greatly weakened both the churches and society and opened the door to compromise and Hitler's Nazi tyranny.[36]

Where was the church in Germany when all this began to happen? Did they not see the storm clouds forming? Did they stand in the gap, did they intercede? Or did they sleep? And when they saw Hitler's horrendous plan come to pass, did they call the church to weep, fast, and pray?

> In 1945 the survivors of the German resistance met at Stuttgart with representatives from sister churches in other countries which had suffered mightily at the hands of Nazis, to proclaim a "confession of guilt." They implored God's forgiveness that they had not prayed more faithfully, believed more intensely, witnessed more courageously, and loved more devotedly.[37]

O America, take note! Beware! Have we not, too, been enfeebled by the rise of humanism and destructive criticism of God's Word? Are we not in our selfish, hedonistic, self-centered pursuits opening the door to evil forces?

Beloved, pray for those in Germany today who truly know the Lord Jesus Christ. As God once ignited the souls of John Hus, Martin Luther, and others, ask Him to ignite the souls of today's believers that they would go forth proclaiming the gospel in all boldness and without compromise. Then, pray that a great sense of emptiness will come upon the German people, and that they will, in turn, be more receptive to the gospel.

And when you pray, Beloved, pray that the Christians in America will awaken lest we, too, have to sign a confession of guilt with bloody hands.

Opening Doors

IN 1951 THE BAMBOO CURTAIN fell, shutting out the world and shutting in the Christians of China. "It is estimated that fifty million people were liquidated by the Communists after they took power ...many Christians would have been in that number."

Now, the closed door to China has been cracked open—an answer to prayer. And what has been revealed through that door is amazing!

The growth of the church in China is unparalleled in history. In 1949, shortly before the door closed, there were less than 2 million Protestants and 3.3 million Catholics in China. In 1992, however, China's State Statistical Bureau estimated there were 63 million Protestants and 12 million Catholics.

Praise God for 140 years of sacrificial seed-sowing by thousands of missionaries.

Praise God also for the Chinese Christians who stood firm in the midst of what was probably the most widespread and harshest persecution the church has ever experienced. This persecution purified and strengthened the church against the more recent efforts to weaken it.

One city, which was the model city for the plan to renounce all religion, is now the most Christian city in China, with Christians officially numbering 300,000.

The Lord also used the massacre of Tianammen Square to end the idolatrous trust in democracy among the more educated as their solution to the oppressive regime of Marxism. As a result, since 1989 large numbers of young people have turned to faith in Christ in their search for truth and hope.

Although many barriers to the gospel have been broken down, a greater harvest awaits. Now is the time for that harvest. China's population is over 1 billion, and the majority have no faith at all. Possibly 500 million have never even heard the gospel, for laws still forbid teaching the gospel to China's children and young people under 18.[38]

Will you, Beloved, join with me in praying for an even greater harvest in China? Tomorrow we'll look at how to intercede for the work in that great land.

Pure and True

ONE OF THE ULTIMATE GOALS of China's Marxist government has been, and still is, the elimination of *all* religious groups.

In the 1950s the Three Self Patriotic Movement (TSPM) among Protestants was used to infiltrate, subvert, and control all organized Protestant churches. During the Cultural Revolution (1966-1976) all religious activity was forced underground. This gave birth to the house-church movement. During Mao's reign of terror, intellectuals and religious believers were cruelly persecuted. An estimated 20 million Chinese lost their lives. Although some restrictions were eased after 1978, there are still strict controls over Christian groups and all unregistered activity is repressed.

Pray for the leaders of the house-church movement. Since the thirteen officially sanctioned seminaries are liberal in theology and are Marxist-oriented, there is a great need for Bible training, especially for the upcoming generation of leaders who are in their twenties and thirties and only recently converted. Pray for the dozens of "secret" seminaries that gather for three months for fellowship, teaching, and preparation for ministry. Pray for their protection. Ask God to cause His people to thoroughly equip and train believers in the Word of God.[39]

Pray also that believers will have discernment and that leaders will have wisdom in correcting false teaching and doctrinal excesses among new converts who are untaught and Bible-less.

Pray especially that these precious Chinese Christians will remain pure and true amid a constant barrage of atheistic propaganda, persecution, mockery, and discrimination. Pray that they will "fear not them which kill the body, but are not able to kill the soul: but rather him who is able to destroy both soul and body in hell" (Matthew 10:28 KJV).

Hunger for His Word

THE TWO FOREIGNERS were with a mission organization, and they had traveled worldwide. They were recent arrivals in China and had managed to smuggle in 150 Bibles. Caught up in the sights and sounds of the recently unveiled jewel of the China mainland, however, they had given little thought as to how they would distribute the Bibles.

As the service they were in came to a close, the foreigners turned around to face a man who had tapped them on the shoulder. The small Chinese man bowed politely and told them, "I live 400 miles inland. I have come here today because the Lord told me that I would receive Bibles. Are you the ones who have the Bibles?"

Springs of joy flowed in their breasts as the Americans were able to say, "Yes, we have brought your Bibles."

Have you ever noticed, Beloved, how precious the Word becomes in lands where persecution and tyranny reign? Can you say that the Word of God is priceless to you, so priceless that you would travel 400 miles, encountering great obstacles and at much risk, to receive a copy? Do you esteem the words of the Book more precious than your necessary food?

In spite of a large increase in the number of Bibles available, there is a famine of the Scriptures in China. This shortage is most acute in inland provinces and among the house churches where most of the spiritual growth has occurred. In some places there are 1,000 or more believers for every Bible. Seven million Bibles have been printed since 1981, but almost all have gone to government-controlled and infiltrated (TSPM) congregations.[40]

As you wait on the Lord today, intercede for Bible couriers to be raised up to take the Word into mainland China. Pray that every Chinese Christian might have access to a copy of God's Word. Also, thank God for His good hand which has so freely provided us with His Word.

Pray for Spiritual Growth

THE TWO SMALL Cambodian children began to cry as their teacher urged them to catch up with the other children who were taking a hike in the Tennessee woods. Terrified, the two fell to the ground screaming and holding on to the underbrush.

Their teacher, in dismay, called off the hike and returned the children to their home. There she learned the reason for their hysterical response. This Cambodian family had survived the massacre in their homeland by escaping through the forest along the border between Cambodia and Thailand. Walking by night to evade detection, they had encountered ultimate horror. Overcome by thirst, they had discovered a pond. As they stooped to drink, they suddenly saw the putrid flesh and smelled the foul odor of rotting corpses in the water. To the two small children, the forest—any forest—still held this terror.

This was the plight of many Cambodians not long ago.

> The terrible genocide perpetrated by the Khmer Rouge in 1975-1978 and the subsequent civil wars have devastated the people. . . . The longing for peaceful transition to democratic government in 1993 is threatened by the continued intransigence of the Khmer Rouge. Pray for a workable and lasting peace with full political and religious freedom.[41]

The Cambodian people have dwelt in spiritual darkness for centuries, and the Cambodian church has struggled to survive. In 1970 there were only 700 believers in evangelical churches. By 1975, the number had grown to 9-12,000, but only 2,000 survived the killings of the Khmer Rouge.

As our globe seems to shrink, we become more and more aware that what touches the other side of the world will eventually touch us. Beloved, pray for the young church in Cambodia. Pray for mature, trained Christian leaders and for more Bible schools. Pray for the one Bible school now in operation in Phnom Penh.

There is a great need among our brethren in Cambodia. Tomorrow we will learn more about them and how we can intercede for them.

NOVEMBER 18

God Is Able

BELOVED, CAN YOU POSSIBLY imagine an entire country being forced into slave labor—a country with no money, no private possessions, no private property? And can you imagine a land where all of the educated, the military, the teachers, and the professing Christians have been killed? It is unthinkable, isn't it? Well, that is what happened in Cambodia. Two million Cambodian people were murdered by the government or died by famine, and 750,000 escaped, leaving all that they possessed behind them.

Even though the future for Cambodia is brighter today, they are a needy, needy people. Buddhism has been the national religion since the fifteenth century, but the Khmer Rouge sought to eradicate all religion. Only since 1990 have Christians been allowed to worship openly, and they are treated as second-class citizens. There has been a revival of interest in Buddhism nationwide.

Are you concerned? Will you do what you can? Will you pray? God forgive us for letting others show more concern than we, the church!

> In Cambodia the needs are enormous. . . . Rehabilitation, orphanages, reconstruction, health care, projects for agriculture, fisheries, water management and education are all ministries where Christians can have significant input. . . . Pray for their health, safety, spiritual freshness and fruitfulness in these ministries. Conditions are difficult and harsh. Pray this land will fully open for other ministries—especially pioneer workers, church planters and Bible teachers.[42]

It seems almost overwhelming, doesn't it, Beloved? That is, until we remember that "the word of the LORD came to Jeremiah, saying, 'Behold, I am the LORD, the GOD of all flesh; is anything too difficult for Me?'" (Jeremiah 32:26,27).

The answer is an emphatic NO! We can pray—and we *know* God will answer.

Answered Prayer

IN 1987 STEVE WAS PART of a Youth With A Mission (YWAM) prayer team. As they camped on Yugoslavia's border and looked across at neighboring Albania, they prayed that God would open a way for them to take the gospel to the people of that closed, Communist country, many of whom had never heard of Jesus.

In 1992, after the Communist government in Albania crumbled and a democratic government was established, God brought 200 Christians from YWAM to the very area the team had prayed over five years earlier. Each team was placed in a village, living with Albanian families and helping them renovate their devastated schools as a way of showing God's love and care for the Albanians. Along with their practical labor, the team members were able to share the gospel and distribute Bibles, and most villagers received the teams warmly.

Steve was on one such team in a predominately Muslim village. They sensed growing spiritual resistance, although their renovations were going well, so the team sought the Lord in prayer and renewed their commitment to extend love to these people. One way they demonstrated this love was by distributing much-needed clothing to every family in the village.

Although the villagers gratefully received the clothing, the next day one woman, perhaps a spiritist, said that in a dream she had learned that the clothes were from dead people and warned the villagers that misfortune would come to them if they wore the clothes.

Beloved, tomorrow we'll look at what God did among this people. For today, take a few minutes to pray for young men and women like Steve and his team who have obeyed the command to go in order that people might hear.

"Faith comes from hearing, and hearing by the word of Christ" (Romans 10:17). Pray that those in Albania might hear!

God's Open Window

THE VERY NEXT DAY, several of the village children, while herding their animals in the nearby mountains, came upon a large, undetonated bomb. Not knowing what it was, the four oldest boys stayed to play with it. The sudden explosion literally shredded three of them to death. The sole survivor made his way down to the village.

Incredible mourning broke out over the village as the eerie sounds of wailing and caskets being prepared penetrated the night air. The team decided to leave, not knowing what the villagers might do in reaction to the tragedy, particularly in light of the spiritist woman's dream.

The next morning the team met to ask the Lord what He would have them do. Albanians traditionally bury their dead at noon on the day after their death. The team realized they must return and show God's love to these people in their time of need and loss.

With fear and trembling they entered the village. There, the Muslim leader met Steve with an embrace. Many of the people had on their new clothing, which also encouraged the team. They then visited each family, brought them food, and prayed with them.

A mullah (Islamic priest) from another village led the first burial with Arabic prayers from the Koran. After the burial, the village leader asked Steve to speak.

Steve prayed and then began to sing an Albanian worship song: "I worship You, Almighty God, there is none like You." God gave Steve the words to say as he shared with the villagers how these boys had been an example, going each day to the "holy hill" (the name the team had given to their place of meeting) to learn about Jesus and give their lives to Him.

The people were very touched. They couldn't understand the mullah, but they understood Steve. As they walked to the next burial, the village leader whispered to Steve, "We have no one who can teach us about God." The leader then asked Steve to come to the mosque the next week to teach the men about the ways of God.[43]

God has opened a "window" in Albania—an opportunity for now! Who will go to the many other villages of that country and introduce our God to hungry, hurting hearts?

A Pattern We Can Adapt

"WITHIN 18 MONTHS of the fall of Communism [in Albania], 16 mission agencies had entered the country for aid projects, evangelism, and church planting. By October 1992, there were over 1,000 believers gathering regularly to worship the Lord in 19 congregations and 17 home groups."

God is working in Albania! But our prayers are needed.

How should we pray? These prayer points suggested by *Operation World* also give us a pattern we can adapt when praying for other lands and other opening doors.

Pray for the growth, maturity, and legalization of Protestant Christianity in the new Albania. Growing pains are acute, and there is a great need for the preparation of leaders.

Pray for groups and ministries working in Albania, such as Youth With A Mission and Operation Mobilization.

Pray for the *Jesus* film as it is shown all over the country.

Pray for unity among the Christians. There is need for trust and close fellowship that will set high spiritual standards.

Pray for the unsaved. A toehold for the gospel has been established in most major towns, but much effort is needed to reach rural and remote areas.

Pray for the development of Christian radio. Over the years, radio has been used to prepare hearts for the gospel.

Pray for the distribution of the Scriptures and good Christian literature. Books, magazines, and leaflets are eagerly sought after. Also, there is a need for a Christian publishing house, for there is a dearth of literature suitable for the atheistic and Muslim cultural worldviews of the majority.

Is your heart moved with gratitude, as is mine, for God's mercy in giving us life in a country with religious freedom? Do we realize what that means?

Let's begin today's prayer with thanksgiving—then ask the God of the impossible to reign in Albania!

Intercede for the Brethren

WHEN WE PRAY, we must remember that God does permit His saints to suffer. Romans 8:35-39, however, assures us that whatever befalls us, we are more than conquerors. No calamity will ever separate us from His love!

Have you ever been tempted just to give up, to throw in the towel? Through gritted teeth, discouraged by circumstances, have you snapped, "That's it, I quit"?

Discouragement desires to be our constant companion, whether in prayer or in service.

Let me tell you about a man from India who had every reason to be discouraged. His story clearly illustrates the truths of Romans 8:35-39.

His white teeth glistened in a smile of glowing radiance as he told about the goodness of the Lord Jesus. He had just been thrown out of jail. He bore the marks of a man with a mission—a mission for his King.

He was an Indian man who had been arrested and put in jail for preaching the gospel to his fellow countrymen. As he related his story, he told of his witness to every man in the jail and of his use of the jailor's bathtub to baptize all the men who believed.

Since he had preached the gospel with such success inside the prison, however, the officials felt they were doing this dear Christian brother too much good. So they threw him out of jail. But that wasn't enough. They took him 25 miles down the road and left him—to get him away from the men he had ministered to in the jail.

Little did they know that they had brought him 25 miles closer to a town he had planned to reach on foot—a town where he would proclaim the gospel of the living Lord Jesus Christ!

O Beloved, how we need to pray for Christians around the world! We must pray that whatever comes their way, they will see it as an opportunity to show those around them the reality of Jesus Christ. Pray that Christians will cease murmuring and learn in everything to give thanks, knowing that this is the will of God in Christ Jesus concerning them (1 Thessalonians 5:18).

Their Need . . . Our Need

GREAT BRITAIN—THE HOME of Wycliffe, Whitefield, Wesley, Carey, Taylor, Mueller, and many others who were used of God to awaken the hearts of men and nations to the reality of Jesus Christ.

Great Britain, a land that is being enveloped in the darkness of its own sin.

> The nation has lost the sense of mission that made it one of the greatest moral and spiritual forces in modern history. The decline of true Christianity and the rise of the permissive society are characteristics of the age. There are now laws that permit homosexuality, witchcraft and abortion. The rise in the crime rate, violence, immorality, suicide, and drug abuse is alarming.

> The rise of New Age and eastern mystical cults has eroded the Judeo-Christian heritage to the point that public opinion is no longer Christian.[44]

Pray for the church in Great Britain, for despite growth, there are serious weaknesses found among evangelicals. A lack of Bible teaching and personal study of the Scriptures has resulted in the average believer being hazy on doctrine, shallow in evangelism, and undiscerning of error among those who claim to base their teaching on God's Word. Also, there is an increase in worldliness and, therefore, little real concern for world evangelism or the support of missionary enterprise.

O Beloved, pray much for these, your brothers and sisters. Ask God to give them a hunger and thirst for righteousness' sake; ask Him to set their hearts ablaze for those who are perishing!

Revival is desperately needed. Historically, every century for the last 800 years has seen a national awakening. The last awakening was in 1859. Pray that Christians would unite to seek such a revival and again bring a blessing to the world.

Do the weaknesses of Great Britain bring to your mind, to your heart, another part of the body of Christ that suffers from the same ills? Yes, pray for us; pray for His body in America. Ask God to work in our lives as He works in the lives of the saints in Great Britain!

Prayer in the Church

WHAT IS YOUR CHURCH life like? How do you and the other members of your church family get along? What are your prayer meetings like?

You know, Beloved, I have become righteously envious of the true church that existed in Communist Russia. Their worship and prayer times made anything we know in America seem pale. They kept their relationships pure because they had to trust each other with their very lives.

The church has always grown best and strongest where the ground is soaked with the blood of martyrs. In Russia, martyrs have numbered in the millions. Millions more were consigned to years of imprisonment or exile or psychiatric "treatments." It is in such places, in such times, that the church is truly the church triumphant.

"In the crowded houses where they met, the congregation frequently stood during the entire service—two to four hours. . . . During the service, the worshipers who were sitting changed places quietly with those who stood.

"But during prayer the Christians always stood or knelt. 'For a human ruler we show respect,' an old woman who has been a Christian since the days of the Czar explained. 'When we talk to the King of the universe, we must stand or kneel.'"

When the church prayed as a body, everyone had an opportunity to pray. Inevitably, there would be mothers praying for their children who faced atheistic hostility in schools. Some would pray for their Christian brothers who had been imprisoned for the sake of Christ.

Beloved, think of it and weep: Prayer was offered, too, for the church in the West that we might be purified and strengthened.

"While one person prays aloud, a sea of prayer surges through the room as other believers whisper their petitions and praise, 'Da Gospodi—yes, Lord,' hear our prayer."[45]

What is it like when your church meets to pray?

God Hears Your Prayers

IT HAPPENED IN THE LATE 1970s in Kiev—a huge conference to prove there was no God. The format was a debate between the top Russian scientists and one of the less educated, "deluded" Christians.

The air was electric with expectancy as 20,000 people took their seats. The few Christians sprinkled throughout the vast conference hall prayed silently as the debate began.

As one of the great Russian scientists began to speak, pointing to his model of the universe, his comrade, another noted scientist, began to argue with him. Soon the debate became mass confusion; the people became angry; some charged the stage, tearing up the scientist's model.

As the great government debaters were ushered away, the lone Christian, anointed by the Spirit, began to speak, simply giving the gospel to the quieted crowd. When he finished, the sweet silence was splintered as 20,000 Russians passionately gave a standing ovation to the one Christian who had spoken at the great conference which had been held to prove, once and for all, that there was no God.

For 70 years, the expressed goal of the Communist Party was to eliminate religion and all expression of faith. Amid the massive killings, imprisonments, torturing, and discriminations God sustained and enabled His church. The very ideology that sought to destroy Christianity was defeated by the prayers of Christians.

In 1984, a seven-year prayer campaign for the Soviet Union was begun, with the specific goal of complete religious liberty and Bibles available for all. By 1990-91 that had been achieved! In 1990, a multiparty democracy was instituted and religious freedom is now constitutionally guaranteed!

Does God hear our prayers, Beloved? Yes, He does! Thank Him for protecting His church in Russia, and for giving her the grace to survive, grow, and triumph!

Continue to pray for Russia and the other nations which were once part of the Soviet Union. Pray that God will establish leaders with His agenda. Pray for the church in Russia to remain pure and strong in light of the flood of Western influence.

Muslims—an Unreached People

Over 1000 years ago a young man with a short beard, long black hair, and prophetic fire in his eyes strode out of the desert. He claimed to have seen visions from God. A Christian relative encouraged him to pursue his destiny as a spiritual leader. Within a hundred years, his band of followers stretched across vast empires and lands.[46]

TODAY THESE FOLLOWERS of Mohammed number over 1 billion people. They represent the single most unreached group in the world . . . and one of the fastest growing.

Most unreached Muslim people live in North Africa, the Middle East, Central Asia, East Asia, and South Asia between the 10th and 40th parallels north, stretching from West Africa across Asia. The phrase "10/40 window" was coined to highlight this area.

"Unreached" people are those who have never heard of Jesus as Savior and have no Christian witness near them. This "10/40 window" contains 90 percent of the most unreached people in the world and the least number of missionaries. The spiritual needs are staggering.

Unprecedented numbers of Muslims have been converting to Christianity in the last few years. Undoubtedly prayer has been a primary reason for this. George Otis, Jr. in *The Last of the Giants*, reports a remarkable incident in a North African village in 1983. One night . . .

> with no prior warning and for no immediately discernible reason—God sovereignly descended upon this coastal township with gracious bounty. Moving from house to house, and communicating through a combination of dreams, visions and angelic visitations, He did not rest until every member of this Muslim community was properly introduced to His begotten Son, Jesus. As might be expected, come daybreak, nearly every villager had a story to tell.[47]

Tomorrow we'll continue this story. Today, ask God to give you the faith to believe that *your* prayers can change the world.

Muslims Can Be Reached

As the Holy Spirit lingered and these simple citizens managed to piece together the magnitude of what had happened to them, a sense of spiritual awe settled over the entire village. In the weeks that followed, their conclusions led to a dramatic wholesale conversion involving some 400 to 450 Muslim villages—a nearly eighteenfold increase in the size of the Algerian national church!

When amazed mission workers, who had had no direct involvement in this extraordinary development, began to investigate . . . they came across a stunning piece of information. It was near this area that, in June 1315, Raymond Lull, a Spanish missionary from Majorca, had been stoned to death by frenzied Muslims after preaching in the open market.

The blood of Martyrs, it has often been said, represents the seed of the Church. Lull, who is generally considered to be the first missionary to the Muslims, certainly believed this. In his book, *The Tree of Life*, he wrote that Islamic strongholds are best conquered "by love and prayers, and the pouring out of tears and blood."[48]

THE "GRAIN OF WHEAT" that fell into the ground that day was watered with the tears of intercessors over the centuries. In the 1960s a team of young Americans prayed on the site of Raymond Lull's martyrdom. They prayed that God would redeem the seed of his life and send a movement of the Holy Spirit.

The sovereign outpouring in that Muslim village has continued for ten years in an Acts-style revival where now thousands of Muslims have proclaimed Jesus Christ as Lord. In spite of intense persecution by family, friends, and government they remain firm in their faith and passionate in their witness.

May we, too, continue to water the fields of Algeria with the tears of our intercessions for an even greater harvest.

Hear God . . . Then Pray

J. OSWALD SANDERS, in his excellent book *Prayer Power Unlimited*, relates this story.

> One night at midnight Mrs. Ed Spahr was awakened and burdened for missionary friends, Rev. Jerry and Mrs. Rose, in Dutch New Guinea working among stone-age culture people. She was so burdened for him, she prayed and next morning wrote a letter telling of it. Later it was learned that he received prayer letters from five prayer partners in five continents saying they prayed for him on that specific occasion.
>
> By adjusting the dateline and time span, it was seen that they all prayed at the same time; at that very time, Mr. Rose was standing with his arms tied behind his back and a huge "stone-age" savage standing before him with a spear ready to pin him to the ground.[49]

As five prayer partners on five continents prayed, another man in the tribe (there were no Christians in the tribe at that time) spoke to the savage, and he walked away.

Dr. Spahr asks: "Could God have made him walk away without the prayer partners? God can do anything He wills, but would He? I don't think He would have. I think it was His desire and will to continue the life of Jerry Rose on earth as a witness through his prayer partners."

The responsibility is awesome, isn't it? God has called His laborers to the harvest in response to someone's prayer; now, He is calling us to intercede on behalf of His servants.

O Beloved, to be led in specific prayer for specific situations, we must constantly keep our eyes on the Master so that we, as His servants, might anticipate His every desire.

May this be our testimony: "He awakens Me morning by morning, He awakens My ear to listen as a disciple. The Lord GOD has opened My ear; and I was not disobedient, nor did I turn back" (Isaiah 50:4,5).

God's Spirit Is Working

IT WAS THE 1940s. Her name was Flora Davidson. A single, Scottish woman, she lived in a two-story house in a city in what is now Pakistan. From a window in the house she could look out to the mountains of Afghanistan. From that vantage point, she spent hours on her knees praying that God would move in that country and open it to the gospel.

If you're like me, Afghanistan was a rare word in your vocabulary until the Russians invaded it in 1980. Suddenly, the Afghans became a people of great interest. Here was a people undergoing immense suffering in a war that took an estimated 800,000 lives, maimed another 1,600,000, and turned 7 million more into refugees. Even after the Soviets withdrew, civil war has continued the devastation.

Yet, in the midst of this horror and destruction, God is bringing forth His people. Currently there is a movement of His Spirit in Afghanistan which has added 3,000 new believers to the Afghan church.

Flora Davidson's prayers are being answered. God began to honor those prayers in the late 1940s when tentmaker missionaries, including Dr. and Mrs. Christy Wilson, began to enter Afghanistan. The Wilsons worked with blind and other visually impaired Afghans for the next 22 years. They were expelled in 1973 because of the large number of Muslims who had proclaimed Jesus Christ as Lord.

The Wilsons continued to pray for these precious friends they were forced to leave, and God gave them a wonderful promise concerning those they had worked with and led to the Lord:

"I will lead the blind by ways they have not known, along unfamiliar paths I will guide them; I will turn the darkness into light before them and make the rough places smooth. These are the things I will do; I will not forsake them" (Isaiah 42:16 NIV).

Tomorrow we'll see how God faithfully kept that promise!

A Light to Those in Darkness

HIS NAME WAS T—. He was totally blind. He was a Christian. Due to the extreme persecution in his homeland of Afghanistan, however, T— had been wavering in his testimony for the Lord Jesus.

One day, he entered a barbershop in Kabul. Although the air was ominously silent, he could feel the presence of many people in the shop. As he entered, he asked the barber, "What are all of these people doing here?"

Roughly denying the presence of any other people, the barber rudely led him to the chair. As T— uneasily sat down, he suddenly felt the barber's razor held tightly against his throat and heard the hateful words, "Are you one of those Christian infidels?"

At that moment, the man who had been wavering in conviction, the man who now had a knife at his throat, made a courageous decision; he began to testify mightily of the Lord Jesus Christ and His power to save.

Barely had T—'s last words escaped his lips, when the Muslim barber ruthlessly slit his throat. He just missed the jugular vein. With the blood dripping from his near-fatal wound, T— crawled out of the shop and made it to the home of believers who took him in and ministered to his wounds.

While he recuperated, five different men, secretly and separately, came to see him; they were the five men who had been sitting in that barbershop, who had witnessed his testimony. They had come to learn more about this Jesus for whom he was willing to die.

As you pray for believers in Afghanistan today, ask your Father to burden *your* heart to share His life with those in *your* world who are groping in darkness!

Beloved, we've spent this month looking at some of the needs of this world and being challenged by the call of our God to stand in the gap. What will be your response? Will you go—on your feet or on your knees—will you go?

DECEMBER

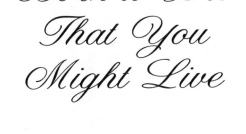

Jesus. Born to die that you might live—and live life abundantly! Go with me on a December journey through the life of Christ and see how He walked . . . how He lived day in and day out! See how you might experience life . . . life as only He can bring . . . life abundant . . . life eternal.

Sometimes God Is Silent

FOUR HUNDRED YEARS of silence. The heavens had been as brass. The prophets were gone. God had ceased to speak audibly to His people. All that was left for them to cling to was the covenant—and the promises. Year after year the people went to the temple to worship, to bring their sacrifices, to say their prayers. Nothing changed.

To some the ritual of worship became routine, boring. It was a part of life. But there were others who clung to the promises given by Jeremiah and Ezekiel—promises of a new covenant. To them it was a way of life with purpose. They were to live for God, to keep His commandments and His regulations blamelessly.

This was how Zacharias and Elizabeth lived, even though it seemed that God had not honored their fidelity and their wholeheartedness. Elizabeth was growing old, and she was barren. Yet they would serve their God.

That was the situation when, one day, the lot fell on Zacharias. Out of all the priests, this time he was the one chosen to go into the temple to replenish the incense burning on the altar in front of the Most Holy Place. How fortunate he was! Some priests were never given this privileged duty, since the assignment was chosen by lot.

As the worshipers gathered to pray, Zacharias entered the Holy Place, guided by the light of the burning candlestick. He passed the table of shewbread. In deep reverence he stood before the veil which kept him from viewing the ark of the covenant. There, at the veil, he stood before the altar of incense.

Suddenly, unexpectedly, 400 years of silence were broken! Gabriel had been sent forth from the presence of God to speak to Zacharias. Zacharias' prayers had been heard! Elizabeth would bear a son! A son who would go forth in the spirit and in the power of Elijah in order to make ready a people who would be prepared for the Lord (Luke 1:5-20).

Have you been praying for a long time? Has God been silent? Have you been tempted to give up? Has your worship become routine, boring? Oh, Beloved, persevere. Wait. God will speak . . . in His time.

God's Good News!

THE PEOPLE NEVER REALLY knew what had taken place that day in the Holy Place. Zacharias had been silenced since that time. He remained unable to speak until the day of John's birth. So almost another year went by, and the people still did not hear from God.

Little did the people realize that a prophet was on his way, a prophet sent from God to prepare them for the coming of the Messiah.

What rejoicing there was when God opened Elizabeth's womb and gave her a son! Neighbors and relatives shared her joy.

When he was eight days old, it was time for his circumcision. His mother said that his name was to be John. Great protest went up because Elizabeth and Zacharias had no relative named John. Those present said, "Name him after his father."

But Zacharias "asked for a tablet, and wrote as follows, 'His name is John.' And they were all astonished. And at once his mouth was opened and his tongue loosed, and he began to speak in praise of God" (Luke 1:63,64).

The silence of nine months was broken—Zacharias could speak! Then the silence of 400 years was broken, for Zacharias was filled with the Holy Spirit and he prophesied. And what God spoke through Zacharias was good news:

> "Blessed be the Lord God of Israel, for He has visited us and accomplished redemption for His people, and has raised up a horn of salvation for us in the house of David His servant—as He spoke by the mouth of His holy prophets from of old. . . . to remember His holy covenant, the oath which He swore to Abraham our father, to grant us that we, being delivered from the hand of our enemies, might serve Him without fear, in holiness and righteousness before Him all our days" (Luke 1:68-75).

Has the good news reached your ears yet? Has God spoken to you? Have you been enabled to serve God without fear, in holiness and in righteousness, in these days?

Salvation Through Christ

WHEN HIS SON was born, Zacharias, filled with the Holy Spirit, prophesied of John's ministry.

> "And you, child, will be called the prophet of the Most High; for you will go on BEFORE THE LORD TO PREPARE HIS WAYS; to give to His people the knowledge of salvation by the forgiveness of their sins, because of the tender mercy of our God, with which the Sunrise from on high shall visit us, TO SHINE UPON THOSE WHO SIT IN DARKNESS AND THE SHADOW OF DEATH, to guide our feet into the way of peace" (Luke 1:76-79).

John the Baptist was to tell the people of the salvation that Christ would bring. This salvation is what Christmas is all about! This is the salvation that God has for men.

Salvation is more than just dying and going to heaven. Salvation is more than living forever. Salvation is more than eternal benefits.

Salvation is forgiveness today for all of your sins—past, present, and future. Salvation is God's provision to free man from life lived under guilt and condemnation.

Salvation is freedom from the kingdom of darkness and all of its fears. Salvation is life in the light of Jesus, who dispels the shadow of death which would keep you in bondage all the days of your life.

Salvation is peace—peace with God, peace of mind, peace of heart. Salvation is being kept in peace as the storms of life rage round about you!

This salvation is for you—not because you merit it, deserve it, or could possibly ever earn it. But because of the tender mercy of our God, salvation has been provided for all men.

Is this salvation, forgiveness, light, life—this peace—yours?

If something seems to be missing in your salvation, why not tell God about it now? Ask Him to show you the answer to your need. He is waiting. He will answer.

In the Fullness of Time

THE FULLNESS OF TIME had come! The Roman government was now permitted, by the Sovereign Ruler of all the universe, to send forth its decree. It was time for the birth of the Son of God! God was to be born of woman, to be born under the law, to be born in Bethlehem Ephrathah.

Out of this city, so small among the clans of Judah, would come Shiloh, the One who would be Ruler over Israel. Conceived by the Spirit of God in a virgin's womb was the One whose "goings forth are from long ago, from the days of eternity" (Micah 5:2).

The fullness of time had come, and most of the world would miss it.

The Roman census had been scheduled for an earlier date. As a matter of fact, it had been rescheduled more than once because of conflicts within Roman jurisdiction and the problems with the Israelites. At least to man these seemed to be the reasons. But what man did not know was that this postponement was of God. It was not yet time to move Mary and Joseph.

Then the word came: Caesar Augustus had issued his decree that a census should be taken of the entire Roman world. Everyone had to register in his own town. Joseph and Mary would have to leave Nazareth and travel south to Bethlehem.

Today, governments are making all sorts of plans, issuing all kinds of decrees involving the lives of multitudes. They are operating as if there were no sovereign God overlooking all of the universe. And yet God reigns in all of His majesty! Although the governments of this world do not know it, He permits them to go only so far, for He knows the time when He will restore the kingdom to Israel. It will be when He, again, will say to His Son, "Come, for all things are ready."

It will be in the fullness of *His* time. And when God comes the second time, it will be to those who eagerly await Him for salvation. Will you be waiting and watching?

"I trust in Thee, O LORD, I say, 'Thou art my God.' My times are in Thy hand" (Psalm 31:14,15).

Jesus' Destiny for All

THERE WAS SO MUCH to treasure in her heart. The times of nursing passed by quickly, for Mary would sit and ponder all that had happened in this last year.

Her fingers caressed the unbelievably soft cheeks. Then she would move her fingers down to play with the corners of her son's precious mouth. Her firstborn—her firstborn son—given to her by God!

Mary couldn't get over what had happened today in the temple when they went to circumcise Jesus and to consecrate Him to the Lord. First, the old man, Simeon. Then the prophetess, Anna. Both of them seemed to have an aura of holiness and joy about them.

She pondered Simeon's words again: "'Behold, this Child is appointed for the fall and rise of many in Israel, and for a sign to be opposed—and a sword will pierce even your own soul—to the end that thoughts from many hearts may be revealed'" (Luke 2:34,35).

Her thoughts turned over and over in her mind. *What was it Simeon had said? A sword shall pierce my soul too! What did he mean? Jesus is destined to cause the falling and the rising of many in Israel? Why would they fall, God? How could this precious baby, this dear son of mine, cause people to speak against Him or to stumble? Oh, I know, He will cause men to rise, for He will tell them of You. He will save Your people from their sins. That is what You told Joseph. That was why we were to name Him Jesus. But how, Lord God, will He cause people to fall?*

When the question was answered in Mary's mind, we do not know. Maybe it was when she remembered what Isaiah had said: "He shall become a sanctuary; but to both the houses of Israel, a stone to strike and a rock to stumble over, and a snare *and* a trap for the inhabitants of Jerusalem" (Isaiah 8:14).

Or maybe it was when she stood at the foot of Calvary and heard jeering taunts that pierced her breast like a sword.

Has Jesus Christ caused you, my friend, to rise or to fall? Do you speak against Him, or do you speak for Him? Is His life foolishness to you?

"Jesus Kept Increasing"

AFTER HIS CONSECRATION, the next event we read of in Jesus' life is His trip to Jerusalem with His parents when he was twelve.

It was the Feast of the Passover, and they had lost Him in the crowd. When they questioned Him later, "He said to them, 'Why is it that you were looking for Me? Did you not know that I had to be in My Father's house?'" (Luke 2:49).

Jesus had been sitting among the teachers in the temple courts listening to them and asking questions! Oh, they were amazed at His understanding and His answers, but they did not know that God Himself had been sitting there with them in the seat of a learner.

Jesus returned to Nazareth with His parents and was obedient to them. We are told nothing about the next eighteen years of His life except one vital sentence: "And Jesus kept increasing in wisdom and stature, and in favor with God and men" (Luke 2:52).

The blind were still blind. The lame were still lame. Israel was still waiting for the Messiah. And what was Jesus the Christ doing?

He was growing in wisdom and stature and in favor with God and with men. He was maturing in four vital areas of life: intellectual, physical, spiritual, and social.

Why? some might ask. Why was He not out healing, delivering, preaching, teaching? He was God. He could have been doing these things! But there was something more needful at *that* time than healing, delivering, teaching, and preaching, something more important even than dying—it was growth, wholeness, balance in life.

Man is not just spirit—he is spirit, soul, and body. Each of these parts of man is to be preserved blameless before the Lord (1 Thessalonians 5:23). Our Lord's ministry was to be a ministry to the whole man. And to be able to accomplish this ministry, He, as a man, needed to know this balance in His own life.

Have you given God the time to make you balanced? Or have you rushed off to do the work of the Lord unprepared, not realizing that you cannot minister to the whole man or the whole woman if you have not taken time to mature in each of these areas yourself?

The Wilderness of Testing

IT WAS AN OPPORTUNE TIME for Satan to tempt Jesus. Jesus had just been baptized by John. God had opened the heavens and said for all to hear, "Thou art My beloved Son, in Thee I am well-pleased" (Luke 3:22). Jesus was on the verge of beginning His public ministry, and He had confidence—the confidence that comes when you know you are in the will of God. But it was a confidence that could not go unchallenged by the enemy.

From the presence of people, from the words of God's blessing, Jesus was led into the wilderness. Now, suddenly, He was shut off in the desert—without food, alone. And for forty days the enemy worked on Him (Luke 4:2). Day in and day out there was no letting up.

How Jesus was tempted during that time, we do not know. The Scriptures simply record what happened on that final day in the wilderness. But before we look at that in tomorrow's devotional, let's see what we can learn for our lives today.

In 2 Corinthians 2:11 God tells us through Paul that we are not to be ignorant of Satan's schemes lest Satan outwit us and take advantage of us.

One of Satan's schemes is to shake your confidence in your relationship with your heavenly Father. How it disturbs the enemy when you know that you have been blessed and chosen of God to do a work for Him! It irritates Satan to have you secure in the knowledge that God is pleased with you.

Satan wants you to think that God is against you and not for you. Or he wants you to feel that you have disappointed God in such a way that God can never use you. He might even whisper in your ear that you are not saved or that you have blasphemed the Holy Spirit and that, therefore, you cannot be saved.

What do you do in times like these? You must take the shield of faith and stand in its protection (Ephesians 6:16). What does God say about you in His Word? What has He spoken in the light? Do not doubt it in the dark hour of testing.

"Submit therefore to God. Resist the devil and he will flee from you. Draw near to God and He will draw near to you" (James 4:7,8).

The Choice of Obedience

FOR FORTY DAYS, Jesus had gone without food. Now He was hungry. So Satan tempted Jesus in the same way he tempted Eve.

The devil had said to Eve: "Eat. Satisfy yourself your way. You will be as gods. Act independently." He wanted Eve to sin. He succeeded.

Now Satan wanted Jesus to sin, so he challenged Jesus to prove Himself as the Son of God, to take things into His own hands.

But Jesus met the enemy's fiery dart with the shield of faith, the precepts of God's Word: "It is written, 'MAN SHALL NOT LIVE ON BREAD ALONE, BUT ON EVERY WORD THAT PROCEEDS OUT OF THE MOUTH OF GOD'" (Matthew 4:4).

Life is not a matter of fulfilling our desires, but a matter of living according to God's words. Jesus chose to trust in the Father and wait upon Him to supply all of His needs.

Satan, however, would not give up!

> Then the devil took Him into the holy city; and he had Him stand on the pinnacle of the temple, and said to Him, "If You are the Son of God throw Yourself down; for it is written, 'HE WILL GIVE HIS ANGELS CHARGE CONCERNING YOU. . . .'" Jesus said to him, "On the other hand, it is written, 'YOU SHALL NOT PUT THE LORD YOUR GOD TO THE TEST'" (Matthew 4:5-7).

Jesus would not be caught in the snare of presumptuous sin— calling God to protect Him when He was doing something against the revealed will of God!

When this tactic failed, Satan tried another. He showed Jesus the kingdoms of the world and said, "I will give You all this domain and its glory; for it has been handed over to me, and I give it to whomever I wish. Therefore if You worship before me, it shall all be Yours" (Luke 4:6,7).

But in this temptation, Satan also failed. Jesus knew there was no crown without a cross. He would not sell His birthright for Satan's mess of pottage.

Beware of the world's tinsel, Beloved, lest you forfeit a crown for it!

Tempted, but Triumphant

WHEN DOES SATAN usually tempt us? Isn't it in times of weakness—physical, mental, emotional—when we are alone, when all is quiet, and when we have time to think, to remember?

Sometimes Satan will seek to wear us down or distract us by some train of thought we cannot seem to shake. Remember, Jesus' temptation went on for forty days! Can you imagine?

Let me share with you what Satan did to me when our board of directors said that they weren't going to build another building until they built a house for us. They felt we needed a house that would give us more privacy and a place to keep ministry guests. However, after the house was built and we were moved in, all I could think about was how I should have designed our home differently.

When we designed it, I'd had an underlying fear that people would criticize, so we did not make it as large as our board of directors had instructed. Why? Because of fear—which was not from God but from Satan. Now the thought of failing in something as vital as designing and building a house almost did me in! The thoughts came at the most inopportune times: when I was praying, when I was teaching, when I was trying to have my quiet time. Whew! At times these thoughts distracted me from things that were vital to our ministry.

I wrestled for days with this. But victory did come!

I think what finally broke Satan's attack was when, embarrassed though I was, I shared my concerns with some dear sisters in Christ and asked them to pray for me. They listened to me with love and understanding and without condemning me for being tempted with such fleshly things. Also, I determined to start praising God for our home just the way it was.

"And when the devil had finished every temptation, he departed from Him until an opportune time" (Luke 4:13).

When Satan returns with another temptation, I know that it will be because he is panicked at the work God will do through me if I will only persevere. When he comes with another temptation, even though it may last awhile, still I can say, "Thanks be to God who always leads us in His triumph in Christ" (2 Corinthians 2:14).

DECEMBER 10

Bow Before Him as Lord

NAZARETH. TOURISTS GO THERE to see the place of Jesus' childhood, to drink from Mary's well. This is where the Son of God came with His mother to help her fetch water. A Son upon whom Mary must have looked with awe, with joy, and yet with sorrow.

And so the people of Nazareth watched this Son of Israel grow in wisdom and in stature and in favor with God and man. Jesus, Joseph's son, was a good lad. How blessed by Jehovah were Mary and Joseph to have such a son as this. Heads surely nodded in agreement as the people passed Him daily on their way to the well to draw the water that sustained them. Little did they realize that He was the fountain of living waters, the One of whom they could drink and live forever.

As tourists leave Nazareth today, I wonder if they look for the brow of the hill where it happened? The son of Mary and Joseph had come to Nazareth where He had been raised. And as was His custom, He entered the synagogue on the Sabbath and stood to read (Luke 4:16). But this time they didn't like what they heard. Oh, the reading of Isaiah was fine. He read with such clarity, such authority. The men of Nazareth shook their heads at the gracious words of this Nazarene as they whispered among themselves, "Is this not Joseph's son?" (Luke 4:22).

When they thought of Him as Joseph's son, they would listen because He was one of them. But when He spoke as the Son of God and took away their cloak of self-righteousness that covered their hard hearts of sin, it was too much! Filled with rage, they rose up and cast Him out of the city and led Him to the brow of the hill in order to throw Him down the cliff (Luke 4:28,29).

What about you? Do you look with sweet sentiment on the baby Jesus as you sing the traditional carols that give you that good feeling of Christmas? And how do you feel about Jesus as He assumes His place as God, uncovering your sin and calling you to righteousness, to submission?

Do you bow before Him as Lord, or do you seek to push Him in anger from the throne of your life because He calls you to conform to Him and does not, will not, conform to your conception of Him?

DECEMBER 11

Forgive and Be Forgiven

"FOR IF YOU FORGIVE men for their transgressions, your heavenly Father will also forgive you. But if you do not forgive men, then your Father will not forgive your transgressions'" (Matthew 6:14,15).

Just preceding this statement, our Lord had given His disciples instructions on prayer: "When you pray . . . Pray, then, in this way: . . . 'forgive us our debts, as we also have forgiven our debtors'" (Matthew 6:6,9,12).

This instruction is part of what we call the Lord's Prayer—a prayer prayed by countless lips in countless churches on the Lord's Day, week after week. What lies in the hearts of those who pray this prayer? What is in your heart as you pray it?

Next Sunday as you sit in church, as you sing carols praising the One who was born to die that you might have forgiveness of your sins, look around you. Is there anyone, *anyone at all*, in your church whom you have not forgiven as your heavenly Father has forgiven you?

And as you sit and think, is there anyone in your family, anyone among your friends, anyone among your acquaintances, anyone at work whom you have *anything at all* against? Can you look at each person and treat him or her with complete love and total forgiveness, so that it is just as if that person had never hurt, never offended, never disappointed, never wounded you?

Walk back down the galleries of your mind. Do you see hanging on those walls the memory of anything that would cause you to murmur or to turn away in revulsion as you remember a particular person? If so, then go with Christ to Calvary and listen to your Savior as He hangs upon that cross, beholding, through eyes filled with the agony of torture and rejection, those who have gladly put Him there. Listen to the words spoken from that cross: "Father, forgive them; for they do not know what they are doing" (Luke 23:34).

Have you claimed God's forgiveness for your sins and your trespasses? Has He forgiven you?

Now, look at the one who has sinned or trespassed against you. Which debt is greater, yours to God or theirs to you? If you have been forgiven the greater, you must forgive the lesser.

One Goal . . . Pleasing God

ARE THERE SOME PEOPLE you just cannot please no matter what you do? There is just no satisfying them no matter how hard you try? You try and try, but everything you do is wrong. You long with all that is within you to show them the reality of your Christianity, but all they can do is find fault with the way you've chosen to live.

Has this caused you to become disappointed, discouraged, defeated? Have you despaired of ever being Christlike enough to win them to your Lord?

Do not despair, Beloved—not if you have sought to live before them in God's strength and according to His precepts of life. Do not give up on being "holy" and think, *What is the use? I'll never be what I should be! I'll never do anything right! I'll never convince them!*

Jesus understands your frustration. He lived among the same type of people. Listen to what He said; it is a word written for you:

> "To what then shall I compare the men of this generation, and what are they like? They are like children who sit in the market place and call to one another; and they say, 'We played the flute for you, and you did not dance; we sang a dirge, and you did not weep.' For John the Baptist has come eating no bread and drinking no wine; and you say, 'He has a demon!' The Son of Man has come eating and drinking; and you say, 'Behold, a gluttonous man, and a drunkard, a friend of tax-gatherers and sinners!' Yet wisdom is vindicated by all her children" (Luke 7:31-35).

No matter what Jesus or His disciples did, they could not please some men. So Jesus understands your frustration. Therefore, may your one goal be to please God.

"If God is for us, who is against us?" (Romans 8:31).

Compassion . . . Like Christ

HAVE YOU EVER HEARD some news that sent you reeling so badly that you had to be alone? That happened to Jesus when He received the news that John the Baptist had been beheaded.

John's disciples had buried his body and then come to tell Jesus. They told of Herod's birthday celebration at which Herodias' daughter had danced for Herod. In his extreme delight, he promised her anything her heart desired. At that point, Herodias saw that her hour of vengeance had come. As she whispered into her daughter's ear, the request was passed on for all to hear, "Give me here on a platter the head of John the Baptist" (Matthew 14:8).

The disciples told the Lord how John's head had been brought into that banquet hall on a platter and given to Herodias' daughter, and of how she had taken it triumphantly and given it to her mother!

John the Baptist, the prophet who would have fulfilled Elijah's role if only they had listened, if only they had believed, had been beheaded at Herod's command (Matthew 17:11-13). It seemed that evil had triumphed over good.

"Now when Jesus heard it, He withdrew from there in a boat, to a lonely place by Himself" (Matthew 14:13). Because He had become flesh, because He could be tempted as we are, because He could be touched with the feeling of our infirmities, grief drove the Sovereign Ruler of the universe to a solitary place.

Grief tore at His soul. Grief over John, who was the greatest among men and yet not recognized as such. Grief over Herodias' triumphant gloating and her blindness. Grief over man's inhumanity to man because of sin's destructive lusts.

He had to get away from men. But they followed Him. And then "He saw a great multitude, and felt compassion for them, and healed their sick" (Matthew 14:14).

May we, no matter how grieved we are because of mankind, always have compassion on them, even as Christ did!

The Word of God . . . Our Standard

"BUT IN VAIN DO THEY WORSHIP ME, TEACHING AS DOCTRINES THE PRECEPTS OF MEN" (Matthew 15:9).

So many Christians are living their lives according to man-made rules. Somewhere along the line we have picked up a code of do's and don'ts for the Christian, and these—rather than the Word of God— have become our standard for living.

How well we know our traditions, and how quick we are to look down our noses and judge as nonspiritual those who do not walk by our code! Yet as we walk within the confines of these do's and don'ts, what are our hearts like? What comes out of our mouths?

It's what comes out of your mouth that makes you clean or unclean: "From the same mouth come both blessing and cursing. My brethren, these things ought not to be this way. Does a fountain send out from the same opening both fresh and bitter water?" (James 3:10,11).

Some Pharisees and teachers of the law had come down from Jerusalem to Galilee where Jesus was ministering. The express purpose of their visit was to criticize Jesus and His disciples because they had broken the Pharisees' tradition. Jesus' disciples ate with unwashed hands and, therefore, they were unclean!

So Jesus proceeded to teach them where uncleanness really came from. "But the things that proceed out of the mouth come from the heart, and those defile the man. For out of the heart come evil thoughts, murders, adulteries, fornications, thefts, false witness, slanders. These are the things which defile the man; but to eat with unwashed hands does not defile the man" (Matthew 15:18-20).

How does your heart compare with your traditions, with your Christian do's and don'ts? Are you like the Pharisees? Are you critical of those who don't follow your particular "Christian" traditions? Does slander come from your mouth regarding them (Matthew 15:3-9)?

Hearing the Whole Counsel

WHAT WOULD MAKE JESUS address Peter as "Satan"? What would make Him say, "Get behind Me, Satan! You are a stumbling block to Me; for you are not setting your mind on God's interests, but man's" (Matthew 16:23)?

Jesus was born for one purpose: He was born to die—to give His life as a ransom so that those who were dead in trespasses and sins might live (Matthew 20:28; Ephesians 2:1).

The time had come in Jesus' life to explain to His disciples that He must go to Jerusalem and there suffer at the hands of the elders, priests, and teachers of the law. This suffering would end in death. But on the third day He would be raised to life!

Apparently, all the disciples heard was "suffering" and "death"! They completely missed His words, "and be raised up on the third day" (Matthew 16:21). And so Peter began to rebuke Jesus, "God forbid it, Lord! This shall never happen to You" (Matthew 16:22).

In return, Jesus addressed Peter as "Satan" and gave His rebuke. Then, He taught them the principle that is true for every man. "If anyone wishes to come after Me, let him deny himself, and take up his cross, and follow Me. For whoever wishes to save his life shall lose it; but whoever loses his life for My sake shall find it" (Matthew 16:24,25).

The work of the cross was God's doing—not Satan's!

It pleased the Father to give His Son as a ransom . . . for you and for me (Isaiah 53:10).

And it pleases the Father when you and I are willing to follow in Christ's stead, to lay down our lives—to give our lives, in a sense, as a ransom for others.

What will you give to God in gratitude, in love, for His unspeakable gift? *Don't listen to Satan as he uses the lips of others to keep you from the cross.*

Think of the pain that would have been spared Peter and the others if they hadn't gotten caught up with Christ's death and missed his words, "and be raised up on the third day."

Life comes only through death!

Jesus Loves the Children!

LITTLE CHILDREN. MANY THOUGHT Jesus was too busy, too important, too occupied in the work of God to be bothered by them. But, oh, how the children wanted to be around Him! For when Jesus was around, there was excitement! And so they would make their way through the forest of tall people, searching and pushing through the flowing garments that blocked their paths.

You could hear their whispers, their giggles, their calls to their playmates, until all of a sudden the forest of people was gone and they stood in the clearing, dazzled by the unexpected light. There He was! Timidly they walked to Him. Would He smile, or would He scold them? Would He even pay any attention to them?

As their little sandaled feet crept closer, they were suddenly brought to a halt by the iron gate of a man's arm. "Don't bother the Master!" And in their young minds they must have thought, *Why do grown-ups always have to be so busy? Why do kids always seem a bother to them?*

Then, just as they were about to run away, Jesus reached out and gently drew one of the children to His side, tucking him under His arm and giving him that special squeeze of love. A tiny smile crept out as the upturned face caught the reflection of the Son's smile.

And Jesus began to speak: "And whoever receives one such child in My name receives Me; but whoever causes one of these little ones who believe in Me to stumble, it is better for him that a heavy millstone be hung around his neck, and that he be drowned in the depth of the sea" (Matthew 18:5,6).

With that, I'm sure, the children's eyes opened wide in amazement while their little arms poked one another. *Hey! We do matter! We're not a bother! See, Jesus is not too busy for us because we are important!*

Children are important. They matter to Jesus so much that God has given you this warning.

Are you careful with children? Do you demonstrate to them the love of God, the character of God? Will it be easy for your children to go to Jesus because they have lived tucked under *your* loving arm?

"What Must I Do?"

JESUS LOOKED AT HIM, and He loved him. But His love did not alter what He said to him. Here was a rich young man with a zeal for the things of God. He had kept the commandments since he had been a boy. Or at least he thought he had kept them! Now, seeing Jesus, he fell on his knees to ask what he must do to inherit eternal life.

"What must I *do*?" Today, so many of us would be so quick to reply, "Why, nothing! It is a gift. All you have to do is *believe* that Jesus is God, that He has died for your sins, that He has paid for your sin in full. You must believe that Jesus Christ was then buried and that He rose from the dead, conquering death by His perfect sacrifice. And you must believe that He lives. If you will accept the Lord Jesus Christ as your Savior, you will be saved."

Doctrinally, our answer would be right. But would our answer be appropriate? Would it be the answer that would bring this rich young man to salvation?

The apostle Paul would later say to a Philippian jailer who asked what he could do to be saved, "Believe in the Lord Jesus, and you shall be saved, you and your household" (Acts 16:31).

But Jesus did not say this to the rich young man. And the rich young man went away lost. Why? Because the rich young man did not do what was necessary to be saved.

"Do? Do, you say! But there is nothing to do to be saved! It is by faith! All you have to do is believe!"

Are you sure there is nothing to do? Carefully read Mark 10:17-30. Ask God to reveal truth to you. Why wasn't the rich young ruler saved? Meditate today upon this passage.

The Doing of Salvation

WHEN THE RICH YOUNG MAN came to Jesus, he called Him, "Good Teacher." With that Jesus replied, "Why do you call Me good? No one is good except God alone" (Mark 10:18).

Why did Jesus pick up on the word "good"? Why did He need to say that there is none good except God?

I believe that Jesus was attempting to bring this young man face-to-face with the fact that He is God. When Jesus quoted the commandments to the young man, He skipped over the first and foremost commandment—the commandment which required men to love God with all and above all! The commandments Jesus did reiterate, the young man had kept since he was a boy. But what about the first and the foremost commandment?

The Scriptures tell us that Jesus looked at and loved this young man. Then, our Lord put His finger on this young man's idol: his possessions, his earthly treasures. He could not forsake his possessions. He could not give them up. He had broken the first commandment, but he was totally unaware of it!

What did the rich young man have to do to be saved? He had to put Jesus first. He had to be willing to leave everything for Christ.

Why? Because Jesus is God, and He must have preeminence in our lives. If you and I are not willing to acknowledge Him as God, and if we are not willing to forsake all for Him, we cannot be saved. That is the "doing" of salvation—not the working but the doing! It is giving God His rightful place as God.

Have you ever done this? When did you do it? If you have never done this, will you do it?

"The kingdom of heaven is like a merchant seeking fine pearls, and upon finding one pearl of great value, he went and sold all that he had, and bought it" (Matthew 13:45,46).

The Last Shall Be First?

DURING ONE OF OUR Family Conference Weekends at Precept Ministries, I decided that I would take the eight through thirteen-year-olds to a neighbor's pool. I wanted to spend some time with them because their young lives are so precious to God.

Because we had a lot of rambunctious boys along, I called for a lineup at the pool so that I could quiet them, give orders, and count noses! What a push there was to be the first in line! Of course, they were thinking, *First in line, first in the pool!*

I watched several of them push and shove for first place, and I could understand their aggressiveness, for my personality is anything but introverted! Then I watched some finagle their way in front of others. The smaller or quieter ones lost the prime places. It seemed unjust, unfair, but I did nothing, for I knew what I would do next!

When the line was finally formed and the count-off was finished, I looked at the hurting faces of those who were to be last in the pool because their number was closer to thirty than one! I looked at other faces, and they didn't care where they were in the line—they were there! They would get in the pool sooner or later! There was no anxiety, only the joy of getting to go.

Finally, I quoted a Scripture and made my brief application, "Thus the last shall be first, and the first last" (Matthew 20:16). And I reversed the line!

This verse hit me again this morning in my quiet time. What a shock it will be when this life is over, when we see so many who seemingly have had it made in this life with their fame, with their position within Christian circles, with their lack of want in any area—for many who were first will be last.

O Father, stamp eternity upon my eyes . . . upon our eyes! May we be able to say, "There is not anything that will keep me from following You freely."

Heart-washings

MY HEART WAS IN CONFLICT. He sat me down in the chair and gently placed my feet in the basin. As he began to wash them, I thought, *No, this isn't right. I should wash his feet first. I'm the woman; he is the man. God's Word says that I was made for him.*

But Jack had taken the initiative. There was no question, no hesitation; he was going to wash my feet first. Then, I would be given the opportunity of washing his in return.

It was so easy to wash his feet! I didn't want him to do a thing, not even to untie his shoes. I wanted to do it all. Now, I could fulfill my role. Now, I could serve him in this act of love as he had served me. As I held his foot in the towel, I bent to kiss that which stood as my earthly shield and protector, that which stood for righteousness, that which stood, in picture form, as my heavenly Lord.

The service proceeded, and the walls of that "Upper Room" in Jerusalem echoed back our hymns of praise and adoration. Not only were feet washed, but eyes, cheeks, even hearts were washed by tears sent from the Spirit of God.

As I washed Jack's feet, I could see that it was only right that he should wash my feet first. He was the man. He was the husband. He was to first wash the feet of his bride. "What I do you do not realize now, but you shall understand hereafter" (John 13:7). Christ sought me, longing to make me His. It was He who gave Himself up for me that He might sanctify me, set me apart, make me holy by cleansing me by His blood and then through the washing of the water of the Word (Ephesians 5:25,26). Although it seemed hard at first for me to let him, it was right that Jack, my lord, should first wash my feet.

"You call Me Teacher and Lord; and you are right, for so I am. If I then, the Lord and the Teacher, washed your feet, you also ought to wash one another's feet" (John 13:13,14).

DECEMBER 21

Keep Watching and Praying

AFTER PRAYING BY HIMSELF in the Garden of Gethsemane, Jesus returned to His disciples. He found them sleeping!

Now was not the time for sleep but for prayer and vigilance. Soon, they, too, would be faced with temptation. And so Jesus, in concern for them, said, "Keep watching and praying, that you may not enter into temptation; the spirit is willing, but the flesh is weak" (Matthew 26:41).

How well Jesus knew the truth that He was imparting to them. He must do the will of the Father (Hebrews 10:7). But the flesh, His body, was weak. And so He went back to wrestle alone in prayer, to watch and pray. Three times Jesus, the Son of God, had to pray, "if it is possible, let this cup pass from Me; yet not as I will, but as Thou wilt" (Matthew 26:39).

Not long ago, I stood in Gethsemane's garden reading these very words and sharing their truths with those we were teaching on our Bible tour of the Holy Land. All of a sudden my heart understood what our Lord was really saying. My soul reached out, grabbing this truth and clinging to it for its very life. For I had recently been rescued from the awful current of temptation which had sought to carry me away and toss me lifeless and gasping among the wreckage of the storm.

I had been tempted in a way in which I had not been tempted in a long time. My flesh had longed to flirt with sin. But in my spirit I knew I couldn't. I didn't want to sin, to walk in disobedience. Why, a few hours earlier, it was the furthest thing from my mind. But then it came—that desire, that longing, that temptation to yield. Only through diligence in watching myself carefully and through persistent praying was I able to say, "Not my will but Thine be done!"

Now, I saw how well Jesus understood the truth that He tried to share with His disciples. Jesus knew. He knew because, even at that moment, He had been wrestling with the weakness of His flesh!

This is my Savior who was tempted in all points such as I. One who can be touched with the feeling of my infirmities . . . my weaknesses.

Have you almost been caught in sin's snare? Are you ashamed for even being tempted? He understands. And He says, "Keep watching and praying."

The Flesh Is Weak

"KEEP WATCHING AND PRAYING . . . the spirit is willing, but the flesh is weak" (Matthew 26:41). But they did not watch, nor did they pray. Instead they slept.

Jesus knew the temptation that Peter would soon encounter. He had told him that Satan had demanded permission that he might sift him as wheat. But Peter was confident. He knew his own spirit. "Even if I have to die with You, I will not deny You" (Matthew 26:35).

Peter was willing to die for Christ. He was not lying. He sincerely meant those words. They came from the depths of his heart.

Now Peter was awakened to participate in a nightmare. Before him stood a large crowd armed with swords and clubs. Suddenly, they seized Jesus. Peter would not have it. His sword was drawn, and in a flash he had severed the enemy's ear! Then the rebuke came. They could not fight! They could not defend themselves! Jesus was to be arrested!

Peter, the warrior, the defender of Jesus, was called to a cease-fire. Yet the enemy marched on. It was too much for his flesh. His flesh was weak. "Then all the disciples left Him and fled" (Matthew 26:56).

Peter was not prepared. Oh, he had been warned, "Keep watching and praying." Instead, he had slept. Peter knew his spirit, but he had not reckoned with his flesh. And so he found himself weeping bitter tears of defeat and condemnation.

Are you aware of the weakness of your flesh? Oh, the zeal is there, and so is the dedication and the commitment . . . but there is also the flesh!

May you, may I, remember to watch ourselves carefully . . . and may we pray much. Only constant vigilance and close communion will keep us from the bitter weeping.

So many who were once standing in zeal are today falling into temptation. Zeal alone cannot keep you from falling. It takes vigilance and prayer.

Keep Standing Firm

IT IS SO MUCH EASIER when what you are doing has the support of those around you! It is easy to go along with the crowd. As a matter of fact, they spur you on. They give you impetus to do what perhaps you wouldn't do if you had to do it by yourself.

Jesus had been arrested and taken to the house of Caiaphas, the high priest. The witnesses gathered, all of them false. One by one, they stepped forward to testify lies without compunction. They were a company of liars.

Finally, Jesus was put under oath. Now He had to speak. His words came, confirming that He was the Son of God, "Hereafter you shall see THE SON OF MAN SITTING AT THE RIGHT HAND OF POWER, and COMING ON THE CLOUDS OF HEAVEN" (Matthew 26:64).

With this, the high priest tore his clothes and accused Jesus of blasphemy. There! The crowd had had it! The high priest had said it. Jesus was guilty! The high priest said to the crowd, "What do you think?" They answered, "He is worthy of death."

Yet every one of them was wrong. And, I believe, if they had gone away to be alone, to think it through, they would have recognized how wrong they were. There was no evidence. They were encouraged by others with the same weaknesses.

As if this were not enough, one, emboldened by the verdict of the high priest, spat in Jesus' face. Others followed his example. Then one hit Jesus with his fist. Others followed. Still others slapped Him and said, "Prophesy to us, You Christ; who is the one who hit You?" (Matthew 26:68). The crowd was enjoying its sport.

He sat alone . . . the only One who was right. Yet He looked like He was the guilty party. At the present, He was unvindicated! But He knew He was right. It was the multitude that was wrong.

Days are coming, Beloved, when if you are going to do what is right, you may have to sit alone. You may have to take the unjust abuse of men—men who are wrong. When it happens, remember that there is One who understands, who sat where you are sitting. And He is now at the right hand of the Mighty One, where someday you will be also.

So sit alone if need be. It won't be long. He is coming soon.

Wrapped in the Father's Arms

TOMORROW IS CHRISTMAS. How do you feel?

Numb . . . busy . . . exhausted . . . pushed . . . guilty . . . frustrated?

Lonely . . . forsaken . . . rejected . . . unloved . . . uncared for?

Disappointed . . . disillusioned . . . filled with despair?

or

Excited . . . loved . . . warm . . . happy . . . secure . . . content?

Full of joy . . . anticipation . . . love . . . gratitude?

Ask God to show you the reasons you feel the way you do. Think about your reasons for a few moments.

Now, Beloved (for that is what you are to God), ask God to show you what to do about your feelings and trust Him to show you.

Sleep well tonight, knowing that you are wrapped in the same tender care that you knew, or that you wish you had known, as a child—protected in your Father's arms of love. Your heavenly Father is holding you closely. Remember that He said He would never leave you nor forsake you (Hebrews 13:5).

Jesus—God's Gift to You

CHRISTMAS! CHRISTMAS IS God saying, "I love you. Look in My manger and see what was born for you . . . what is given by Me. Come. See. It is My Son. My only begotten Son. He means all the world to Me. He is there as My gift to you on My Christmas tree. It's Calvary. Hush! Listen! Can you not hear the carols being sung? They were composed for you, to tell you over and over again that I love you."

"What is man that Thou dost magnify him, and that Thou art concerned about him?" (Job 7:17).

"I have loved you with an everlasting love; therefore I have drawn you with lovingkindness" (Jeremiah 31:3).

"But God demonstrates His own love toward us, in that while we were yet sinners, Christ died for us" (Romans 5:8).

"For God so loved the world, that He gave His only begotten Son, that whoever believes in Him should not perish, but have eternal life" (John 3:16).

"See how great a love the Father has bestowed upon us, that we should be called children of God" (1 John 3:1).

"Lo, for my own welfare I had great bitterness; it is Thou who hast kept my soul from the pit of nothingness, for Thou hast cast all my sins behind Thy back" (Isaiah 38:17).

"May the beloved of the LORD dwell in security by Him, who shields him all the day, and he dwells between His shoulders" (Deuteronomy 33:12).

"Behold, I have inscribed you on the palms of My hands" (Isaiah 49:16).

"If God is for us, who is against us? He who did not spare His own Son, but delivered Him up for us all, how will He not also with Him freely give us all things? . . . nor height, nor depth, nor any other created thing, shall be able to separate us from the love of God, which is in Christ Jesus our Lord" (Romans 8:31,32,39).

God says to you, "What more can I say? What more can I do? What more can I give to show My love to you?"

Is Your Faith Faulty?

THE PASTOR STOOD before the coffin and pointed his finger threateningly to the congregation. "This will never happen again in this church. This woman never should have died. It is your fault."

A mist of guilt rolled over the congregation, blocking out the warmth and the light of the Son that was meant to comfort those who sorrowed. Someone in the church had lacked faith. Someone had made a negative confession. And so this young mother had died, leaving her husband and her young children without a keeper of the home.

The true story above could be repeated in numerous ways as similar pronouncements come from pulpit after pulpit: "Your daughter wouldn't have died in that accident if someone had prayed properly." . . . "What you confess with your mouth is what you get; you can be healed by the faith of a positive confession." . . .

And so guilt, condemnation, and anxiety rest like a heavy cloud over many a church, over many a Christian, as they are told that their lack of faith or their negative confession permitted disease or brought premature death.

If this is true—and it is not—their loved one's times were apparently not in God's hands (Psalm 31:15), but in the hands of their own faith and confession, or in the faith and confession of other believers!

Just recently a precious man said to me, "I lost my children and my wife some time ago. When I heard this teaching, I began to think, 'Maybe if I had only prayed differently or had spoken differently they would still be alive.' " Trouble and confusion had hung as shades over his eyes until truth pulled the cords; then, the blinds went up, and the light dispelled his darkness. Finally, he understood the prophecy from Isaiah 53:4, "Surely our griefs He Himself bore, and our sorrows He carried."

We will look at this verse in depth tomorrow, but let me first ask you a question.

Beloved, are you a student of God's Word? Have you learned for yourself to compare Scripture with Scripture, or do you simply live by what you hear others preach?

Does Jesus Heal Today?

DOES JESUS HEAL TODAY? Are miracles still possible? Does my faith or my positive or negative confession determine the length of my own life or of another's life or health? Did Christ, who was born to die, carry all of our physical sicknesses to the cross and there atone for them so that through faith we can be healed of all that would afflict us?

For the next two days we will look at Christ's ministry to mankind in His life and in His death. May God, by His Spirit, lead us into truth through a study of His Word as we compare Scripture with Scripture.

> And when Jesus had come to Peter's home, He saw his mother-in-law lying sick in bed with a fever. And He touched her hand, and the fever left her. . . . And . . . they brought to Him many who were demon-possessed; and He cast out the spirits with a word, and healed all who were ill in order that what was spoken through Isaiah the prophet might be fulfilled, saying, "HE HIMSELF TOOK OUR INFIRMITIES, AND CARRIED AWAY OUR DISEASES" (Matthew 8:14-17).

Now, compare these verses with Isaiah 53:4: "Surely our griefs [sicknesses] He Himself bore, and our sorrows He carried; yet we ourselves esteemed Him stricken, smitten of God, and afflicted."

According to the verses in Matthew, when did Jesus bear or take our infirmities and carry away our diseases? Does Jesus heal today? Yes. Are miracles still for today? I believe so. But is all healing, are all miracles, from God? No. Satan can heal and perform miracles also. We are warned of this fact in 2 Thessalonians 2:9,10.

I believe the Word teaches that Jesus did and can heal. But I do not believe the Scriptures teach that physical healing of these temporal bodies is ours because of His atonement. You may possibly retort, "But what about the verse that says that by His stripes we are healed?" Tomorrow, we will look at that verse.

Today, it is my prayer that God will use these lessons to free those of you who are under bondage—the awful bondage that this false teaching brings when you or your loved ones are not healed.

The Greatest Healing

IT WAS THE PROPHET ISAIAH who told us that we would be healed by Christ's stripes. Listen to these magnificent words of promise:

> Surely our griefs He Himself bore, and our sorrows He carried; yet we ourselves esteemed Him stricken, smitten of God, and afflicted. But He was pierced through for our transgressions, He was crushed for our iniquities; the chastening for our well-being fell upon Him, and by His scourging we are healed (Isaiah 53:4,5).

We saw yesterday that Christ bore our sicknesses (griefs) and carried our sorrows of pain as He healed the sick and set free those possessed of demons. "Yet we ourselves," God's Israelites, "esteemed Him stricken, smitten of God, and afflicted."

What a paradox it was! Christ came and manifested to Israel—to the world—His miraculous powers of healing, His complete authority over Satan and his kingdom; yet at the cross of Calvary, they taunted Jesus with statements like, "He believes in God, let God rescue Him" (see Matthew 27:43). They were statements that implied that Jesus was being smitten by God. What audacity! What sin lay in their darkened hearts! What blindness!

Then Isaiah goes on to explain the reason for, the purpose of, the cross. He was pierced through for our transgressions. He was crushed—killed—for our iniquities. Our deserved chastening fell on Him, that we might have peace, reconciliation with God. By His scourging or stripes we are healed.

Healed? Healed of what?

Peter tells us in his first epistle: "And He Himself bore our sins in His body on the cross, that we might die to sin and live to righteousness; for by His wounds you were healed. For you were continually straying like sheep, but now you have returned to the Shepherd and Guardian of your souls" (1 Peter 2:24,25).

By His stripes we were healed of our sins . . . of their power and their dominion over us (Romans 6).

What a healing! What a Savior!

It Is Finished!

THERE HE STOOD—God in the flesh—being scourged by men whose very breath He controlled. The leather straps coiled around His body like a serpent striking the flesh with its fangs of bone and metal. Just as each hook caught His flesh, the arm of the soldier would wrench back his whip, flipping the flesh from Jesus' back and abdomen. There Christ stood as the New Covenant was being written in His blood.

"I gave My back to those who strike Me, and My cheeks to those who pluck out the beard; I did not cover My face from humiliation and spitting. For the Lord GOD helps Me, therefore, I am not disgraced" (Isaiah 50:6,7).

Why did God permit His Son's appearance to be "marred more than any man, and His form more than the sons of men" (Isaiah 52:14)? Why the scourging? Why not just the crucifixion, horrible as it was?

Because the crucifixion was not enough. We had broken God's holy law, and we were indebted to Him by virtue of our unrighteousness. And so God wrote out that certificate of debt in the flesh of His Son. Then God took that certificate of debt and nailed it to the cross (Colossians 2:14). Finally, from Calvary's cross the cry came, "*Tetelestai* (It is finished!)."

In Jesus' day, when a debtor finally paid off his debt, the word *tetelestai* was written across the certificate of debt and nailed to the door of the debtor's home where all could see and know that his debt had been "paid in full."

God has written out your certificate of debt. He has engraved your sins in the body of His only begotten Son so that by His stripes you might be healed . . . healed so that you might die to sin and live to righteousness. Have you been healed? Do you live a righteous life?

"No one who is born of God practices sin, because His seed abides in him; and he cannot sin, because he is born of God. By this the children of God and the children of the devil are obvious: anyone who does not practice righteousness is not of God, nor the one who does not love his brother" (1 John 3:9,10).

Glorify His Name

"LET GOD RESCUE HIM." But God did not rescue Jesus. He let Him die. And if God had rescued Him, where would we be? We would be lost, for there would have been no sacrifice for our sins. Jesus was our substitute. He was the One who died for us, in our place, and thus He paid the penalty for our sins. He was born to die.

Let me ask you a question. Is it always to God's glory and to man's good for God to rescue us from our difficult circumstances? And if it is not, are you willing not to be rescued but to suffer?

> And those passing by were hurling abuse at Him, wagging their heads, and saying, "You who are going to destroy the temple and rebuild it in three days, save Yourself! If You are the Son of God, come down from the cross." In the same way the chief priests also, along with the scribes and elders, were mocking Him, and saying, "He saved others; He cannot save Himself. He is the King of Israel; let Him now come down from the cross, and we shall believe in Him. HE TRUSTS IN GOD; LET HIM DELIVER Him now" (Matthew 27:39-43).

And so the word also comes to the followers of Jesus: "Come down from the cross . . . save yourself . . . let God rescue you." But God does not always remove the instrument that would bring us to death of self. And if we were saved from all unpleasant situations, how would others in the same situations see the sufficiency of our God for those situations and thus be saved themselves? If we save ourselves, we cannot save others. Let God rescue me? "Now My soul has become troubled; and what shall I say, 'Father, save Me from this hour'? But for this purpose I came to this hour. Father, glorify Thy name" (John 12:27,28).

O Beloved, whatever your trial, your difficulty, your circumstance, will you not ask God to glorify His name in whatever way it pleases Him? Will you not say, "Rescue me, Father, only if it is Your will? Otherwise, I will be faithful unto death, for I know that if I am obedient and remain at this cross, You will rescue and save others!"

His Call...
"Follow Me"

THERE WAS NO ESCAPE for Jesus. He tasted it all. He drank the dregs of the cup of suffering. He partook of temptations, of trials, of testings. He learned obedience through the things He suffered, even though He was the Son of God. There was no escape.

Why was there no escape? Because you and I need a great High Priest who can be touched with the feeling of our infirmities (Hebrews 4:15). We need a Priest who can understand our temptations because He has been there.

There was no escape for Jesus. Will there be escape, then, for us, His children? It seems that this is what many are seeking in Christianity, for this teaching makes popular preaching. But is this what God has for His children? Escape?

If we are to be priests in Christ's stead, in His place, as His representatives (Revelation 1:6; 5:9,10; 1 Peter 2:9), how can we minister to people, to the world, unless we have been touched with the feeling of their infirmities? Their trials, testings, afflictions, sufferings, discomfort?

"Just as it is written, 'FOR THY SAKE WE ARE BEING PUT TO DEATH ALL DAY LONG; WE WERE CONSIDERED AS SHEEP TO BE SLAUGHTERED.' But in all these things we overwhelmingly conquer through Him who loved us" (Romans 8:36,37).

Why, then, are we trying to escape? What kind of priests do we want to be? He was born to die that we might live, and we were born to die that others might live.

> "The hour has come for the Son of Man to be glorified. Truly, truly, I say to you, unless a grain of wheat falls into the earth and dies, it remains by itself alone; but if it dies, it bears much fruit. He who loves his life loses it; and he who hates his life in this world shall keep it to life eternal. If anyone serves Me, let him follow Me; and where I am, there shall My servant also be; if anyone serves Me, the Father will honor him" (John 12:23-26).

O Beloved . . . follow Him who died for you.

Notes

March

1. Geoffrey Bull, *God Holds the Key* (London: Hodder and Stoughton Publishers).
2. If you are having difficulty spending time alone with your Shepherd, may I suggest that you get my little booklet, *A Quiet Time Alone with God*, available from Precept Ministries, P.O. Box 182218, Chattanooga, TN 37422. Many people have been helped by it.
3. Much of the information about sheep has been drawn from W. Phillip Keller's book, *A Shepherd Looks at Psalm 23* (Grand Rapids, MI: Zondervan, 1988).
4. Phyllis Thompson, *Madam Guyon: Martyr of the Holy Spirit* (London: Hodder and Stoughton, 1986), 156.
5. Leslie T. Lyall, *John Sung* (Chicago: Moody Press, 1964), 42-43.

April

6. Peter Gillquist, "The Christian Life: A Marathon We Mean to Win," *Christianity Today,* October 21, 1981.
7. Ibid.
8. Ibid.

May

9. Irving Jensen, *Jensen's Survey of the Old Testament* (Chicago: Moody Press, 1978), 467.
10. G. Campbell Morgan, *The Minor Prophets* (Old Tappan, N.J.: Fleming H. Revell, 1960), 154.
11. W. E. Vine, *An Expository Dictionary of New Testament Words* (Nashville: Thomas Nelson, 1978), 688.
12. Charles L. Feinberg, *The Minor Prophets* (Chicago: Moody Press, 1978), 260.

August

13. Roger, Steer, *George Müller: Delighted in God!* (Wheaton: Harold Shaw, 1975).
14. See August 11.
15. F. J. Huegel, *The Cross of Christ, the Throne of God* (Minneapolis: Bethany House, 1965), 9-10.
16. Ibid., 78.
17. Ibid., 79.

September

18. R. C. Trench, *Synonyms of the New Testament* (Grand Rapids: Wm. B. Eerdmans, 1948).
19. Bernard Palmer, *Run for the West* (Elgin, Ill.: David C. Cook, 1979), 82, 121.

October

20. Myrna Grant, *Vanya* (Altamonte Springs, FL: Creation House, 1974), 51-59.
21. William J. Anderson, "God's Victorious Grace," *TFC Today* (Toccoa Falls College, Toccoa, GA), Winter 1978, 16-17.
22. Dixie Kemp, "Beauty for Ashes," *TFC Today*, Evangelical Press Association.
23. Quoted from the audio tape, "Evidence Not Seen," recorded at Precept Ministries by Darlene Rose. The story is also available in book form: Darlene Diebler Rose, *Evidence Not Seen* (New York: Harper and Row, 1988).

24. Myrna Grant, *Vanya*, 83-88.
25. Myron S. Augsburger, *Faithful Unto Death* (Waco, TX: Word Books, 1978), 24.
26. Nell Mohney, *The Inside Story* (Nashville: The Upper Room, 1979), 80.
27. Corrie ten Boom, John and Elizabeth Sherrill, *The Hiding Place* (Lincoln, VA: Chosen Books, 1971), 214-215.
28. Mohney, *Inside Story*, 58.
29. From Darlene Rose's tape. Also included in *Evidence Not Seen* by Darlene Rose.
30. Norman Grubb, *Rees Howells, Intercessor* (Fort Washington, PA: Christian Literature Crusade, 1964), 145-147.

November
31. Much of the information and many of the prayer points in this month's devotionals are drawn from *Operation World* by Patrick Johnstone (Grand Rapids, MI: Zondervan, 1993). There is also a children's version entitled *You Can Change Your World* by Jill Johnstone. Another excellent source of information for prayer for the nations is The Sentinel Group, P.O. Box 6334, Lynnwood, WA 98036.
32. F. Kefa Sempangi and Barbara Thompson, *A Distant Grief* (Glendale, CA: Regal Publications, 1979), 99-100.
33. Ibid., 91.
34. Ibid., 119-120.
35. David Beam and Frank Waggoner, *Unto the Least of These* (Guatemala Evangelical Ministries).
36. Johnstone, *Operation World*.
37. James and Marti Hefley, *By Their Blood* (Grand Rapids, MI: Baker Book House, 1987), 219.
38. Quotations and information from *Operation World*.
39. Ibid.
40. Ibid.
41. Ibid., 145.
42. Ibid., 146.
43. The story used these last two days was taken from *On Line* (Youth With A Mission, Winter, 1993).
44. Johnstone, *Operation World*.
45. Quotations from Anita and Peter Deyneka, Jr., *A Song in Siberia* (Elgin, IL: David C. Cook Publishing Co., 1977), 54-55.
46. "Breaking Through the 10/40 Window," *OM Indeed*, April-May 1992.
47. George Otis, Jr., *The Last of the Giants* (Tarrytown, NY: Fleming Revell Company, 1991), 157.
48. Ibid., 157-158.
49. J. Oswald Sanders, *Prayer Power Unlimited* (Chicago: Moody Bible Institute, 1977), 157.